China Restored

China Restored

The Middle Kingdom Looks to 2020 and Beyond

ERIC C. ANDERSON

 PRAEGER

AN IMPRINT OF ABC-CLIO, LLC
Santa Barbara, California • Denver, Colorado • Oxford, England

Library of Congress Cataloging-in-Publication Data

Anderson, Eric C. (Eric Curt)
  China restored : the Middle Kingdom looks to 2020 and beyond /
  Eric C. Anderson.
    p. cm.
  Includes bibliographical references and index.
  ISBN 978–0–313–38517–9 (hard copy : alk. paper) — ISBN 978–0–313–38518–6
  (ebook)
1. China—Foreign relations. 2. China—Military policy. 3. China—Economic
policy. 4. China—Cultural policy. I. Title.
JZ1734.A93   2010
320.60951—dc22   2009050889

ISBN: 978–0–313–38517–9
EISBN: 978–0–313–38518–6

14 13 12 11 10   1 2 3 4 5

This book is also available on the World Wide Web as an eBook.
Visit www.abc-clio.com for details.

Praeger
An Imprint of ABC-CLIO, LLC

ABC-CLIO, LLC
130 Cremona Drive, P.O. Box 1911
Santa Barbara, California 93116-1911

This book is printed on acid-free paper ∞

Manufactured in the United States of America

For Melanie . . . of course

Contents

Acknowledgments

I started following developments in China when I was shipped off to South Korea as an intelligence officer in the U.S. Air Force. Tasked with tracking developments in North Korea following the collapse of the Soviet Union, it quickly became apparent in order to understand some of Pyongyang's behavior one had to monitor events in Beijing. This proved to be no easy feat. Chinese military activity was generally uninteresting, and Beijing's foreign policy was largely framed by the Chinese Communist Party's effort to cast off the long shadow of Tiananmen Square. Some of my colleagues suggested I was wasting my time, others argued I was looking to the future—albeit a bit before the U.S. policy community actually cared what happened in China on a day-to-day basis. Needless to say, much has changed in the intervening 20 years.

My part-time hobby became a full-time occupation in 2002. The unfortunate sudden demise of my counterpart at the U.S. Pacific Command's Joint Intelligence Center resulted in my being drafted to serve as the organization's senior intelligence analyst for Northeast Asia. Aware of the fact I had an uphill battle on my hands, but not quite sure how the war would be won, I went in search of allies and skilled analysts. While I wish there were space to list everyone who contributed to the effort, that is simply not the case. I apologize if you are not here. That said, I owe the following people a special thanks: Mark Admiral, Dan Brown, Lacey Chong, Cortez Cooper, Mike Coullahan, Joe Chennler, Eric Croddy, Andy Drake, Evan Esaki, Mike Fitzmorris, Hunter Grimes, Ed Lamm, Mark

McCullough, Kerry McQuistin, Alex Miller, Donald Pruefer, Jason Rudrud, Jack Savage, and Tom Woodrow.

In addition to these fine analysts, I have had the opportunity to work with a number of people who made this text possible. Jeff Engstrom culled through a mountain of academic and media sources to find many of the articles cited in this book. Robert Hutchinson, a senior editor at Praeger/ABC-CLIO, kept the project on path and within strict timelines. Cindy Hargett kept me paid and suffered through a stack of endless book orders. Finally, Steve Moore, willingly engaged in multiple obscure conversations concerning China and helped ensure I provided the reader information those of us too close to the subject assume is common knowledge.

I also owe a debt of gratitude to my parents—Jim and Audrey Anderson—who have listened to my prattle about China for years, and to my father and mother-in-law—Len and Barbara Togman—the most recent victims of my musings.

I want to offer a special thanks to my wife, Melanie Sloan. For the last year Melanie has been compelled to listen to my grumbling about Chinese press reports and obscure official publications. Melanie is my sounding board. Without her comments and feedback I would never have finished this project or many other reports on time.

Finally, I want to thank the other two members of our family, Ainsley Anderson and Cheyenne. We adopted Ainsley about the time I was beginning to work on Chapter 4. Rather than becoming a distraction, she served as an inspiration—the smiles she offers every morning make the rest of the day a much more pleasant event. And then there is Cheyenne—the furry member of the family. As someone who works at home on a regular basis, it is always a treat to have a counterpart sitting by my feet through endless revisions—offering a nuzzle and friendly wag of the tail. Every author needs a Cheyenne to provide company and an excuse to ponder while taking yet another tour of the neighborhood.

Introduction

Heaven is above, earth is below, and that in between heaven and earth is called China. Those on the peripheries are the foreign. The foreign belong to the outer, whilst China belongs to the inner. Heaven and earth thus make it possible to differentiate the outer from the inner.

—Shi Jie, 1040, "On the Middle Kingdom"

China has "come of age" on the global stage. Like the 1988 Summer Olympics that heralded South Korea's arrival in the international arena, the 2008 games will ultimately be remembered as the moment Beijing resumed her rightful place in the sun. While U.S. businesses have long predicted this would be the case, American academicians and politicians have proven more reticent. A survey of recent academic and policy debates concerning China's future reveals fundamental differences over where the country is headed, Beijing's objectives in the coming 10 years, and what this all means for Washington. For some participants in this discussion China remains a developing nation struggling with demographic, economic, political, and security challenges that threaten the nation's very survival.[1] On the flip side of the coin are those who declare China is a rising giant —a nation whose economy and diplomatic influence could eclipse the United States by 2025.[2]

I contend China's future is most likely to be found somewhere between these two extremes. The Chinese Communist Party is not about to depart the dance, but China's leaders are finding it increasingly difficult to dictate who accompanies them to the floor. This does not mean, however, China's leaders are preparing to announce plans for formation of a new democracy. Instead, I would argue the Chinese Communist Party is intent on preserving its place atop the nation's political hierarchy through a perpetuation of Deng Xiaoping's economic miracle. To this end, China's leadership is intent on abetting the nation's re-emergence as the "Middle Kingdom."

This objective is neither so dangerous—nor benign—as the title might suggest. China's vision for the Middle Kingdom should not be confused with Moscow's apparent bid to recapture the "glory" that was the former Soviet Union. Beijing is not beset with delusions of imperial grandeur. Rather, I will show China is governed by pragmatists who seek to re-establish a sphere of influence conducive to continued economic development. As such, I agree with John Mearsheimer, a distinguished political scientist at the University of Chicago, who argues, "China is likely to try to dominate Asia the way the United States dominates the Western Hemisphere. Specifically, China will strive to maximize the power gap between itself and its neighbors . . . and to ensure that no state in Asia can threaten it."[3] Like Mearsheimer, I also believe Beijing is not about to engage in a campaign of territorial conquests—rather, China will simply want to dictate the boundaries of acceptable behavior within Asia in much the same way Washington does in the Americas.

This focus on explaining China's future through the prism of the Middle Kingdom is not accidental or the product of wishful thinking. Careful examination of Chinese and international academic, journalistic, and official studies have led me to this conclusion. In some senses, China's leaders are engaged in a very modern campaign of rolling back history. They fully intend to erase the last vestiges of the "century of humiliation"[4] and regain a respected position among the world's great nations. Beijing does not, however, appear intent on a race for global domination. While China's efforts to achieve regional dominance may occasionally appear dangerously close to head-to-head worldwide competition with the United States, I argue this is a matter of Western perception—a case of misreading intentions.

This is not to dismiss Washington's concerns, or belittle Beijing's accomplishments. The real problem here is discerning the difference between efforts intended to facilitate regional aspirations and developments with global implications. In a world of satellite communications, outsourced manufacturing, and escalating energy and resource prices, China must reach beyond her borders and Asia in order to ensure accomplishment of less grandiose ambitions. This means Beijing is compelled to explore outer space and foster relations with governments in Africa, the Middle East, and South America. As we shall see, this global outreach is not an attempt to realize Lenin's "highest stage of capitalism"[5]—imperialism—but rather the act of a nation intent on regaining her historical position—of achieving the status worthy of the Middle Kingdom.

ASPIRATIONS FRAMED BY HISTORY

China—when rendered in original historic characters—literally translates as the "middle country" or "middle kingdom." While certainly no act of humility, this self-imposed title speaks volumes about how the Chinese view themselves and the territory they inhabit. For the average Chinese citizen, China is more than just a political boundary etched on widely distributed maps. China is thousands of years of cultural, economic, military, and political experience and learning. China, as a result, is thus thought to have once achieved a deserved status as the center of the cognitive world—the place between heaven and earth. For many Chinese, over the last two millennia only the late emperors of the Qing dynasty and their eventual successors have ruled a China that was perceived to have not lived up to this billing.

Colonial expansion by rising European, Asian, and American powers, coupled with the Qing dynasty's inability to modernize, ultimately led to China's international decline.

This withering did not fundamentally, however, alter the extraordinary power and gravity of the world's largest population and oldest continuing civilization. Humiliation at the hands of Western and Japanese "barbarians" did not eliminate the glory that is China, it simply placed Beijing in a state of suspended animation. A long slumber, if you will, that was only to be briefly interrupted by the apparently aimless flailing of domestic and foreign politicians.

While much has been written on Mao's internal transgressions—from the Great Leap Forward to the Cultural Revolution—and China's place in the Cold War—from Korea to Vietnam—for the moment I am more concerned with understanding China's *weltanschauung* before Beijing became embroiled in modern day capitalism and communism. Any discussion of a re-emerging Middle Kingdom must return to a study of China's "international relations" prior to the 1800s.

According to John Fairbank, the venerable Harvard professor, China's historical foreign policy objectives are best characterized as follows:

1. China has historically shown a preference for regional "dominance"
2. This "dominance" is based on demonstrating and winning appropriate respect for China's "superiority"
3. China appears to uses this "superiority" to dictate a sense of harmonious co-existence[6]

China's foremost political objective has been to defend herself from Inner Asia, the broad stretch of land that encompassed everything north and west of the Great Wall—what is currently Mongolia, Russia, and Kazakhstan. For Beijing, the Great Wall marked the dividing line between "less civilized" nomadic peoples and the cultured/educated world.[7] The "civilized"—with few exceptions—stayed on their side of the Wall. Military adventures outside the gates were largely confined to defeating emerging threats and subjugating problem areas. Even these ventures were markedly different from the "crusades" and campaigns in the West, as the "civilized" Chinese typically avoided feudal domination in favor of "tributes" who were left to govern as they saw fit. The only restraint? Acceptance and recognition of the Chinese regime—a relationship we have come to understand as "peaceful co-existence."[8]

What is truly remarkable about this extended dominance of the "known world" was China's apparent lack of interest in expanding her territorial holdings. With the exception of modern Mongolia and Taiwan, China largely chose to live within her borders. Unlike Genghis Khan, Alexander the Great, the Caesars, or Napoleon, China did not seek to lay claim on distant foreign lands. In fact, once China had established unquestioned hegemony in East Asia, the emperors apparently found little need to pursue greater conquest.

How was this possible? Rather than impose military rule, the Chinese sought to extend their influence via culture, education, and "divine inspiration." Tribute states were brought into China's fold through instillation of the Confucian values used to govern the Chinese.[9] This cultural imperialism served to ingrain popular acceptance of China's place atop the political hierarchy. Or so ancient Chinese scholars and some contemporary Western academics would have us believe. As it turns out, the truth is less infused with visions of Confucian glory[10] and more grounded in political and economic reality.

Scholars now largely agree China maintained a sphere of influence in Asia through employment of a wide spectrum of national capabilities. While ancient Confucian scholars may have wanted to believe "barbarians" recognized the emperor as the mediator between heaven and earth, policy-makers within the royal court were typically more pragmatic. For these "realists," the Confucian theories of hierarchical relationships were little more than myths intended to justify the emperor's place atop the Chinese political system—the theories and stories served little purpose beyond the Great Wall.[11] Instead, the Chinese were found to have employed a number of more traditional methods associated with achieve foreign policy objectives. These included: military expeditions; alliances; diplomatic missions; and trade.[12]

It is this use of trade—particularly within the "tribute system"—which appears to have caused some Western scholars to conclude the Chinese were able to convince outsiders of the emperor's, and therefore China's, inherent superiority. As it turns out, the truth is less glamorous. In addition to standard merchant business deals,

> China's foreign trade took another important form ... "tributary" trade or exchange of gifts. Foreign rulers sent tributary missions to the Chinese court, the Chinese would present a certain amount of Chinese products, in return for the foreign tribute, and both sides would gain. For the foreign countries, the major motive was economic. The highly profitable trade with China was seen as more than adequate compensation for their superficial recognition of Chinese superiority.[13]

In essence, then, the Chinese "tribute system" was little more than a purchase of trade rights. Those coming from outside the Wall would offer the required gifts and token recognition; in exchange, the Chinese would open the door to lucrative business rights.

This tribute system thus ensured internal loyalty to the emperor—afterall, the foreigners "clearly understood" his superiority—and served to "influence" the neighbors through establishment of economic ties.

Not surprisingly, scholars have found this "tribute system" was apparently in practice beyond the Great Wall. A Japanese academic has published a number of articles in which he argues the "tribute system" operated in several dimensions. More specifically, he found that many of those paying tribute to China in turn expected tribute from their neighbors. As a result, the tribute system served to establish a loose confederation of political integration ranging across Asia—a sequence of concentric circles with China at the center.[14]

Perhaps John Fairbank best summed the entire process—from internal politics to external relations—when he wrote, " ... the doctrine of the emperor's superiority, symbolized in tributary ritual, had many uses. When force was available, it rested on force; when Chinese power was lacking, it could rest on the retrospect of Chinese power; or it could rest solely on the lure of trade."[15] The end product was a loose coalition of nations with a single, widely recognized power center. A phenomenon not easy to duplicate and maintain. Consider, for example, the former Soviet Union's inability to successfully emulate this relationship with the Warsaw Pact, or Washington's continuing struggle to do so with Latin or South America. In any case, this "tribute system" and its domestic political benefits came to an end after the Anglo-Chinese "Opium War" of 1842.[16] I now contend it is about to resurface—with considerable assistance from the Chinese Communist Party.

STEPPING INTO THE FUTURE

China's emergence from the Cultural Revolution and Deng Xiaoping's unbridled ambitions concerning his nation's economic revival renewed academic debates about Beijing's ultimate intentions. For some scholars, Deng's tentative first steps were little more than a poorly conceived campaign to bootstrap China out of poverty. Other Western analysts offered less benign explanations for Deng's efforts. For instance, in 1983 an American academician wrote,

> ... the year 1982 witnessed significant developments in Chinese domestic and foreign affairs .... Abroad, the People's Republic of China ... struck a more independent, nationalistic note. Beijing consciously moved to a more equidistant position diplomatically between the United States and the Soviet Union ... diplomatic overtures to the Third World also increased.[17]

The unstated conclusion, China was preparing for a multi-polar world
—an international community absent two competing ideologies or a
single hegemon.

China's obvious lack of demonstrable national power, however, left
Beijing in a seemingly interminable waiting game. Certainly progress
toward China's emergence as a respected international actor would
come with the demise of the Soviet Union, Beijing's fostering of a
domestic "economic miracle," and rebuilding of the People's Liberation Army (PLA). But as a whole, there was little China's leaders could
point to as justification for a revival of national pride. This struggle
with what it meant to be Chinese was reflected in the publication of
texts like *The Ugly Chinaman*,[18] which purported to expose the
nation's decrepit cultural underpinnings.[19]

Even as Chinese intellectuals struggled with crafting language
intended to depict China's emergence from its century of humiliation,
politicians in Beijing were laying the foundation for grander ambitions. In February 1992, the National People's Congress passed legislation unilaterally declaring China was the outright owner of
contested territories in the East and South China Seas. At first blush,
this would appear simply an act of legal bravado—until one considers
the areas claimed in this legislation included the Paracel, Senkaku and
Spratly Islands . . . and Taiwan. Furthermore, the law declared China
had the right, "to adopt all necessary measures to prevent and stop
the passage of vessels through its territorial waters" and for PLA
"warships or military aircraft to expel the intruders." As a Western
academic was to later note, China's subsequent actions "indicated
the law had not been passed simply for domestic purposes. In May,
1992, for example, Beijing granted oil-exploitation rights in [one of
the] disputed areas."[20]

Perhaps it is most useful to think of the 1992 legislation as simply
the formalization of Deng's broader vision. In addition to his press
for China's economic revival, during the early 1990s Deng Xiaoping
also issued what has come to be known as the "24 character strategy."
Deng's 24 character strategy directed China's diplomatic and military
apparatus to "observe calmly, secure our position; cope with affairs
calmly; hide our capacities and bide our time; be good at maintaining
a low profile; and never claim leadership." This new strategy suggested the re-emergence of the Middle Kingdom—a dominant force
in Asia that would "arrive" by carefully maximizing future options
though avoiding unnecessary provocations, shunning excessive

international burdens, and building-up China's power over the long-term.[21]

This careful balancing of economic, military, and political agendas did not go unnoticed at home—or abroad. In 1996, a group of young Chinese authors published *China Can Say No*[22]—a largely polemical text which nonetheless won popular acclaim for boldly asserting Beijing should prepare to resume its rightful place under the sun.[23] Not surprisingly, as the Chinese were "rediscovering" themselves—the rest of the world was engaged in the process of "discovering" China. In 1993, *Foreign Affairs* published Nicholas Kristof's piece, "The Rise of China," the first of a continuing dialogue the magazine has abetted in the intervening years.[24] But none of this early work really answered the question, where is Beijing ultimately headed? In fact, some Western analysts were largely dismissive of China's re-emergence. This sentiment was best captured in 1999, when *Foreign Affairs* published Gerald Segal's article, "Does China Matter?"[25]

As it turns out, China does matter—at multiple levels. Consider, for a moment, Minxin Pei's thoughts on an ascending China's strategic consequences for the West. According to Minxin Pei, an adjunct senior associate in the China Program at the Carnegie Endowment for International Peace, Beijing's rise will be hard to manage because:

1. Despite its enormous progress in terms of economic reform and modernization, China has maintained a distinctly authoritarian political system, and its leaders who have vowed to never adopt a "Western style" democracy

2. Beijing's world view is unalterably ingrained in realism, which sees the world as an anarchical place where states compete for power and influence; and their security an only be enhanced through acquisition of power and influence

3. Chinese nationalism projects fear and suspicion onto the outside world; it simultaneously fosters xenophobia and chauvinism[26]

A grim prognosis, but one that serves to make the point—Washington can not afford to ignore Beijing.

Despite Minxin Pei, and similar naysayers, by 2003 it had become obvious to a number of scholars that China was not going to attempt striking out on its own.[27] In an article published in *International Security*, Alastair Iain Johnston—the Laine Professor of China in World Affairs at Harvard–observed Beijing is, in fact, very much a vested member of the international community. As Johnston found in his examination of China's record on four major international "normative regimes"—sovereignty, free trade, arms control, and national self-determination—Beijing had crafted a foreign policy remarkably similar to that exercised by much more established members of the existing international order.[28] All of which suggested Beijing had reason to maintain the international system as it presently existed.

In 2005, David Shambaugh, the Director of George Washington University's China Policy Program, took this argument a step further when he wrote, "the traditional underpinnings of international relations in Asia are undergoing profound change, and the rise of China is a principle cause."[29] Shambaugh then goes on to provide a list of the other catalysts for change in the region, which included:

- The relative decline of U.S. influence and authority in Asia
- The expanding normative influence of the Association of South East Asian nations and the growth of regional institutions
- Increased technological and economic interdependence throughout the region
- The amelioration of several formerly antagonistic bilateral relationships—remarkably Japan and China[30]

Shambaugh argues these changes have fostered a new regional posture for Beijing. In place of the suspicion, isolationism, and animosity Beijing engendered in the late 1970s and early 1980s, we now find a China positioned to assume a leadership role in the Far East. Why? According to Shambaugh, this "China emerging" can be attributed to four factors: (1) Beijing's participation in regional organizations; (2) China's establishment of strategic partnerships and deepening bilateral relations; (3) the expansion of regional economic ties; and (4) the reduction of distrust and anxiety in the security sphere.[31]

This is not to say "all is well" in the security sphere—or, for that matter—when it comes to economic integration. While Shambaugh would have us believe China's military modernization is driven by a desire to field a force comparable with Beijing's new international stature and a wish to retain the capabilities necessary to deter Taiwan independence, he admits these motivations don't reassure the neighbors. As Shambaugh notes, two issues on the military front are particularly troublesome for China's Asian counterparts—(1) Beijing's development of power projection capabilities; and (2) the potential for this force to be used against Taiwan.[32] Neither concern can be wished or denied away. Despite Hu Jintao's "peaceful rising" campaign, his Asian neighbors remain worried about where the Chinese are headed. Is Hu setting the stage for Beijing to serve as the capital for a Chinese empire? Or is Hu facilitating China's re-emergence as the Middle Kingdom—a senior mentor with benign aspirations for guiding the development of an entire region? (Please note I am not suggesting Hu and his counterparts are altruists . . . the Chinese Communist Party is well aware Asia's rise is to their benefit—and necessary for their survival.)

A few words of clarity are in order at this point. As used here, "empire" refers to a Western concept of governance. That is, an empire is a single political unit charged with governing an extensive territory—that includes colonies or similarly militarily and politically subjugated subordinates. A Middle Kingdom redux would provide the neighbors Chinese "direction and guidance," but not abet "imperial" aspirations. China's neighbors would be allowed to continue to exist as independent states—they would, however, be expected to pay tribute to Beijing in the form of recognizing China's "due role" atop regional associations and organizations.

Clearly, this is a slippery slope. How do we know when acquiescence to Chinese leadership is in danger of becoming coerced acceptance of Chinese dictatorship? A hard question to answer, but an issue scholars are beginning to openly debate. In seeking to address these concerns, Shambaugh argues we need to consider two questions:

1. Does China's growing power and influence inexorably come at the expense of the United States?
2. What is the extent to which the national interests and policies of the United States and China coincide or diverge on a host of regional issues?[33]

If we can argue that Beijing's growing power and influence do not come at a marked cost to Washington's international leadership—and we find the United States and China share significant national interests and policies on regional issues—there is reason to believe China is headed toward re-emerging as a true Middle Kingdom. If, however, China's emergence as a regional power comes as win-lose proposition for the United States—and Beijing pursues regional interests that are inimical to the United States, we are witnessing the birth of a Chinese empire.

Is there a way to foster the former, while preventing the latter? Scholars focused on global and regional economic relations suggest this is indeed possible. As Alastair Iain Johnston notes:

The globalization discourse recognizes that the main factors that will constrain states and sovereignty in the future—their domestic economic choices, domestic cultural choices, even domestic political choices, and their foreign policies—may have less to do with material power distributions and more to do with a state's openness to global capital, information and technology flows. China analysts mostly agree that globalization is a double-edged sword, with adverse effects for state sovereignty and autonomy in a range of policy areas.[34]

Students of regional economic relationships come to a similar conclusion. In a paper published in 2004, Byung-Joon Ahn, a professor of political science in South Korea's prestigious Yonsei University, wrote, "Economic and political imperatives are diverging in East Asia. By and large, economic imperatives are working toward interdependence, but political imperatives are working toward nationalism within and between East Asian countries."[35]

The current Chinese leadership appears to recognize this limitation and is struggling to craft an appropriate policy response. In November 2003, Zhen Bijian, Vice President of the Central Party School—and purported Hu Jintao close advisor—introduced the concept of China's "peaceful rising." The "peaceful rising" strategy envisions China's future as being directly linked with other regional powers. According to Chinese Premier Wen Jiabao, "peaceful rising" is intended to "take full advantage of this opportunity of world peace to develop and strengthen ourselves ... China's rise cannot be achieved without the support of the rest of the world. We must maintain our opening-up policy and we must develop economic and trade exchanges with all friendly countries on the basis of equality and mutual benefit."[36] In an apparent effort to assure outside observers, an editorial in the *People's Daily* explained:

Western realpolitikers believe a nation's rise always implies a shift in hegemony and is thus doomed to confrontation with existing powers and that the rise of a new power with such historical trauma as China's will pose a greater threat to world security. Bearing this in mind, the Chinese government seems to have

added a qualifier to make the world understand its political intention: peaceful rise, in an attempt to prove that China can rise
peacefully.[37]

As we have seen, this language is far from accidental. The Chinese are
painfully aware of their own history—and of the fact many Westerners
believe Beijing is intent on correcting for the grievances of the past by
inflicting a political and economic cost on the neighbors and, potentially, the rest of the world. In announcing this new strategy, and then
immediately providing clarification, Beijing is trying to head off such
conclusions.

This pre-emptive strike was not limited to comments made to
reporters or newspaper editorials. In June 2005 Zhen Bijian spoke to
an audience in Washington, DC. During this presentation he argued,
"By unswervingly [adhering] to a development path of peaceful rise,
we seek to become a modern socialist country that is prosperous,
democratic and culturally advanced, and a responsible big country
playing a constructive role in international affairs which doesn't seek
hegemony or leadership of the world."[38] Put more simply, China is
not seeking to replace Moscow as Washington's global competitor.
Or, as a Chinese professor in Shanghai put it, "explicit in [peaceful ris-
ing] is the notion that China's economic and military development is
not a zero-sum game and that China represents less of an economic
competitor than economic opportunities."[39] A Canadian professor
offered this assessment, "discussions about the 'peaceful rise' of China
need to be understood in . . . context: its emergence as a major economic power with a global reach cannot but evoke the specter of hegemonic transition and its political fallout. Chinese leaders, however,
are clearly uninterested in assuming the mantel of global hegemon."[40]

So what do the Chinese want? Perhaps the easiest way to answer
that question is to examine the factors driving Chinese behavior. First,
China continues to demonstrate significant suspicions about perceived great power challenges to Beijing's sovereignty. Second, China
continues to be intent on protecting her own sovereignty from a
repeat of the "century of humiliation." Finally, China wants to be recognized as a having attained the status of a great power.[41]

Given these objectives, one has to ask how Beijing is realistically
intending to accomplish the task at hand. More than one scholar has
suggested in "peaceful rising" and similar policy declarations China
is laying the groundwork for an Asian version of the United States'
Monroe Doctrine.[42] Like Washington's 1823 implied declaration of

regional dominance, Beijing's press for reestablishment of a Middle Kingdom comes before she is ready to economically, militarily, or politically force the issue. But like the United States and the Monroe Doctrine, all of this only seems a matter of time—and probably not the 50-plus years it took for Washington to achieve the prowess sufficient to back its verbal declarations.

So where does this leave us? It would appear Beijing is likely headed toward Middle Kingdom rather than empire. The dominant role economic growth plays in the Chinese Communist Party's continued legitimacy strongly suggests China's leaders have no other option. (As one Western scholar put it: economic and military developments will place ultimately overwhelming strains on the present system of Party rule."[43]) Momentary inflammation of nationalist pride may serve to mobilize a population in crisis—but with 1.3 billion citizens focused on achieving improved economic advancement, Beijing can ill-afford to repeatedly engage in such dangerous dalliances. Thus, we foresee the re-emergence of China as the Middle Kingdom.

In this role China will serve as the dominant policy leader for Asia—but will not dictate behavior through blunt applications of military force. Instead of unleashing the People's Liberation Army, Beijing is positioning to employ economic and political might. As such, China will re-emerge as a respected as a "senior" member of the international community, but not at a win-lose cost to Washington. Absent a desire to assume the mantel and cost of serving as a global hegemon, Beijing has few choices but abet the well-being and continuance of the existing—largely U.S.-friendly—international economic and political order.

CHAPTER 1

China Matters

China is better understood as a theoretical power—a country that
has promise to deliver for much of the last 150 years but has consistently disappointed .... China matters about as much as Brazil
for the global economy. It is a medium-rank military power, and
it exerts no political pull at all.

—Gerald Segal, *Does China Matter?* 1999[1]

The debate over whether Beijing will emerge as Washington's
global "peer competitor"[2] is finished. The near collapse of the West's
financial system, the U.S. military's struggle for lasting victories in
Afghanistan and Iraq, and Washington's perceived inability to reach
a political solution to America's economic woes, have secured Beijing
a respectable place on the international stage. China's mounting
economic, military, and political prowess have earned the country a
$2.1 trillion foreign exchange reserve[3], staked a claim to regional lead-
ership in Asia, and now suggest successful governance of a large
territory and population does not require the exercise of liberal
democratic principles. In short, China has arrived—and the United
States will need to learn to live with her new counterpart.

How sure can one be of this assumption? After all, only 10 short
years ago *Foreign Affairs*—the U.S. Council on Foreign Relations'
flagship publication—went to newsstands with an article boldly titled:
"Does China Matter?" In the magazine's featured essay, Gerald Segal,
the former director of studies at the International Institute for Strategic Studies in London, argued China was "overrated as a market,
a power, and a source of ideas."[4] According to Segal's data, in 1997

China accounted for approximately 3.5 percent of global gross domestic product (GDP)—ranking seventh in world, parked firmly between Brazil and Italy. He then went on to argue China only accounted for 3 percent total world trade in 1997 and about 11 percent of total Asian trade during the same time period. Finally, Segal highlighted relative pittance China received in foreign direct investment in 1997—$45 billion dollars, 80 percent of which reportedly came from ethnic Chinese. His conclusion, "in terms of international trade and investment... Beijing is a seriously overrated power."[5]

No more. In 2007, China became the world's third largest economy —leapfrogging over Germany. According to Beijing's National Bureau of Statistics, in 2007 China accounted for 6 percent of global gross domestic product, generating $3.32 trillion in goods and services.[6] China also accounted for approximately 6 percent of total world trade and foreign direct investment in the nation grew to $82.7 billion.[7] Perhaps most telling, however, has been Beijing's dramatic accumulation of foreign capital. In 2007, China's foreign exchange reserves were estimated to total over $1.53 trillion.[8] As a means of placing China's economic performance in context, consider that in 2006 China's foreign reserves were approximately $1.07 trillion, and in 1992 that figure was only $19.4 billion. More astoundingly, China's foreign exchange reserves only surpassed the $100 billion mark in 1996. It took another five years for Beijing's foreign exchange holdings to reach $200 billion, and it was not until 2004 that China amassed over $500 billion in this account.

While this trend has slowed as a result of the global financial crisis, there are signs China's economy—unlike its Western competitors— will continue to expand during an otherwise global contraction. Why? First, Chinese consumers have money to spend—and a demonstrated willingness to do so. (The most remarkable example, in January 2009 Chinese consumers for the first time purchased more vehicles than did Americans—790,000 vehicles were sold in China during January 2009, versus 657,000 in the United States.[9]) Second, Beijing promptly moved to contradict domestic economic decline by rapidly approving a $586 billion stimulus package.[10] Third, foreign investors still perceive China as an underdeveloped economic opportunity. For example, consider sovereign wealth fund investments trends in Asia.

Like financial analysts in the Western world, sovereign wealth fund managers are in search of maximum return on one's investment. For investors in Asia, the target of choice is China. Singapore's Temasek

Holdings is a case in point. According to Temasek, between March 31, 2006 and March 31, 2007, the Singapore-based fund transitioned from placing 34 percent of its investments in other Asian nations, to 40 percent.[11]

The primary beneficiary of this transition in investment patterns? China. During 2005 Temasek investment in Singapore accounted for 49 percent of the firm's moneys. In 2006, that figure was 44 percent, and in 2007, 38 percent. During the same timeframe, Temasek's investments in Northeast Asia (China, South Korea, and Taiwan), grew from 8 percent in 2005, to 19 percent in 2006, and 24 percent in 2007.[12] Developments at the end of 2007 suggest this trend is going to continue. Temasek announced in early December 2007 it will be providing half of the funding for a new, $2 billion China-focused private equity venture being set up by a Goldman Sachs Group partner. This fund is reportedly geared toward purchasing stakes in state-owned Chinese companies.[13]

WHAT IS A "PEER COMPETITOR"?

The demise of the Soviet Union in 1991 left U.S. national defense strategists searching for a worthy adversary. While military commanders were confronted with a veritable herd of third world "rogue regimes," these hostile forces were largely deemed unworthy of long-term dialogue and planning. (A dismissive attitude Washington came to rue in 2004.) In late 1990s, however, it became fashionable to warn about the potential emergence of a "peer competitor"—an adversary who could challenge the United States on something approaching equal terms.

Arguably, the most concise definition of what constitutes a "peer competitor" for Washington appeared in a 2001 Rand Corporation study. According to the authors of *The Emergence of Peer Competitors: A Framework for Analysis*:

For a state to be a peer, it must have more than a strong military. Its power must be multidimensional—economic, technological, intellectual, etc.—and it must be capable of harnessing these capabilities to achieve a policy goal. For a peer to also be a competitor, it must have the desire to challenge the status quo and the rules of the international system

> that are largely upheld by the United States, the current
> hegemon. (Szayna, et al., 2001, p. xii)
>
> There is considerable controversy as to the reason military
> thinkers began debating the rise of "peer competitors." Critics
> argue the concept won an audience in the Pentagon because
> the "rogue nation" focus was simply insufficient for continued
> expansion of defense spending. Instead, the skeptics continue, U.S.
> military planners sold the idea of emerging "peer competitors"—
> China and Russia—as a means of justifying the procurement of
> new, high-tech weapons. (Klare, November 1997)

A similar trend is developing at sovereign wealth funds charged with
investing petrodollars. In an August 2007 interview with *The Wall
Street Journal*, Badar Al-Sa'ad, managing director of the Kuwait
Investment Authority, stated he is cutting his organization's investment in the United States and Europe from 90 percent of holdings,
to less than 70 percent. In what could be read as an expression of sentiments found throughout the Middle East, Al-Sa'ad rhetorically asked
The Wall Street Journal reporter, "why invest in 2% growth economies
when you can invest in 8% growth economies?"[14] As for potential targets of interest in China, Hong Kong bankers claim the sovereign
wealth funds have been investigating natural resources and the financial sector.[15]

So China presents an alluring target for foreign investors, but what
about the country's long-lamented banking problems? For years,
Beijing's critics hounded the Chinese government for abetting and
disguising an "alarmingly" high percentage of non-performing loans.
As Segal put it, "by conservative estimates at least a quarter of
Chinese loans are non-performing ... ordinary Chinese would be
alarmed to learn that their money is clearly being wasted."[16] In his
text, *The Coming Collapse of China*, Gordan Chang takes a similar
approach—going so far as to suggest the loan problem could contribute to a dramatic change in Chinese governments.[17] Why these grim
forecasts? According to Segal, this was an issue that "the current
leadership understands well but finds just too scary to tackle
seriously."[18]

It now seems China's public detractors underestimated Beijing—
in spades. The Chinese Communist Party has been engaged in an

extensive effort to address—and, by all appearances, resolve—the non-performing loan problem. The first step was to follow a procedure used during the 1997–89 Asian financial crisis and transfer some of the non-performing loans to asset management companies. In 1999, Beijing established four asset management companies that were paired with the "big four" banks."[19] Financial analysts believe the asset management firms initially "purchased" between $170 and $200 billion in non-performing loans at book value.[20]

The second step occurred in 2003, when the Chinese government established Central Huijin—an investment office within the State Administration of Foreign Exchange. In late 2003, Central Huijin "invested" $45 billion from China's foreign exchange reserves in 2 banks—The Bank of China and the China Construction Bank. (A week after announcing this move, the Finance Ministry quietly decided to write-off a $41 billion stake in the two banks in an additional effort to help alleviate their non-performing loan problem.[21]) This fiscal transfer resulted in Central Huijin owning 100 percent of the Bank of China and 85 percent of the shares issued by the China Construction Bank. As it turns out, this purchase gave Central Huijin almost exclusive claim to returns realized from the initial public offering of these banks in 2005—a tidy profit according to some Western analysts. In any case, Central Huijin's realized return on its investments at the end of 2004 was estimated to be almost $6 billion—not bad for a firm that had been open for little more than a year.[22]

The third move in Beijing's war on non-performing loans took place on the regulatory front. In 2003, Beijing sought to resolve the problem of poor business practices associated with the non-performing loans by standing up the China Banking Regulatory Commission to supervise and control the country's financial institutions. Unable to close this political loophole, in 2004 Chinese authorities resumed their efforts to resolve the non-performing loan problem through further transfers to the asset management companies. Accordingly, these firms purchased another $34 billion in non-performing loans from the Bank of China and the Construction Bank of China—this time at 50 percent of book value.[23]

What did all this do for the non-performing loan problem? By 2006, the "big four" were reportedly confronted with a non-performing loan ratio of 9.3 percent.[24] Dollar figures associated with this statistic remain in dispute. Ernst and Young Global issued a revised report in May 2006 claiming the "big four" were then confronted with approximately $133 billion in remaining non-performing loans.[25] The China

Banking Regulatory Commission offered a more nuanced report, declaring the non-performing loan ratio for all state-owned banks was 9.5 percent, but that the same figure for joint-stock banks—specifically the Bank of China, Construction Bank of China, and Industrial and Commercial Bank of China—was actually 3.1 percent. The official Chinese banking regulatory authority also stated overall non-performing loans had declined in value to a total of $160 billion. Western accounting firms immediately dismissed this figure by issuing reports stating the number was likely closer to $475 billion.[26]

While Chinese authorities may never completely resolve the country's non-performing loan problem—and there are growing concerns Beijing's economic stimulus campaign in 2009 may have given new life to this dilemma[27]—they certainly appear to understand targeted bailouts. At the end of 2006, the Chinese "big four" financial institutions reported the following non-performing loan ratios: Bank of China—4.04 percent; Construction Bank of China—3.39 percent; Industrial and Commercial Bank of China—3.79 percent . . . and the Agricultural Bank of China—26.17 percent.[28] The Agricultural Bank of China's dilemma—an estimated $114 billion in bad loans—has not gone unnoticed, both in and outside China.[29] In fact, there are rumors the Agricultural Bank of China is preparing to join the other "big four" with a public stock listing in 2010,[30] and that the China Investment Corporation—Beijing's sovereign wealth fund—is slated to participate in the official effort to address the Bank's non-performing loan problem.[31]

Two years ago we may have been tempted to dismiss all of this as little more than "blue smoke and mirrors." I hardly suspect that is no longer the case. The U.S. subprime crisis is now credited with toppling Iceland's government,[32] causing riots in Eastern Europe,[33] and potentially saddling taxpayers and stockholders with losses totaling $2–4 trillion. (The International Momentary Fund forecasts bank losses from toxic U.S.-originated assets at $2.2 trillion. Nouriel Roubini, the economist widely recognized for predicting the U.S. financial crisis, estimates banks will write down at least $2.5 trillion—$3.6 trillion beyond the $1.1 trillion in losses reported in 2007 and 2008.[34]) And Washington remains unable to rapidly craft a politically acceptable means of addressing the crisis.[35] At this point, the U.S. government has thrown $700 billion at its banking sector—the Troubled Asset Relief Program—engaged in a political showdown over an $800 billion stimulus package, and the Federal Reserve has essentially rendered borrowing money a cost-free proposition. All of which is to say the

Chinese non-performing loan problem now seems under control and a little more than minor glitch in Beijing's long-term plans for economic development.

And did I mention China now owns more than $1 trillion of Washington's debt, and is increasingly less interested in acting as a major creditor for the United States?[36] Speaking with the *New York Times*, an economist employed at the Royal Bank of Scotland put it this way, "all the key drivers of China's Treasury purchases are disappearing—there's a waning appetite for dollars and a waning appetite for Treasuries and that complicates the outlook for interest rates."[37] In other words, a China faced with diminished import earnings, a slowing economy, its own stimulus package, and low U.S. Treasury note interest rates is exhibiting less appetite for our debt. Does this matter? Well, as more than one economist has observed, a loss of foreign interest in U.S. national debt is going to drive up the cost of borrowing in America—by as much as 100–200 basis points.[38] Imagine paying 8 percent interest on a car or home loan . . . now I suspect people are beginning to think China matters.

So it would appear Gerald Segal was wrong about China's economic prospects, her importance in world markets, and Beijing's ability to clean up an ailing banking industry. But what about China's military? There is little disagreement that the People's Liberation Army (PLA) in the mid 1990s was poorly prepared for a modern—or any—armed conflict. In 1999, a Chinese military officer described the PLA as a boxer suffering, "short arms and slow feet." While Beijing maintained a force of over 2.8 million uniformed personnel, the PLA was largely restricted to conducting onshore operations within marching distance of China's territorial borders. China lacked air and sea lift, she had few over-the-horizon intelligence gathering capabilities, and essentially planned for conducting single-service military operations.[39] Given this situation, researchers at Rand declared, "China [in 1999] is indisputably not a 'peer competitor' of the United States." Nonetheless, Rand warned, China was also "not just another regional power."[40]

According to the Rand analysts, in 1999 China exhibited four characteristics that separated the PLA from other regional powers. First, China had nuclear weapons that could reach targets within the United States. Second, the Chinese military had fielded a greater number and variety of theater-range ballistic missiles than any other force then confronting the U.S. military. Third, the PLA's absolute size was daunting in its own right. And, finally, China's geographic expanse largely precluded the paralyzing synergistic attacks the U.S. armed forces had used so effectively in Operation DESERT STORM.[41] China may not have been prepared for combat, but she was not about to be rolled like a common drunk.

Suffice it to say, 10 years down the road things have changed. While China is still not prepared for a head-to-head conflict with the U.S. military, the PLA's regional capabilities are anything but "short" or "slow." Equipped with satellite-based surveillance assets, top-of-the-line Russian fighter aircraft, a rapidly modernizing navy, and more than 1,300 short- and medium-range ballistic missiles, the PLA can capably locate, track, and engage any military force operating within 500 miles of the Chinese coastline. Furthermore, Chinese commanders' are learning to field and fight a military that realizes the effect and efficiency inherent in joint warfare. Finally, Beijing's focus on downsizing the PLA, while simultaneously addressing logistics shortfalls, suggests the Chinese military is preparing to show up ready for battle long before sufficient U.S. forces can be moved into the theater.

China, in fact, explicitly and openly acknowledges this is the case. In Beijing's 2008 national defense white paper, the authors declare:

> China's national defense policy for the new stage in the new century basically includes: Upholding national security and unity, and ensuring the interests of national development; achieving the all-round, coordinated and sustainable development of China's national defense and armed forces; enhancing the performance of the armed forces with informationization as the major measuring criterion; implementing the military strategy of active defense; pursuing a self-defensive nuclear strategy; and fostering a security environment conducive to China's peaceful development.[42]

In order to successfully accomplish the many and difficult missions suggested by this policy Beijing goes on to report, "driven by preparations for military struggle, the [PLA] accelerated the development of weaponry and equipment, stepped up the development of the arms and services of the armed forces ... optimized its system, and reduced the number of personnel by 700,000."[43] The result? According to former U.S. Director of National Intelligence Michael McConnell, the Chinese are "building their military, in my view, to reach some state of parity with the United States ... they're a threat today; they would become an increasing threat over time."[44] The U.S. intelligence community thinks China's military capability matters.

Which brings us to Segal's final point—China's political relevance . . . at home and abroad. In 1999, Segal contended the Chinese Communist Party (CCP) "is devoid of ideological power and authority."[45] While Segal goes on to argue this ideological void is a domestic problem because it abets the rise of religions and cults, he was much more scathing about how the CCP's abandonment of communist orthodoxy played abroad. Segal would have us believe that, "bizarre as old-style Maoism was, at least it was a beacon for many in the developing world. Now China is a beacon to no one."[46]

Apparently concerned he had not made this point with sufficient vehemence; Segal then takes aim at what he perceives as Beijing's irrational isolationist tendencies. Arguing that China is "bereft of friends," Segal goes on to declare, "China is alone because it abhors the very notion of genuine international interdependence." Why does Beijing pursue this lonely course of action?

> No country relishes having to surrender sovereignty and power to the Western-dominated global system, but China is particularly wedded to the belief that it is big enough to merely learn what it must from the outside world and still retain control of its destiny. So China's neighbors understand the need to get on with China but have no illusions that China feels the same way.[47]

Needless to say, in the last 10 years things have changed. Not only has the Chinese Communist Party survived at home, Beijing is now considered the harbinger of a new form of governance.

The Chinese Communist Party's ability to outlive its Soviet counterpart can, in no small part, be attributed to Beijing's pursuit of her constituents' economic wants and needs. In fact, the CCP's continued place atop China's political hierarchy can be directly linked to an abandonment of the ideological fervor that unleashed the Great Leap Forward[48] and the Cultural Revolution.[49] By choosing to abandon Mao's revolutionary teachings for "reform and opening," Deng Xiaoping and his successors saved the Chinese Communist Party— but appear to have stripped it of an ideological touchstone.

I use the word "appear" above purposefully. While the Chinese Communist Party may no longer espouse "communist" rhetoric, it certainly is not absent an ideology. As a scholar at the Massachusetts Institute of Technology so ably put it: "being pragmatic is an ideology in and of itself."[50] Perhaps this is best explained by citing quotes attributed to Deng Xiaoping—the father of China's opening and reform policy:

- "Poverty is not socialism. To be rich is glorious."
- "It doesn't matter if a cat is black or white, so long as it catches mice."[51]

Quite simply, China's leadership chose to adapt rather than die. In a series of incremental policy experiments, the Chinese Communist Party has fostered economic development by allowing for performance-based remuneration, private property rights, and marketplace competition. While Western critics will argue Beijing—particularly when it comes to rule of law—has a long way to go and may result in nothing but decay,[52] many Chinese and members of the international community appear less skeptical.

How do we know the average Chinese citizen appears satisfied with their leadership's pragmatic approach to governance? In June and August 2005, a Western public polling organization[53] discovered 76 percent of Chinese respondents agreed, "the free enterprise system and free market economy work best in society's interests when accompanied by strong government regulations." Furthermore, of the 20,791 respondents in 20 countries, the Chinese "ironically, [were] the country that showed the highest level of support for the free enterprise system . . . with 74 percent agreeing that it is the best system. Others that were nearly as enthusiastic were the Philippines (73 percent), the United States (71 percent), and India (70 percent)."[54] In short, it appears the average Chinese citizen believes Beijing has chosen wisely in opting to abandon communism for capitalism—but do they agree this should be the government's top priority?

The answer to that question appears an emphatic yes. A survey of approximately 2,000 Chinese citizens conducted during the summer of 2006[55] caused the Chicago Council on Global Affairs to announce:

- The Chinese believe their country is already a significant power and express strong support for its economic and military ascendance. Asked about their country's global influence today, the Chinese give themselves a mean rating of 7.8 on a zero-to-ten scale, second only to the United States—8.6. Asked how influential they will be in 10 years, the Chinese give themselves an 8.3, the same as the United States, followed by Russia (7.5) and the European Union (7.3)

- The Chinese do not put increasing their global influence at the top of their foreign policy priorities. When presented a list of 11 foreign policy goals, the Chinese tend to place more importance on economic concerns. Protecting the jobs of Chinese workers is the top objective (chosen as very important by 71 percent), followed by promoting economic growth (64 percent very important) and securing adequate energy supplies (61 percent very important). The goal of building superior military power in Asia came last—seen as very important by 40 percent of Chinese respondents[56]

These findings reiterate the point we made above—the average Chinese citizen finds pragmatism an entirely reasonable approach to governance, even if this means "suffering" strong government regulation of the marketplace.

So it appears Segal was wrong about the Chinese Communist Party's domestic relevance and appeal, what about on the international front? Are the Chinese still "bereft of friends?" Well, this depends on how one defines friend. If we adhere to Webster as the standard, "one attached to another by affection or esteem," the Chinese are not alone in appearing friendless. The existing international system—based on principles enunciated in the Peace of Westphalia—is a relatively chaotic environment that offers few rewards for demonstrations of "affection." Beijing does; however, seem to be earning considerable esteem—while Washington's regard in the international community appears on the wane.[57]

The argument for China's emerging esteem in the international community was most clearly articulated in a 2004 article titled "The Beijing Consensus." Written by a member of Kissinger Associates, "The Beijing Consensus" opens by contending, "China's rise is already reshaping the international order by introducing a new physics of development and power."[58] China, according to the author, "relies less on traditional tools of power projection . . . and leads instead by the electric power of its example and bluff impact of size."[59] In place of the Washington Consensus, he continues, we now have the Beijing Consensus—a set of theorems that reject Washington's prescriptive dictates in favor of innovation, pragmatism, and sustained development.

What is the Beijing Consensus? It is said to consist of three theorems about "how to organize the place of a developing country in the world." More specifically, the Beijing Consensus is said to advocate:

1. Developing countries employ bleeding- rather than trailing-edge technology so as to create change that moves faster than the problems change causes.

2. Employment of new governance tools—instruments that reflect the fact it is impossible to control chaos from the top. This second theorem is said to "demand a development model where sustainability and equality become first considerations, not luxuries."

3. An emphasis on self-determination—an approach to international relations that "stresses using leverage to move big, hegemonic powers that may be tempted to step on your toes."[60]

The fundamental essence of the Beijing Consensus is "to tackle problems before they arise."[61] Sounds good, but is anyone buying? After all, the China model would appear to advocate economic development with little regard for democratic principles.

Acolytes of Joseph Nye's "soft power"[62] theory seem to believe China is surrounded by admiring—but wary—shoppers. In a study released in April 2008, the Congressional Research Service (CRS) declared: "China is seen to be trying to project soft power by portraying its own system as an alternative model for economic development, one based on authoritarian governance and elite rule without the restrictions and demands that come with political liberalization."[63] While CRS concludes China has limited success in this marketing effort—others believe Beijing is making significant headway.

In May 2007, two scholars at the Stanley Foundation argued China was "at the verge of a return to great power status . . . it is already, or soon will be, a dominant player in East Asia . . . and is playing an increasingly global role."[64] The potential extent of this global role—specifically as a role model—was further highlighted by the financial crisis that began to unfold in the summer of 2007. Looking over the debris, Roger Altman, a former U.S. Deputy Treasury Secretary, concluded: "this damage has put the American model of free-market capitalism under a cloud. The financial system is seen as having collapsed; and the regulatory framework, as having spectacularly failed."[65] The winner: China. For while China's economy will also suffer a slowdown, it's financial system was largely unexposed to disaster. As such, Altman continues, "Beijing will be in a position to assist other nations financially and make key investments . . . at a time when the West cannot."

THE WASHINGTON CONSENSUS

In 1989, John Williamson, an economist at the Peterson Institute for International Finance, drafted a paper titled, "What Washington Means by Policy Reform." Williamson declared he had identified "what would be regarded in Washington as constituting a desirable set of economic policy reforms." These were:

- Fiscal discipline—"large and sustained fiscal deficits are a primary source of macroeconomic dislocation in the form of inflation, payment deficits and capital flight"
- Public expenditure priorities—health and education are regarded as "quintessentially proper objects of government expenditure;" defense spending is largely unassailable as the "ultimate prerogative of sovereign governments;" but, subsidies are "regarded as prime candidates for reduction or preferably elimination"
- Tax reform—with a focus on developing a broad tax base and moderate marginal tax rates
- Reasonable interest rates—interest rates should be market-determined and positive so as to discourage capital flight and/or increase savings
- Reasonable exchange rates—exchange rates should be determined by market forces, or be consistent with macroecnomic objectives . . . the former is preferred
- Favorable trade policy—access to imports at "competitive prices" was deemed important to export promotion—free trade was deemed ideal, but could be restricted by a need to promote "infant industries" or as a means of protecting a venerable economy
- Welcome foreign direct investment—"a restrictive attitude limiting the entry of foreign direct investment is regarded as foolish"

- Encourage privatization—"private industry is managed more efficiently than state enterprises"
- Emphasize deregulation—as a means of "promoting competition"
- Institutionalize property rights—"fundamental for the satisfactory operation of the capitalist system"

Williamson's bottom line is that "the economic policies that Washington urges on the rest of the world may be summarized as prudent macroeconomic policies, outward orientation, and free-market capitalism." (John Williamson, 1990, "What Washington Means by Policy Reform," *Latin America: How Much Has Happened?* Peterson Institute for International Finance, Washington, DC.)

A distressing observation, but Altman is not finished. He offers no solace for those worrying China's rise. According to Altman, "there could hardly be more constraining conditions for the United States and Europe." Why?

First, the severe recession will prompt governments there to focus inward ... Second, unprecedented fiscal deficits and difficulties in the financial systems will also preclude the West from engaging on major international initiatives ... Third, the economic credibility of the West has been undermined by the crisis.[66]

It is this third point—the collapse of Washington's economic credibility—that Altman appropriately highlights as the largest problem. As he notes, the "soft power" resident in Adam Smith's *laissez faire*, market-based capitalism is now much diminished. The ongoing perceived nationalization of banking in the United States and Europe, coupled with a popular demand for stringent regulation on multiple fronts, strongly suggests Beijing—not Washington—was headed down the right path. The bottom line for Altman—and this author— "China's global influence will thus increase, and Beijing will be able to undertake political and economic initiatives to increase it further."[67]

Where does this lead on the political front? For that answer we turn to Azar Gat, The Weizman Professor of National Security at Tel Aviv

University. In 2007, Gat published an article titled "The Return of Authoritarian Great Powers." According to Gat, liberal democracies face two great challenges: radical Islam and the rise of nondemocratic great powers.[68] More specifically, Gat argues the West is confronted with the emergence of China and Russia as "authoritarian capitalist" rather than "communist" regimes. According to the professor, "capitalism's ascendancy appears to be deeply entrenched, but the current predominance of democracy could be far less secure."[69] As such, Gat would have us believe that a form of governance largely banished by the Second World War may now be in the midst of a resurgence.

Is this a reasonable argument? Is China little more than a modern-day equivalent of 1939 Germany or Japan? And what about Egypt, Singapore or Venezuela? Are these contemporary versions of Mussolini's Italy—erstwhile democracies tottering on the edge of authoritarian dictatorship? Gat provides a discomfortingly vague response. Rather than dispute the potential historical analogies, Gat chooses instead to explain why fascist Berlin and imperialist Tokyo are no longer with us. Germany and Japan, he contends, were defeated because they were "medium-sized countries with limited resource bases and they came up against [a] far superior . . . economic and military coalition."[70] This certainly is not the case with China. So what about the future?

In the world according to Gat, "democracies generally outdo other systems economically. Authoritarian capitalist regimes are at least as successful—if not more so—in the early stages of development, but they tend to democratize after crossing a certain threshold of economic and social development."[71] This is an argument proponents of liberal democracy have clung to for years. Wait, they bid, China will someday emerge as the world's largest democracy. A similar statement is made concerning Russia—and then we are treated to a quick litany of examples typically including Spain, South Korea and Taiwan.

Why this optimism? Good question. Gat is certainly unable to definitively explain why we should conclude liberal democracy will prevail in a contest with authoritarian capitalism. He readily admits China's economic transformation has been a boon for global development—to say nothing of lifting between 200 and 400 million Chinese out of poverty. And, Gat wishfully declares "China may still eventually democratize, and Russia could reverse its drift away from democracy."[72] But why should Beijing and Moscow follow this path rather than staying the course? This Gat cannot answer. Instead he wistfully points to Washington as "the single most important hope for the future of liberal democracy." The bulwark of the United States' strengths are "considerable potential to grow—both economically and in terms of population."

But what—as events in 2008 appear to indicate—if Gat is wrong? What happens if the United States is not able to sustain economic growth? What happens if Altman is right and China uses this moment of international economic crisis to secure her reputation as a viable alternative to the West and its coercive "Washington Consensus?" Would Gat and other proponents of liberal democracy still be willing to come to a similar conclusion? Certainly there indications of a shift away from Adam Smith and deregulation in America and Europe. In no small sense, economic angst and terrorism-driven security concerns now appear to be curtailing American enthusiasm for liberal democracy. For no small number of U.S. citizens desire a steady—and even authoritarian—hand at the tiller.

This domestic shift to the right comes with a growing realization the financial crisis of 2008 may have served to significantly diminish the United States' stature on the international stage. As Bush administration officials told the *Wall Street Journal* in October 2008, "the financial crisis could further undermine the U.S.'s role as the world's only superpower and affect the reshaping of international institutions."[73] This appears a widely shared assessment. For instance, in *Global Trends 2025: A Transformed World*, the National Intelligence Council (NIC) declares, "the international system ... will be almost unrecognizable by 2025 owing to the rise of emerging powers, a globalizing economy, an historic transfer of wealth and economic power from West to East, and the growing influence of non-state actors." The NIC goes on to argue, "although the United States is likely to remain the single most powerful actor, the United States' relative strength ... will decline and U.S. leverage will become more constrained."[74]

The new dominant players—Brazil, Russia, India and China (BRICs)—according to the NIC, "are not following the Western liberal model ... but instead are using a different model, 'state capitalism' ... a system of economic management that gives a prominent role to the state."[75] Nor, it seems, does the NIC believe the BRICs are inevitably headed for liberal democracy. In a classic example of intelligence community hedging the NIC decrees:

We remain optimistic about the long-term prospects for greater democratization, even though advances are likely to be slow and globalization is subjecting many recently democratized countries to increasing social and economic pressures with the potential to undermine liberal institutions.[76]

In short, there is widespread acceptance of the argument Washington is not likely to remain securely atop the global power hierarchy—and that liberal democracy is by no means a foregone evolutionary political conclusion. As Robert Reich once so ably observed, "democracy needs capitalism . . . capitalism doesn't need democracy."[77]

All of which brings us back to Segal. It now appears the Chinese Communist Party has not only maintained, but enhanced, its appeal both at home and abroad. Instead of being "bereft of friends," Beijing now finds itself surrounded by would-be suitors—all of whom seem to believe China matters. This is not to say, however, China is suddenly going to become the most popular kid on the block—or that the neighborhood is going to dramatically change. Recall our admonishment concerning use of the term "friend" when referring to relations in the existing international community. China may have won esteem, but she is not an object of affection. Furthermore, Beijing seems to understand that her esteem is best served by preserving the current international order.

I hasten to note this is not a unique observation. In their April 2008 report on China's employment of "soft power," the Congressional Research Service concluded Beijing's "interests appear to have benefited more substantially by operating within the current global system, of which the United States is the chief architect, than by challenging it."[78]

Why acquiesce to an international system which appears tailored to Western rather than Chinese values and norms? John Ikenberry, the Albert G. Milbank Professor or Politics and International Affairs at Princeton University, would have us believe it is because the existing international order is "a Western-centered system that is open, integrated, and rule-based, with wide and deep political foundations."[79] Academic scatology at its finest.

Let's take a quick look at how China likely perceives the existing international order. First, while the current global power structure is certainly "Western-centered," it was only secured in such a manner during the last 200 years—and this imperialism was reinforced by the Bretton Woods Agreement . . . a negotiation the CCP was not invited to attend. Second, the existing system is "open"—but only if one agrees to play by the West's rules. For instance, China has been compelled to join a jumble of ineffective United Nation's bodies, had to appeal for membership in the World Trade Organization, and still cannot get Washington to recognize Beijing's claim on Taiwan. Third, the system is integrated—only if one: (a) is not a Muslim fundamentalist state; (b) acquiesces to the West's definition of who is a terrorist; and, (c) accepts that capitalism and Bretton Woods' spinoffs are the most efficient means of governing international finance. Fourth, the system is "rule-based"—but only if one accepts that rule number one is "might makes right" . . . or some derivative thereof.

Admittedly, the West's insistence on maintaining a Westphalian system has been embraced in Beijing—but only because the Chinese Communist Party has found it to their advantage to do so. Finally, the system has "wide and deep political foundations." Again, think about this from Beijing's perspective. The international system has Western "wide and deep political foundations." Historians are quick to note the Judeo-Christian, Greek and Roman tradition was not widely adopted in Asia—and yet we are to believe the Chinese are going to permanently accept these values as the only logical foundation for the international political system? Martin Jacques, the author of *When China Rules the World*, certainly does not believe that is the case . . . and uses a 500-plus page text to document the evidence supporting his argument.[80]

PRAGMATISM AS AN IDEOLOGY

So why do the Chinese choose to operate within the existing international system? Time for a return to our earlier observation on the Chinese Communist Party's adoption of pragmatism as an ideological foundation. If we assume the Chinese leadership is rational—and there is no reason to believe otherwise—than Beijing has to realize it is to her advantage to quietly accede to functioning within the existing system. Keep in mind, the Chinese Communist Party's primary goal is to remain in power, and that to do so its leadership must be perceived as fostering economic development. The current international economic system certainly appears tailor-made for this agenda.

The Chinese have figured out that a Bretton Woods world is exactly what they need. The original Bretton Woods agreement worked because the United States was the world's largest economy—and had accumulated a remarkable stockpile of gold as a result of payments made during World War II. (The United States reportedly held $26 billion in gold reserves at the end of World War II, 65 percent of the international total estimated to be approximately $40 billion in 1945.) And, more importantly, because Washington was willing to facilitate development of a trading pattern that enriched the recovering economies in Europe and Japan at the United States' expense.

While Europe struggled with a balance of payments problem between 1945 and 1950, the Marshall Plan and U.S. efforts elsewhere served to revive the international economy. In 1950, the balance of payments reversed direction—with moneys flowing out of the United States and back into central banks throughout Europe. Although this could have resulted in a run on Washington's gold stockpile, most nations chose to forgo converting dollars to hard metal. Why? *U.S. trade deficits kept the international economy liquid and promoted further economic development in exporting countries.* Furthermore, with gold set at a fixed price, holding dollars was more lucrative than acquiring a bank vault of bullion. Dollars could be used to earn interest—gold holdings were simply not as easy to convert into a return on one's investment.[81] Keep these observations in mind as we proceed. The lessons learned in London, Paris, and Rome were to be carefully studied and applied in Beijing.

Over the ensuing 50 years the original Bretton Woods agreement has largely come apart at the seams. This is not to say, however, the fundamental economic principles underlying Bretton Woods have been buried and forgotten. In 2003, Michael Dooley, David Folkerts-Landau, and Peter Garber released a paper titled, "An Essay on the Revived Bretton Woods System."[82] According to the authors, the international economic and political system existent during the original Bretton Woods system is best understood as consisting of a "core" and "periphery." The United States served as the core, while Europe and Japan constituted an emerging periphery. According to Dooley, Folkerts-Landau, and Garber, "the periphery countries chose a development strategy of undervalued currencies, controls on capital flows, trade reserve accumulation, and the use of the [core] as a financial intermediary that lent credibility to their own financial systems. In turn, the U.S. lent long term to the periphery, generally through foreign direct investment."[83]

As Dooley, Folkerts-Landau, and Garber understood economic history in 2003, the collapse of Bretton Woods I was the result of growing prosperity in Europe and Japan. However, they go on to argue, the subsequent period of free floating exchange rates was "only a transition during which there was no important [economic] periphery."[84] As Dooley, Folkerts-Landau, and Garber put it, "the communist countries were irrelevant to the international monetary system." Europe and Japan, Dooley, Folkerts-Landau, and Garber contend, have now been replaced by an "Asian periphery" that is proceeding down the same path as their predecessors in Berlin, Paris, and Rome. That is, "the dynamics of the international monetary system, reserve accumulation, net capital flows, and exchange rate movements, are driven by the developments of these periphery countries"—with the United States again serving as the "core."

Why Washington at the center? According to Dooley, Folkerts-Landau, and Garber:

Asia's proclivity to hold U.S. assets does not reflect an irrational affinity for the U.S. Asia would export anywhere else if it could and happily finance any resulting imbalances. But the U.S. is open; Europe is not. Europe could not absorb the flood of goods, given its structural problems and in the face of absorbing Eastern Europe as well. So Asia's exports go to the U.S., as does its finance.[85]

In short, Dooley, Folkerts-Landau, and Garber contend the economic relationships critical for Bretton Woods have simply undergone a geographic transfer. In the broader picture, the periphery still uses trade imbalances with the United States to finance domestic economic development. In turn, the periphery supports American spending by investing in the United States; purchasing corporate and government debt that American consumers no longer have the cash to acquire.

This symbiotic relationship—and thus the existing international system—has certainly worked for the Chinese. The question now confronting decision makers is will it last? On this question the jury remains out, but is not sequestered. Some members of the academic community contend Beijing is simply using the current system to stack the deck in China's favor.

For instance, Aaron Friedberg, a professor of politics and international affairs at Princeton, argues China pursues mercantilist policies and uses the existing system as a "muffling influence on American strategy."[86] According to Friedberg, Beijing primarily accomplishes this objective through the establishment of business relationships with American corporations—who can then be "rewarded or punished" into working for China's agenda back in the

United States. A second option Friedberg notes, is for the Chinese to engage in financial diplomacy. United States dependence on Chinese purchases of our Treasury notes as a means of underwriting Washington's deficit spending also renders Americans vulnerable to "financial blackmail." That is, the Chinese could threaten to cease purchasing our debt, or rapidly sell same, thereby sending the American economy into a tailspin. In either case, Friedberg's point is the same—China's economic growth and participation in the existing international system "provide it with an increasing array of instruments with which to try to exert influence on other countries and, if it chooses, to carry forward a strategic competition with the United States."[87]

This argument is carried to its logical extreme by those who assert China will ultimately destabilize the world economy as a result of the Chinese Communist Party's self-serving agenda. In this scenario, Beijing's single-minded pursuit of economic growth results in distorted trade, huge financial imbalances, and contentious competition for scarce resources.[88] Adherents to this argument postulate evidence of Beijing's willingness to overturn the applecart are manifested in China's "predatory" trade policy, artificial suppression of the renminbi's value, and her efforts to "lock-up" oil, gas, and copper supplies. The difference, they continue, between Washington and Beijing is that although "the United States has seen a prosperous global economy as a means of expanding [U.S.] power ... China sees the global economy—guaranteed markets for its exports and raw materials—as a means to promote domestic stability."[89] When the international system no longer meets that goal? Time for a change, likely in a manner Beijing deems most favorable for the CCP's longevity.

According to Chinese authorities, Beijing's "financial nuclear option" would be executed through a rapid sell-off of U.S. government securities. The associated consequences—a dramatic decline in the value of the dollar, collapse of the Treasury bond market, and a potential U.S. economic recession—are considered to be so anathema to Washington that American politicians are thought more willing to accept Beijing's demands than risk the "fallout."

As might be expected, there is considerable debate about China's willingness to execute this strategy, particularly in light of Beijing's substantial U.S. Treasury note holdings and the damage a rapid sell-off would inflict on the Chinese economy. Chinese officials, in fact, have gone to great lengths to downplay any discussion of the financial "nuclear option." For instance, in August 2007 the People's Bank of China tried to refute rumors of such a plan by releasing a statement declaring Beijing is "a responsible investor in international financial markets" and that "U.S. dollar assets, including American government bonds, are an important component of China's foreign exchange reserves." (Ambrose Evans-Pritchard, August 10, 2007, "China Threatens 'Nuclear Option' of Dollar Sales," *The Telegraph*, London; Jeff Manson, March 29, 2008, "Clinton Says China Holdings Threaten U.S. Security," REUTERS; and Sim Chi Yin and Bhagyashree Garekar, August 13, 2007, "China Says It Will Not Dump U.S. Dollar Assets," *The Straits Times*, Singapore)

On the other side of the coin are those who hold China is a responsible member of the international community, and can be expected to maintain the existing system. Advocates of this school like to open the discussion by citing Deng Xioping's three tasks for China in the 1980s: (1) oppose hegemonism and preserve world peace; (2) work on China's reunification with Taiwan; and (3) step up the drive for China's four modernizations.[90] These tasks, China's fans argue, are indicative of a nation bent on operating within the international system, not one focused on toppling the *ancient regime*.

Perhaps the best statement of this position is offered by Alastair Iain Johnston. In a 2003 scholarly article titled "Is China a Status Quo Power?" Johnston declared:

> ... it is hard to conclude that China is a clearly revisionist state operating outside, or barely inside, the boundaries of a so-called international community. Rather, to the extent that one can identify an international community on major issues, [China] has become more integrated into and more cooperative within international institutions than ever before.[91]

Nor, Johnston continues, can he find definitive evidence that "China's leaders are actively trying to balance against U.S. power to undermine an American-dominated unipolar system and replace it with a multipolar system."[92] Johnston is not alone in coming to this conclusion. In 1997, a U.S. Air Force officer argued, "China is pursuing impressive military modernization programs, but they continue to be based on attempts to improve her world status and provide a viable defense of her homeland."[93] In other words, even members of the U.S. military perceive Beijing's actions as those of a responsible member of the international community.

But what happens when we take Beijing off the global stage and instead ask her to perform closer to home—does China behave like a responsible member of the international community when dealing with other nations in East Asia? This question has generated considerable controversy. Writing in 1999, an officer at the U.S. Air War College argued, "China is driven by culture, history, and new found nationalism to become East Asia's hegemon."[94] Historians focused on China argue to the contrary. They foresee a mature China essentially reviving the ancient "tribute system." This system, as one academic noted, would feature a combination of patron-client ties, economic interdependence, security agreements, cultural assimilation, political ritual, and benevolent governance.[95] And what about the Chinese themselves? How do they see their relations unfolding with Asia? Scholars have found "Chinese across the professional spectrum regularly claim that because of China's past horrific encounters with foreign imperialism and hegemony, it will never exert the same on others."[96]

So who is right? The hawks or the doves? For the moment, it appears China is widely perceived to be a responsible actor—even when it comes to dealing with her neighbors. In 2005, Robert Sutter, a visiting professor of Asian Studies at Georgetown University's School of Foreign Service, observed, Beijing's "greater embrace of globalization means that the Chinese leadership has come to a more sophisticated view of U.S. power and Asian affairs, recognizing how China benefits in the face of U.S. global leadership in Asia."[97] For Sutter, China's behavior in Asia was intended to serve five long-term objectives:

1. Help secure China's foreign policy environment while Beijing is focused on economic development and political stability.

2. Promote economic exchange that facilitates China's development.

3. Support Chinese efforts to isolate Taiwan and secure a flow of advanced arms and military technology.

4. Calm regional fears and reassure the neighbors about how an increasingly powerful and influential China will act.

5. Boost China's regional and international power and influence as a means of helping to secure an ambiguous world order.[98]

Certainly, these are not completely benign objectives, nor, however, do they suggest the rise of a regional hegemon or imperial power. If Sutter is right, Beijing is behaving like a responsible member of the international community—and the neighbors should be able to see that is indeed the case.

If recent analysis from David Kang, a professor at Dartmouth College, and the Rand Corporation is correct, that is exactly how China's neighbors perceive Beijing. Kang's 2007 study of political relations in East Asia comes to two conclusions: (1) China's neighbors are not seeking to balance Beijing, they are accommodating her; and, (2) this accommodation is due to a "constellation of interests and beliefs—a particular mix of identities and the absence of fear."[99] The absence of fear? Come on, this is China we're talking about—the most populated nation on the plant, a nuclear power with a communist government—how can the neighbors not fear Beijing? Kang agrees —at first blush this makes no sense. Conventional theories about international relations—and human interaction—frequently posit the acquisition of power causes fear in others. And yet, public opinion polls in Asia—with the exception of Japan—reveal a tendency to view China's rise in a favorable manner. Furthermore, the polls reveal little support for a confrontational approach in dealing with China.[100] This brings us to the issue of accommodating China. According to Kang, a majority of Asia sees little reason to not accommodate Beijing, as "these states . . . view the likelihood that China will use military force in the region as low."[101]

Now even I am skeptical. It seems hard to believe that the China of 2009—equipped with modern air, ground, and naval weapon systems —is not perceived as likely to employ this equipment in a coercive manner. But that is exactly what Rand discovered during a study of how six U.S. allies and major security partners have responded to China's rise over the last 10 years. According to Rand:

• East Asia is not gradually falling under China's hegemony.

• China is not gradually and surreptitiously pushing the United States out of the region.

- Regional states are not climbing on a Chinese bandwagon.
- East Asian nations are not modernizing their militaries in an effort to balance Chinese power.
- China's military modernization has not even sparked a regional rush to expand military budgets or force structures.[102]

In short, the Rand study verifies what the previous scholarship had argued—China is widely perceived as a responsible member of the international community, even in East Asia. This is a surprising finding. Traditional approaches to understanding international relations suggest a dominant or rising power should be seeking to establish herself as a hegemon or, at least, as the head of a competing power group—and that this ambition should make the neighbors very nervous.

HIERARCHY, NOT HEGEMONY

There is, however, a significant possibility the traditional approaches to understanding international relations are wrong—at least when it comes to explaining China's behavior. Rather than subscribing to a mindset that demands a balance of power, or an international hegemon, Chinese leaders appear to view the world in a hierarchical manner. I understand this will be no easy argument. Consider, for instance the work of Henry Kissinger—the most prominent advocate and practitioner of balance-of-power politics. "The relations of the principle Asian nations to each other," according to Kissinger, "bear most of the attributes of the European 'balance-of-power' system of the nineteenth century. China is on the road to superpower status. The other Asian nations are likely to seek counterweights to an increasingly powerful China."[103]

But just perhaps—as the Rand study indicates—Kissinger was wrong about Asia. Rather than applying the tired European model to this situation,[104] we should be seeking alternative explanations. To that end, I propose we use Asian history to help explain China's current behavior in much the same way Kissinger used European history to rationalize Moscow's approach to dealing with Washington. Furthermore, I propose we move away from Kissinger's theories and consider more contemporary arguments being floated in political science.

In 2007, David Lake, a professor of political science at the University of California in San Diego, published an article titled "Escaping from the State of Nature: Authority and Hierarchy in World Politics."

As Lake observes in his opening sentence, "international relations theory has long assumed that the modern international system is a state of nature devoid of political authority."[105] This assumption he continues, leads to the logical conclusion that the international system is anarchic—no state possesses authority over another. And yet, Lake notes, historically that has not been the case. Instead he argues, there have always been a wide variety of hierarchical relations within the international system—to include: empires protectorates, spheres of influence, and "other relationships in which the sovereignty of the subordinate polity is ceded in whole or in part to a dominate state."[106]

This type of hierarchical relationship emerges when one state recognizes that another has the political authority—"rightful rule"—to command certain forms of behavior. As Lake puts it, political authority has been established when "the subordinate state recognizes both that the dominant state has the right to issue certain commands and that it should, within the limits of its abilities, follow those commands or suffer the appropriate consequences."[107] Why is this important? To answer that question, Lake explains the difference between anarchy and hierarchy within an international system. Anarchy, he explains, is a situation wherein "none is entitled to command; none is required to obey." Hierarchy, on the other hand, exists when some are so entitled—via political authority—and others—by dint of recognizing that authority—are so required.[108] This emphasis on political authority is not accidental. As Lake makes clear, regimes that rely on coercion rather than authority are typically called tyrannies.[109] As far as Beijing seems to be concerned, a state that relies on authority in today's international system might best be referred to as China.

In his study of China's relations with other states in East Asia, David Kang comes to a very similar conclusion. In fact, he contends one of the reasons Beijing's neighbors have relatively little fear of China's intentions can be explained by the hierarchical relationships that existed in the region for over a 1,000 years. Kang explains the relationship this way:

> The traditional international order in East Asia encompassed a regionally shared set of norms and expectations that guided relations and yielded substantial stability. In Chinese eyes—and explicitly accepted by the surrounding nations—the world of the past millennium has consisted of civilization (China) and barbarians

(all other states). In this view, as long as the barbarian states were willing to kowtow to the Chinese emperor and show formal acceptance of their lower position in the hierarchy, the Chinese had neither the need to invade . . . nor the desire to do so. Explicit acceptance of the Chinese perspective on the regional order brought diplomatic recognition from China and allowed the pursuit of international trade and diplomacy.[110]

This explanation covers the ground, but leaves one uncomfortable issue to be addressed: exactly what does it mean to "kowtow to the Chinese emperor?" Kang explains the kowtow as a largely ritual act that involved the regular dispatch of "tribute missions" and a *pro forma* request for the emperor to approve of any change in leadership in the lesser states. (This later process is known as "investiture.") Kang then goes on to note—and I emphasize this—"*Kowtowing to China did not involve much loss of independence, since these states were largely free to run their internal affairs as they saw fit, and could contact foreign policy independently from China.*"[111] In other words, as long as one at least formally recognized the status quo you were free to pursue selfish national interests with little fear of being clobbered by the big kid on the block.

Kang is not alone in explaining historical national relationships in Asia this way. John Fairbank, explains China's historical foreign policy objectives as follows:

1. China has historically shown a preference for regional "dominance."
2. This "dominance" is based on demonstrating and winning appropriate respect for China's "superiority."
3. China appears to uses this "superiority" to dictate a sense of harmonious coexistence.[112]

China's foremost political objective has been to defend herself from Inner Asia, the broad stretch of land that encompassed everything north and west of the Great Wall—what is currently Mongolia, Russia, and Kazakhstan. For Beijing, the Great Wall marked the dividing line between "less civilized" nomadic peoples and the cultured/ educated world.[113] The "civilized"—with few exceptions—stayed on their side of the Wall. Military adventures outside the gates were largely confined to defeating emerging threats and subjugating problem areas. Even these ventures were markedly different that "crusades" and campaigns in the West, as the "civilized" Chinese typically avoided feudal domination in favor of "tributes" who were left to govern as they saw fit. The only restraint? Acceptance and recognition of the Chinese regime—a relationship we have come to understand as "peaceful coexistence."[114]

WHERE IS CHINA HEADED?

Having thus established the framework for a new, or different, manner of evaluating Beijing's behavior, we are ready to examine China's actions over the last 10 years and predict where she is heading in the coming decade. We start this exercise by observing that in place of the suspicion, isolationism, and animosity Beijing engendered in the late 1970s and early 1980s, we now find a China positioned to assume a leadership role in the Far East. Why? According to David Shambaugh, this "China emerging" is manifested in four forms: (1) Beijing's participation in regional organizations; (2) China's establishment of strategic partnerships and deepening bilateral relations; (3) the expansion of regional economic ties; and (4) the reduction of distrust and anxiety in the security sphere.[115]

This is not to say "all is well" in the security sphere—or, for that matter—when it comes to economic integration. While Shambaugh would have us believe that China's military modernization is driven by a desire to field a force comparable with Beijing's new international stature and a wish to retain the capabilities necessary to deter Taiwan independence, he admits these motivations don't reassure the neighbors. As Shambaugh notes, two issues on the military front are particularly troublesome for China's Asian counterparts—(1) Beijing's development of power projection capabilities; and (2) the potential for this force to be used against Taiwan.[116] Neither concern can be "wished" or "denied" away. Despite Hu Jintao's "peaceful rising" campaign, his Asian neighbors remain worried about where the Chinese are headed. Is Hu setting the stage for Beijing to serve as the capital for a Chinese empire? Or is Hu facilitating China's reemergence as the Middle Kingdom—a "senior mentor," with benign aspirations for guiding Asia into the mid twenty-first century?

Perhaps the easiest way to answer that question is to examine the factors driving Chinese behavior. First, the Chinese Communist Party wants to be recognized as a responsible member of the international community—both at home and abroad. Second, China is positioning herself to equip, train, and maintain a modern military required by a Westphalian world—but which is less threatening to the neighbors. Finally, China is seeking to "sell" her governance model—from economic development to serving a domestic constituency—as a direct competitor to the version of liberal democracy Washington has long sought to peddle across the planet.

This, as I have noted elsewhere, is no mean agenda, and has been the cause of alarm and planning in Washington. Such reactions are wise—it is better to wander into the wilderness prepared—but, as we shall see, largely unnecessary. Beijing's plans for the future should not be confused with Moscow's apparent bid to recapture the "glory" that was the former Soviet Union. Beijing is not beset with delusions of imperial grandeur. Rather, we argue China is governed by pragmatists who seek to reestablish a sphere of influence conducive to continued economic development.

This objective is neither so dangerous—nor benign—as some might suggest. On her way to achieving these goals Beijing will have to act as Washington's "peer competitor." That means we can expect China to seek means of securing her energy supplies—and to participate in international peacekeeping operations. We can expect China to deploy military forces abroad—and to back away from her confrontation from Taiwan. We can expect Beijing to challenge our leadership in the United Nations—and to facilitate U.S. nuclear nonproliferation efforts around the globe. We can expect Beijing to bridle at efforts to condemn her human rights record at home, while simultaneously advocating Chinese socialism abroad. In short, Washington is now confronted with a contemporary who understands the benefit of maintaining the current international system, but is not enamored of the existing leadership.

CHAPTER 2

Harmonious World

Peace, opening-up, cooperation, harmony and win-win are our policy, our idea, our principle, and our pursuit. To take the road of peaceful development is to unify domestic development with opening to the outside world, linking the development of China with that of the rest of the world, and combining the fundamental interests of the Chinese people with the common interests of all peoples throughout the world.

White Paper on China's Peaceful Rise, Dec. 22, 2005[1]

The contention China desires establishment of a regional hierarchy rather than competing global hegemonies presents an interesting dilemma for policy-makers burdened with Cold War mindsets. A regional hierarchy based on political authority—rightful rule—is a novel concept for many of our elder statesmen. Imagine arriving at the State Department or Pentagon prepared for crafting policies aimed at balancing spheres of influence only to be told one's peer competitor is no longer an adversary or enemy. In no small number of ways that is exactly what is happening with China.

Evidence of this transition came to the fore during Hillary Clinton's trip to Asia in February 2009. Rather than confront Beijing with the usual litany of human rights complaints, the new secretary of state chose to focus on the global economic crisis, climate change, and regional/international security threats such as North Korea's nuclear program.[2] Clinton's comment on this new approach is telling, "We have to continue to press them" on human rights. "But our pressing on those issues can't interfere with the global economic crisis, the global climate-change crisis and the security crisis."[3] In remarking on this relatively abrupt change in Washington's "normal" approach to Beijing, the *Washington Post* opined, "Clinton's willingness to break a diplomatic taboo—generally U.S. officials will claim to seek progress on human rights, even if they may not mean it—appears to be part of a determined effort by the new administration to clear the linguistic fog of international diplomacy."[4]

Other pundits were not as kind. In an editorial titled "Not So Obvious," the *Washington Post* declared, "Ms. Clinton's statement will have an effect: It will demoralize thousands of democracy advocates in China, and it will cause many others around the world to wonder about the character of the new U.S. administration."[5] Anne Applebaum, a syndicated columnist was even more scathing. "A cozy relationship with China's current rulers won't guarantee everlasting Asian stability .... President Obama was right, in his inaugural address, when he told 'those who cling to power through corruption and deceit and the silencing of dissent' that they should know they are 'on the wrong side of history.' Now, he and his secretary of state need to enact practical policies to drive home that rhetorical lesson."[6] And, the *Wall Street Journal* offered this comment, "At best, Mrs. Clinton's comment is a serious rookie mistake. At worst, it's a slap to dissidents in China, including at least 12 who were placed under house arrest during her visit."[7]

I provide this response to Clinton's remarks as an indication of the degree to which Cold War perspectives continue to frame Washington's foreign policy dialogue. Think I'm kidding? In her column on Clinton's trip Applebaum argues, "Grandiloquent human rights speeches ... have been a hallmark of American foreign policy since at least 1956, when we didn't come to the aid of Hungarians taking part in a rebellion we helped incite."[8] What's important to understand here is that this focus on human rights is almost globally perceived as a veil for Washington's broader criticism of a competing political system—one whose values do not explicitly mirror our own. That said, occasionally someone slips and comes close to blatantly stating this is the case. For instance, in the *Wall Street Journal* editorial on Clinton's remarks we find the following comment: "Beijing's bad rights record already interferes with U.S.-China ties. The same non-transparent judicial system that jails dissidents can hurt U.S. businesses and businessmen."[9] In other words, we're not just concerned about human rights; we believe the Chinese may be a fundamental threat to our way of life.

I would also note this concern is not limited to the American media. Many of these same assumptions have won a voice in mainstream American foreign policy circles. Consider comments found in a 2008 report from the U.S. Secretary of State's International Security Advisory Board. Writing on "China's Strategic Modernization," the board declared, Washington "is viewed as China's principle strategic adversary and as potential challenge to the regime's legitimacy."[10] The board goes on to note, "it is essential that the United States better understand and effectively respond to China's comprehensive approach to strategic rivalry, as reflected in its official concept of "three warfares." This is followed by the dire warning:

> If not actively countered, Beijing's ongoing combination of Psychological Warfare (propaganda, deception, and coercion), Media Warfare (manipulation of public opinion domestically and internationally), and Legal Warfare (use of "legal regimes" to handicap the opponent in fields favorable to him) can precondition key areas of strategic competition in its favor.[11]

In short, during the Bush administration the State Department's International Security Advisory Board believed China was a strategic adversary who was willing to use every trick in the book to come out on top of the game.

The International Security Advisory Board is not alone in coming to this conclusion. In January 2009, the American Enterprise Institute (AEI) issued a report with an equally Cold War-era assessment of China's underlying motivations and international agenda. According to the authors of "An American Strategy for Asia," Beijing's leaders "appear to see themselves as locked in a long-term, multifaceted strategic competition with the United States."[12] The goal of China's "authoritarian" regime? According to the AEI analysts, Beijing seeks to "constrict America's presence, alliances, access, and influence in Asia and to limit the autonomy of Asian democracies."[13] To accomplish these objectives, the authors argue, "Beijing will likely continue its present, generally cautious, policies, seeking to expand its influence ... while avoiding any direct challenge or confrontation."[14] The bottom line for AEI: China is committed to a set of policies that masks Beijing's ambition to "restore what its leaders see as their country's 'rightful place' at the apex of an Asian and possibly a global hierarchy."[15]

And how do the Chinese publicly claim to perceive the situation? In his meeting with Clinton on February 21, 2009, Chinese President Hu Jintao thanked the U.S. Secretary of State for making Asia her first overseas trip. He went on to declare her trip "shows the new administration attaches great importance to developing relations with Asia and with China. I greatly appreciate it. I believe, madam secretary, that during your tenure you will make positive contributions to the growth of U.S.-Chinese relations."[16] A polite welcome, probably facilitated by the fact China's leadership knew they were going to be spared the usual harangue on human rights—and thereby a none-too-subtle attack on Beijing's chosen form of governance.

But China's leadership is seeking more than a simple acceptance of its right to exist within a Westphalian international system. That, for Beijing, is a given. What China's leadership is now trying to accomplish is nothing less an overhaul of her global reputation. Beijing's maturation over the last decade includes more than a mere repudiation of Mao's support for revolutionary causes. To use a much-abused phrase, China is now intent upon being recognized as a "responsible international actor." What does this mean? Good question. There is apparently no fixed definition for what constitutes a "responsible international actor"—save the state in question is not a "rogue" or member of the axis of evil.

Allow me to try and address this shortfall. The term "responsible international actor" appears to have evolved from then-Deputy Secretary of State Robert Zoellick's call for China to become a "responsible stakeholder" in the existing international system.[17] So what is a responsible international stakeholder? According to an AEI fellow, a responsible international actor "works to protect and strengthen the international system as it is currently constituted; they do not merely derive benefits from it."[18] That is to say, a responsible international actor seeks to maintain peace and stability, to facilitate removal of undesirable regimes, dissuade employment of force—or threat of force, and, increasingly, to help bailout flailing international financial institutions.[19]

Other scholars have suggested a responsible international actor fills these roles and serves to help arrest the proliferation of nuclear technologies[20] and should be willing to restrict conventional arms sales to states considered equally mature.[21] Finally, there is a school that holds a truly responsible international actor meets all of these expectations and recognizes the preeminent authority of international treaties—to include using the United Nations as the ultimate arbiter of international law and interstate disputes.[22] As this discussion should make clear, being labeled a responsible international actor is no mean feat, and the bar for successful achievement of this status is constantly being raised. Nonetheless, I think it is safe to argue China is indeed now a responsible international actor.

ROBERT ZOELLICK'S DEFINITION OF A "RESPONSIBLE STAKEHOLDER"

Robert Zoellick's September 2005 speech outlining Washington's desire for Beijing to become a responsible stakeholder in the international system included seven criteria by which China's efforts on this front could be evaluated. These criteria are listed below . . . the definitional quotes are from a 2007 paper by Dan Blumenthal, then a fellow at the American Enterprise Institute.

An open and rules-based economy:

- "Responsible stakeholders work to open and liberalize new markets and abide by the rules of the international trading system."

Economic development and assistance:

- "Promotion of openness, lack of corruption, good governance, and furtherance of collective rather than purely national goods are all expected of a responsible stakeholder."

Energy security:

- "Responsible stakeholders rely upon the oil market, not mercantilism, for their supply. They share responsibility for security of supply, which means contributing to the stability of supplier regions."

Counterproliferation:

- "Responsible stakeholders understand that certain regimes . . . are the greatest proliferation threats. The 'great powers' should use all tools of statecraft to prevent those regimes . . . from obtaining weapons of mass destruction."

Peacekeeping and enforcement:

- "For responsible stakeholders, intervention becomes necessary in unstable states from which terrorist threats could emanate. Peacekeepers and enforcers have to be nation builders as well and therefore sensitive to human rights."

Human rights:

- "Responsible stakeholders recognize that they have a moral imperative to stop genocide and civil war."

Asian security:

- "The principles of openness, transparency, good governance, and the peaceful resolution of disputes, should characterize Asian security."

(Excerpts from: Robert Zoellick, September 21, 2005, "Whither China: From Membership to Responsibility;" and, Dan Blumenthal, June 11, 2007, "Is China at Present (or will China Become) a Responsible Stakeholder in the International Community.")

Certainly the Chinese would like us to believe that is the case. In an effort to counter international concerns about China's growing economic, military, and political might, in 2003 Beijing began to insist the nation is engaged in a "peaceful rise." According to Chinese Premier Wen Jiabao, China's rise "will not come at the cost of any other country, will not stand in the way of any other country, nor pose a threat to any other country."[23] Other Chinese sources have argued "peaceful rise" could be summed a Beijing's vow to not "seek hegemony" and focus on a policy of "calming, enriching, and befriending neighbors."[24] In any case, it seems "peaceful rise" appears intended to create an environment conducive to continuing China's economic development.

This ceaseless effort to win recognition as a responsible international actor has even crept into Beijing's biannual defense white papers. For instance, in *China's National Defense in 2008*, Beijing declares she "will never seek hegemony or engage in military expansion now or in the future, no matter how developed [China] becomes."[25] Admittedly, there seems little comfort to be derived from quotes included in such official documents—but compare this statement with following lifted from Washington's 2006 *National Security*

Strategy and one begins to see why China's leaders thought it was important to put such a declaration in print.

> ... the first duty of the United States Government remains what it always has been: to protect the American people and American interests. It is an enduring American principle that this duty obligates the government to anticipate and counter threats, using all elements of national power, before the threats can do grave damage. The greater the threat, the greater is the risk of inaction—and the more compelling the case for taking anticipatory action to defend ourselves, even if uncertainty remains as to the time and place of the enemy's attack.
>
> To forestall or prevent such hostile acts by our adversaries, the United States will, if necessary, act preemptively in exercising our inherent right of self-defense. The United States will not resort to force in all cases to preempt emerging threats. Our preference is that nonmilitary actions succeed. And no country should ever use preemption as a pretext for aggression.[26]

While not explicitly referenced in the Chinese defense paper, the point is made. The Bush administration's so-called preemptive strike doctrine will not be an official policy in Beijing.

It is important to note that in 2004 Chinese leaders began avoiding the "peaceful rise" phrase. Stung by international critics who claim use of the word "rise" reveals China's continued goal of "amassing national power,"[27] Beijing has sought a less inflammatory title for this new policy. Instead of "peaceful rise," Chinese leaders began referring to "peaceful development," and then ultimately adopted President Hu Jintao's "harmonious world."[28] This latter phrase was thought to be more subtle and yet remain an expression of China's ultimate intent.

Beijing's focus on economic development and coming to terms with the neighbors is hardly accidental. The Chinese Communist Party (CCP) leadership is painfully aware of the requirement to continue China's economic growth or face extinction. The result has been an official transition from "peaceful rise" to "peaceful development," and now "harmonious world." According to a former U.S. deputy assistant secretary of defense, "there is a strong consensus in China that the policy will help Beijing to increase the middle class and sustain ... economic transformation of the country, all of which require foreign capital and cooperation."[29]

That said, Hu's policy does not suffer for a want of domestic critics. Traditional Chinese "leftists" argue Beijing should be more focused on development at home, and Chinese "rightists" contend the CCP should be emphasizing a global ideological campaign based on the ideals of democratic socialism. Neither extreme is thought to be capable of derailing Hu's efforts, but are said to be a thorn in the Chinese president's persistent moves to develop a long-term policy consensus among China's top leaders.[30] For the time being Hu appears to have prevailed—at least on the international front. We shall return to his domestic economic challenges in the following chapter.

LOOKING FORWARD TO 2020

For more than a century...China was threatened, bullied, invaded, and exploited...Given such a history of suffering, the Chinese want nothing but the important basics: that is, independence, unification, peace, and development.
                              —Zheng Bijian, *Bo'oa Forum for Asia*, 2003[31]

Hu's approach to international and domestic affairs is commonly attributed to Zheng Bijian, one of China's leading thinkers on ideological questions. A former member of the CCP's senior ranks, in 1992 Zheng served as Hu Jintao's deputy at the Central Party School. In that role Zheng worked closely with Hu in overhauling the school —turning it into a center for educating the next generation of Chinese leaders. The relationship between Hu and Zheng, however, is apparently more than simply that of two bureaucrats climbing the ladder of success. Zheng is now widely thought to have laid the intellectual foundation for Hu's "harmonious world" policy.

In any case, China's focus on fostering a "harmonious world" is a further evolutionary step in Beijing's *weltanschauung*—world view. Under Mao Zedong, the "Great Helmsman," China pursued "self-reliance," resulting in a foreign policy that greatly constrained Beijing's international relations, while simultaneously promoting the emergence of Maoist revolutionary parties. Chinese diplomacy at the time could best be summed as "Mao...reject[ing] the rules of the international system and [seeking] to over throw it, pursuing change through revolution."[32]

While Mao's support for Kim Il-sung in the Korean War and Ho Chi Minh in Vietnam's long conflict with France and United States are symbolic of this commitment to revolutionary change, Beijing was not exclusively focused on toppling the existing global order. In 1954, Chinese Premier Zhou Enlai and Indian Prime Minster Jawaharla Nehru jointly issued the now well-known "Five Principles of Peaceful Coexistence." These five principles—as we shall see—have had a staying force that suggests China's current leadership believes Mao's approach to international affairs is not completely inapplicable in the twenty first century. The "Five Principles of Peaceful Coexistence" are as follows: mutual respect for sovereignty and territorial integrity; mutual nonaggression; noninterference in each other's internal affairs; equity and mutual benefit; and peaceful coexistence.[33] As students of Beijing's current foreign policy will attest, all five of these principles regularly appear in Chinese statements from time-to-time, particularly the call for respect of sovereignty and internal affairs.

MAO'S THREE PRINCIPLES FOR FOREIGN POLICY

In 1949, Mao Zedong enunciated three principles that were to serve as the basis for Chinese foreign policy until Deng Xiaoping began his reform and opening campaign:

- "Start up the fire in a new stove"—initiate diplomatic relations with every country on a new basis.
- "Clean house first and then invite guests"—consolidate Chinese Communist Party control at home and then develop foreign relations.
- "Leaning to one side"—favor the Soviet Union.

The purpose of these three principles: to address how Beijing would establish China's new foreign policy; delineate how China would deal with the United States and other Western states; and, stipulate how China would treat the Soviet Union and other socialist countries. (Quansheng Zhao, 1996, *Interpreting Chinese Foreign Policy*, Oxford University Press, Oxford, pp. 46–47.)

Looking back, Chinese and Western scholars now agree that Mao's foreign policy dictates did little for the country's economic wellbeing or her international stature. Given Beijing's current emphasis on pragmatism, one has to ask why Mao chose such a path. In his groundbreaking work on Chinese foreign policy, Quansheng Zhao, a research associate at the Fairbank Center for East Asian Research at Harvard University, contends there are three explanations for China's behavior at the time:

1. Preoccupied with national survival, China was exceptionally sensitive to perceived outside threats.
2. The Chinese Communist Party leadership regarded their revolution as an element of a global transition.
3. Mao, and many other Chinese leaders, remained conscious of China as the Middle Kingdom—and by extension the center of a global revolution.[34]

The result was a Chinese foreign policy that was isolationist, protectionist, and revolutionary—a contradictory mix that made Beijing an inscrutable challenge for almost every diplomat, regardless of who they were dispatched to represent. As the Sino-Soviet split demonstrates, even Moscow—Beijing's erstwhile comrade in fomenting a global socialist revolution—found it almost impossible to do business with Mao's China.

This isolationist philosophy began a slow thaw under Deng. In pursuit of the "reform and opening" that would promote China's economic revival, Deng adopted what might be thought of as a voyeur's approach to foreign policy—directing Chinese leaders to be observant and silent.

Deng's tentative approach to foreign affairs was definitively captured in his "24 character strategy." Deng's strategy directed China's diplomatic and military apparatus to "observe calmly, secure our position; cope with affairs calmly; hide our capacities and bide our time; be good at maintaining a low profile; and never claim leadership." For a number of years, this guidance resulted in statesman who sought to avoid unnecessary provocations, shun excessive international burdens, and seek any means of building-up China's comprehensive national power.[35] It did little, however, for enhancing China's reputation on the world stage.

Deng's emphasis on quietly bidding one's time served to restrict China's participation in multilateral or even bilateral relationships. Concerned multilateral institutions could be used to punish or constrain Beijing; Deng was a wary participant in a limited number of intergovernmental and nongovernmental organizations.[36] Nonetheless, he recognized the value of engaging the international community and sought to balance caution and pragmatism. The result is evident in Deng's three best-known principles:

1. China's economic development requires a peaceful international environment.
2. China must never head an alliance that could become a target of international contention.
3. China must maintain a low profile and meet foreign challenges with great self-constraint.[37]

This cautious approach also characterized Deng's guidance concerning relations with the United States. In the early 1990s, Deng issued a 16 character instruction that provided the following marching orders for his diplomats charged with engaging Washington: increase mutual trust; reduce trouble; enhance cooperation; and, avoid confrontation.[38] Quite simply, under Deng the Chinese avoided entangling alliances and bid their time as his policy of reform and opening served to revive a long-moribund domestic economy.

China's reluctant engagement in bilateral and multilateral forums reached a turning point with Jiang Zemin's struggle to end Beijing's post-Tiananmen isolation. In a subtle challenge to Deng's international passivity, Jiang urged his countrymen to "gear up with the world" and expounded on ideas like "developing China as a comprehensive power."[39] Furthermore, Jiang and the CCP leadership came to the realization international organizations and relations could serve Chinese economic, military, and political objectives. The result, in the mid 1990s Beijing commenced a concerted effort to engage the outside world—particularly in multinational forums.

China's relationship with the Association of Southeast Asian Nations (ASEAN) is a demonstrative case-in-point.[40] In 1995, Chinese leaders opened a sequence of annual meetings with senior ASEAN officials. In 1997, Beijing facilitated establishment of ASEAN+3—annual meetings with the 10 ASEAN countries plus China, Japan, and South Korea. This was followed by ASEAN+1, annual meetings between ASEAN and Chinese leaders. Similar incremental processes were used to engage the European Union and ultimately lead to the establishment of the Shanghai Cooperation Organization.[41]

While Jiang's efforts to expand China's international outreach are little remembered, he was remarkably successful in undoing Mao's isolationism and Deng's caution. By the time Jiang departed the presidential office in 2003, China had so significantly increased its involvement in international institutions and organizations, that Beijing is now a signatory to almost all major international regimes—including membership in the World Trade Organization.[42]

All of which leads us to Hu's "harmonious world" which he introduced in 2005. While there are debates as to the concept's origin—some argue it was derived from "peaceful rise,"[43] others insist Hu was seeking a means of addressing the challenges he had confronted upon entering office[44]—the international community was provided a concise overview of the policy's objectives during the United Nation's 60th anniversary summit.

Speaking before the United Nations' General Assembly in New York, Hu laid out a three-point proposal for building a harmonious world.

1. Multilateralism is the best means for realizing common security. According to Hu, "we must abandon the Cold War mentality, cultivate a new security concept featuring trust, mutual benefit, equality and cooperation, and build a fair and effective collective security mechanism."

2. Mutually beneficial cooperation should be upheld to achieve common prosperity. Hu argued, "we should work . . . to establish and improve a multilateral trading system that is open, fair, and non-discriminatory."

3. The spirit of inclusiveness must be upheld to build a world where all civilizations coexist harmoniously. Hu's logic, "we should endeavor to preserve the diversity of civilizations in the spirit of equality and openness, [and] make international relations more democratic."[45]

Chinese and Western scholars who have examined Hu's proposals come away with two broad observations. First, Hu's harmonious world "suggests an increasingly confident China relinquishing its aloofness to participate and undertake greater responsibility in international affairs."[46] Second, that Hu's foreign policy is very much a product of China's domestic arena. As a professor emeritus from the London School of Economics put it, China's current foreign policy reflects "the need to try and provide an international environment that provides security and the public goods necessary for the country's continued economic development."[47]

In fact, when Hu's three proposals are examined for general trends it appears the current Chinese president has simply provided for an evolution of Deng's three principles. The U.S. Council on Foreign Relations goes even further, arguing there are three areas where "harmonious world" has clearly come to the fore. These are:

- Settling border disputes with neighboring countries.
- Increasing economic relations throughout Asia.
- Membership in Western and regional institutions.[48]

In short, Hu's objectives are largely Deng's—China's economic development is paramount, and to accomplish this objective Beijing must operate within a favorable international environment. All of which suggests through 2020—and beyond—Beijing is ultimately intent on realizing five national priorities: economic development; domestic stability; maintenance of Communist Party control; recognition as a great nation; and territorial integrity.

EMPLOYING REASSURANCE AND DETERRENCE[49]

China is the beneficiary of the current international order, particularly economic globalization. China stands for reform, rather than violence, in the efforts to establish a new international political and economic order.
—Zheng Bijian, Brookings Institution, June 16, 2005[50]

As we look forward to 2020, it now appears Chinese leaders are intent on employing two means of achieving their foreign policy objectives—reassurance and deterrence. I will address the reassurance campaign below; the deterrence discussion will have to wait until we examine China's military modernization efforts. In any case, the reassurance element of Hu's foreign policy is clearly evident in Beijing's efforts to realize the three key components of Hu Jintao's "harmonious world" policy.

PEACEFUL RESOLUTION OF BORDER DISPUTES

China's leadership is insistent the international community "should persist in settling . . . disputes peacefully through consultations and negotiations on the basis of equality." This emphasis on employment of diplomacy includes a warning against "willful use or threat of use of military force."[51] At first glance, this appears little more than a heady dose of propaganda. The CCP leadership has certainly demonstrated a historical willingness to employ force when confronted with territorial challenges. Beijing's dispute with New Delhi in 1962, border clashes with Pyongyang in 1968–69,[52] Moscow in 1969, and ongoing altercations with Hanoi and Taipei all provide evidence of China's decision to employ force when challenged on territorial claims.

There is, however, a second body of evidence suggesting China may be less territorially ambitious than popularly believed. In fact, a recent study of Asian border disputes since 1949 reveals China has settled 17 of her 23 territorial disagreements with substantial compromises— usually receiving less than 50 percent of the contested land.[53] This willingness to compromise comes as surprise to many observers, and deserves a clarification.

As it turns out, China's territorial disputes can be separated into three categories: frontier, homeland, and offshore islands. With 14 neighbors arrayed along a 13,700 mile border, China is no stranger to contested frontiers. Since 1949, China has been confronted with 16 disputes along her land border. Many of these confrontations arose as a result of the ambiguity surrounding China's borders when the People's Republic was formally established. Furthermore, ethnic minorities along China's borders and logistical difficulties associated with supporting military activity in remote locations presented multiple opportunities for perceived land grabs. How has China done in resolving these disputes? As of 2008, all but two had been put to rest —the remaining problem areas are with India and Bhutan.

In seeking to explain China's demonstrated willingness to peacefully resolve frontier disputes, Chinese and Western scholars point to issues associated with internal political stability. When confronted with internal political instability, these scholars argue, the People's Republic of China has sought to secure frontier areas by fostering better relations with neighboring states.[54] However, there is also reason to believe some of these disputes were resolved as an element of China's efforts to emerge as a respected member of the international community. In any case, there is little evidence to suggest China is pursuing imperial ambitions along its frontiers.

The second major category for Chinese territorial disputes involves claimed elements of the homeland. Prior to 1997, China had three disputed areas historically linked to the nation's Han Chinese majority—Hong Kong, Macao, and Taiwan. In the intervening 10 years, Hong Kong and Macao have been returned to the People's Republic of China, Taiwan remains the significant outlier. There is little, to no, reason to believe disputes over China's perceived homeland territories are likely to be resolved through concessions.[55] With the CCP's legitimacy inexorably linked to reunification of pre-1911 China, it is highly unlikely this intransigence concerning Taiwan will change in the foreseeable future.

The final category of disputed territory—offshore islands—largely focuses on the fate of four island groups and the South China Sea. Since 1949 China has only compromised in one of these disputes, the White Dragon Tail. Beijing's claims to the Paracel, Senkaku, and Spratly islands remain contentious problems. The cause of this standoff: primarily rights to natural resources—fish and possibly oil—and potential military basing rights.[56] China perceives these island groups as potential forward staging points for forces charged with maintaining her economic growth by conducting surveillance and securing sea-lanes of communication.

While the aforementioned islands constitute touchstones for this ongoing dispute, the larger problem is China's claim to the near entirety of the South China Sea. This claim is based on Beijing's reading of the 1982 United Nations Convention on the Law of the Sea—and abetted by her claims to islands in the South China Sea that serve to facilitate this perceived sea grab. Beijing's decision to join the ASEAN members in signing the 2002 Declaration on the Conduct of Parties in the South China Sea offered a glimmer of hope on this front, but only a glimmer. In the 2002 Declaration, the signatories "reaffirmed" their commitment to purposes and principles of the United Nations Charter, the 1982 United Nations Convention on the Law of the Sea,[57] 1976 Treaty of Amity and Cooperation in Southeast Asia,[58] the Five Principles of Peaceful Coexistence, and other universally recognized principles of international law.[59] The parties also:

- Reaffirmed their respect for and commitment to the freedom of navigation in and over flight above the South China Sea as provided for in the 1982 United Nations Convention on the Law of the Sea.

- Agreed to undertake to resolve their territorial and jurisdictional disputes by peaceful means, without resorting to the threat or use of force.

- Accepted the need to exercise self-restraint in the conduct of activities that would complicate or escalate disputes—to include refraining from inhabiting presently uninhabited reefs.[60]

As the 2002 Declaration noted, the overall intent was to establish "a code of conduct in the South China Sea [that] would promote peace and stability in the region."[61]

WHY BEIJING OBJECTS TO U.S. NAVY SURVEY OPERATIONS

The March 10, 2009 run-in between Chinese fishing boats and a U.S. Navy oceanographic survey ship is not the first time Beijing has vehemently responded to this type of operation in China's exclusive economic zone. Angry Chinese reactions to these survey operations can be traced back to 2002—when Beijing bitterly complained about the USS *Bowditch* conducting similar activities in the Yellow Sea. (September 27, 2002, "China Protests US Vessel in Yellow Sea," Voice of America.)

Quite simply, the Chinese government regards such U.S. surveillance as both illegal and unjust: illegal because, in Beijing's view, the missions violate the Chinese interpretation of Article 58 of the U.N. Convention of the Law of the Sea concerning Exclusive Economic Zones. According to China, these zones are near-sovereign security spaces for military activity as well as economic purposes. The operations are unjust according to Beijing because the actions appear as an aggressive, "in-your-face" military intimidation by an arrogant superpower. (Michael Swaine, March 11, 2009, "The U.S.-China Spat at Sea," Carnegie Endowment for International Peace, Washington, DC; and Swaine, June 26, 1998, *Exclusive Economic Zone and Continental Shelf Act*, Adopted at the third session of the Standing Committee of the Ninth National People's Congress, Beijing.)

Or, as I put it in a March 13, 2009 article in the *Huffington Post*, "one can understand Beijing's press to cease the survey operations. China contends such U.S. Navy seabed mapping is really intended to facilitate submarine operations in the event of a conflict. Beijing believes such operations also serve to enhance our monitoring of Chinese submarine deployments and training. To explain the Chinese sensitivities, allow me to place the shoe on the other foot. Imagine how the U.S. Department of Defense would react if the Chinese were conducting similar survey operations 75 miles off San Diego or Norfolk. I believe the term apoplectic would be appropriate should such an event come to pass." (Eric Anderson, March 13, 2009, "China Matters, Now ... An Open Letter to the President," *Huffington Post*, New York.)

The bottom line, China's leadership will not soon forget her "century of humiliation," and thus is prone to take a very reactionary response to such operations, or any perceived foreign provocation apparently intended to threaten China's sovereignty.

The actual success of the 2002 Declaration remains in question. Merchant ships and commercial airlines have been provided freedom of navigation,[62] the signatories have refrained from employing force when engaged in disputes, and all parties appear to have ceased building new outposts on previously uninhabited reefs and atolls. But the potential for friction remains high. For instance, Vietnam is constantly on the watch for China expanding her claims in the South China Sea—a task complicated by Taiwan's military presence on Taiping Island and Taipei's decision to expand and improve the runway there between 2005 and 2008.[63]

Hanoi is not alone in causing Beijing angst on this front. In early March 2009, Manila further roiled the already troubled waters by passing legislation laying claim to waters that included isles Beijing has previously declared a part of China.[64] The Philippine move was further exacerbated by the March 10, 2009 run-in between five Chinese fishing boats and a U.S. Navy survey ship. In the aftermath of this incident a Chinese naval officer apparently felt compelled to declare the People's Liberation Army Navy has "the strength to defend the South China Sea from a force point of view." The officer, a former Commander of Beijing's East China Sea Fleet went on to note, "China is committed to maintaining peace and stability in the

South China Sea, but will never allow foreign provocation."[65] In other words, China was willing to abide by the 2002 Declaration—but there are limits to every agreement.

Given this insistence on retaining and assertively defending claims in the East and South China Sea, why did Beijing compromise on the White Dragon Tail Island? According to Chinese scholars, Mao ordered the island's transfer to Hanoi in 1957 as a means of aiding North Vietnam's conflict with the United States.[66] The CCP's current focus on protecting and abetting China's economic growth suggest such acts of generosity have come to an end—particularly in the South China Sea. Beijing will seek all means possible of protecting her claims to possible oil and natural gas deposits in the area, and will insist her claims to large areas in the South China Sea— which sit atop one of the world's busiest commercial sea lanes—are sacrosanct.

This sensitivity to any perceived competing claim to her self-declared territorial possessions and exclusive economic zones will include continued vehement rejection of the United States'—or any other international actor's—unsanctioned effort to conduct oceanographic surveys within these areas. Chinese officials will continue to argue they established the legal foundation for rejecting unilateral exercise of such "freedom of navigation operations" in 1998, when Beijing issued the *Exclusive Economic Zone and Continental Shelf Act*. According to Article 3 of this Act, "the People's Republic of China shall exercise sovereign rights for the purpose of exploring and exploiting, conserving and managing the natural resources of the waters superjacent to the seabed and of the seabed and its subsoil."[67] Article 12 is even more specific, declaring:

> The People's Republic of China may, in the exercise of its sovereign rights to explore, exploit, conserve and manage the living resources of the exclusive economic zone, take such measures, including boarding, inspection, arrest, detention and judicial proceedings, as may be necessary to ensure compliance with its laws and regulations.
>
> In the event of a violation of the laws and regulations of the People's Republic of China in the exclusive economic zone or the continental shelf, the People's Republic of China shall have the right to take the necessary investigative measures in accordance with the law and may exercise the right of hot pursuit.[68]

It is this document Beijing is referring to when Chinese authorities claim U.S. survey operations are illegal activities. And it is this document that Chinese authorities believe grants them permission to forcibly halt such activities.[69] I would note, however, even on this sensitive subject the Chinese have opted to display a bit of pragmatic "flexibility." Rather than outright reject the possibility of such survey operations in her exclusive economic zone, Beijing simply refers to Article 9 of the 1998 *Exclusive Economic Zone and Continental Shelf Act.*

According to Article 9, "All international organizations, foreign organizations or individuals that wish to conduct marine scientific research in the exclusive economic zone or on the continental shelf of the People's Republic of China shall be subject to approval of the competent authorities of the People's Republic of China and shall comply with the laws and regulations of the People's Republic of China."[70] By highlighting this stipulation, Chinese authorities appear to be rhetorically asking, "Who is really being unreasonable here?" From Beijing's perspective, China is in compliance with the International Law of the Sea—it's the interlopers who won't follow clearly publicized procedures that appear to cause all the problems.

What have we learned from this conversation? While Beijing is willing to peacefully resolve many territorial disputes, this flexibility disappears when issues that might threaten the Chinese Communist Party's future grasp on power arise. This sensitivity explains China's reaction to questions concerning Taiwan, and applies to her approach to handling claims within the South China Sea and/or China's maritime exclusive economic zone. In short, Hu's China does indeed seek to reside within a "Harmonious World," but there are clear limits on how far anyone should push the limits when it comes to territorial issues.

Increasing Economic Relations throughout Asia

China's economic relations with Asia continue to mature and expand. China is no longer simply engaged in the import of raw material or export of cheap manufactured goods or agricultural products. A leading participant in the globalized manufacturing process, China is one more—albeit one of the largest—cog in what has become known as the "disassembly line."[71] What does this mean? Here's one author's take:

While China was becoming the world's factory, its Asian neighbors were terrified there would be no room left for them in world trade. Contrary to their fears, trade has increased, though their roles have changed dramatically. Because of the popularity of the disassembly line model, developing countries have found they have unexpected new roles to play in the global economy. Bangladesh or Vietnam might not have the manufacturing sophistication to turn out and entire laptop computer or a whole car suitable for export . . . but they certainly have factories capable of making simple components that then can become pieces of those complex products. Developing countries without high-technology capabilities have made themselves the origins of supply chains—doing the first, simple steps . . . before the goods move on to the next step . . . often on to assembly in China.[72]

According to the World Bank, this process has proceeded down a path that might be compared to a rising tide—it lifts all boats. In 1988, developing countries provided just 14 percent of rich countries' manufactured imports, in 2006 that figure reached 40 percent, and in 2030 is expected to climb beyond 65 percent.[73]

As the World Bank data indicates, this "disassembly line" manufacturing process has done wonders for China's economic relations throughout Asia. In 2005, the China Business Forum found Beijing was quickly becoming the "largest export market" for other Asian nations.[74] A survey of newspaper headlines reveals just how quickly.

In August 2008, Tokyo's Finance Ministry released data showing China had replaced the United States as Japan's biggest trading partner.[75] In May 2008, the Australian Minister for Trade went before reports to disclose similar findings.[76] In March 2008, India announced China had replaced the United States as New Delhi's largest trading partner.[77] In February 2008, ASEAN declared its 10 members and China had become each other's fourth-largest trading partners.[78] All this comes less than five years after South Korean and Taiwan announcements concerning equivalent developments. The bottom line: China is not just on its way to increasing trade relations with Asia—as of 2008, Beijing is the predominant trading partner throughout Asia.

Nor, one should note, is this situation likely to change in the foreseeable future. China's membership in the Asia-Pacific Economic Cooperation (APEC) facilitates further development of Asian regional trading relations. APEC, created in 1989, is the first high-level multilateral economic arrangement in the Pacific Rim. Encompassing 21 economies, APEC was initially derisively referred to as little more than a "talk shop."[79] However, when APEC members signed the "Bogar Goals" in 1994 the stage was set for "open trade and investment in the Asia Pacific" by 2010 for "industrialized economies" and by 2020 for "developing economies."[80]

In 1996, the APEC "member economies" adopted the Manila Action Plan to ensure implementation of efforts intended to realize the Bogar Goals. In 2001, APEC pushed for China, Taiwan, Russia and Vietnam's membership in the World Trade Organization. Quite frankly, APEC is poised to accomplish an agenda as sweeping as the North American Free Trade Agreement (NAFTA). Only, in this case Washington will not be the winner—APEC seems headed down a path apparently in direct correlation with Beijing's overarching objectives.

CHINA'S RESPONSE TO ASIAN FINANCIAL CRISES

Initiated by two rounds of currency devaluations in the summer of 1997, the Asian financial crisis demonstrated the economic vulnerability of regional "tigers," and generated lingering animosity over the manner in which the United States, Japan and International Monetary Fund's (IMF) responded to various governments' request for assistance. The financial turmoil that began in July 1997 caught Washington by surprise—and the Clinton administration was slow to react. Tokyo earned widespread enmity when then-Prime Minister Hashimoto responded to requests for stimulus spending by declaring "Japan needs to worry about its own self-interest." And the IMF was soundly criticized for apparently insisting on reforms in a "colonial manner" through a bureaucracy that refused to tailor its demands to meet each nation's individual situation. China, on the other hand, came out of the crisis smelling like a rose.

China won high acclaim from her Asian neighbors for three reasons. First, Beijing avoided further escalating the crisis by pledging to not devalue the renminbi. As China's vice minister of foreign trade and economic cooperation told an audience in Honolulu in January 1998, "we evaluated the pros and cons and decided that it [was] in the best interests of China not to devalue. This might [negatively] affect China's competitive position, but we have more important things to do." Second, Beijing used the IMF framework and/or bilateral channels to provide Thailand and other Asian countries with over $4 billion in aid. Finally, China sought to boost domestic demand and stimulate economic growth, thereby easing pressure on the overall Asian economy.

The feedback? A widespread perception that China was indeed a responsible international actor. As George Yeo, Singapore's minister for information put it: "The determination of the Chinese government to not devalue the renminbi in order to not destabilize Asia further will be long remembered. (Richard Halloran, 27 January 27, 1998, "China's Decisive Role in the Asian Financial Crisis," Global Beat Issue Brief Number 24, Global Beat, New York; Wayne Morrison, March 3, 1999, "China's Response to the Asian Financial Crisis: Implications for U.S. Economic Interests," CRS Report for Congress, Congressional Research Service, Washington, DC; Shalendra Sharma, April 2002, "Why China Survived the Asian Financial Crisis?" *Brazilian Journal of Political Economy*, Volume 22, Number 2, pp. 32–58.)

Beijing is taking a similar tack in 2009. In April 2009, Beijing announced the establishment of a $10 billion China-ASEAN investment cooperation fund. The fund would be used for projects focused on infrastructure construction, energy and resources, information and communications. In addition, China announced a plan to offer $15 billion in credit to ASEAN countries, including $1.7 billion in loans with preferential terms for cooperation projects. (April 12, 2009, "China Rolls Out Assistance Blueprint for ASEAN," Xinhua, Beijing.)

It is appropriate to note this apparent effort at establishing the Asian equivalent of the European Union seems unlikely to occur in the next 10 years. Western scholars point to four reasons for the slow-motion progress on this front:

1. The continuing contentious state of Sino-Japanese relations.
2. Continued territorial disputes—including the Senkaku and Spratley Islands, and Taiwan.

3. Significant disparities in the regional distribution of power—i.e., China versus the Philippines.

4. Uncertainty about the future longevity of some regimes in the region—i.e., Indonesia, North Korea, and even the People's Republic of China.[81]

Given these limitations, it seems safe to assume East Asia is closer to achieving a NAFTA-type arrangement than emerging as the "Asia Union." The potential for such a development is closer than most casual observers realize. In August 2009, China's Commerce Minister and his counterparts from the 10-member Association of Southeast Asian Nations (ASEAN)[82] signed an investment agreement completing the negotiation process for a Free Trade Area that is to go into effect January 1, 2010. The agreement is intended to provide a free, transparent and just investment mechanism for investors throughout ASEAN and China. Beijing is currently ASEAN's fourth largest export market, and the third largest source for good flowing into ASEAN.[83]

Membership in Western and Regional Institutions

Deng's cautious approach to participation in international organizations has clearly been abandoned by the current CCP leadership. China is now a member of over 130 regional and "Western" institutions. While some of these organizations offer little more than photo opportunities, others serve to facilitate achievement of Beijing's economic, political, and security agendas. A partial listing of the international organizations with Chinese membership follows:

- Asia-Pacific Economic Cooperation
- Association of Southeast Asian Nations +1 and +3
- Bank for International Settlements
- Caribbean Development Bank
- Group of 77
- International Atomic Energy Agency
- International Bank for Reconstruction and Development
- International Chamber of Commerce
- International Civil Aviation Organization
- International Criminal Police Organization

- International Development Association
- International Federation of Red Cross and Red Crescent Societies
- International Finance Corporation
- International Fund for Agricultural Development
- International Hydrographic Organization
- International Labor Organization
- International Maritime Organization
- International Monetary Fund
- International Olympic Committee
- International Red Cross and Red Crescent Movement
- International Telecommunication Union
- Organization for the Prohibition of Chemical Weapons
- Permanent Court of Arbitration
- Shanghai Cooperation Organization
- United Nations
- Universal Postal Union
- World Customs Organization
- World Health Organization
- World Intellectual Property Organization
- World Meteorological Organization
- World Tourism Organization

There is considerable debate as to the reason for China's "sudden" interest in all these organizations. One school of thought holds Beijing's pursuit of membership in regional and "Western" organizations is a direct effort to foster a stable international environment and thereby facilitate China's economic development. Advocates of this argument contend economic development is key to the CCP's continued survival—and thus Beijing has pragmatically abandoned isolation and stand alone independence.

A second school of thought posits China's membership in international organizations is little more than an attempt to redraw the world in Beijing's image—or at least to cast off the vestiges of "Cold War thinking" and perceived U.S. dominance. Advocates of this argument hold China is seeking to change an "unfair" existing international order that: (1) largely exists to serve the national interests of Western developed nations; (2) is dominated by Western great powers to the detriment of the developing world; and (3) is biased against socialist governmental systems.[84] The solution, China joins a wide variety of international organizations and then uses its economic and military clout to quite literally change the world.

A third school takes an entirely different approach. While China's widespread participation in regional and Western institutions at first appears the work of a single-minded bureaucracy that has managed to discover the means of maximizing political profits to be gleaned from international organizations, studies of China's behavior across time suggest a different conclusion. Western political scientists have discovered participation in multiple international forums has a socializing effect on what were previously perceived as "rogue" states.

In 2007, Stanford University published an extensive study of China's participation in international organizations. Rather than arguing this membership has unilaterally worked to Beijing's advantage, this study contends China's interaction with leading international organizations such as the Conference on Disarmament, World Bank, World Trade Organization, UN Committee Against Torture, and the World Health Organization have promoted Beijing's gradual socialization into the community of nations.[85] This finding jibes with the argument the international community—and thus Washington—is better served by encouraging China's membership in multiple regional and global organizations than by pressing to contain or isolate Beijing. In short, China's foreign policy objective—at least in this case—appears to serve everyone's best interests.

Finally, there is a school of thought that contends China's membership in a wide array of international organizations is driven by an effort to shape the strategic context, prevent the emergence of unfavorable coalitions, and provide Beijing a voice in an ever-widening range of issues. Advocates of this theory argue, "China's goal is to install itself as the hub of a whole group of multilateral organizations." From this position China could seek to limit membership and define agendas such that a broad range of international bodies all appear to support Beijing's posture on a particular subject or potentially contentious treaty arrangement.[86]

Regardless of which school one chooses to join, it seems clear China has come to recognize the value of participating in international organizations and is unlikely to back away from this approach to interacting with other nations in the foreseeable future. It also seems likely that this membership is indeed a two-way street, with China's participation possibly influencing developments in Beijing in a manner as significant as the CCP's impact on the organizations in question.

PURSUING A GLOBAL PRESENCE THROUGH FOREIGN AID

China's peaceful rise brings ... opportunities for development, conditions for peace, and space for cooperation.
—Zheng Bijian, *Bo'ao Forum for Asia*, April 18, 2004[87]

In addition to directly pursuing Hu's "harmonious world" agenda, Chinese leaders have long sought to burnish Beijing's international reputation through the provision of foreign aid. Contrary to popular perception, China has been a donor to the developing world for over 50 years. Between 1950 and 1985, China provided foreign assistance to 87 nations—a list that included 16 regimes in Latin America, 20 in Asia, and 46 in Africa.[88] While the size of these aid packages typically paled in comparison to assistance offered by Western governments, Beijing's donations were considered important for fostering China's claim to developing world leadership, fending off recognition of Taiwan, and fomenting Maoist revolution.

China's increasing role in the international community has also witnessed an expansion in Beijing's foreign assistance programs. Unfortunately, a lack of official and reliable data make the scope of China's foreign aid difficult to quantify. For instance, the Congressional Research Service reports Beijing claims to have provided approximately $970 million in foreign assistance in 2006—but this figure likely does not include loans, the main source of Beijing's overseas aid.[89] A New York University study found grants only constituted 3 percent of Beijing's total foreign assistance.[90] When loans and state-sponsored investment is included in the calculation, in 2007 the Chinese promised a global total of $31 billion in economic assistance. This was a threefold increase over similar promises in 2005, and 20 times greater than what Beijing had offered in 2003.[91]

Just as the size of China's foreign aid has grown over the last decade, so have the number of objectives Beijing is thought to pursue via economic assistance. While some observers argue China remains altruistically focused on assisting the developing world, most China-watchers insist foreign aid serves a much larger number of purposes for Beijing. These include:

- Stabilizing China's periphery—and isolating Taiwan.
- Facilitating the development of regional trade.
- Securing natural resources.
- Expanding Beijing's international influence.
- Demonstrating China's "great power" status.[92]

It is only fair to note some of Beijing's largess is driven by a desire to serve common global interests. As such, one can argue China uses foreign aid to accomplish objectives Beijing shares in common with the West—including, developing the world to alleviate poverty; improve national and international governance; and create global economic opportunity.

Ascribing such broad humanitarian concerns as one of the underlying causes for Chinese foreign aid is not unreasonable, but likely misses the primary reason for Beijing's expanding economic assistance program. China, like all other nations, primarily employs foreign assistance as a means of achieving other national economic and political objectives. In Beijing's case, these objectives are largely focused on fostering China's continued economic development and securing the CCP's place atop the nation's political hierarchy.

Even Zheng Bijian is forthright about China's need to protect and foster her national interests. In a September 2004 interview, Zheng declared, "there must be prerequisites and guarantees for peaceful rise. The most fundamental are state sovereignty and security ... Only with this fundamental prerequisite and guarantee and in a peaceful international environment will it be possible for us to concentrate on development, on providing a good life for the 1.3 to 1.5 billion Chinese people."[93]

A case in point? China's assistance for African nations. Beijing's economic miracle has been sustained by ready access to natural resources, specifically industrial metals and oil. While Southeast Asia and the Middle East have been the historic primary sources for these goods, rising prices and resource scarcity is pushing China in search of alternative suppliers—as one economist put it, "resource-rich Africa can deliver."[94] To that end, at the African Development Bank summit in May 2007 Beijing pledged to double its aid to Africa and to provide $5 billion in loans and credit by the close of 2010. In addition, Beijing has established the African Development Fund that is slated to eventually accumulate another $5 billion.[95]

CHINA AND FOREIGN DIRECT INVESTMENT

In 2002, the CCP initiated a "go-out" policy, a plan to establish between 30 and 50 "national champions" from the most promising and/or strategic state-owned enterprises by 2010. These firms were intended to pursue four goals: (1) help China shift away from an almost exclusively export-driven economy to one that includes outward foreign direct investment; (2) assist in building Beijing's political capital and international influence; (3) gain access to technology and know-how necessary for meeting—or exceeding—global competitive standards; and (4) secure energy and resources needed to sustain China's economic miracle. (Accenture, 2005) The program has succeeded beyond Beijing's expectations—with over 7,000 Chinese enterprises now invested in 160 countries and regions around the world.

The policy, however, is not without problems. For example, consider the situation Beijing confronts in Africa. With over 700 Chinese companies now involved in cooperative ventures in Africa, (1) China's leadership has found it increasingly difficult to coordinate among a vast array of associated corporate and government bureaucracies; (2) distance and time differences have significantly hindered regulatory oversight; and, (3) corporate entities have developed a tendency to pursue profit-oriented decisions that may conflict with the agenda of other Chinese actors in the region.

Furthermore, it has become evident that Chinese corporations operating off the mainland are generating what heretofore might have been dismissed as "capitalist" or "imperialist" concerns. Beijing has discovered Chinese firms tend to not be familiar with local customs, laws or institutions. In a bid to maximize profits, the Chinese firms seek to lower labor costs by reducing wages, allowing for marginal working conditions, and skimping on safety measures. Finally, the Chinese firms have been known to engender fears of outsider dominance within a particular industry.

In short, Beijing's "go-out" campaign has served to move Chinese businesses offshore and expand market opportunities, but at a political cost the CCP appears to not have expected. Chinese businesses now frequently find themselves treated in a manner once reserved for Americans and Europeans—as a source of cash and employment, but not a trusted agent.

China has historically offered access to this type of promised foreign aid through three venues: grant aid—aid in kind or zero interest loans (90 percent of which are ultimately written off)—concessional loans—debts with subsidized interest rates—and commercial loans and/or investment.[96] The primary focus of this aid is the development of infrastructure to facilitate resource extraction, telecommunications, and transport.[97] And the primary recipients? Not surprisingly, given their petroleum and industrial metals stores, Angola, Nigeria and Sudan.

This snapshot of China's apparent aid priorities in Africa immediately gives rise to a number of questions. First, is China deliberately undercutting Western efforts to curtail human rights violations on the African continent by aiding rouge governments? Second, is access to Chinese aid going to abet Africa's wholesale return to debtor status? Finally, why are African nations turning to China—when Western assistance is available and comes with a proven track record?

Considerable time and effort has been expended investigating these questions. The findings are somewhat unexpected. First, there is no clear evidence China's aid to "rogue" states like Sudan has resulted in a further degradation of the recipient government's human rights record. In fact, some economic data shows aid and trade links with China may actually serve to incrementally improve the life of average citizens in the target states. According to analysts working for the Organization for Economic Cooperation and Development (OECD), the intensified aid and trade links with China have resulted in higher economic growth rates, better trade terms, increased export volumes, and higher public revenues.[98] This is far from saying "all is well," but any quality of life improvement in some of these nations is to be preferred over the status quo.

Second, there is little evidence Chinese aid is returning Africa to a debtor status. The Heavily Indebted Poor Countries Initiative that commenced in 1996, and associated Multilateral Debt Relief Initiative begun in 2006, removed approximately $43 billion in debt from the shoulders of struggling African citizens.[99] China's recent loan aid programs have provoked fears the cycle is about to start anew—with poor governments borrowing more than they can ever hope to pay back.

The data, again, is less condemnatory. To date, Beijing has conservatively written off an estimated $2.13 billion in debt, with a further debt cancellation of approximately $1.28 said to be in the works.[100] This debt relief has been an outstanding public relations tool for Beijing—and may expand in scope as Western nations curtail lending in the wake of the 2007–08 financial crisis. Quite frankly, there is room to argue China's aid program not only garners popular support . . . it also allows for two positive press events—the first to provide the loan, the second to relieve the debt.[101]

This brings us to the question of why governments are increasingly seeking development from the Chinese instead of Western donors. In addition to the fact China has a demonstrated tendency to simply write-off what had previously been declared a loan, the Congressional Research Service found:

1. China offers assistance without the political and/or economic conditions Western donors frequently place on aid—China's policy of "noninterference in other countries' domestic affairs" typically wins international support because it is considered respectful of other nations' sovereignty.

2. Beijing has proven capable of delivering aid in a rapid manner— often bypassing the lengthy processes designed to protect social and environmental safeguards.

3. Chinese aid is often delivered at lavish events of great symbolic value to the recipient state's leadership.

4. Beijing has been willing to tackle projects other aid donors have avoided because of technical difficulties or hardships.[102]

Quite simply, China has become the donor of choice because Beijing is willing to offer near-immediate rewards in exchange for a potentially lucrative relationship years or even decades in the future. It is only fair to note this development is not exclusively of China's making. As one scholar found, "developmental assistance offered by established [Western] donors has become less generous and less attractive, while emerging donors' aid has become more generous and more attractive."[103]

BEIJING'S DIPLOMATIC OUTREACH

China does careful global geopolitical calculations in which it tries to objectively analyze its geopolitical assets and liabilities. It then works out a long-term plan to enhance its assets and minimize its liabilities.[104]

—Kishore Mahbubani, *Spring* 2008

The final element of China's global "reassurance" campaign is to be found in Beijing's diplomatic corps and its expanding efforts to reach a global audience. Chinese diplomats—unlike many of their Western counterparts—have become noted as pragmatic representatives who seek to avoid foreign audiences through employment of ideological and/or doctrinaire messages.

In fact, since 1996 Beijing has forged a diplomatic strategy with two broad purposes:

1. To maintain the international conditions necessary to facilitate China's focus on domestic capabilities (primarily economic development).

2. To reduce the likelihood the United States or other nations will use their current material advantage to truncate China's ascent and frustrate Beijing's international aspirations.[105]

This diplomatic strategy is said to consist of two elements: reassurance and partnership. We have already examined at length the reassurance element of this strategy; let's turn for a moment to what the Chinese mean by international partnership.

CHINA AND LATIN AMERICA

Beijing has not limited her outreach efforts to Asia. Over the last six years China has also sought to establish a diplomatic foothold in Latin America. The ideological foundations for this outreach effort were outlined in a White Paper released in November 2008, the White Paper declares: "the Chinese government views its relations with Latin America ... from a strategic plane and seeks to build and develop a comprehensive and cooperative partnership featuring equality, mutual benefit, and common development."

According to Beijing, the goals of China's policy on Latin America are:

- Promote mutual respect and mutual trust.
- Deepen cooperation and win-win results.
- Draw on each other's strengths to boost common progress.

> • Establish the one China principle as the political basis for the establishment of relations between China and Latin America.
>
> Commenting on the White Paper, Michael Shifter, vice president for policy and director of the Andean program at the Inter-America Dialogue, observed "there is nothing surprising in the policy paper . . . it . . . sets out in general terms a framework for what the Chinese government is doing and plans to do in the region." (Wendell Minnick, November 13, 2008, "China Issues First White Paper on Latin America," DefenseNews.com.)

Beijing's growing participation in multilateral international organizations, and almost universal normalization of diplomatic relations, springs from an effort to cultivate partnerships. China's focus on partnerships is intended to "enhance its attractiveness to the other great powers while retaining flexibility by not decisively aligning with any particular state or group of states."[106] In order to accomplish this objective, Beijing has emphasized:

1. Establishing bilateral relationships without targeting a third party.
2. Promoting economic intercourse.
3. Focusing on shared concerns instead of disagreements.
4. Rendering official visits—particularly military-to-military exchanges and leadership summits—routine.[107]

Harkening back to China's approach to operating on the international stages—as a member of a regional hierarchy rather than a participant in balance of power politics—this *realpolitik* approach to foreign policy and the practice of diplomacy is unlikely to change in the foreseeable future. What has changed, however, is the manner in which China practices international diplomacy.

China's Diplomatic Corps

Chinese diplomats used to be an isolated lot. Frequently unfamiliar with local culture, customs, or language, these official representatives of the People's Republic would hide behind the doors and walls of their diplomatic compound. No more. China's Foreign Service now appears intent on only employing the best and the brightest. As a dean at the National University of Singapore declared, Chinese embassies are trumping their international counterparts "through the powerful combination of enhanced geopolitical acumen and better professional diplomacy."[108]

What constitutes "better professional diplomacy?" According to the author of *Charm Offensive: How China's Soft Power Is Transforming the World*, over the last 15 years China's Ministry of Foreign Affairs has sought to retire older, more ideological diplomats, strongly encourage regional specialization, and demand enhancement of language skills. This effort is coming to fruition. As of 2005, approximately half of China's 4,000 diplomats were less than 35 years old. Many of these newer employees had studied local languages at overseas universities, and all were subject to repeat assignments within a particular geographic area.[109]

The result is a diplomatic corps that is repeatedly praised as professional, knowledgeable, and accessible. This final attribute is commonly cited as a stark contrast with American embassies. As a Singaporean scholar put it, "while Chinese diplomats walk around freely without escort, American diplomats live and work in a fortress-like compound, and venture outside only rarely and with great care in many countries."[110] Needless to say, the Chinese are thought to be using these differences to Beijing's advantage—seeking to cultivate ties where Americans are perceived as being unwilling or unable, to tread.

POPULAR PERCEPTION OF U.S. DIPLOMATIC PRESENCE OVERSEAS

In his book *Hot, Flat, and Crowded*, Thomas Friedman, a three-time Pulitzer Prize recipient and author of *The World Is Flat*, describes the U.S. consulate in Istanbul, Turkey, as follows: a 22-acre facility, with buildings constructed on a solid rock hill. Per State Department regulations, walls surrounding the buildings are at least 100 feet away from the facilities and are capable of withstanding bombings and ramming. Guard booths have been placed at the perimeter of the facilities, and windows and doors are bulletproof—and designed to resist forced entry.

As Freidman sarcastically notes, "All that is missing was a moat filled with alligators and a sign that said in big red letters 'Attention! You are now approaching the U.S. consulate in Istanbul. Any sudden movements and you will be shot without warning. ALL VISITORS WELCOME.'"

The Turkish impression of this new U.S. consulate? The facility is so secure, "they don't let birds fly there." I have been struck with a similar sentiment when visiting U.S. diplomats in Bangkok, Manila, and Seoul. They work within armed fortresses that markedly resemble maximum security prisons. Not exactly the most accommodating approach to public diplomacy. The real dilemma, of course, is balancing post 9–11 protection requirements with this outreach effort. The question at hand— how to weigh risk versus gain? Should we be willing to potentially expose diplomatic personal to terrorist attacks in an effort to win the battle for overseas hearts and minds? Or should we "cocoon" the State Department employees and hope the world —after passing through pat-downs and a metal detector—will come to us?

Aggressive Public Diplomacy

According to the U.S. State Department, public diplomacy is focused on promoting national interests through understanding, informing and influencing foreign audiences.[111] While the most visible element of China's push on this front—the planned establishment of Confucius Institutes to offer Chinese culture and language classes —has received considerable public attention, the full scope of Beijing's outreach effort is less well known.

Consider, for example, the main objectives for Chinese public diplomacy. Beijing seeks to employ public diplomacy as a means of:

1. Publicizing China's assertions to the outside world.
2. Forming a desirable image of the Chinese state.
3. Issuing rebuttals to "distorted" overseas reports about China.
4. Improving the international environment surrounding China.
5. Exerting influence on the policy decisions made in foreign countries.[112]

THE $6.5 BILLION OUTREACH CAMPAIGN

China is the midst of a "overseas propaganda" campaign that seeks to rival CNN or the BBC. Armed with a reported $6.58 billion, Chinese authorities are diligently working to establish an English language news channel modeled on *al-Jazeera*. The goal? To provide Beijing's take on current issues and events. This international outreach also includes an upgrade for Xinhua, China's official news agency. There are now reports Xinhua is planning to standup a 24-hour news channel that would compete with CNN. In the words of one CCP Politburo Standing Committee member, it is time for Chinese officials to go out and "vigorously sing the praises of the achievements of the CCP, socialism, the reform policy, and the glories of the great motherland." (Willy Lam, January 22, 2009, "Chinese State Media Goes Global: A Great Leap Outward for Chinese Soft Power?" *China Brief*, Volume 9, Number 2, The Jamestown Foundation, Washington, DC.)

Clearly, this is no modest agenda. And the Chinese leadership is pursuing all means available for disseminating its message. Historically, Beijing sought to practice public diplomacy by employing periodicals, selective contacts with foreign correspondents, and English-language radio broadcasts. By 2004, the Chinese leadership was seeking to diversify its means of communicating with foreign audiences. Accordingly, Beijing has issued instructions to:

1. Boost external publicity through the Internet.
2. Expand cultural exchanges by unifying these events with external publicity.
3. Make the external cultural industry more competitive and influential.
4. Adopt a more positive attitude toward foreign media and reporters.
5. Strengthen external publicity activities by studying communications marketing.
6. Make concentrated efforts to publicize important issues on a priority basis.[113]

RISE OF THE CONFUCIUS INSTITUTE

The most visible element of China's public diplomacy is the ever-expending chain of Confucius Institutes. Run by the Ministry of Education, the Confucius Institutes are charged with "promoting friendly relationships with other countries and enhancing the understanding of the Chinese language and culture"—by fostering and supporting initiatives led by local nongovernmental organizations and/or universities. The first Confucius Institute—located in Tashkent, Uzbekistan—was established in June 2004 as a pilot program. The first operational Confucius Institute opened in Seoul, South Korea, on 21 November 2004. As of November 2008, there were over 300 Confucius Institutes operating in almost 80 countries. According to the Chinese Ministry of Education, by 2010 there should be 500 Confucius Institutes, and 1,000 by 2020.

The Confucius Institutes are intended to be a low-key means of expanding international familiarity with Chinese culture. This helps to explain their low funding priority in Beijing, and the fact that foreign Confucius Institute partners are often tasked with covering more than half of the start-up and annual operating costs. Rather than "planting flag poles" through the purchase or construction of physical structures, the Institutes are typically established within universities or similar educational organizations. Operating with limited funds and small staffs, the Confucius Institutes have yet to demonstrate the successes associated with Germany's Goethe Institutes or the French Alliance Francaise. As one scholar notes, however, "the founding of the Confucius Institutes is, by and large, an image management project . . . to promote the greatness of Chinese culture while . . . counterattacking public opinion that maintains the . . . 'China threat'." (Xiaolin Guo, January 2008, "Repackaging Confucius," Institute for Security and Development Policy, Stockholm, Sweden; and, Ingrid d'Hooghe, July 2007, "The Rise of China's Public Diplomacy," Netherlands Institute of International Relations, The Hague.)

In short, China's modern public diplomacy—and diplomatic representation—is "not your father's Oldsmobile." Developments on both fronts over the last 10 years strongly suggest Beijing has come to understand and practice strategic communication—getting the right message to the right audience through the right medium at the right time. Furthermore, the very breadth of this effort is indicative of a global campaign intended to paint China in the hues Beijing selects, not those imposed by external critics. This increasingly sophisticated application of diplomatic tools is certain to expand in scope and message over the coming decade.

SO WHERE IS BEIJING HEADED OVER THE NEXT 10 YEARS?

China's diplomatic and economic outreach bespeaks a nation focused on regional relations rather than global domination. As we have seen, Hu Jintao is intent upon continuing Deng Xiaoping's reform and opening—and to expanding China's reputation as a responsible international actor. In fact, I would contend that over the last ten years Beijing has pursued her economic development and diplomatic outreach in a manner that suggests a maturing regional actor whose behavior is puzzling for the Cold War-trained policy makers in Washington.

This is particularly evident in the "realist" or "neoconservative" circles who dominated the foreign policy conversation during the George W. Bush administration. For example, in 2001 John Mearsheimer wrote, "A wealthy China would not be a status quo power, but an aggressive state determined to achieve regional hegemony."[114] As a result of this prevailing *weltanschauung*, Washington pursued what can best be described as a containment policy in regard to China. As such, means of slowing Beijing's economic growth were debated, and China's military modernization program was deemed cause for considerable alarm.

I would note not all members of the academic or policy communities adopted this hard-line perspective. Other China watchers advocated engagement rather than containment. Furthermore, proponents of this more collegial option suggested China's economic development and military modernization could have a stabilizing influence on the region.[115] It would be fair to say this line of reasoning was not warmly received in Washington between 2000 and 2008. The favored pejorative term used to describe these engagement advocates: "panda hugger."

Back to our topic at hand, why the hard-line approach? As Mark Beeson, a prominent British academic wrote in 2009, "The idea that hegemonic competition and transition are inescapable, cyclical features of the interstate system has been suggested by scholars operating from a number of perspectives."[116] In other words, analysis of China's "rise" had been largely pigeonholed within a Cold War context. Leading American scholars and policy makers were operating under a mindset that suggested a need to contain China for the same reason Washington had found it necessary to surround and, ultimately, go to war with Vietnam—the quarantine and eradication of communism.

We now have reason to believe this construct is inappropriate when dealing with China. To explain why I come to this conclusion we have to quickly turn to Robert Gilpin, a leading proponent of the hegemonic paradigm. According to Gilpin, changes in distribution of power within the existing international system—particularly when it involves economic might—serve to undermine the balance and cause the rising state(s) to seek a means of changing the status quo in a manner that is more favorable to their interests.[117] That, however, is not what has happened in East Asia. Instead, as we have seen above, China is emerging on the international stage without demanding the United States step aside. Nor, we should note, is Beijing seeking to establish a hegemonic dominance in Asia.

To drive this point home, let's return for a moment to our discussion of China's economic and diplomatic rise in Asia. As *The Economist* reported in March 2007, Beijing's economic development has not come at the expense of her neighbors.[118] China's role as a final stop on the global "disassembly line" has actually served to benefit her less-well off, and wealthy, regional counterparts. Some economists go so far as to argue China's economic development was one of the reasons Asia rebounded from the Asian financial crisis of 1997–98.[119] Furthermore, China—unlike Japan—has made herself open to foreign investors, a development that served to even spur economic expansion in South Korea and Taiwan.

Turning to the diplomatic element of this equation, we have already highlighted China's willingness to peacefully resolve most of her border disputes. We have also discussed China's growing enthusiasm for bilateral and multilateral engagement, and her decision to plug into the existing international diplomatic order—including wholesale participation within the United Nation's family of organizations. In short, while Washington has been accused of assuming an increasingly unilateral approach to international affairs, Beijing has been reaching out. As Mark Beeson reminds us:

> Nowhere has the juxtaposition [between Washington and Beijing's approach] been more stark than in China's ever closer relations with ASEAN. Whereas the U.S. has frequently snubbed ASEAN, China has established a Free Trade Agreement, signed ASEAN's treaty of Amity and Cooperation, and taken a much softer line on contentious issues like the potentially resource-rich Spratly Islands.[120]

Beijing is reaching out to her neighbors, and not just in a "charm offensive." Hu actually seems to be implementing his "harmonious world" policy by beginning at Beijing's doorstep, and the neighbors—as we noted in Chapter 1—have been impressed and appear reassured they have little to fear from this reemerging China.

So we are back to the debate over "rightful rule" and hierarchical relationships. If you recall, I have previously argued a hierarchical relationship exists in international affairs when one state recognizes that another has the political authority to command certain forms of behavior. I have also contended that China is in the midst of realizing this status in Asia. I am not alone. At the conclusion of his examination of the factors covered in this chapter, Beeson offered the following observation:

> ... China has rapidly reasserted herself at the center of a more coherent and integrated East Asian regional order, and [her] neighbors, whether they like it or not, are increasingly dependent on China for their own well being and development. In such circumstances, China is beginning to enjoy a degree of "structural" power of a sort that has until recently been predominantly associated with the United States.[121]

Beeson is unsure if China is not ultimately intent upon becoming a regional hegemon, but for the foreseeable future he concludes such a grab for power is probably not to Beijing's benefit. In fact, Beeson's closing argument harkens back to John Fairbank. Beeson suggests "the only 'realistic' response to [the] looming environmental crisis is one that involves admittedly unlikely forms of cooperation in a region that is synonymous with fiercely protected sovereignty."[122] Fairbank, as you will recall, held China historically used her hierarchical superiority to "dictate a sense of harmonious coexistence." Remarkably similar conclusions, reached 40 years apart, using data separated by centuries.

So what does China want in the coming 10 years? To answer that question at this point in our investigation I turn to Robert Sutter, a former National Intelligence Officer for East Asia. In his book, *China's Rise in Asia: Promises and Perils*, Sutter suggests China's "activism and clearer focus on Asia" point to five long-term goals:

1. Help secure China's foreign policy environment while Beijing is focused on economic development and political security.

2. Promote an economic exchange that facilities domestic economic development.

3. Supports efforts to isolate Taiwan and secure access to advanced arms and military technology.

4. Increase Chinese contacts and calm regional fears about Beijing's rising power and influence.

5. Secure an "ambiguous world order"—one absent U.S. hegemony or regional efforts contrary to China's interests.[123]

According to Sutter, "China's approach to [her] neighbors has a geoeconomic emphasis that seems to mesh well with the prevailing priorities of Asian leaders."[124] In other words, China's "harmonious world" and hierarchical approach to regional relations works because it correlates with the neighbors ambitions. Given the beneficial consequences of maintaining this harmony, I have no reason to believe China plans to stray from this path over the coming decade.

Beijing's "harmonious" approach to dealing with the international community is also evident on a global scale. In late January 2009, China's leaders began to make it quite clear they had lost faith in Washington's ability to responsibly oversee the international financial system. At the annual global gathering of economic and political leaders in Davos, Switzerland, Wen Jiabao forthrightly blamed the U.S.-led financial system for the ongoing global economic slump. According to China's Premier, "excessive expansion of financial institutions in blind pursuit of profit," a failure of government supervision, and an "unsustainable model of development, characterized by prolonged low savings and high consumption," were directly to blame for the crisis.[125]

This finger-waving lecture, however, was quickly followed by a Chinese call for Beijing and Washington to cooperate in efforts to "fight the financial crisis and promote constructive and cooperative bilateral relations."[126] Speaking with reporters from the *Financial Times* on February 2, 2009, Wen declared, "we believe that to maintain cooperation between China and the United States serves world peace, stability, and prosperity."[127] What Wen did not tell the reports was that China was indeed working on a plan that would require Washington's cooperation while simultaneously cutting the U.S. apron strings with the international financial system.

That announcement came in late March 2009, when Zhou Xiaochuan, the governor of the People's Bank of China, released a paper calling for the establishment of a new "super-sovereign reserve currency" to replace the dollar. In his paper, Zhou said the new currency reserve system should be controlled by the International Monetary Fund as a means of avoiding the "inherent vulnerabilities and systemic risks in the existing international monetary system."[128] Interestingly, despite the fact China currently holds the world's largest foreign exchange reserve, the new "super-sovereign reserve currency" is to be supranational. According to Zhou, the global dominance of a few currencies—the dollar, euro and yen—leaves the international financial system more volatile and vulnerable. In short, Zhou was not proposing the renminbi replace the dollar.

Zhou's solution—expand the use of "special drawing rights." Special drawing rights were an IMF creation in the 1960s. Under this system, the supranational currency has a value determined by a basket of major currencies. Nations would gain access to these special drawing rights through increased contributions to the International Monetary Fund. As the *Wall Street Journal* observed, this would increase the role and powers of the IMF—indicating "that China and other international developing nations aren't hostile to international financial systems—they just want to have more say in running them."[129]

As it turns out, the *Wall Street Journal* was right on the mark. During the last week of March 2009 Beijing made clear it would be willing to make more money available to the IMF so as to increase the institution's ability to assist nations ailing as a result of the current financial crisis, but only for greater IMF voting rights. As an economist for Deutsche Bank told the *Journal*, "China sees this as a good opportunity to increase [Beijing's] influence."[130] International financial analysts watching Beijing's apparent power play agreed the request seemed reasonable, but also warned a larger role for China could result in greater scrutiny of banking practices in Europe and the United States. They specifically pointed to a statement People's Bank of China deputy governor Hu Xiaolian made in late March 2009 as evidence of their claim. According to Hu, "under the current situation, [China feels] the IMF particularly needs to strengthen its surveillance of the economic and financial policies of the major reserve-currency-issuing nations."[131]

So what does China want? This bid for a greater voice in governing the international financial system is indicative of China's broader efforts to level the playing field. Beijing is not seeking to dictate or dominate the conversation, she is simply attempting to ensure non-Western voices have a say at the table. While the proposal to move away from the dollar to an IMF-governed special drawing rights system would diminish Washington's role, China is not attempting to replace the United States. Instead, it really does appear China is seeking to realize a rebalancing of the entire international system—such that, she is able to secure an "ambiguous world order"—one absent U.S. hegemony or regional efforts contrary to China's interests. A "harmonious world" come to fruition.

CHAPTER 3

The "Moderately Prosperous Society"

As a large developing country with a population of over one billion, China cannot afford and should not expect to rely on the international community. Its only option is to rely on its own strength. That is to say, it must (1) fully and consciously draw on its own institutional innovation, (2) tap the growing domestic market, (3) translate its hefty savings into investment, (4) improve the quality of its citizens' lives, and (5) address its resource shortages and environmental problems through the advancement of science and technology.

—Zheng Bijian, Bo'ao Forum for Asia, 2003[1]

Had the Chinese leadership strictly focused on establishing a "harmonious world" with little thought to conditions at home it seems unlikely this text—or any other study of China's future—would be necessary. Beijing, however, has managed to avoid Moscow's fatal myopic focus on impressing or threatening the neighbors. Instead, the Chinese Communist Party has come to the realization it has obligations at home and abroad. The scope of this domestic responsibility was remarkably evident in Hu Jintao's report to the 17th National Congress on October 15, 2007. Speaking to an audience gathered at the Great Hall of the People, Hu declared, "building a moderately prosperous society in all aspects is a fundamental goal for the Party

and the state to reach by 2020."[2] This pledge to pursue continued
national development should not have come as a surprise; Hu was simply following in Deng Xiaoping's footsteps.

In 1987, Deng outlined what became known as the "Three-Step
Development Strategy." According to Chinese scholars, step one of
this strategy called on Beijing to abet a doubling of the 1980 gross
national product[3] (GNP)—and that all Chinese would have sufficient
food and clothing—by the close of the decade. Step two called for
the Chinese leadership to quadruple the 1980 GNP by the end of
the twentieth century. Step three—to increase per-capita GNP to
the level of the medium-developed countries by the mid-twenty-first
century—marks the current state of Deng's dream.

As we shall see, the Chinese Communist Party has done an admi-
rable job in meeting Deng's tasking. But significant problems have
emerged along the path to moderate prosperity. As Hu admits in his
report to the 17th National Congress, "while recognizing our
achievements, we must be well aware that they fall short of the expectations of the people." The litany of shortfalls according to Hu
include:

> ... economic growth is realized at an excessively high cost of
> resources and the environment. There remains an imbalance in
> development between urban and rural areas, among regions,
> and between the economy and society ... There are still many
> problems affecting people's immediate interests in areas such as
> employment, social security, income distribution, education,
> public health, housing, work safety, administration of justice
> and public order; and some low-income people lead a rather dif-
> ficult life. More efforts are needed to promote ideological and
> ethical progress ... A small number of Party cadres are not honest
> and upright, their formalism and bureaucratism are quite con-
> spicuous, and extravagance, waste, corruption and other undesir-
> able behavior are still serious problems with them.[4]

How to fix these problems? In true Chinese Communist Party-
style, Hu laid out the path forward—complete with references to
Mao, Marx, socialism and harmony.

FOUR CARDINAL PRINCIPLES

In 1979, Deng Xioping presented the "four cardinal principles," policy decisions on which no debate would be allowed. The four cardinal principles are:

1. The principle of upholding the socialist path.
2. The principle of upholding the people's democratic dictatorship.
3. The principle of upholding the leadership of the Chinese Communist Party.
4. The principle of upholding Marxist-Leninist-Mao thought.

In his 2007 speech to the 17th National Congress Hu Jintao reminded his audience that these principles remain an ideological touchstone for the Chinese Communist Party—a foundation for continuing Deng's reform and opening without blatantly sacrificing the socialist tenets Mao had fought to impose on the country.

Hu's fixes come in the form of a formulaic statement—a tedious repetition of the obvious for some, but essential for understanding why the Chinese Communist Party now seems more a bastion of capitalism than a harbinger of the workers' paradise. In what he calls the "scientific outlook on development," Hu declared, "we must always adhere to the Party's basic line of taking economic development as the central task and upholding the four cardinal principles, and the reform and opening up policy."[5] Why? Hu is quite blunt on this point. "Taking economic development as the central task is vital to invigorating our nation and is the fundamental requirement for the robust growth and lasting stability of the Party and the nation."[6] In short, Hu and his fellow Chinese Communist Party leaders, have come to the simple conclusion they must facilitate domestic economic development or follow their socialist counterparts in Moscow to the rubbish heap of history.

ESSENTIAL ELEMENTS OF A "MODERATELY PROSPEROUS SOCIETY"

While there is a temptation to declare Beijing is now in league with Gordon Gekko—"greed is good, greed works"—Chinese leaders argue there are multiple essential elements of a moderately prosperous society. As outlined in Hu's October 15, 2007 address to the 17th National Congress these are:

- Economic—The goal is to quadruple the per-capita gross domestic product (GDP) of the year 2000 by 2020, increasing China's comprehensive national strength and international competitiveness.
- Political—Socialist democracy and the legal system will be improved and the rule of law will be enforced more thoroughly as a fundamental principle.
- Cultural—In cultural development, the education level, scientific knowledge, ethical code and physical fitness of the whole nation will be improved to promote the comprehensive development of the people.
- Sustainable development—The capacity for sustainable development will be strengthened and resource use efficiency will be improved to achieve harmony between the development of man and nature.

(October 25, 2007, "Buzz Phrases From the 17th National Congress of the Communist Party of China," *Beijing Review*, Beijing.)

The evidence suggests Hu and company have taken this lesson to heart. China's track record—at least on the monetary front—is nothing short of astounding. Over a 30-year period, China's annual gross domestic product (GDP) has averaged an approximately 9 percent growth rate.[7] Per capita income has gone from $175 in 1978 (measured in 2000 dollars) to more than $2,000 today. During the same time period, the incomes of an additional 250 million Chinese have risen above Beijing's poverty level of $1 a day.[8]

Table 3.1   China's Average Annual GDP Growth Rates, 1960–2007[9]

Time Period	Average Annual GDP Growth Rate
1960–1978 (pre-reform)	5.3%
1979–2007 (post-reform)	9.3%
1990	3.8%
1992	14.2%
1994	13.1%
1996	10.0%
1998	7.8%
2000	8.4%
2002	9.1%
2004	10.1%
2006	10.7%
2008	9.0%

This economic growth has depended on China's domestic development and her participation in the international market place. Over the last five years, however, the primary drivers for China's continued growth have reversed. In 2003, over half of Beijing's annual GDP expansion could be attributed to domestic investment and private consumption. By 2007, that figure appeared in danger of being reversed—with exports serving as the primary driver for China's continued economic growth.[10] To put this development in context, consider the fact economists estimate domestic consumption—public works to housing—only account for approximately 40 percent of China's annual GDP growth rate, the remainder is generated by exports.[11]

China's focus on exports is clearly evident in international trade data. A case-in-point is provided by Beijing's trade record in 2007. During the year in question China's global trade surplus surged 48 percent to a new record of $262.2 billion. Chinese exports in 2007 were up 25.7 percent, for a total of $1.22 trillion, while Beijing's imports expanded 20.8 percent to $955.8 billion.[12]

Not surprisingly, this mounting trade surplus has also done wonders for China's foreign exchange reserves—now estimated to be over $2 trillion.[13] The rapid growth of China's foreign exchange reserves can be directly attributed to economic globalization and Beijing's monetary policy.[14] This policy both holds down labor costs—thereby making Chinese-manufactured goods the option of choice for many consumers—and centralizes the accumulation of foreign capital. As a means of keeping the yuan valued against the dollar at a level perceived sufficient to stimulate export growth,[15] China "sterilizes" incoming dollars by compelling domestic recipients to convert their earnings into renminbi (literally, the "people's currency") at a carefully maintained exchange rate.

The foreign currency is then shuttled through the finance system to the People's Bank of China (the central bank), and finally to the State Administration for Foreign Exchange (SAFE) where it is reinvested—usually in the United States—to stimulate further consumption.[16] While this process costs the national government money at the time of transaction, the net result is a long-term gain for China via increased exports and an associated growth in gross domestic product.

Quite simply, Beijing has decided the increased earnings from exports and associated domestic job creation outweighs the opportunity cost of forging a more *laissez faire* monetary policy.[17] Needless to say, this policy has generated significant political heat in the West, and elsewhere—where governments and popular pundits like to complain Beijing's fiscal management addresses China's employment concerns at the cost of other nations' jobs.[18]

The means by which China has perpetuated this economic development has drawn more than just international criticism—it has come with a significant cost at home. As Zheng Bijian told a European audience in 2004:

> As China enters the twenty-first century it faces three big development challenges. The first is that of natural resources . . . oil, natural gas, water and arable land . . . The second challenge is the environment. Serious pollution, the wasteful use of resources, and low rates of recycling are bottlenecks for sustainable economic development. The third is the lack of coordination between economic and social development.[19]

This list of "challenges" is proving a real burden for Hu and the Chinese Communist Party leadership. Beijing has discovered it is one thing to recognize one's problems—it is quite another to actually remedy the shortfalls.

NATURAL RESOURCES

The People's Republic of China is the world's second largest oil consumer—falling only behind the United States (China became a net importer of oil during the 1990s, and in 2008 almost 50 percent of the country's consumption relied on imports). China's economic growth can be almost directly correlated with Beijing's seemingly ceaseless third for oil, which is thought to increase by 3.5–4.5 percent per year. At this rate, China's need for imported oil is projected to increase at least 60 percent by 2020.[20]

Beijing's petroleum consumption rates have been attributed to a number of factors, including poor insulation of housing, factories, and other commercial spaces; inefficient manufacturing techniques; and Chinese consumers—whose appetite for personal transportation in the form of automobiles is just beginning to skyrocket. The bottom line: China is significant participant in the international petroleum market, and there is no expectation of diminished interest in the foreseeable future.

All of which begs the question, where will Beijing find the oil necessary to continue fueling China's demand for this "black gold"? There is universal agreement the solution is not to be found at home. China's proven oil reserves are insufficient to meet her needs. At current production rates these domestic reserves are unlikely to last beyond 2030. In fact, the International Energy Agency predicts that by 2030, Chinese oil imports will equal or surpass current U.S. foreign petroleum purchases.[21]

As we have previously noted, China's growing future dependence on oil imports has caused Beijing to seek supplies abroad. China has now acquired stakes in exploration and production in Canada, Iran, Iraq, Kazakhstan, Russia, Sudan, Saudi Arabia, Venezuela, and West Africa. Despite these diversification efforts, China has become increasingly dependent on Middle East oil. In 2008, 58 percent of China's oil imports came from the region. By 2015, 70 percent of Beijing's oil is expected to come from the Middle East.[22]

Furthermore, China's search for oil could prove a real challenge for Beijing's "harmonious world" campaign. As the Institute for the Analysis of Global Security reported in 2008,

> In the South China Sea, China is involved in territorial disputes with Malaysia, the Philippines, Taiwan, Vietnam and Brunei over access to energy in the Spratly and Paracel Islands. In the East

China Sea, where rich oil and gas reserves are believed to exist, rivalry is developing between China and Japan over access to energy resources. China has already begun the exploring process for gas reserves on its side of the East China Sea. The Japanese government claims that some of the reserves are actually on its side of the demarcation line and has accused China of attempting to extract hydrocarbons from its water ... Another source of tension is access to Russian oil. For many months, China and Japan have been involved in a bidding war over a major pipeline deal to deliver Russian oil from Eastern Siberia. China's plan calls for a pipeline running to the Manchurian city of Daqing, while Japan is insisting on a pipeline that would run to Nakhodka, the Russian coastal area opposite to Japan ... In the Western Hemisphere China concluded oil and gas deals with Argentina, Brazil, Peru, and Ecuador. But its main country of interest is Venezuela, U.S.' fourth largest oil supplier. A series of oil agreements signed in early 2005 allow Chinese companies to explore for oil and gas and set up refineries in Venezuela. Chinese state-owned oil companies have also begun seeking ambitious oil deals in Canada, the top petroleum supplier to the U.S.[23]

In short, China's quest for oil could prove a long-term problem, not only for Beijing, but also for her neighbors and other major petroleum consumers in the international community.

China's search for oil is likely to be closely accompanied by a bid for sources of potable water. Water usage in China has quintupled since 1949, and demand is unlikely to diminish in the foreseeable future. Compared with the United States, China is confronted with a water nightmare. China is estimated to have about 7 percent of the world's water resources, and roughly 20 percent of the global population. The country also suffers a severe regional water imbalance, with about four-fifths of the water supply in the south.[24]

And then there are man-made problems. Industry in China uses 3 to 10 times more water than manufactures producing similar goods in developed nations. Furthermore, Beijing insists on maintaining Chinese grain self-sufficiency, despite the fact this agricultural demand is also depleting the nation's aquifers.[25] Couple these demands with the fact that up to one-third of all river water and a majority of China's largest lakes suffer pollution levels that render the contents unsuitable for even industrial use, and one has a real recipe for disaster.[26]

China's solution, for the moment, is to seek alternative water sources at home. For instance, in September 2007 the *New York Times* reported Chinese leaders are "reaching back to one of Mao's unrealized plans: the $62 billion South-to-North Water Transfer Project to funnel more than 12 trillion gallons northward every year along three routes from the Yangtze River basin ... The project, if fully built, would be completed in 2050. The eastern and central lines are already under construction; the western line ... remains in the planning stages."[27]

In addition to these "water movement" projects, China is considering options like shifting an even larger portion of the rural population into cities—eliminating small farms and thereby increasing agricultural efficiency—and constructing a large desalinization plants.[28] The problem with these options, increased fuel consumption to power the urban areas and generate the flow levels required at the water-making facilities—a very real Catch-22 for the Chinese leadership.

POLLUTION

China's economic miracle has also been accompanied by a legacy of seemingly unprecedented environmental pollution. The Chinese Ministry of Health now admits pollution has made cancer China's leading cause of death. Scientists report only 1 percent of the nation's 560 million city dwellers breathe air the European Union considers safe. And the World Health Organization has found China's population suffers more deaths from water-related pollutants than the nation's toxic urban air.[29] China's State Oceanic Administration reports over 80 percent of the nation's sea areas are polluted to some extent.[30]

To make matters worse—at least from a capitalist's perspective—China's pollution problems are now eating into the nation's economic development. In 2006, China's State Environment Protection Agency announced the country's environmental damage costs Beijing approximately 10 percent of the overall gross domestic product. This data is not a state secret. China released the figures in a white paper titled, "Environmental Protection in China (1996–2005)."[31]

China's pollution problems are increasingly becoming a global concern. As the *New York Times* put it: "Sulfur dioxide and nitrogen oxides spewed from China's coal-fired power plants fall as acid rain on Seoul and Tokyo. Much of the particulate pollution over Los Angeles originates in China."[32] Given these reports, there is no end to the debate over China's potential contribution to global warming. And worse appears yet to come. The International Energy Agency in 2007 reported China was likely to overtake the United States as the largest producer of greenhouse gases by 2008.

Beijing has not taken this threat lightly. As indicated by the release of the 2006 white paper, Chinese authorities are publicly committed to addressing the problem. As of 2005, official Chinese spending on pollution treatment had reached over $20 billion a year,[33] and there have been nascent political efforts to address the issue on a longer-term basis. For instance, in 2004 Hu Jintao endorsed "comprehensive environmental and economic reporting"—known as "Green GDP." The project was intended to calculate the cost of pollution in each of China's provinces and report same every year.

While "Green GDP" died as a result of provincial leadership non-cooperation, the Chinese government has taken other steps in the right direction—including an announced effort to use 20 percent less energy to achieve the same economic activity realized in 2005. Beijing has also required overall emissions of mercury, sulfur dioxide and other pollutants be reduced by 10 percent by 2010.[34]

The real problem here, adhering to expensive policy options during economic downturns. In late 2008, media sources began reporting on signs China was abandoning its nascent green movement in favor of maintaining employment. As the research director at a Chinese think tank observed, "With the poor economic situation, officials are thinking twice about whether to close polluting factories, whether the benefits to the environment outweigh the dangers to social stability."[35]

SOCIAL UPHEAVAL

China's economic miracle hangs menacingly—like the proverbial Sword of Damocles[36]—over the CCP's collective leadership heads. Deng Xiaoping's decision to largely abandon Mao's socialist/communist economic policies in favor of capitalist principles almost certainly saved the CCP from eventual extinction, but at a considerable political cost for Beijing's current leaders.

Deng's "reform and open door" policy spurred China's economic revival, lured foreign investment, and won the CCP widespread support from a domestic constituency. But Deng's pragmatism—captured in slogans like "black cat or white cat, it is a good cat if it

catches the mouse," or "to get rich is glorious"—promoted the establishment of an economic system that no longer promises to rise all
boats in a common manner. This change is evident in tangible and
intangible manners. I tell my friends, one is more likely to see a Max
Mara outfit than Mao suit in Shanghai today. And, there is growing
evidence China's new moneyed class expects a say in the political
process.

Jiang Zemin—China's president from 1993–2003—essentially
declared this was the case in his decision to impose the "Three Represents" theory on the Chinese Communist Party. Speaking before the
Party Congress in November 2002, Jiang declared:

> ... the Party must always represent the requirements of the
> development of China's advanced productive forces, the orienta-
> tion of the development of China's advanced culture, and the
> fundamental interests of the overwhelming majority of the people
> in China.[37]

While there is considerable debate as to exact meaning of Jiang's
words, many Western observers chose to interpret the first clause of
this statement—"*represent the requirements of the development of China's
advanced productive forces*"—as a demand the Chinese Communist
Party expand beyond a historic focus on the proletariat. More specifically, the Three Represents is thought to require the Chinese Communist Party become more democratic—by allowing private
entrepreneurs to join its 73 million-person ranks.[38]

Regardless of how one chooses to interpret the Three Represents, it
is now clear that when Hu Jintao began his service at China's helm he
inherited an increasingly divided society. Today, China is best
described as a country suffering regional development disparity, a failing social welfare system, massive unemployment, structural poverty,
and growing social unrest. As a pair of Chinese scholars so aptly
noted, "The rapid pace of development has disrupted the formation
of the pluralistic yet cohesive society that Beijing had hoped for;
instead, a highly divided society has emerged."[39]

The degree to which Beijing is confronted with a house divided is
perhaps most evident in reports of social unrest. In a startling bit of
honesty, between 2001 and 2006 the Chinese Ministry of Public Security published data on national and local "mass incidents." When considered in a cross-temporal framework, the resulting picture is a
veritable textbook example of mounting societal unhappiness.

For instance, between 1993 and 1999 there was a 268 percent increase in reported mass incidents—from 8,700 to 32,5000. Between 1999 and 2006 that figure nearly doubled again—from 32,500 to 58,000. Disquieting developments for any regime, less a communist system that had previously prided itself on championing an egalitarian society.

In 2006, the Ministry of Public Security ceased providing the annual summaries. As was the case when the flow of data began, no explanation for the change in reporting procedures was provided, but one suspects Beijing's pre-Olympic games sensitivities were the primary cause. The CCP's well-crafted efforts to present China in the most positive manner probably included a sweeping decision to cease admitting incidents of public unrest. This line of reasoning has certainly found a home at Amnesty International, who argued in their April 2008 study, "China: The Olympics Crackdown," "it is increasingly clear that much of the current wave of repression is occurring not in spite of the Olympics, but actually because of the Olympics."[40]

In any case, the Ministry of Public Security data spurred a plethora of academic and media speculation as to the underlying causes for this steady climb in Chinese "mass incidents." The simplest explanation wins my vote—demonstrations work. A popular Chinese expression

Table 3.2   Incidents of Social Unrest in China

Year	Number of Incidents
1993	8,700
1994	10,000
1995	11,500
1996	12,500
1997	15,000
1998	24,000
1999	32,500
2000	40,000
2001	N/A
2002	50,400
2003	58,000
2004	74,000
2005	87,000

holds, "making a great disturbance produces a great solution, small disturbances produce small solutions. Without a disturbance, there will be no solution." It would seem the Chinese have taken this saying to heart.

That the CCP's constituency believes demonstrations work is insightful, but does not address the fundamental concern—why are Chinese citizens taking to the streets with increasing regularity? To answer that question, we turn to academic evaluations of the social dynamics at play. Some of the earliest work in this area came from a political scientist working at the Rand Corporation.

BUSY PREDICTING CHINA'S COMING COLLAPSE

Beijing's economic success has spawned a cottage industry focused on predicting the Chinese Communist Party's demise. The most popular work on this front is Gordon Chang's *The Coming Collapse of China*. Published in 2002, the book predicts Beijing's ruling party is unlikely to survive another decade. According to Chang—an attorney and amateur political scientist—the Chinese Communist Party will be overwhelmed by changes associated with the country's World Trade Organization accession. Chang specifically laid the blame on China's continued support for state-owned enterprises and an "astounding" $540 billion in non-performing bank loans. Chang was hardly breaking new ground—his comments on China's non-performing loan problem were largely lifted form Nicholas Lardy's 1998 *Foreign Affairs* essay, "China and the Asian Contagion."

Chang was not alone. In 2002, Joshua Kurlantzick published an article in *The New Republic* that declared, "Ultimately, China's economic façade probably will crack. And when it does, the consequences may be disastrous." Kurlantzick goes on to contend, "Washington's finest minds have prepared for a rising Middle Kingdom, spending little time contemplating what would happen if China's economy were to implode." (Joshua Kurlantzick, 16 December 2002, "Is China's Economic Boom a Myth?")

In a 2004 article titled, "China Rethinks Unrest," Murray Tanner, a Rand scholar takes direct aim at conventional wisdom. Rather than arguing "it's the economy, stupid," the author instead reveals the incidence of public protests "has, at times, risen during periods of inflationary high growth, recession, and recovery—a serious challenge to any simple economic determinist explanation of social unrest."[41] In other words, the Chinese citizenry's decision to head for the streets cannot be solely correlated with domestic economic conditions.

How then to explain the rise in public demonstrations? According to the author of "China Rethinks Unrest," the CCP's constituency is both sensitive to economic conditions and is exhibiting signs of a shifting political culture.

> A quarter century of gradual, progressive political reform is forging a new culture . . . that is more open, assertive, and even "developed." China's citizens are now simply much less willing to tolerate unjust, corrupt bureaucrats, and the population is far more willing to take complaints to the streets.[42]

If this observation is accurate, China's leadership is indeed in trouble. Recall that former Chinese Premier Zhu Rongji once declared "development is the fundamental principle, and the key to resolving all problems China is facing. We must maintain a comparatively high growth rate in our national economy."[43] It now appears Zhu may have accounted for less than half of what currently ails his successors.

CRACKING DOWN ON CORRUPTION

Citizen outrage over official corruption in China has drawn a swift—and, at times, brutal—response from Beijing. In 2005, the CCP reportedly disciplined more than 115,000 of its members—turning 15,000 over to the courts for prosecution (*Washington Post*, February 14, 2006). Furthermore, Chinese officials maintain "execution for corruption is proportionate and accords with 'China's national condition'" (*International Herald Tribune*, August 2, 2007). To this end, Beijing has gone so far as to even execute the former head of its State Food and Drug Administration.

This crackdown on corruption is unlikely to diminish in the foreseeable future. In August 2008, Chinese officials were provided a draft revision of the country's criminal law that would punish relatives who benefited from an official's illegal behavior. The proposed revision also doubled the penalty for accepting bribes from 5 to 10 years.

Rand followed up on this line of reasoning during testimony before the U.S.-China Economic and Security Review Commission on April 14, 2005. During his presentation for the commissioners, Tanner argued, "it seems increasingly clear that the lagging development of China's political and legal institutions bears at least as much of the blame for rising unrest as does the economy."[44] According to Tanner, these political and legal shortfalls were particularly evident in: (1) the lack of effective channels for redressing citizen grievances; (2) weak government oversight and enforcement of laws; and (3) pervasive corruption.

Following in Rand's footprints, the Carnegie Endowment for International Peace provided a second look at potential causes for increased social unrest in China. Like his counterpart at Rand, the Carnegie Endowment fellow swiftly concluded, "the simplest economic explanation of social unrest—that faltering growth causes unrest—fails to explain the [Chinese] trends."[45] Instead of linking the rise in "mass incidents" to economic dissatisfaction, the argument again focused on personal disruptions caused by "modernizing investment" and structural "reforms."

This focus on economic and structural explanations for China's mounting social unrest gave rise to lists of citizen grievances. On the economic side these are now said to include:

- Low and unpaid wages.
- Layoffs and unpaid back wages.
- Loss of worker benefits.
- Union representation—specifically efforts to form independent labor organizations.
- Environmental degradation.
- Access to water.
- Tolls and fees—particularly those levied by local officials.
- Land condemned for public use.
- Ethnic tensions.[46]

On the structural front, Chinese citizen protests were said to be largely linked to corruption and malfeasance. In these cases complaints focused on:

- Local abuse of fees and tolls.
- Real estate project "fundraising"—local approval for the collection of money—frequently not repaid—from ordinary citizens by developers and business leaders in return for paper promising higher rates of return than offered by official financial organizations.
- Land confiscation and asset stripping.
- Enterprise workplace abuse.
- Sale of official positions.
- Inadequate government oversight mechanisms.[47]

Finally, some Chinese citizens were said to be publicly venting as a result of being caught between both economic and structural shortfalls. This is particularly the case for those unfortunate enough to be residents of China's two "rust belts" or the nation's increasingly moldy "breadbasket." Beijing's pre-1980s decision to concentrate industrial sectors in isolated areas devoid of rapid access to port facilities—first in Manchuria and then to landlocked provinces—has led to the formation of the northeast and interior rust belts. Just as troublesome, the marked difference in rural and urban family incomes resulted in a flight from the nation's richest farmlands.

CHINA'S XINFANG SYSTEM

Public demonstrations are the most visible, but a less prevalent means of expressing discontent. The average Chinese citizen is much more likely to employ the country's *xinfang* (Letters and Visits) system when seeking official assistance in righting a perceived wrong. In the *xinfang* system, a citizen may petition authorities through employment of a letter, phone call, or personal appearance.

In place since 1951, the CCP's variant of this ancient right of petition has undergone at least two major revisions over the last 15 years. The first occurred in October 1995, when the State Council issued the "Regulations of Petition." The second—and more significant—revision took place in 2005, when the State Council provided a new version of the regulations. The 2005 revision of the regulations was intended to serve two purposes: (1) to better control the petitioners; and (2) to compel local officials into taking more responsibility for dealing with petitions.

Chinese officials certainly take care to publicly stress the importance of heeding *xinfang* appeals. For instance, in March 2006 China's top legislator declared "the National People's Congress Standing Committee ... paid great attention to letters and visits and put the complaints wisely aired by ordinary people as its supervision priorities." Nonetheless, the success of the petition process remains very much in question.

A 2005 study found only 0.2 percent of petitioners resolved their problem through the *xinfang* system, and Chinese scholars have repeatedly argued the process is ineffective for solving legal problems and therefore should be scrapped.

Despite these grim findings, the *xinfang* system survives. Why? For the common citizen the system provides a means of "venting," even if little comes from their efforts. In the 2005 study, 90.5 percent of the petitioners said they had traveled to Beijing for the "purpose of "informing the Central Government" about existing problems; 88.5 percent stated they simply wanted to "apply pressure on local governments to get problems solved;" and 81.2 percent admitted they "knew that the Central Government cannot solve the problems directly, but they were hoping to obtain an official directive. (Li Li, Nov. 10, 2005, "Life in a Struggle," *Beijing Review*.)

For the CCP, the *xinfang* system provides: (1) an information collection source; (2) helps central authorities monitor the performance of local officials; (3) helps address violations of citizens' rights; and (4) serves a propaganda function by convincing petitioners their case lacks any basis in policy or law. (Carl Minzer, 2006, "*Xinfang*: An Alternative to Formal Chinese Legal Institutions," *Stanford Journal of International Law*, pp. 103–179.)

In any case, Chinese citizens continue to employ the *xinfang* system, with an average of 10–13 million appeals a year—approximately 600,000 of which make it to the top bureaucracy in this process, the State Bureau for Letters and Calls.

This geographic element of China's social unrest problem is possibly the most pressing issue Beijing will have to confront in the coming 10 years. While joblessness in urban areas is estimated to range as high as 15 percent, residents of the Chinese "rust belts" are said to face unemployment figures starting at 25 percent. This problem has been further exacerbated by the steady demise of state-owned enterprises—the very foundation of China's "iron rice bowl."[48] Beijing's decision to allow for the failure of many state-owned enterprises resulted in the loss of approximately 27.8 million factory jobs between 1999 and 2004.[49] Further shuttering of these unprofitable enterprises could cause another 6–10 million Chinese to lose their jobs by 2010.

CCP sensitivity to the plight of these former state-owned enterprise employees can be traced to the fact the workers are more likely to be urban residents, and therefore have greater access to the facilitators of social unrest"—specifically, union activists, reporters, lawyers, and intellectuals. As a result, for the CCP this urban pool of unemployed presents the threat of an organized, dissatisfied mass with access to pubic communication systems; all the ingredients necessary for creation of a solidarity movement similar to found in 1980s Poland.[50]

The same cannot be said of China's unemployed rural population. Beijing's piecemeal development of China's transportation infrastructure—and maintenance of "communist" land ownership practices—has contributed to preservation of seemingly unimaginable poverty in the midst of the planet's greatest economic bootstrapping. One begins to get a feel for the scale of this problem when we consider the fact the income gap between urban and rural areas in China has done nothing but expand over the last 20 years. In the mid-1980s this income gap favored urban residents at a 1.8:1 ratio. That is to say, for every 1.8 yuan a city dweller earned, his rural counterpart only took home 1 yuan. In the mid-1990s this income gap had widened to 2.5:1, in 2006 it was 3.28:1, and by 2010 the gap could be 7:1 or 8:1.[51]

Now keep in mind China has an estimated 750 million rural residents, nearly 350 million of whom still live below the official poverty line of $1 a day.[52] More than half of this total rural work force is presently considered an excess labor pool. And, to make matters worse, if China's rural productivity reaches the levels demonstrated in developed countries only 40–60 million of these 750 million rural residents will be required to attain the level of agricultural output achieved in 2005.[53]

HUKOU HOUSEHOLD REGISTRATION SYSTEM

The *hukou* system is a lingering remnant from China's economic and social policies in the 1950s. Developed as a means of limiting internal movement and the size of urban populations—two perceived elements of political instability—the *hukou* system was implemented in 1958. Under this system, individuals and households were registered by occupation and place of birth. The result is anyone who was registered as a rural resident in 1958 would remain as such, as would all subsequent generations. The same was true for urban households.

The problem for Beijing, under the original *hukou* system urban residents received additional government services—education, grain subsidies, and medical care—while rural populations were left to grow their own food and make do with "barefoot doctors." This difference in treatment can be explained by the fact that China's communal farms of the time provided work opportunities not available to the "poorer" urban areas.

In 1983, the CCP sought to reform the system by allowing rural residents to live and work in "market towns." In 1984, the system was again revised, granting rural residents the right to legally work in cities, as long as they had their own source of funds, food, and housing—and registered with local security bureaus. These revisions did not go unchallenged. While urban areas desired access to the cheap labor rural residents provided, the city governments did not want to pay for the social services migrants desired. The compromise, an ID card that could be used to get a job and thereby allow employers to ignore where the employee was legally registered.

The revised *hukou* system is still in effect—with Beijing remaining able to oust the migrant labor population whenever economic and/or political conditions so demand.

China's continued rural poverty can primarily be attributed to three factors. First, the average farmer only has access to paltry plot of arable land. Once source claims at least 70 million of these farmers are landless or till less than 260 square yards.[54] Second, over-farming and environmental mismanagement have degraded the yield of over a third of China's farmland. Third, CCP economic development programs have focused on urban populations—depriving farmers of education, health care, and infrastructure development.

Chinese leaders are aware of these rural problems—and have taken steps to address the underlying issues. But not rapidly enough to avoid a fourth, related dilemma, China's approximately 150–200 million person migrant labor pool.[55] Eager to escape the countryside's grinding poverty, up to a fifth of China's rural population has gone in search of jobs in metropolitan areas.

Deng's economic reform and opening generated a surge in migration from China's farms to her coastal cities. Drawn by the promise of better paying jobs in construction and labor-intensive, export-focused industries, this sea of *gastarbeiter* became a ready target for unscrupulous employers and scapegoats for urban problems including crime and congestion.[56] Add to these woes the migrants' denial of social services by China's *hukou* household registration system—and one begins to see how Beijing's rural population is a continuing leadership nightmare.

There are signs things could be looking up for China's rural residents. Hu's tendency to use the rural population as a base of support for the CCP suggests the *hukou* system could be significantly revised prior to his departing office in 2012. In the interim, Hu and the CCP leadership have sought to correct for the disparity in urban-rural incomes by revising China's agricultural land-use policies. In October 2008, Beijing announced a plan to double—by 2020—the disposable income available to the approximately 750 million people still residing outside urban areas. In addition, the CCP promised to boost social services in the countryside, modernize agriculture, and integrate rural and urban economies. While Western observers dismissed much of the plan as "rather minor," they did herald a reform aimed at consolidating farmland.[57]

Under China's current laws, farmers do not own the land they till—it remains government property—but instead hold 30-year leases. Furthermore, the farms have tended to be small, averaging about 1.66 acres.[58] Needless to say, these plots are difficult to farm in a profitable manner, thereby contributing to size of China's migrant labor pool. Under the new plan farmers would be allowed "to lease their contracted farmland or transfer their land use rights."[59] To facilitate this process, markets for land leasing and rights transfer will be established so that farmers can publicly sub-contract, exchange and swap their rights. According to the new policy, all land-use rights transfers must be voluntary, with adequate payment.[60] The overarching goal: gradual consolidation of small plots into larger farms in a manner that boosts rural incomes without inciting violence—and without surrendering the principal of state-ownership of all property.

HU JINTAO'S BID FOR A HARMONIOUS SOCIETY

Beijing's efforts to address the plight of seemingly forgotten residents is but one element of a broader policy Hu began to publically espouse in 2005. Aware that China's economic growth has resulted in mounting social unrest, the Chinese President made a sequence of speeches announcing his commitment to fostering a "Harmonious Society." In October 2006, the Chinese Communist Party formally endorsed Hu's program—proclaiming "China is a harmonious society in general, but there are many conflicts and problems affecting social harmony. We must always remain clearheaded and be vigilant even in tranquil times."[61]

Given the litany of problems confronting Hu and his fellow travelers, this turn of events should have come as no surprise to professional China watchers. Quite simply, Hu was admitting he is confronted with fundamental socialist paradox. That is, while the nation's overall GDP has demonstrated unprecedented growth—the results have not been equitably distributed. The solution: rather than welcoming the rise of political opponents that might generate the policy debates necessary to address Beijing's many challenges, the Chinese Communist Party set about resolving the crises on its own.

I would hasten to note Hu's "harmonious society" campaign is probably best understood as a continuing refinement of the objectives resident in Deng's reform and opening movement. At their basest level both "harmonious society" and "reform and opening" are intended to accomplish one thing—preservation of the Chinese Communist Party. The preeminent objective for any CCP leader is survival of the country's communist party. In an effort to stave off the domestic political challenges that might arise, Beijing has been quick to crush potential contenders and seek a means of placating its 1.3 billion person constituency. This focus on survival helps explain CCP reactions to the Falun Gong and Beijing's incessant drumbeat in support of economic development.

Before we turn to Beijing's efforts on the economic front, a short comment is in order on the Falun Gong. On July 20, 1999, Beijing banned the Falun Gong and declared the movement's practitioners a highly organized political group "opposed to the Communist Party of China and the central government, [that] preaches idealism, theism and feudal superstition."[62] The vehemence of this condemnation is probably best explained by China's history—specifically, the Taiping Rebellion.

Between 1851 and 1864 China was convulsed by the Taiping Rebellion, an armed attempt to topple the Qing dynasty. The Taiping Rebellion was led by Hung Xiuquan, a farmer's son who—inspired by Christian missionaries—reached the conclusion he was the younger son of Jesus sent to found the Heavenly Kingdom on earth. Hung tapped a nerve within the Chinese peasantry that eventually led to his 1853 capture of Nanjing and rule over southern areas populated by approximately 30 million people. Hung and his Heavenly Kingdom of Great Peace were ultimately defeated by a coalition of Qing, French and British forces, but Chinese leaders learned a valuable lesson—never allow a religious movement to blossom unchecked. The CCP leadership has clearly studied Chinese history, and is not about to allow the Falun Gong or any other faith-based organization become a potential political adversary.

The same anticipatory response appears resident in China's 30-year focus on economic growth and development. Working in accord with an updated version of Deng's grand strategy for economic development (outlined at the 1997 15th Party Congress), Chinese leaders are striving to provide a per capita GDP that seduces all-but the most ardent critic.[63] To achieve this goal, the CCP has sketched a three-step development strategy (1980–1990, 2000, 2010–2050) that is further divided into three petit stages (2010, 2020, 2050). This grand strategy for economic development began in 1980, and has since proceeded in ten-year increments—with each stop intended as a measuring stick for progress.

As of 2005, Beijing had already surpassed its target for 2010. In 2005, China's per capita GDP reached approximately $1,700.

Table 3.3   China's Grand Strategy for Economic Development[64]

Year	GDP per Capita
1980	$100
1990	$200
2000	$800
2010	$1,600
2020	$3,200
2050	$12,800

In 2006 that figure was $2,000, and in 2007 it was an estimated $2,200. In January 2008, a Chinese government think tank boldly predicted that by 2010 the nation's per capita GDP would reach almost $3,000—roughly double the figure demanded by the CCP's economic grand strategy.[65] The impact of the 2007–08 global financial crisis on this prediction remains to be seen, but one suspects China's GDP in 2010 will still exceed the 1997 benchmarks and be touted as further evidence of the CCP's sound leadership.

Given these figures, one has to wonder why Hu essentially admitted significant shortfalls in the Chinese Communist Party's governance by declaring his "harmonious society" policy in 2006. As we have seen above, China's growth has not been absent hiccups and problems—particularly in its growing consumption of oil, generation of pollution, and mounting social unrest. But do these issues really warrant a nationwide press for a "harmonious society?" Surely Beijing could have found a way to at least buy-off or suppress the dissenters, cover up the pollution, and purchase petroleum from a myriad of unsavory sellers?

The response to this rhetorical query is, of course, yes. But that would fail to capture the true extent of the problems confronting Hu and his fellow party elders. The full scope of Beijing's governance challenges was perhaps best enunciated in a 2003 Rand Corporation study titled *Fault Lines in China's Economic Terrain*. According to the study's authors, China's leadership is confronted with significant issues across eight domains: unemployment, poverty, and social unrest; economic effects of corruption; HIV/AIDS and epidemic disease; water resources and pollution; energy consumption and prices; fragility of the financial system and state-owned enterprises; possible shrinkage of foreign direct investment; and, Taiwan and other potential conflicts.[66]

The bottom line: Rand found that adverse developments within these eight domains "would [cause] a decline in China's annual rate of economic growth, conservatively estimated at 1.0–1.3%."[67] I would note this seemingly minor decrement does not capture the cumulative impact of all eight domains—but rather is an estimate based on adverse developments in one or two of the areas. Should, for example, Beijing actually go to war over Taiwan the secondary effects in the remaining seven domains could essentially halt China's economic growth. This becomes evident when Rand's findings are laid out in tabular form as I have done below.

When the correlation between China's "economic fault lines" and GDP growth are considered in this manner, the breadth of Hu's domestic policy nightmare becomes even clearer. As the Rand scholars conclude:

> To mitigate the stresses engendered by these fault lines will demand an enormous and continuing array of consultations, negotiations, and transactions among China's central and provincial governments and the Communist Party apparatus. This demanding process is likely to preoccupy China's new collective

Table 3.4   Impact on China's Economic Growth—By Domain[68]

Domain	Decrement to Economic Performance
Unemployment, poverty, and social unrest	0.3–0.8%
Economic effects of corruption	0.5%
HIV/AIDS and epidemic disease	1.8–2.2%
Water resources and pollution	1.5–1.9%
Energy consumption and prices	1.2–1.4%
Fragility of the financial system and state-owned enterprises	0.5–1.0%
Possible shrinkage of foreign direct investment	0.6–1.6%
Taiwan and other potential conflicts	1.0–1.3%

leadership during the next decade, predisposing it to avoid external distractions and to maintain equable relations with the United States.[69]

Looking at this study five years after its publication, one can safely declare Hu's effort to address these issues has not caused Beijing to "avoid external distractions," but does help explain the CCP's focus on fostering a harmonious society and a harmonious world. We have already examined the latter—let's now turn to the former.

China's leadership announced formal plans to pursue a policy focused on building a "harmonious socialist society" during the October 2006 Sixth Plenum of the 16th Chinese Communist Party's Central Committee. Under the new policy, all government entities in China were instructed to "exert their efforts in resolving matters concerning the intense mass reactions resulting from the expropriation of land and implementation of house demolitions for urban construction ... and actively prevent and properly address the mass incidents triggered by internal contradictions among the people and maintain public interest and social stability."[70] In one fell-swoop, Hu and his CCP cohorts were demanding Chinese officials address the six major social risks confronting Beijing: the "three agricultural issues" (agriculture, peasants, and rural backwardness) and the "three disparities" (rich-poor, rural-urban, and east-west).[71] No mean task—regardless of one's political orientation or system of governance.

To fully comprehend Hu's objective, however, we need to review a speech the Chinese President made on February 19, 2005. In remarks at the CPC Central Committee Party School, Hu declared "this period is a crucial stage for [China's] economic and social development ... Independent thinking of the general public, their newly-developed penchant for independent choices and thus widening gap of ideas among different social strata will pose further challenges to China's policy makers."[72]

In order to meet this challenge, Hu continued, Chinese leaders needed to foster development of a "harmonious society." According to the Chinese president, "a harmonious society should feature democracy, the rule of law, equity, justice, sincerity, amity, and vitality."[73] To meet this goal, Hu instructed the CPC leadership to pursue seven objectives:

- Strive for sustained, rapid and coordinated economic growth.
- Develop socialist democracy.
- Actively enforce the principle rule of law.
- Strengthen ideological and ethical buildup.
- Maintain social equality and justice.
- Establish a fine-tuned social management system.
- Beef up environmental protection.[74]

While not subject to the academic and media analysis that would accompany a similar pre-announcement from a European or American politician, this ambitious agenda even caused Chinese scholars to warn against unrealistic expectations.

As Beijing was preparing for the October 2006 Sixth Plenum of the 16th Chinese Communist Party's Central Committee, policy "experts" told reporters that eight challenges stood between Hu and his "harmonious society." According to the experts—an associate chief editor of a government-owned publisher and a researcher at the Chinese Academy of social sciences—these challenges are:

- A growing gap between rich and poor.
- Corruption.
- A lack of protection mechanisms for some social groups.
- Unemployment.
- An inadequate social security system.
- Unsustainable economic growth and its related environmental pollution.
- Backwardness in science, education, culture, medical care and sports.
- A general lack of management skills.[75]

Not surprisingly, these eight challenges are markedly similar to the economic and structural shortfalls commonly identified by Western scholars. The question, then, is how does Hu go about conquering this mountain?

REALIZING THE "HARMONIOUS SOCIETY"—CHINA'S HEALTH CARE REFORM

The Chinese Communist Party has announced an ambitious effort to address its constituents' long-standing concerns about access to affordable health care. The 1985 launch of Deng's market-oriented reforms included a commercialization of health care that left many Chinese scrambling to pay their medical bills. A 2005 study by the State Council's Development Research Center found that in 1978 patients covered 20 percent of their medical fees, 25 years later that figure had risen to 52 percent. In 2007, World Health Statistics revealed government/private expenditure for health care in China was split 38 percent to 62 percent. In comparison, the government/patient split in Great Britain was 86.3 percent/13.7 percent . . . and in the United States the same figures were 44.7 percent/55.3 percent.

On April 6, 2009, the State Council announced a three-year health care plan intended to diminish patient costs and expand rural health care options. The $124 billion plan, which charges local governments with assuming 60 percent of the total cost, includes a promise to provide universal access to basic health insurance, improved primary health care facilities, and equitable access to basic public health services.

China's goals for the health care reform program:

- More than 90 percent of the population will have some form of basic medical insurance by 2011.
- Construction of 2,000 county-level hospitals, build 29,000 township hospitals, and the upgrade of 5,000 township medical facilities.
- Train 1.37 million village doctors and 160,000 community doctors.
- Establishment of a universal medical records database.

To lower prescription costs—the largest complaint about the current system—Beijing will promote implementation of an essential medicines program for state-run hospitals, clinics, and pharmacies. This program is intended to hold down treatment expenses by strictly controlling prices for drugs on the essential medicines list. As the vice director of the National Development and Reform Commission summarized the program, "we will gradually cut the profit margin of drugs sold at medical institutions . . . and implement zero profit margin for drugs sold at local public clinics." (Yuan Ye and Jiang Guocheng, April 7, 2009, "China Unveils Ambitious Plan to Overhaul Health Care Sector," Xinhua, Beijing.)

IN PURSUIT OF SUSTAINABLE ECONOMIC GROWTH

We must regard development as the top priority of the CCP in governing arid rejuvenating the country. Development is of decisive significance for building a moderately prosperous society in all respects and speeding up socialist modernization. We must firmly commit ourselves to the central task of economic development, concentrate on construction and developing the productive forces. We must better implement the strategy of rejuvenating the country through science and education, the strategy of strengthening the nation with trained personnel and the strategy of sustainable development.

—Hu Jintao, October 15, 2007[76]

Chinese officials understand the "three agricultural issues" and "three disparities" present a formidable challenge for national policy makers. Furthermore, as noted above, concerns about energy, pollution, and water are being factored into CCP economic models. How can we be sure of this? In 2006, the State Council's Development and Research Center[77] released a study identifying major problems that will confront Chinese leaders in the coming 5–10 years. According to the report, Beijing is headed for an economic bottleneck created by energy shortfalls, environmental problems, excess labor, unemployment, and water shortages. If the scholars at the Development and Research Center are correct, these issues will converge in the 2015 time frame.[78]

This does not mean Chinese leaders should despair—or that China's economic growth is going to come to an abrupt halt in the foreseeable future. Why this optimism? A number of factors come into play when answering this question. I think, however, three variables are at the top of the list. The first is China's remarkable rise in productivity since 1978. The second is Beijing's political approach to fostering growth, and the third is China's remarkable domestic savings rate.

RISE IN PRODUCTIVITY

One of the earliest efforts to uncover the secret behind China's rapid growth came in 1996, when the International Monetary Fund (IMF) dispatched a research team to examine the sources of Beijing's economic miracle. On their return, the IMF team reported:

> Although capital accumulation—the growth in the country's stock of capital assets, such as new factories, manufacturing machinery, and communications systems—was important, as were the number of Chinese workers, a sharp sustained increase in productivity (that is, increased worker efficiency) was the driving force behind the economic boom.[79]

The IMF team went on to note Chinese productivity increased at an annual rate of 3.9 percent between 1979 and 1994—during a comparable period U.S. productivity only grew at a rate of 0.4 percent. How did Beijing accomplish this feat? According to the IMF, five factors contributed to the productivity growth: (1) introduction of profit incentives; (2) decollectivization of agriculture; (3) allowing establishment of small businesses; (4) opening the door to foreign investors and traders; and (5) freeing many enterprises from constant intervention by state authorities.[80] The IMF's bottom line: "such explosive growth in productivity is remarkable ... and enviable, since productivity-led growth is more likely to be sustained."[81]

In November 2005, Goldman Sachs Economic Research Group picked up where the IMF left off. In a study titled, "China's Ascent: Can the Middle Kingdom Meet Its Dreams?" Goldman Sachs analysts argued "China's growth has been driven by productivity gains as much as, if not more than, factor accumulation."[82] Typically, "factor accumulation" is focused on money, machinery, factories, and human resources. If we are to believe Goldman Sachs—this sustained increase in productivity can be directly correlated with Beijing's "gradualist and pragmatic approach" to the transition from a centrally controlled economy to one largely dominated by market competition. That is to say, rather than "shocking" the economy with a sudden shift to private enterprise, or micro-managing the process with a detailed blueprint, China reintroduced Adam Smith's "invisible hand" through gradual state withdrawal from the marketplace.

For the analysts at Goldman Sachs, changes in five areas have been "crucial" for China's success. These five areas are:

- Market oriented reforms—policy changes that progressively gave greater rein to market forces. This process began with agriculture and has now extended to industry and even the services sector.
- The great leap outward—Deng's open door policy that eventually allowed for extensive foreign direct investment.
- Better definition of private property rights—Beijing's transfer of resource control that ultimately appears headed for outright legal ownership of property.
- Decentralization and competition among regional economies.
- Prudent macro management—Beijing's improving skills in managing macroeconomic issues associated with China's growth.[83]

Given these developments, and Beijing's commitment to accelerating domestic reforms in conjunction with integration into the international economy, Goldman Sachs predicted China's growth "in the high altitude of 8–9 percent per annum over the next 5 years."[84] In short, the Chinese leaders appeared on course for 2010, but what about 2015 or 2020? Can Beijing maintain sustainable economic growth over a longer time period?

FOSTERING GROWTH

The answer to that question appears largely affirmative, particularly in light of China's savings rate and carefully managed monetary policy. In fact, a paper drafted by two members of the World Bank in 2007 makes just such an argument. In a conference focused on China's exchange rate policy, the paper's authors contend Beijing's economic growth is primarily attributable to three factors:

- China's high and rising savings rate coupled with a state-managed monetary supply.

- Respectable rates of industrial progress—thereby increasing production capacity.
- Increasing production of manufactured goods—that directly contribute to a balance of trade in China's favor.[85]

The problem with depending on this approach to stimulating an economy, according to the authors: (1) it may be impossible over time to maintain the required savings rate and (2) the focus on industrial, vice service, sector growth will ultimate create fewer and fewer jobs as manufacturer efficiency improves. The bottom line: if Beijing adheres to current policy and practices China's GDP growth rates could slow to approximately 8 percent by 2015 and 7 percent in the 2015–2025 time frame.[86]

All of which returns us to the Chinese Communist Party's focus on maintaining sustainable economic growth into the future. Clearly, China needs to determine a means of continuing high productivity rates. We see this happening with the increased mechanization of the country's industrial sector, but at a cost to employment opportunities. Every year Beijing is confronted with the problem of finding jobs for an additional 20 million people. In 2006, only 11 million of those would-be employees found jobs.[87] Increased mechanization and employee efficiency is not going to help resolve this headache for China's policy makers.

One option is to increase China's presence in the international service sector. While China is expected to suffer a 10 percent decrement in industrial sector contributions to the country's GDP by 2035, the service sector is estimated to offer a 20 percent increase to Beijing's GDP during the same time frame.[88] Furthermore, service sector industries typically cannot wholesale mechanize jobs out of existence, increasing the possibility of greater employment options. An added bonus—no small issue in China's case—service sector industries typically require fewer imports, consume less energy, and generate fewer pollutants. Finally, increased service sector development and employment may help to diminish Beijing's concerns about establishing offshore military capabilities. If China can generate economic growth without depending on material imports and exports there is a possibility Beijing may see less need for an expanded air or naval force—cyber protection, in this case, is an entirely different matter.

THE CHINESE SAVINGS MYTH

There is a widespread belief China's savings rate—approximately 45–50 percent of earnings—can be directly attributed to household penny-pinching. Economists now believe this is an erroneous assumption. While Chinese household savings rates are high—an average of 25 percent of disposable income—over the last 10 years the bulk of increased savings in China have come from business enterprises.

Savings in China 1996–2006 (% of GDP)

Year	1996	2000	2002	2004	2006
Source					
Gross Domestic Savings	40.7	36.9	37.6	43.0	50.6
Households	20.1	14.8	16.3	15.4	15.3
Enterprises	15.6	15.3	14.4	19.8	28.3
Government	5.0	6.8	6.9	7.8	7.0

Why this increase in enterprise savings? In a 2007 conference paper, two economists at the World Bank pointed to four causes: (1) the post 1997 Asian economic crisis reform and restructuring of China's state-owned enterprises has actually rendered a majority of these firms profitable; (2) rapid entry and growth of foreign and private firms; (3) China's WTO entry—and the resulting diminution in onerous regulations; (4) Retention of profits rather than payouts in dividends—particularly with state-owned enterprises. (Bert Hofman and Louis Kuijs, October 19, 2007, "Rebalancing China's Growth," Paper presented at the Conference on China's Exchange Rate Policy, Peterson Institute for International Economics, Washington, DC, pp. 6–7.)

A second option is to maintain China's focus on industrial production, but for consumers at home. A significant contributor to the pressures Beijing faces from abroad is China's perceived mercantilist economic policies. This is true if one is discussing China's material exports—or her newly established sovereign wealth fund. The international community is alarmed by the profusion of cheap Chinese products—and the subsequent loss of domestic manufacturing jobs. The same community of nations is worried China stands poised to buy sensitive or strategic national assets. The solution, get Chinese consumers to purchase more and save less. Easier said than done.

SAVINGS RATE

I come to this conclusion for three reasons—China's inadequate supplemental income program, her rising medical costs, and Beijing's continuing struggle with education.

- *Addressing retirement concerns*: Among the challenges facing Hu and his CCP colleagues is China's inadequate social security net. If Chinese are going to be convinced that spending is a good thing, they must also be assured savings are not required to meet basic educational, medical, or retirement needs. To that end, in January 2007 the government announced it would establish a nationwide basic social security system that will, for the first time, cover historically neglected rural areas.[89] Under the new system, up to 3.5 percent of China's rural population would now be guaranteed a minimum monthly income.

- *On the medical front*: During his March 2008 speech before the National People's Congress, Premier Wen Jiabao announced the expansion of China's rural medical care system. The central government announced its intention to provide $1.3 billion in subsidies for this program—a $750 million increase from the previous year.[90] In China's cooperative medical care system, launched in 2003, a rural participant pays $1.3 a year—additional contributions come from the central government, county, or municipality. Despite Beijing's good intentions, the system is hardly adequate. According to Chinese data, in 2003 the average rural income was $328 a year—the average annual medical bill for the same population was $280. As a result, in 2003 almost 75 percent of people living in China's rural areas chose not to seek medical treatment. Under the new system families are reimbursed 25 percent of their total medical expenses—or approximately $95.[91] These fiscal limitations on care are coupled with a shortage of doctors and facilities. The long story made short, only about half of China's population currently has access to the medical care program.

- *And in education*: If China is to advance into a service economy, improve industrial productivity, or even provide new opportunities for its rural population, Beijing must seek to improve the country's educational system. To that end, during his March 2008 speech Wen also promised to spend $11 billion on education during the coming year. This is a 41.7 percent increase over the previous 12 months.[92] According to Wen, "education is the bedrock of China's development, and fairness in education is an important form of social fairness. We need to make education a strategic priority and accelerate the development of all types of education at all levels."[93] Beijing's new educational initiative includes providing compulsory free education through 9th grade and a move to recruit more teachers. Chinese sources indicate rural schools are presently confronted with a faculty shortfall approaching 50 percent and that almost 310,000 of the nation's current teachers do not have the academic degrees required by national standards.[94]

Beijing's promises—while certainly inspiring—are unlikely to meet the bill. Social spending in China remains relatively paltry. As a means of comparison, consider that in 2006 China spent $9.6 billion on health care, $15.6 billion on education, and $50.6 billion on defense.[95] This is not to say the CCP leadership is ignoring its expanding responsibilities on the social security front—Wen Jiabao's March 2008 speech also included acknowledgments of a need to create 10 million more jobs—one just has to wonder if his comments on the need for continued military spending were as poorly received in China's hinterlands as they were in Canberra, Tokyo and Washington.

GRAPPLING WITH THE FINANCIAL CRISIS OF 2007–09

Whether we can turn the pressures into momentum, transform challenges into opportunities and maintain stable and fairly fast economic development is a test of our ability to ride out the complications and a test of the party's ability to govern.

—Hu Jintao, November 30, 2008[96]

China's leaders are understandably concerned about potential fallout from the global financial crisis that began in the summer of

2007. While Beijing's estimated $2 trillion in foreign exchange reserves and the country's relative exclusion from Western financial institutions promised to spare China the worst of this crisis, a downturn in consumer spending in Europe and the United States is now beginning to strike close to home. In late October 2008, Western press sources began to run stories suggesting up to 2.7 million factory workers in southern China could lose their jobs with the withering of Western consumer demand for clothes, electronics and toys.[97] In early November, the BBC claimed job losses had prompted "tens of thousands" of migrant workers to pack railway stations in southern China. According to the BBC, an estimated additional 130,000 passengers a day were passing through the rail stations en route rural homes after losing their jobs.[98] Similar figures appeared in a *Wall Street Journal* article printed in early December.[99]

By early January 2009, Western press reports suggested the unemployment problem was leading to broader questions about Beijing's ability to meet rising demands for greater political opportunities. In an article published on January 13, 2009, the *Washington Post* went so far as to argue:

> As a global recession takes hold and China's economy continues to slow, growing legions of unemployed workers are becoming increasingly bold in expressing their unhappiness—expanding a debate over how to protect the Chinese economy into long-fought disputes over other issues such as freedom of expression and equality before the law.[100]

The story then claims, "Unemployment is now estimated to be at its highest levels since the Communist Party took over in 1949."[101] At this stage old China hands should be scratching their heads—"highest levels since the Communist Party took over in 1949"? My suspicion is that this bit of hyperbole likely only cleared the editors due to a lack of historical perspective and accurate employment statistics.

In fact, China has probably witnessed higher unemployment rates—and much more recently than 1949. To help explain this statement, keep the following statistic in mind—in order to keep pace with a growing employment pool, economists estimate China's GDP must annually increase by approximately 8 percent.[102] Over the last 20 years there have been two cases when this did not occur. The first took place in 1989 and 1990, when China's GDP only expanded by 4.1 and 3.8 percent, respectively.[103] The resulting unemployment was said to be

a major contributing factor to the demonstrations that ultimately cul-
minated in the Tiananmen Square democracy protests.[104]

China's GDP growth rates again fell below the "magic" 8 percent
rate during the Asian financial crisis. In 1998 China's annual GDP
was reported to increase at a rate of 7.8 percent. In 1999 it slowed to
7.1 percent.[105] The result, soaring unemployment figures. According
to Wang Tao, an economist employed at UBS, between 1997 and
2002 some 35 million urban workers were laid off because of the
financial crisis and restructuring of state-owned enterprises. The
major difference between this situation and events of the late 1980s
—no widespread demonstrations. Wang goes on to note unemployment associated with the current economic crisis is also "unlikely" to
result in large-scale unrest. This time Beijing has more resources and
has publicly committed to stimulus efforts aimed at resolving the
problem in a rapid manner.[106]

So much for the historical element of this argument—now let's look
at the problem with Chinese unemployment figures. Some of you will
recall that I previously stated joblessness in urban areas is estimated to
range as high as 15 percent, while residents of the Chinese "rust belts"
are said to face unemployment figures starting at 25 percent.[107] The
Chinese government, on the other hand, reports unemployment in
China as a whole stands at between 4.0 and 4.5 percent.[108] The Chinese Academy of Social Sciences claims the figure is actually closer
to 9.4 percent.[109] A researcher at the Central Party School in Beijing
argues urban unemployment was actually at 12 percent in December
2008 and could reach 14 percent in 2009.[110] And a survey of 15 provinces in January 2009 indicated 15 percent of the total migrant labor
pool—or 20 million people—were unemployed at the time.[111] The
problem with all these figures—(1) none of them match, (2) there is
no authoritative source for the data; and, (3) there is no consistency
in Chinese or Western reporting.

How, in a country that prides itself on accurate record keeping, did
such a situation arise? First, as a matter of national pride, Chinese
authorities are reluctant to suggest the CCP is failing to meet all of
their constituents' needs. Second, China's official urban unemployment figures fail to include migrant workers, who are not registered
in the cities. Third, because of registration concerns, many migrant
workers are employed under-the-table, making it almost impossible
to accurately track changes in the fate of this 200 million-person labor
pool. So how many migrant laborers were unemployed in early 2009?
According to the CCP's office on rural policy, the figure probably was

close to 20 million—with a potential to reach 25 million by year's end.[112]

Even in a country of 1.3 billion these are not minor figures—but hardly worthy of grim prognosis resident in the January 13, 2009 *Washington Post* story. Chinese authorities are well aware of the unemployment problem and are seeking to address the issue before it breeds a repeat of 1989 Tiananmen Square. As early as November 2008, Chinese authorities were telling Western reporters, "It's extremely important to maintain employment stability."[113] During the same time period, Public Security Minister Meng Jianzhu publicly warned police chiefs they "should be aware of the challenge brought by the global financial crisis and try their best to maintain social stability."[114] By December 2008, Beijing was engaged in a nationwide consumer reassurance campaign—placing a slogan on the nightly television news that read, "Face the challenge with Unwavering Confidence."[115]

Not surprisingly, these news stories on China's unemployment woes were accompanied by a series of reports suggesting a decline in Beijing's overall economic growth rates. In late October 2008, the Chinese National Bureau of Statistics announced the nation's GDP growth rate in the third quarter of 2008 had dropped to 9 percent—down from the 10.1 percent reported in the second quarter of 2008.[116] By early November, Western economists were predicting China's economy could expand by as little as 5.8 percent in fourth quarter of 2008, a little more than half the grow rate reported during the same time period in 2007. A Shanghai-based economist told the *New York Times*, "It's tough to be optimistic . . . the three engines of growth—exports, investment, and consumption—have all slowed down."[117] By late November 2008, the World Bank had lowered estimates of China's GDP growth for 2009 to 7.5 percent.[118] In March 2009, the World Bank dropped that figure to 6.5 percent.[119]

As might be expected, the CCP leadership did not take this threat to their careers and place atop China's political hierarchy lightly. On November 9, 2008, Beijing announced it would begin implementing a $586 billion economic stimulus package. According to the State Council, this stimulus package included easing credit restrictions, expanding social welfare services, and launch of an infrastructure construction program—that includes airports, railways, and roads.[120] Perhaps the best indication of how seriously Chinese leaders were taking this problem, however, was simply the size of the stimulus package. The $586 billion is roughly equivalent to all central and local government spending in 2006.[121]

While this move to truncate the impact of the global financial crisis was not surprising, Beijing's candor concerning the need for this spending package was a further sign China's leaders understand they must address the concerns of a domestic constituency. In its announcement of the stimulus package, the State Council declared, "In expanding investment, we must be fast and heavy handed."[122] In January 2009, China's leaders were traveling the country with the message, "our aim is to be the first to recover from the financial crisis. We must have faith and determination."[123] And by March 2009, Wen Jiabao went so far as include the following statement in his opening remarks to the annual National People's Congress: "In China ... maintaining a certain growth rate for the economy is essential for expanding employment for urban and rural residents, increasing people's incomes and ensuring social stability."[124]

WHY FOCUS ON INFRASTRUCTURE?

China's focus on infrastructure development as a means of stimulating economic growth is not without warrant. Since 1986, when transportation was designated a top priority in Seventh Five-Year Plan, China has invested heavily in projects intended to facilitate economic development. According to the Chinese National Bureau of Statistics, in 1994 Beijing spent $39 billion on communications, power, sanitation, and transportation projects. In 1998 that figure climbed to $88 billion, and in 2003 about $123 billion.

The results have been laudatory—but hardly sufficient for a country with a land mass equivalent to the United States. In 1984, for instance, China had approximately 32,000 miles of railway. By 2008 that figure had reached 48,000 miles, but after adjusting for land area, the country still has one of the lowest rail-to-population ratios in the world.[1] A similar comment can be made about China's road network. While low speed, two lane roads link many rural and urban areas, high-speed, paved expressways are still a growth enterprise. Over the last 10 years China has constructed some 30,000 miles of expressway—a remarkable leap from essentially nothing. Beijing now plans to add another 23,000 miles of expressway by 2020; a development that would surpass the 47,000 miles of interstate currently existent in the

United States. (Andrew Batson, November 11, 2008, "China Bets Highways Will Drive Its Growth," *Wall Street Journal*, New York.)

The bottom line: China's infrastructure spending is an investment in the nation's future economic growth. Confronted with significant air, power, road, rail and sanitation shortfalls, Beijing is not repeating the overbuilding that squandered Japanese taxpayers' monies in the 1990s, nor is China engaged in the construction of a giant "bridge to nowhere."

So what does $586 billion buy the CCP? This depends on who you ask. An economist with Morgan Stanley in November 2008 estimated the stimulus package could result in a continuation of 8–9 percent economic growth rates in 2009. Without Beijing's intervention the Morgan Stanley analyst predicted China would witness a 5–6 percent growth rate in 2009.[125] Other analysts were less optimistic. As a reporter for *Forbes* noted, less than half of the designated funds (approximately $220 billion) were truly new spending. The remainder was largely drawn from previously allocated funds.[126] The stimulus package included anticipated expenditures like $146.4 billion for post-earthquake reconstruction in southwestern China, tax breaks for corporate capital investment, export rebates, and land reform measures aimed at addressing the urban-rural income gap.

Gordon Chang, the author of *The Coming Collapse of China*, was even more condemnatory. In an essay published in the *Weekly Standard* Chang argued, "Despite the initial global fanfare greeting the announcement, the program seems unlikely to reverse the economic downtrend."[127] Chang's criticisms: (1) the stimulus was not big enough; (2) by focusing on infrastructure construction the program would not have much impact until 2010 or 2011; and, (3) only 1 percent of the $586 billion appeared directly targeted on social services. Chang's conclusion: "the Chinese economy will thus remain heavily dependent on exports and investment—and be unsustainable in the long run."[128]

Writing for the *Wall Street Journal*, Calla Wiemer, a visiting scholar at the University of California Los Angeles, offered a much different perspective. Wiemer, an economist who has also taught for the National University of Singapore, contended Beijing's stimulus plan includes "a mix of consumption and investment-boosting elements."[129] While Wiemer agreed more railroad construction would do little to help rebalance China's economy, she noted the plan would also serve to help stimulate consumption—either directly or indirectly. As evidence for her position, Wiemer points to Beijing's announced intention to focus elements of the plan on health and education spending; and to provide support for social security, pensions, and income support. Her observation: "spending in these areas not only supports public consumption directly, it stimulates private consumption as well by relieving households of the need to save to finance retirement or self-insure against mishap."[130] Wiemer's bottom line, "China's stimulus package is good news for the world at large . . . a growing consumer market to be tapped in the years ahead."

The World Bank came to a remarkably similar conclusion. In their *East Asia and Pacific Update* released in April 2009, World Bank analysts concluded "the forceful stimulus policies will help dampen the downturn."[131] Overall, the World Bank observed:

> China has fared better than many other countries because it does not rely on external financing, its banks have been largely unscathed by the international financial turmoil and it has the fiscal and macroeconomic space to implement forceful stimulus measures.[132]

The World Bank's forecast for Beijing was equally rosy—"China's economy should continue to grow significantly in a very challenging external environment."[133] Why? In addition to the stimulus package, the World Bank highlighted Beijing's efforts to "rebalance growth toward consumption and services, away from investment, exports, and export-oriented manufacturing."[134]

On April 11, 2009 the *Wall Street Journal* ran a front page article that seemed as equally as effusive. The first line in the *Journal* story read, "China's massive $586 billion government stimulus program appears to be kicking in . . . the world's third-largest economy may be turning the corner."[135] Among the signs the stimulus package may be working: China's demand for raw materials were up, crude oil-imports were at a one year high, and car sales had reached a monthly record in March 2009. The *Journal*—no obvious fan of socialism in any guise—went on to declare,

> Overall, it appears that the state's push has helped keep China from slipping into a downward spiral . . . The impressive size of China's stimulus announced in November, gets some credit for

that... But the vestiges of China's command economy have also proved useful.[136]

That's right; the *Wall Street Journal* was offering praise for China's authoritarian intervention in the marketplace. More specifically, the *Journal* cited Beijing's ability to direct bank lending and investment spending in a manner that expedited delivery of the stimulus spending.

While international acclaim for Beijing's economic rescue efforts likely earned accolades for Hu's advisors, there is also a high probability Chinese officials were cognizant of the contending evaluations of their stimulus efforts—and likely had ordered similar analysis be conducted at home. The results of this feedback cycle became evident in early March 2009, when National Development and Reform Commission Director Zhang Ping held a press conference to outline the revised stimulus package. While overall spending rates remained at $586 billion—there were tweaks in the "investment portfolio."

Beijing's revised spending priorities appeared to favor those who argued China needed to do more to stimulate domestic consumption —and address long-standing shortfalls in the country's social safety net. In fact, Zhang seemed to be alluding to such a decision when he told the attending reporters, the government's focus would be to reshape the country's economic growth pattern.[137]

While the changes to Beijing's stimulus package are not of a magnitude to draw international attention, they are further indication of the CCP's sensitivity to domestic opinion—and factions there within.

Table 3.5   Spending Priorities in Beijing's Stimulus Plan[138]

Category	Old % of Investment	New % of Investment
Social Welfare	1%	4%
Sustainable Environment	9%	5%
Technology Advances	4%	9%
Earthquake Reconstruction	25%	25%
Civilian Projects	7%	10%
Rural Civilian Projects	9%	9%
Infrastructure	45%	38%

As Cheng Li, a senior fellow at the Brookings Institution, observed in March 2009, the current international financial crisis has revealed rifts within a CCP. In an article published in *Foreign Policy*, Li notes China's top decision-making bodies—the Politburo and its Standing Committee—are now run by "two informal coalitions that compete against each other for power, influence, and control over policy."[139] According to Li, these coalitions can be characterized as the "populists" and the "elitists."

The populists—currently led by Hu and Wen—are largely products of the Chinese Communist Youth League, and thus are known as *tuanpai*. Most of these individuals served as local and provincial leaders, often in the poorest inland areas. The *tuanpai* have a well-earned reputation for organizational and propaganda skills, but have little experience in international finance. As Li puts it, these former skills were not highly prized under Jiang Zemin, but "are considered critical now as the risks of social unrest and political tensions rise."[140] The elitists—presently championed by Wu Bangguo, chairman of the national legislature, and Jia Qinglin, head of a national political advisory body—are commonly referred to as "princelings." The princelings are primarily children of former high-ranking officials, and largely grew up in wealthier coastal regions while pursuing careers in foreign affairs, finance, technology, and trade.[141]

The key point here? Of the six fifth generation leaders serving on the politburo, three are populists and three are elitists. The differences in their factions may help to explain the modifications to the stimulus plan. For as Li so ably argues:

> To a great extent, the [difference between populists and the elitists] reflects the country's competing socioeconomic forces: Princelings aim to advance the interests of entrepreneurs and the emerging middle class, while the [populists] often call for building a harmonious society, with more attention to vulnerable social groups such as farmers, migrant workers, and the urban poor.[142]

Given the revisions evident in Beijing's stimulus package, it would appear the populists won this round—but not by much. I caution, however, about making too much of this evident difference in leadership priorities. While the two groups may be playing to differing constituencies, their overall objective is the same—preservation of the existing political system. There may be disagreements over how much money to place in one stimulus program or another, but there is clearly no difference over the need for such a spending package. All of which has caused economists to argue Beijing's stimulus plan is money well spent. As one Chinese economist put it, "you can say it is wasteful now, but it is not wasteful over the long term."[143]

In any case, as best Western sources can tell this official effort to nip the problem in the bud appeared to work. In August 2009, the *Wall Street Journal* reported fears of migrant unrest in China had faded.[144] While Beijing's official media continue to acknowledge the employment situation remained tough—with an estimated 5 million migrants still searching for jobs—the economic downturn had not spurred massive demonstrations. Why? As one Deutsche Bank analyst argued, Beijing's concerns about a repeat of 1989 were a primary driver behind the country's large stimulus package. The analyst goes on to note, however, that now the CCP realizes "the risk of social unrest due to unemployment was grossly overestimated," the government is unlikely to push for a similar measure in 2010. As the analyst put it, "Why should the government spend another few trillion renminbi to deal with a much lower political risk?"[145]

CHINA'S WAY AHEAD–AT HOME

Predicting the Chinese Communist party's demise is a morbid parlor game played with considerable regularity. Participants in this academic blood sport come from both sides of the political aisle. Conservatives like to argue Beijing's mishandling of China's financial system will ultimately cause the "house of cards" to topple,[146] while liberals contend the end will be linked to a demand for greater individual and political freedoms.[147] To date, neither side has been right. It would appear that Beijing's politics of the pragmatic have also won the day at home. In fact, I would argue that the maturity we now witness in Beijing's foreign policy came after significant practice on the domestic front. China's leaders realized their staying power hinged on an ability to improve the economic lot of their constituents—and they have delivered . . . at least in some cases.

There are obvious limits to this argument. As Hu observed in his October 2007 report to the Seventeenth National Congress of the CCP, much work remains to be accomplished. As Hu put it, "China's development shows a series of new features . . . the economic strength has increased markedly, but the overall productivity remains low, the capacity for independent innovation is weak, and the long standing

structural problems and extensive mode of growth are yet to be fundamentally addressed."[148] Quite simply, China has done much to bootstrap herself out of poverty, but at a cost to the environment, social
stability, and potentially the nation's political system.

What does one do in such a situation? For Hu, the answer is to be
found in an eight-fold plan:

1. Enhance China's capacity for independent innovation.
2. Accelerate transformation of the mode of economic development.
3. Balance urban and rural.
4. Improve energy, resources, ecological and environmental
   conservation.
5. Promote balanced development among regions in China.
6. Improve the basic economic system and modern market system.
7. Deepen fiscal, taxation and financial restructuring and improve
   macroeconomic regulation.
8. Expand opening up in scope and depth and improve our open
   economy.[149]

This is not an agenda for the lazy or weak of heart. But we should
also recognize this is not a list developed for an American audience
whose focus tends to extend no further than the next congressional
or presidential election. Hu is laying out an agenda he believes will
drive China's domestic development over the next 10 years—and he
expects his successors to follow in his footprints, just as he did with
Deng Xiaoping and Jiang Zemin.

I, for one, would argue Hu has set off in the right direction. As a
collection of longtime China watchers observed in 2000, Beijing
must resolve economic, ethnic, political, and urban/rural concerns
if the Communist Party is to remain comfortably atop China's
domestic hierarchy. Nor they cautioned, should we make too much
of arguments concerning China's long term stability.[150] In a
thoughtful moment, one of the China-watchers added this comment,
"any prediction of stability in China must of necessity be a relative
one and a contingent one." The relative and contingent problems
to be tackled 10 years ago: economic reform, China's financial system, greater participation in decision making, room for open discourse, and a transparent means of dealing with corruption and
malfeasance.[151]

China's leaders have succeeded in managing and/or muddling-through these challenges over the last 10 years. According to the World Bank China appears poised to emerge from the current global economic crisis with her banking system intact and GDP activity in the positive column. China's non-performing loan problem remains an issue—but one that Beijing has taken by the horns . . . and with a greater degree of success than Washington can currently claim of efforts to heal the West's ailing financial system. Opportunities for political participation in China are growing—but as Susan Shirk wrote in 2007, China's leaders remain insecure and concerned about their political survival.[152] Democracy—at least the American variant thereof—is unlikely to appear in China anytime soon. Finally, it is safe to say Beijing is seriously engaged in a campaign to reduce official corruption and malfeasance. In short, Hu's bid for a "harmonious society" appears to be working for the moment—and I see no reason to believe it is in serious danger over the coming 10 years.

Perhaps use of the term "muddling-through" above was a bit too glib. Yes, China's leadership has struggled with transitions over the last 10 years, but not in a manner that has appeared potentially regime-ending. Apart from Gordon Chang's incessant "coming collapse" rhetoric, one learns of few serious scholars who are willing to contend—as Jack Goldstone did in 1995—that "China shows every sign of a country approaching a crisis . . . all . . . as the state rapidly loses its capacity to rule effectively."[153] How did Beijing escape this fate? By adapting and evolving. China's leadership opted to retain an authoritarian political system, but have maintained and expanded opportunities for popular participation in its operation.[154] China's leaders have struggled with economic and environmental issues, but managed, nonetheless, to accumulate $1.9 trillion in foreign exchange reserves. In short, China's institutional and policy adaptations have helped shore up Beijing's political authority and create an environment conducive to rapid growth and potentially abetted the emergence of a new political ideology.

It is this adaptability—reflected in a willingness to experiment and learn—that has made the CCP resilient and a potent regional leader in the decade to come. The political risks the Chinese political leadership have been willing to assume during the implementation of Deng Xiaoping's reform and opening are daunting when considered with hindsight at hand. The results, however, have been downright amazing. China's neighbors have been watching, and more than a few are now jealous. How they choose to repeat the lessons remains to be seen. Will Burma or North Korea be willing to take as many chances with equally high risk to their regime or the nation's population? Only time will tell. But for the moment, I am comfortable concluding that China's domestic path has been set—and Beijing will brook little interference that fundamentally threatens this attempt to realize the moderately prosperous society.

CHAPTER 4

Where Next for the People's Liberation Army?

Economic globalization and world multi-polarization are gaining momentum ... The rise and decline of international strategic forces is quickening ... new emerging powers are arising. Therefore, a profound readjustment is brewing in the international system.

—China's National Defense in 2008[1]

While one can wonder at the degree of political risk-acceptance the Chinese Communist Party (CCP) has exhibited over the last 30 years, there is no reason to believe Beijing is anything but a rational actor. As we have seen, China's international outreach efforts have been focused on abetting the achievement of long-term goals, and Beijing's domestic policies bespeak a ruling elite who understands their survival is contingent upon meeting constituency demands. Given this demonstrated pragmatism, one should not be terribly surprised to discover China is engaged in an ongoing effort to modernize the People's Liberation Army (PLA)—much to Washington's oft-verbalized dismay.

I suspect that absent the events of September 11, 2001, Washington and Beijing would now be engaged a new Cold War. I come to this conclusion for a number of reasons, but two stand out. First, at the close of Bill Clinton's presidency the U.S. Defense Department was a monstrously large bureaucracy in search of a mission. The Soviet Union's demise and an academic argument over "the end of history,"[2] had left the Pentagon searching for a *raison d'être*.[3] Furthermore, despite continuing military commitments in the Balkans and Middle East, Washington was engaged in an earnest discussion about realizing a "peace dividend" by slashing the Department of Defense budget and further scaling back the Air Force, Army, Navy and Marines. This vision might well have come to fruition had there not been this place called China. Beijing's militaristic response to the 1996 Taiwan presidential campaign, and China's subsequent decision to refocus the PLA on martial rather than commercial obligations,[4] was a tangible justification for continued expansive U.S. defense spending.

As a senior intelligence analyst serving with the U.S. Pacific Command at the time, I can personally attest to the "sudden" level of interest China began to draw in Navy circles. Historically, the Defense Department's analysis of China had largely been relegated to a few specialists and a collection of hobbyists. Parked in dusty corners, these individuals were normally left to pursue their own eclectic interests—only to be gainfully employed during a crisis or other unexplained development. In fact, at most U.S. official agencies charged with monitoring events in Northeast Asia the North Korea shops were inevitably equal in size—or larger—than the China desk. In 2000 that changed—in a relatively abrupt manner. Suddenly, China mattered and there were a lot more questions than answers.

American politics is the second reason I believe Washington was poised for a Cold War with China in 2000. As one of my fellow scholars argued at the time, "Informed U.S. analysts both within and outside the military rarely conclude that China will pose a significant danger to U.S. security interests anytime soon. The most ardent U.S. critics of China tend to be politicians, not military planners."[5] Allow me to cite two examples of what I mean. In 2000, Congress established the U.S.-China Economic and Security Review Commission—a bipartisan body charged with monitoring, investigating, and submitting to Congress an annual report on the national security implications of the bilateral trade and economic relationship between the United States and the People's Republic of China. This commission is specifically tasked with studying the following eight areas: proliferation practices, economic transfers, energy, U.S. capital markets, regional economic and security impacts, U.S.-China bilateral programs, World Trade Organization compliance, and the implications of restrictions on speech and access to information in the People's Republic of China.

During the same year, Congress tasked the Defense Department with providing an "Annual Report on Military Power of the People's Republic of China." This requirement was explicitly outlined in Section 1202 of the National Defense Authorization Act for Fiscal Year 2000. The legislation stipulates the Secretary of Defense will submit a report "on the current and future military strategy of the People's Republic of China. The report shall address the current and probable future course of military-technological development on the People's Liberation Army and the tenets and probable development of Chinese grand strategy, security strategy, and military strategy, and of the military organizations and operational concepts, through the next 20 years."[6]

It is safe to contend some of this political interest in China is directly attributable to both fear of the "red menace" ("ChiComs," as some of my conservative counterparts like to say) and liberal concerns about human rights abuses. As a result, by 2000 members from both sides of the aisle were expressing dismay that a more confident, but still authoritarian China—a state still not worthy of being labeled a "responsible international actor"—could present a future threat to the United States.[7] In short, members of both the U.S. military and Congress were increasingly convinced China was/is the new Soviet Union. As such, Washington—and all other non-communist states in Asia and across the planet—needed to be on alert . . . needed to be watching for the emergence of a new military threat to democracy and capitalism.

I also hasten to note, however, this was not a unanimous opinion. In 2005, former Secretary of State Henry Kissinger authored an op-ed for the *Washington Post* in which he argued: "Various officials, members of Congress and the media are attacking China's policies, from the exchange rate to military buildup, much of it in a tone implying China is on some sort of probation. To many, China's rise has become the most significant challenge to U.S. security."[8] Kissinger went on to observe:

It is unwise to substitute China for the Soviet Union in our thinking and to apply to it the policy of military containment of the Cold War. The Soviet Union was heir to an imperialist tradition, which, between Peter the Great and the end of World War II, projected Russia from the region around Moscow to the center of Europe. The Chinese state in its present dimensions has existed substantially for 2,000 years. The Russian empire was governed by force; the Chinese empire by cultural conformity with substantial force in the background. At the end of World War II, Russia found itself face to face with weak countries along all its borders and unwisely relied on a policy of occupation and intimidation beyond the long-term capacity of the Russian state.[9]

To which I can only add, hear, hear. China is not the Soviet Union, and her military modernization efforts need to be considered with that fact in the forefront of one's mind. Please note I am not suggesting we ignore the PLA's ongoing transformation. China could inflict tremendous damage on Taiwan or any other perceived threat. I am, however, willing to argue China's military modernization campaign is the work of a "responsible international actor"—one who realizes that in a Westphalian world each state must look out for itself, or become a victim. Given China's modern history, one can be assured Beijing is seeking the former and not the latter.

WHAT A LONG STRANGE TRIP IT'S BEEN . . .

In 1999, a Chinese military officer described the People's Liberation Army as a boxer suffering, "short arms and slow feet." Although Beijing maintained a force of over 2.8 million uniformed personnel, the PLA was largely restricted to conducting onshore operations within marching distance of China's territorial borders. China lacked air and sea lift, she had few over-the-horizon intelligence gathering capabilities, and essentially planned for conducting single-service military operations.[10] As researchers at Rand put it, "China today is indisputably not a 'peer competitor' of the United States." Nonetheless, Rand warned, China was also "not just another regional power."[11]

According to the Rand analysts, in 1999 China exhibited four characteristics that separated the PLA from other regional powers. First, China had nuclear weapons that could reach targets within the United States. Second, the Chinese military had fielded a greater number and variety of theater-range ballistic missiles than any other force then confronting the U.S. military. Third, the PLA's absolute size was daunting in its own right. And, finally, China's geographic expanse largely precluded the paralyzing synergistic attacks the U.S. armed forces had used so effectively in Operation DESERT STORM.[12]

Suffice it to say, 10 years down the road things have changed. While China is still not a "peer competitor" for the United States' military, the PLA's regional capabilities are anything but "short" or "slow." Equipped with satellite-based surveillance assets, top-of the-line Russian fighter aircraft, a rapidly modernizing navy, and more than 1,300 short- and medium-range ballistic missiles, the PLA can capably locate, track, and engage any military force operating within 500 miles of the Chinese coastline. Furthermore, Chinese commanders are learning to field and fight a military that realizes the effects and efficiencies inherent in joint warfare. Finally, Beijing's focus on downsizing the PLA, while simultaneously addressing logistics shortfalls, suggests the Chinese military is preparing to show up ready for battle long before sufficient U.S. forces can be moved into the theater.

PREPARING FOR A NEW WORLD ORDER

Statements within the 2008 national defense white paper indicate China believes the international system is about to undergo a tectonic shift. Beijing's decision to highlight "globalization," "multi-polarization," and "emerging developing powers" is anything but accidental. China perceives American power as being on the decline—and Beijing's star on the rise. This evolving world order opens doors for the Chinese, but also presents new security challenges and risks. Nonetheless, Beijing continues to declare, "China will never seek hegemony or engage in military expansion now or in the future, no matter how developed it becomes." (*China's National Defense in 2008*, pp. 3–8.)

In the pages that follow we will examine how the PLA made this remarkable transformation, and what it means for the United States and other actors within Asia. To accomplish this task, we will examine the strategic guidance Beijing has issued for PLA commanders and how those orders have been realized over the last 10 years. We will also discuss how China is paying for this modernization.

NATIONAL SECURITY AND MILITARY MODERNIZATION

China's national defense policy for the new stage in the new century basically includes: Upholding national security and unity, and ensuring the interests of national development; achieving the all-round, coordinated and sustainable development of China's national defense and armed forces; enhancing the performance of the armed forces with informationization as the major measuring criterion; implementing the military strategy of active defense; pursuing a self-defensive nuclear strategy; and fostering a security environment conducive to China's peaceful development.

—China's National Defense in 2008[13]

Beijing's decision to not publish a national security strategy—or at least a document similar to that released in Washington—does not mean the Chinese leadership have abrogated a responsibility to delineate broad security directives for the People's Liberation Army. In fact, the Chinese Communist Party since 1949 has promulgated at least five sets of "military strategic guidelines," the highest level of national guidance and direction available to the PLA. According to the PLA's National Defense University, "the military strategic guidelines are the fundamental military policies of the Party and the nation. They are the overall principles for planning and guiding the development and utilization of the armed forces."[14]

There is a discernable historical evolution within these "military strategic guidelines." Under Mao Zedong, the PLA was directed to prepare for "People's War"—protracted, large-scale land warfare that envisioned invading Russian or even U.S. forces being drawn deep into Chinese territory, enveloped, and slowly destroyed through attrition. The demise of the Soviet Union and subsequent demonstration of U.S. military capabilities in DESERT STORM, convinced Chinese leaders the time had come to dramatically rethink Mao's guidance. As such, Deng Xiaoping and his successors have advocated development of "military strategic guidelines" focused on fighting small-scale, regional conflicts along China's periphery.

Given the sweeping impact of these leadership directives on the PLA, the issuance of a new set of "military strategic guidelines" are a rare and significant event. Jiang Zemin promulgated his "military strategic guidelines" in January 1993. Known as the "Military Strategic Guidelines for the New Period" these directives constitute the national military strategy the PLA sought to implement for almost 15 years.

"MILITARY STRATEGIC GUIDELINES"

New "military strategic guidelines" are not likely to initially appear in a single speech or document. Rather they are compiled from a collection of speeches or publications which the PLA consider "strategic guiding thoughts" or "strategic guiding ideology" that serve as the basis for priorities, programming, planning, adjustments, acquisition, and resource allocation. More specifically, "military strategic guidelines" for any particular period provide official judgments covering the following five areas:

- Assessment of the international environment and potential impact of same on China's security.
- China's overall national security objectives and domestic objectives, and the relationship of military objectives to these.
- The most likely type of conflict for which the PLA must prepare.
- Ideological and political basis for the guidelines.
- Broad guidance to the PLA on how it will prepare, reform, or adjust to meet the challenges facing China.

Western scholars contend Jiang's decision to issue a new set of "military strategic guidelines" in 1993 was driven by three key assessments:

1. The major change to the international order following the Soviet Union's demise and collapse of other communist regimes in Eastern Europe.
2. Evolving domestic concerns—specifically:
   - China's continued effort to "reform and open up."
   - A priority on economic development.

- Beijing's requirement for a stable domestic, international and peripheral environment to succeed.
- The People's Liberation Army's requirement to modernize within the context of other national objectives.

3. The changing nature of warfare and the self-recognized PLA inadequacies to successfully operate within this new environment.[15]

The PLA's strategic-level missions and objectives under the "Military Strategic Guidelines for the New Period" were five-fold:

- Defending national territory and sovereignty.
- Securing the nation's maritime rights and interests.
- Maintaining China's unity.
- Ensuring internal stability.
- Maintaining a secure and stable external environment, particularly on China's periphery.[16]

While all of this direction appears relatively generic to any national-level security directive, it is the type of war the PLA must be prepared to fight which truly set Jiang's 1993 proclamation apart from the previous four sets of military strategic guidance. In Jiang's words:

Since the founding of our country, [the PLA] has always implemented the military strategic guidelines of the active defense. Under the new historical conditions, exactly what kind of military strategic guidelines should we be carrying out? We believe that we should continue to carry out the military strategic guidelines of the active defense ... At the same time, along with the development and changes to the situation, we should bestow the military strategic guidelines of the active defense with the new content at this appropriate moment.[17]

Under this guidance, the PLA since 1993 has been instructed to work towards being ready to fight and win "local wars under modern high-tech conditions." More specifically, the PLA is charged with transitioning its modernization efforts from late industrial age warfare to a long-term program of developing "information age" combat capabilities. The Chinese military was ordered to shift from a focus on heavy armor and land-battles to the electronic ether and spaced-based warfare.

GULF WAR "LESSONS LEARNED"

The PLA has been a keen observer of U.S. military operations, using lessons learned to supplement and update Chinese strategic thought and planning. This has been particularly true with U.S. operations in the Persian Gulf region—specifically DESERT STORM and OPERATION IRAQI FREEDOM.

Key PLA lessons learned from these operations include:

- The centrality of information on the battlefield, and the impact of attacking key nodes rather than across a broad front of activity.
- The importance of offensive action, preemptive strikes, surprise, and deception.
- The value of high-tech weaponry. More specifically, that weapon systems needed to integrate information technology, increased firepower effects and range, higher accuracy, and greater mobility and survivability.
- The importance of "real-time" Command, Control, Communications, Computers, Intelligence, Surveillance and Reconnaissance (C4ISR), long-range precision strike, and advanced electronic warfare capabilities.
- The combat-multiplying effect of joint operations.
- The need for timely, comprehensive logistics support.

The descriptor "local wars under modern high-tech conditions" has changed slightly over the intervening years, becoming "local wars under modern informationalized conditions" in 2002. This semantic change aside, the bottom line for the PLA since 1993 has remained unchanged—the military is to focus modernization efforts on developing the capabilities necessary to fight 21st Century conventional warfare in a manner the United States first demonstrated during Operation DESERT STORM in 1991.[18]

The People's Liberation Army has been tasked with developing the joint warfighting capabilities—including precision strike and synergistic operations—codified for the U.S. Department of Defense in the

Goldwater-Nichols reforms of the 1980s. This tasking, however, also includes a "leapfrog" vision of modernization which requires the PLA to recognize the trials and errors of the U.S. campaign for joint operations. More specifically, the Chinese call for "informatization" is a press to realize the combat efficiencies and effectiveness resident in the ever-evolving U.S. C4ISR common operating picture.

WHAT IS "INFORMATIZED WARFARE"?

According to the People's Liberation Army Academy of Military Science, battlefield information technology is a comprehensive integration of modern computer, communication and command capabilities. Scholars at the Academy also contend information technology is the "sum total" of the ability to acquire, and employ data.

Chinese military scholars hold informationized warfare is reflected in:

- Weapon systems developments—specifically, control, reaction speed, precision and destructive might.
- Battlefield common operating pictures—integration of command and control (C2) and intelligence.
- Command and control—widespread fielding and employment of computers.

"Informatization" at the operational level appears focused on providing an integrated platform for joint war zone C4ISR connectivity, and for peacetime (C2) within the PLA's Military Regions. According to official Chinese media, the 11th Five-Year Program tasks the PLA Informatization Work Office to move the PLA toward a "perfect universal transmission . . . and processing platform."[19]

Recent programs to establish integrated joint communications and data transfer capabilities attest to the priority placed on this effort, and China's information technology sector is certainly capable of providing an effective architecture commensurate with the high level of resource commitment. As one senior PLA General notes, success in "informatized warfare" hinges primarily on "national information strength"—both in terms of global perception management efforts and domestic capabilities in key information technologies.[20]

One of the primary tasks in "informatized warfare" is to transform traditional modes of mobilization to fit the conditions of modern warfare—the concept of "People's War" in a new era. For this reason, the modernization and reorganization of militia and reserve forces is to great extent focused on bringing in high-technology qualified reservists and militia members—both to form new high-tech units (such as information and electronic warfare detachments), and to leaven existing or transforming units with more capable engineers and computer technicians.[21] The urban militia in particular is clearly evolving to provide the war fighting force with high-tech support, providing access to an increasingly tech-savvy workforce.[22]

NON-CONTACT WARFARE

According to Chinese military thinkers, "non-contact warfare" provides for the use of kinetic options—missile strikes and employment of precision-guided munitions—without the more traditional engagement of opposing ground forces. Chinese military strategists contend the "state of the art" for warfare in the twenty-first century is to be found in the integration of air and space technologies. More specifically, Chinese authors argue the United States has developed a "seamless" integration of air and space combat operations that has moved theories on space warfare from discussion of "support" to an emphasis on offensive and defensive operations. According to the Chinese, this is particularly evident in the theory of "non-contact warfare," which the PLA holds is the art of employing "all kinds of long range precision strike forces, with space combat systems as the principal agent, to attack the important targets of the opposing states in order to carry out a highly concentrated and precise sudden assault."

The Chinese rubric for this over-arching transformation of the military is the "Revolution in Military Affairs," or RMA. According to Chinese military thinkers, RMA is:

...the close integration of the present technologies...with
advanced thinking of operations and military structure and
organization so as to make the most of the potential of present
technologies and lead to [a] revolutionary leap in the military
capability.[23]

THE REVOLUTION IN MILITARY AFFAIRS AND "INFORMATIZING"

Western analysts frequently note difficulty in explaining the
relationship between the PLA's "revolution in military affairs"
and repeated Chinese references to defense "informatization"
campaigns. In an effort to resolve these difficulties the U.S.
Director of National Intelligence's Open Source Center (OSC)
in May 2008 published a short study titled, "PRC Military
Terminology: 'RMA with Chinese Characteristics.'"

According to the OSC authors, "PRC media use the phrase
'Revolution in Military Affairs (RMA) with Chinese characteristics' to describe the process by which China's military and
national defense industry is attempting to transform itself into a
military capable of winning a limited, local high-tech war. The
Chinese concept is built on the Western idea of RMA—the adoption of advanced military concepts and the incorporation of
information technology ('informatization')—but also seeks to
raise the general modernization level of China's military to a level
comparable with those enjoyed by Western militaries even before
they adopted the RMA concept."

The OSC analysts go on to note, "As in the West, China aims
to improve its ability to win a high-tech war by transforming its
military through the incorporation of information technology
and overhauling its military's organization and doctrine." And,
that Chinese authors contend "the 'essence and core of the revolution in military affairs with Chinese characteristics is to bring
about the informatization of national defense and army building'" According to the Chinese writers, "informatization"
involves "many different elements and aspects, the more crucial
of which are the development of weapons and armaments, opti-
mization of the military's structure and organization, and

innovations in military theories." They go on to argue, all these elements have to "come together to constitute an organic entity."

As such, for the Chinese "informatization" appears a key element of the revolution in military affairs—modernization of the PLA in a manner intended to realize the synergistic benefits of simultaneous command, control, communications, and intelligence, surveillance and reconnaissance.

This "leap in military capabilities" is to transform PLA operations by accomplishing four objectives:

1. Greatly strengthening information superiority—symbolized by the domination of battlefield awareness on both sides of the conflict;

2. Integrate, by "system of systems" application, force employment so as to make the most effective use of all weapons available to the commander;

3. Combine the employment of precision-guided and long-range munitions with state-of-the art intelligence to increase effectiveness; and,

4. Develop and field digital simulation systems and computer-assisted decision-making systems which "greatly" enhance the efficiency of operational commanders.[24]

Given the breadth and depth of changes to military operations envisioned in RMA, it is not surprising to find Chinese strategists less than optimistic about how long it will take to implement the vision outlined in the 1993 "Military Strategic Guidelines." As one PLA author summed the situation confronting his contemporaries, "the realization of ... RMA will be a long process. American experts think it takes at least decades."[25]

In fact, Chinese military thinkers are not the only ones who understand the road to realizing the revolution in military affairs is a long and arduous path. In the 2006 White Paper on National Defense, Beijing outlines a three-step process to achieving the end state desired in Jiang's 1993 "Military Strategic Guidelines for the New Period." According to the 2006 White Paper:

China pursues a three-step development strategy in modernizing its national defense and armed forces, in accordance with the state's over-all plan to realize modernization. The first step is to lay a solid foundation by 2010, the second is to make major progress around 2020, and the third is to basically reach the strategic goal of building informationalized armed forces and being capable of winning informationalized wars by the mid-21st Century.[26]

Despite the daunting nature of this task, the PLA is clearly intent on realizing the stated objective. Evidence of this commitment is resident at all levels of the military decision-making/execution cycle—what the Chinese refer to as "peacetime army building." This includes development of operational concepts, force structure decisions, and equipping and training the force.

REITERATING THE TIME LINE FOR MILITARY MODERNIZATION

China's National Defense in 2008 once again provides the 50 year time-line for military modernization. The verbiage has been cleaned up and toned down—we no longer read about being able to win informationalized wars by the mid-twenty-first Century—but the goals remain the same:

... lay a solid foundation by 2010, basically accomplish mechanization and make progress in informationization by 2020, and by and large reach the goal of modernization of national defense and armed forces by the mid-twenty-first century. (*China's National Defense in 2008*, p. 9.)

While Jiang's dictates helped transform the PLA, there is growing evidence Hu Jintao has an even grander vision for China's military forces. On December 24, 2004, Hu announced a new set of guidelines for the PLA. These "Historic Missions" have broadened the Chinese definition of security and identified four tasks for the PLA:

1. To reinforce the armed forces' loyalty to the Chinese Communist Party.[27]

2. To help ensure China's sovereignty, territorial integrity, and domestic security in order to continue national development.

3. To help safeguard China's expanding national interests.

4. To help ensure world peace.[28]

Hu's "Historic Missions" are significant as they: (1) represent an adjustment to China's military strategic guidelines; (2) expand China's definition of national security to include new geographic regions and function areas—specifically, beyond territorial integrity to maritime, space and the electromagnetic spectrum—and (3) are a statement of aspirations rather than capabilities.[29]

PURSING AN "ACTIVE DEFENSE"

While Western and Chinese defense scholars have dedicated considerable effort to understanding the PLA's focus on Jiang's guidelines and Hu's latest revisions of these marching orders, Beijing has not abandoned its insistence the armed forces are postured for an "active defense" of the nation. This seemingly "benign" tenant of Chinese military doctrine can be traced to Mao Zedong's thoughts on warfare—and is hardly as "passive" as the title might suggest. In his writings, Mao emphasized mobility, surprise, dispersion, flexibility, concentration, the alert shifting of forces, and retaining the initiative.

As such, active defense calls for a quick reaction before enemies are ready to strike. The goal here is two-fold. First is to minimize damage to China' own infrastructure, by conducting the war at enemy's backyard. Second is to create a psychological or political shock to the enemy, by upsetting an adversary's strategy and expectations, and acquiesce in a new status quo that is much more favorable to China.

Beijing reiterates China's adherence to this doctrine in the 2008 national defense white paper. In the document, Beijing declares, "China implements a military strategy of active defense. Strategically, it adheres to the principle of featuring defensive operations, self-defense and striking and getting the better of the enemy only after the enemy has started an attack." (*China's National Defense in 2008*, p. 10.)

A review of Chinese military publications and academic tracts reveals Hu's new guidance inexorably links the PLA with China's economic development efforts.[30] This linkage should not come as a surprise. As the first task of the "Historic Missions" implies, the PLA remains the Party's army—and as such shall be used to ensure the CCP remains atop China's political hierarchy. By allowing economic development to supplant socialist ideology over the last 25 years, China's leaders tacitly accepted the premise their continued survival hinges on meeting the population's economic expectations. The PLA's second priority is to "raise the flag of peace, *development*, and cooperation."

For the military, Beijing's focus on economic progress translates into the following guidance: "the army must use its power to make sure the party's ruling status is consolidated, provide solid strategic support for defending national interests, and bring into full play the army's role in maintaining world peace and promoting common development."[31] All of which can be boiled down to a simple declaration—the PLA will defend against and defeat challenges to China's economic development—on mainland China, and off.

As such, Chinese military thinkers now claim:

> The armed forces need to cope with traditional security threats, and also need to cope with nontraditional security threats; need to safeguard the state's survival interests, and also need to safeguard the state's development interests; need to safeguard the homeland security, and also need to safeguard the overseas interests security; need to safeguard the overall state interests of reform, development, and stability, and also need to safeguard world peace and promote common development.[32]

This is truly a case of remarkable "mission creep." Over the last 30 years the PLA's strategic function has evolved from defensive, terrestrial, mechanized wars of attrition to potentially offensive, offshore campaigns employing kinetic and non-kinetic weapon systems.

We note this guidance is incorporated in Beijing's 2008 defense white paper. According to authors of *China's National Defense in 2008*, the PLA is now charged with "enhancing the capabilities of the armed forces in countering various security threats and accomplishing diversified military tasks."[33] In addition to requiring the military to "win local wars in conditions of informatization," these "diversified tasks" include:

- Counter-terrorism
- Stability maintenance
- Emergency rescue
- International peacekeeping[34]

As the 2008 white paper bluntly states, this new tasking "takes military operations other than war as an important form of applying national military forces."[35] This is not a throw away line. The 2008 white paper goes on to insist training for military operations other than war is an "important" element for the PLA's "comprehensive development."[36] In short, the PLA has been specifically directed to pursue all aspects of Hu's "Historic Missions," and we expect training, manning, and equipping programs will be tailored to accomplish this strategic objective.

ANTI-PIRACY PATROL FIRST TEST OF HU'S "HISTORIC MISSIONS"

China's decision to dispatch three People's Liberation Army Navy ships to the Gulf of Aden in December 2008 is a clear indication of a commitment to Hu's new military strategic guidelines. On December 28, 2008, Beijing responded to the ongoing piracy threats off the Somali coast by dispatching two destroyers and a replenishment ship. As over 1,200 Chinese flagged commercial ships pass through the Gulf annually, this deployment sought to support China's economic development—specifically, her ability to generate earnings through imports and exports.

The deployment was not without cause. As of December 2008 over 40 Chinese vessels had been attacked. Recognizing the ongoing danger posed by pirates to China's trade with Europe through the Suez Canal, and to her oil imports from Sudan, Yemen, and possibly Oman, Beijing decided to act. In doing so, China joined the United States, United Kingdom, Russia, India, Malaysia and other countries seeking to end the piracy threat.

This truly was a "Historic Mission," as China has not engaged in this type of activity in over six centuries. Furthermore, Beijing is clearly cognizant of the "responsible actor" message the deployment is sending. China only dispatched the ships after the United Nations Security Council passed four resolutions authorizing action, and an invitation from the Somali Prime Minister to join other nations in policing the waters. (Yan Hao and Bai Ruixue, December 26, 2008, "Chinese Fleet to Escort Ships off Somalia," Xinhua, Beijing.)

EVOLVING MILITARY KINETIC CAPABILITIES

Taking informationization as the goal of modernization of its national defense and armed forces and in light of its national and military conditions, China actively pushes forward with the revolution in military affairs with Chinese characteristics.

—China's National Defense in 2008[37]

On the kinetic front, the People's Liberation Army has been tasked with developing the warfighting capabilities—including precision strike and synergistic joint operations. The breadth of this commitment becomes apparent when placed in a historic context. As an analyst who worked in the U.S. Department of Defense Office of Net Assessments summed the process:

In just over two decades, China has transformed itself from having a navy of World War II era landing ships, patrol boats, shore-based aircraft, and submarines with limited range . . . into a high-tech force capable of at least area denial, anti-access missions and possibly also power projection.[38]

China's focus on developing a military capable of countering and eventually defeating a modern opponent is most evident in Beijing's weapons acquisition, development, and fielding efforts. The 1991 Gulf War, 1999 NATO campaign in the Balkans, and 2003 invasion of Iraq all served to reinforce the criticality of this equipment modernization effort. As the 2009 Department of Defense annual report to Congress on Chinese military power notes, this focus on weapon systems is a central element of Beijing's "laying the foundation for a force able to accomplish broader regional and global objectives."[39]

Given the breadth of China's military modernization campaign, there are four broad categories in which weapons systems can be

placed. While some platforms could be placed within all four categories — particularly C4ISR systems—this taxonomy is useful as a
means of highlighting areas Chinese military and political decision
makers believe they need to address. These four categories are:

- Anti-Access and Integrated Air Defense
- Precision Strike and Over the Horizon Targeting (OTHT)
- Nuclear Deterrence and Anti-Ballistic Missile Defense
- C4ISR and Counter-C4ISR Warfare

ANTI-ACCESS AND INTEGRATED AIR DEFENSE

China's historic doctrinal approach to defending against a hypo-
thetical invader was to lure the adversary into the vast country and
fight a war of attrition. This strategy—dictated by Beijing's then-
rudimentary military equipment and skill, has been significantly
revised. China now seeks to destroy an adversary outside of its
territorial land and sea borders.[40] A key element of this strategy is
the Joint Anti-Air Raid Campaign—a plan devised as a result of
lessons learned while observing U.S. air power successes during the
1991 Gulf War and the 1999 Balkan conflict. The Joint Anti-Air Raid
Campaign centers on the fielding and operation of a modern, integrated air defense system capable of effective offensive counter-air
and defensive counter-air. As such, this campaign calls for attacking
an adversary's airbases and carriers using long-range precision strike,
and defending vulnerable targets at home through employment of
fighters, anti-aircraft systems, ship-borne surface-to-air missiles, and
airborne early warning and command assets.

PRECISION STRIKE AND OVER-THE-HORIZON TARGETING

Weapon systems capable of precision strike and over the horizon
targeting provide China the ability to attack an adversary's basing or
other critical infrastructure at long range. These targets could be fixed
in place—airbases and ports—or mobile—such as aircraft carriers. In
either case, the intent remains the same—to locate and destroy or dis-
able an adversary before they are capable of significantly disrupting
Chinese operations.

China possesses, and is developing, a number of weapons platforms —missiles and airframes—capable of long range, precision targeting. The ability to project power with precision facilitates destruction of an adversary's key centers of power. In Chinese doctrinal writings, these nodes have been identified as an adversary's economic, military, and political bases, command centers, communications and transportation hubs, and troop concentrations.[41]

China has both ground- and sea-based over-the-horizon radars to track targets far from its shores. On land, China has SKY-WAVE over-the-horizon backscatter (OTH-B) radars for surveillance of the East and South China Seas.[42] These radars are useful to detect U.S. aircraft carriers and provide early warning. On the sea, China has the Russian-built Mineral-ME/BAND STAND radar, which provides over-the-horizon targeting capabilities on its newer destroyers through the use of a data link. An advanced phased array radar from the Ukraine has also been deployed on Luyang II DDG.[43]

All of the precision strike and over-the-horizon weapons and systems are to be linked together to conduct what the PLA terms a "Joint Firepower Campaign." This campaign is intended to integrate strike aircraft and conventional ballistic and cruise missiles into a precision attack supported by a C4ISR infrastructure that defeats an adversary and accomplishes significant operational or even strategic objectives. PLA doctrine emphasizes these campaigns are designed to attack the enemy at all depths in the battlespace.

NUCLEAR DETERRENCE

Beijing contends China's small, but potent, nuclear arsenal serves three missions — strategic deterrence, prevention of nuclear coercion, and conferment of great-power status.[44] While this nuclear arsenal appears to have served these purposes in the past, China's leadership is increasingly concerned by anti-ballistic missile systems, such as the U.S. terminal high-altitude area defense, that pose the greatest challenge to the deterrence value of China's small arsenal. This concern could drive development of alternative delivery systems and may pressure the Chinese into fully exploring a "nuclear triad" similar to that found in the U.S. armed forces.

In the near- to mid-term, the proliferation of nuclear armed states could force China to reassess its nuclear strategy due to increased vulnerability from countries other than the United States. China shares borders with four known nuclear powers—India, North Korea, Pakistan and Russia. These close to-home potential threats could cause the Chinese to reconsider shorter-range nuclear delivery systems—including short- and medium-range ballistic missiles.

To ensure the efficacy of its nuclear forces, China will respond to current and future challenges by increasing the size, scope, and survivability of its nuclear forces. In terms of procurement, China will focus on sub-launched and mobile systems versus static ICBM silos. This emphasis on mobility will give the Chinese nuclear arsenal additional flexibility and survivability. Similarly, China is phasing out liquid-fueled missiles in favor of solid fuel designs and has made significant strides in increasing range and accuracy to enhance lethality.

C4ISR, SPACE, AND SPACE WARFARE

In addition to airborne early warning and command platforms mentioned previously, China is developing satellite and Unmanned Aerial Vehicle (UAV) technology to enhance the PLA's C4ISR capabilities. China is using its resources to enhance the nation's space and terrestrial information gathering infrastructure.

China is developing a credible space-based ISR capability with electro-optical, synthetic aperture radar, and signals collection platforms. China has launched a pair of Jingbing-5 SAR satellites in the last two years, and has plans for a future eight-satellite constellation composed of four radar (HJ-1A/B) and four electro-optical satellites (HJ-1C) with resolutions of 3 feet or less. The PLA also relies on foreign commercial satellite imagery as well as civilian meteorology and land mapping satellites.[45] One of the primary difficulties China faces in conducting precision, over-the-horizon strike operations is real-time Intelligence, Surveillance, and Reconnaissance (ISR) data relay and fusion. In order to address this shortfall, China will need to develop and field a space-based data relay capability.

COUNTER-C4ISR AND COUNTER-SPACE WARFARE

While seeking to enhance its own C4ISR capabilities, China is simultaneously searching for ways to deny anadversary those same options. This effort includes anti-C4ISR platforms such as anti-satellite (ASAT) missiles; direct energy weapons (DEW); jamming devices; missiles designed to destroy airborne and terrestrial ISR platforms; and the use of cyber warfare to disrupt the computer net-works that are the backbone of C4 systems.[46] China recognizes the highly integrated C4ISR systems that make the United States such a formidable opponent are also one of its greatest vulnerabilities.

Counter-Space Platforms: Recognizing it cannot currently compete with U.S. space dominance, China's response has been to develop asymmetric capabilities to deny or even destroy American space assets. Recent advances on this front include the 2007 direct ascent, kinetic kill vehicle ASAT test, as well as the production of directed energy weapons and jammers designed to blind or deafen U.S. space-based sensors.

The Chinese ASAT test of January 2007 signaled an emerging counter-space capability. The test showed China can destroy satellites in low-earth orbit with a kinetic kill. That the missile was likely fired from a road mobile launcher[47] and had to close with a target that had a velocity of 4.6 miles per second demonstrates considerable technical prowess in tracking, command, and control.[48]

China will probably continue to develop these capabilities—specifically addressing the range and scope of ASAT systems—so as to destroy satellites in medium-earth orbit and geosynchronous orbit. Months before the ASAT test, media reports surfaced concerning a Chinese laser that had "painted" a U.S. satellite, temporarily blinding the system.[49] In the future, DEW—including high-powered microwaves and lasers—could be used to disrupt or even destroy U.S. satellites. This DEW "soft kill" renders sensitive electronic components unusable, a potentially more politically acceptable approach than the physical obliteration of a kinetic kill. "Soft kill" options do not create a field of space debris dangerous to other nations' systems.

EXPLAINING CHINA'S ASAT TEST

Beijing's January 11, 2007 test of a direct-ascent hit-to-kill interceptor against an aging Chinese weather satellite caused many Western analysts to conclude the PLA was publicly demonstrating a capability to shutdown Washington's "eyes and ears" in space. Two years after the fact, this assessment seems a leap to worst case assumptions. Rather than a purposeful attempt to send U.S. decision makers a message, it now appears the Chinese ASAT test was not caused by external events or domestic politics—instead, the January 2007 "shot heard around the world" reflected the maturation of a technology program.

A number of factors suggest the ASAT test was the result of poor internal coordination, bureaucratic infighting, and failure to anticipate international reaction. According to researchers from the Union of Concerned Scientists and New America Foundation who spent eight months in China focused on this issue:

- Interviews with Chinese scientists reveal Beijing's hit-to-kill program began in the 1980s—and could have been used to counter Soviet and/or U.S. missiles and/or overhead systems.
- Chinese budgetary restrictions prevented the program from proceeding at anything other than a modest pace—while Washington and Moscow developed and tested ASAT capabilities, Beijing's efforts were essentially on a back burner.
- Accidental destruction of the Chinese Embassy in Belgrade in 1999 revived high-level interest in the hit-to-kill program.
- Program managers were finally ready to test in 2006—and felt pressured to demonstrate they had produced something that worked. A satellite was chosen over a missile intercept as the satellite was thought an easier target.
- Appropriate paperwork was submitted.
- The bureaucratic review failed to completely "endgame" the consequences of the test, probably as a result of coordination failures among relevant civilian and military agencies.
- In the test aftermath there was near unanimity the event was a net negative for Chinese security interests—the cost to Beijing's international reputation was higher than anyone in China expected.

While I have no means of corroborating these findings, related developments suggest the findings above are accurate. For instance, the Chinese Foreign Ministry made no comment on the test for 12 days and no further tests have occurred. (Gregory Kulacki and Jeffery Lewis, October 1, 2007, "Understanding China's Anti-Satellite Test," Union of Concerned Scientists and New America Foundation, Washington, DC.)

STRIVING TO REALIZE THE REVOLUTION IN MILITARY AFFAIRS

The People's Liberation Army's modernization campaign bespeaks a concerted effort to realize the revolution in military affairs.[50] What is RMA? In their seminal article, "Strategy and the Revolution in Military Affairs: From Theory to Policy," Steve Metz and James Kievet hold the current RMA is characterized by four types of change:

- Extremely precise, stand-off strikes
- Dramatically improved command, control, and intelligence
- Information warfare
- Nonlethality[51]

The tasking for the PLA, however, also includes a "leapfrog" vision of modernization, which requires the Chinese armed forces to meet and then surpass existing U.S. standards. More specifically, the Chinese call for realizing the revolution in military affairs is a press to realize, or develop a means of defeating,[52] the combat efficiencies and effectiveness resident in the ever-evolving U.S. C4ISR common operating picture.

For the PLA, the revolution in military affairs and "informatizing" is applicable at the strategic, operational, and tactical levels of war. At the strategic level, this press for "revolutionary" modernization includes establishment of U.S.-like national command structures and integration of all the state's instruments of power—diplomatic, information, military and economic. At the operational level, this Chinese military modernization appears focused on providing an integrated platform for joint war zone C4ISR connectivity, and for peacetime command and control within China's military regions. According to official Chinese media, the 11th Five-Year Plan tasks the PLA Informatization Work Office to move the PLA toward a "perfect universal transmission ... and processing platform."[53] Similar efforts are likely underway at the tactical level.

Recent programs to establish integrated joint communications and data transfer capabilities attest to the priority placed on this effort. It is important to note this prioritization is more than simply political rhetoric. As one senior PLA general notes, success in informationized warfare hinges primarily on "national information strength"—both in terms of global perception management efforts and domestic capabilities in key information technologies.[54] China is fostering rapid development of this "national information strength."

Despite the daunting nature of this task, the PLA is clearly intent on realizing the stated objective. Evidence of this commitment is resident at all levels of the military decision-making/execution cycle—what the Chinese refer to as "peacetime army building." This includes development of operational concepts, force structure decisions, and equipping and training the force.

EVOLVING NON-KINETIC CAPABILITIES

> This guideline lays stress on deterring crisis and wars. It works for close coordination between military struggle and political, diplomatic, economic, cultural and legal endeavors, strives to foster a favorable security environment, and takes the initiative to prevent and defuse crises, and deter conflicts and war.
>
> —China's National Defense in 2008[55]

It is imperative to remember Beijing is not just focused on kinetic solutions to potential conflicts. The U.S. military prowess displayed during OPERATION DESERT STORM convinced China's military thinkers of the need to confront a modern adversary on and off the traditional battlefield. The full extent of Chinese efforts on this "second front" became clear with the 1999 publication of *Unrestricted Warfare: Assumptions on War and Tactics in the Age of Globalization*. Written by a pair of colonels in the People's Liberation Army Air Force, *Unrestricted Warfare* argued "the new principles of war ... no longer use armed forces to compel the enemy to submit to one's will, but rather are using all means, including the armed force or non-armed force, military and non-military, and lethal and non-lethal means to compel the enemy to accept one's interests."[56]

According to the PLA authors, "unrestricted warfare," was conflict that "transcends all boundaries and limits." More specifically, they contended unrestricted warfare,

> ... means that all weapons and technology can be superimposed at will, it means that all boundaries lying between the two worlds of war and non-war, of military and non-military, will be totally destroyed, and it also means that many of the current principles

of combat will be modified, and even that the rules of war may need to be rewritten.[57]

Before proceeding, I hasten to note the authors were careful to insist a "trend toward no limits . . . is not intemperate use of measures, and even less is it absolutist use of measures, or the use of absolute measures."[58] Rather, the two colonels argue unrestricted warfare serves to dramatically expand a conflict's battlespace. As such, the new battlespace could include:

- Trade Warfare—i.e., trade barriers, trade sanctions, and embargoes.
- Financial Warfare—i.e., restriction on access to capital or targeting currency values.
- Ecological Warfare—i.e., using technology to influence the state of rivers, oceans, the crust of the earth, polar ice caps, and/or the ozone layer.
- Psychological Warfare—i.e., spreading rumors to intimidate the enemy.
- Resources Warfare—i.e., hoarding or plundering natural resources.[59]

The bottom line for *Unrestricted Warfare*—"the major threat to [any state's] national security is already far from being limited to the military aggression of hostile forces against the natural space of one's country."[60] This contention is based upon the authors' assumption the concept of territorial sovereignty envisioned by the Peace of Westphalia has been rendered obsolete by globalization. As the two PLA colonels put it, "it is not only the United States, but all nations which worship the view of modern sovereignty, that have already unconsciously expanded the borders of security to a multiplicity of domains, including politics, economics, material resources, nationalities, religion, culture, networks, geography, environment, and outer space."[61] In short, the authors of *Unrestricted War* contend modern warfare requires more than kinetic targeting of sovereign soil—the battlespace of 2010 encompasses hearts, minds, economics, the electromagnetic spectrum, and extra-terrestrial interests.

While I cannot authoritatively state *Unrestricted Warfare* resulted in a dramatic change in Chinese warfighting doctrine, the text does appear to have won an influential audience in Beijing. In 2004,

Chinese press reports began to openly discuss PLA preparations to conduct "legal," "media," and "psychological" warfare—options that had appeared as examples of expanding conflict domains in *Unrestricted Warfare*.[62] Considered "important indicators" of a nation's preparation for "modern warfare,"[63] these three areas reflect Beijing's increasing focus on non-kinetic conflict. Why legal, media and psychological warfare? PLA internal journals argue "three warfare" is intended to first abet taking the political imitative, and second to maximize the effectiveness of military actions.[64] As such, PLA authors argue the "three warfare" must be implemented throughout the entire course of a conflict—and that these non-kinetic options may be employed at the strategic, operational, or tactical level of war.[65]

The PLA does not appear to have widely publicized its definitions of legal, media, and psychological warfare. That said, a review of PLA and Taiwan news sources reveals legal warfare is intended to highlight "the just, legitimate, and inevitable nature of our military actions in future operations according to domestic laws, international laws, and laws governing armed conflicts."[66] Military thinkers on Taiwan argue Chinese media warfare is designed to "win the support of the media both at home and overseas." The Taiwan authors go on to contend, Chinese "media warfare" includes "directional propaganda activities and commentaries via the media aimed at various important and sensitive issues is an important way to support efforts in national politics, diplomacy and military struggle."[67]

To date I have not located an official definition of "psychological warfare" as envisioned within the construct of the "three warfare." Western scholars who have examined Chinese writings on psychological warfare contend at the strategic level these operations would be characterized by "coercion, which will take the form of intimidation achieved through demonstrations and use of force."[68] Preparations on Taiwan to counter Chinese psychological warfare suggest this is an accurate evaluation of PLA intentions. In 2005, Taiwan's psychological warfare week featured the following defensive themes: "identifying the threats from enemies; knowing the various types of warfare; upgrading military intelligence security; boosting patriotic morale; and streamlining military discipline."[69]

A note of caution before leaving this discussion on kinetic and non-kinetic capabilities. Chinese military thinkers clearly believe both options are necessary in modern warfare. This is not an "accidental" development. The PLA has carefully monitored U.S. operations over the last 20 years and can be expected to employ the lessons learned in any future conflict.

EVALUATING PROGRESS CHINA'S IN THE MILITARY MODERNIZATION CAMPAIGN

> Regarding military training as the basic approach to furthering the comprehensive development of the military and raising combat effectiveness, the PLA is working to reform training programs, methods, management and support, and create a scientific system for military training in conditions of informationization.
> —China's National Defense in 2008[70]

China's civilian and military leadership understand simply procuring modern equipment will not alone serve to realize the broad directives provided in Jiang's "Military Strategic Guidelines for the New Period" or Hu Jintao's "Historic Missions." In order to win "informatized wars," the PLA must realistically train using the new equipment and weapon systems. To that end, since at least 2005 Chinese leaders and the PLA General Staff Department[71] have increasingly emphasized training objectives calling for integrative exercises resulting in joint, synergistic employment of China's armed forces.[72]

The extent to which the PLA attempts to follow these training objectives can be inferred from reports capturing highlights from different exercises conducted throughout the country over the course of a year. However, perhaps the single best means of determining what the PLA is expected to accomplish during a coming year is through an examination of General Staff Department (GSD) training directives issued before the commencement of an annual exercise cycle. These GSD directives are intended to translate party leadership strategic guidance into operational objectives readily understood by command and staff officers throughout the People's Liberation Army.

PLA TRAINING GUIDANCE

While inklings of the PLA's shift to focusing on training for integrated joint operations appeared in training guidance for 2004, the first direct statement of this requirement showed up in 2005.

The 2005 GSD training directives appeared in *Jiefangjun Bao*—the official newspaper of the People's Liberation Army General Political Department—on January 15, 2005 under the title "The General Staff Headquarters makes Plans for this Year's Military Work in a Bid to Comprehensively Enhance Units' Combat Power." Beneath this cumbersome moniker rests a clear indication of how the PLA is to begin focusing on joint operations. The degree, however, to which this was a nascent concept for the Chinese military only become apparent halfway through the *Jiefangjun Bao* article, when the author notes, "the Academy of Military Science and relevant units should provide theoretic guidance for integrated training." Nonetheless, the PLA is urged to "promote the strategic mission of the revolution in military affairs" and military units are directed to:

- Practice commanding, coordination, and support under realistic combat conditions—particularly in electronic warfare environments.
- Recognize the fundamental role of joint operations in informationalized conditions by promoting integrated training.
- Standardize training in accordance with law in order to more effectively monitor the quality and evaluation processes.[73]

A year later, the concept of integrated joint operations appears to have reached more solid ground on the training front. On January 18, 2006, *Jiefangjun Bao* reported the GSD had disseminated the "2006 Military Training Directives" at the beginning of the new year. These directives declared:

- The "principle task" of the PLA in 2006 was to carry out military training with realistic scenarios.
- The GSD also called for "practical results" in the following aspects of military training:
  - Intensifying realistic combat training, strengthening tactical and technical training, and having a "good grasp" of operational services, logistics, and equipment support.
  - Exploring integrated training and continuing to "deepen" the theories of integrated joint operations and training.
  - Stressing joint training and conducting joint campaign and tactical exercises and specialized training.

- Enhancing officers' and soldiers' knowledge of informationalized technologies and their ability to solve problems with their
"informationalized knowledge."
- Developing a "military training management system" in order
to strengthen control over the process and quality of military
training and to push training management toward "standardi-
zation, procedure, and precision."
- Giving "full play" to the regulating role of training evaluation
and examination.
- Intensifying training of high-caliber talent, particularly
of command personnel and specialized technical personnel.[74]

In the 2007 directives the GSD gives even greater prominence to
integrated joint operations. More specifically, the General Staff
Department's four main training tasks for 2007 are identified as:

- Stepping up research on military training under informationalized conditions.
- "Thoroughly and solidly" developing training in a complex
electromagnetic environment.
- Focusing on improving units' integrated joint operations capabilities under informationalized conditions.
- Continuing to explore integrated training, which includes training that integrates the key factors of joint operations under informationalized conditions.[75]

The 2008 training directives proved a deviation from this trend—
but only because the GSD ordered PLA commanders to expand
their efforts by training for a variety of combat and noncombat roles
envisioned in Hu's "Historic Missions." According to analysts at the
U.S. Director of National Intelligence's (DNI) Open Source Center,
the January 21, 2008 *Jiefangjun Bao* article "indicates that the
PLA is ready to initiate at the highest level the new [military strategic guidelines] envisioned by . . . Hu Jintao in 2004."[76] More specifically, the Open Source Center assesses the 2008 training
directives seek to prepare the PLA to realize Hu's vision of the military's "Historic Missions"—a focus on expanded geographic range,
greater readiness to conduct priority missions like combating terror-
ism, and strengthening participation in bilateral and multilateral
military partnerships.

While the GSD 2008 training directives also break with the previous four years by not explicitly referring to "integrated joint operations," the PLA is nonetheless ordered to exercise skills sets that directly support this objective. To this end, the training directives call for the PLA to:

- Focus on honing intelligence, reconnaissance, command, control and communications support as "key" skill sets.
- "Intensify" exercising operational tasks required for cross-service missions.
- "Deepen regional coordination training"—a vague concept thought to require drills that hone sustainment and supply operations.[77]

The 2008 training directives also reinforce the PLA's requirement to prepare for combat on a battlefield characterized as a "complex electromagnetic environment." This focus is evident in both a stipulation to "accelerate the pace of building complex electromagnetic training environments and facilities," and in a demand the PLA broaden all units' knowledge of complex electromagnetic environment concepts and principles. Finally, the 2008 GSD training directives renewed attention on training commanders operations in high-tech environments and once again called for realistic drills, including preparations for contingencies that are unpredictable—such as "sudden incidents" and natural disasters.[78]

Perhaps the most coherent statement of Beijing's focus on preparing the People's Liberation Army for joint operations on the modern battlefield appeared in July 2008. *Jiefangjun Bao* reports indicate that in late July 2008 the PLA was issued a revised version of the official Outline for Military Training and Evaluation (OMTE). This document, last updated in 2001, is the authoritative long-term plan for Chinese military training.

According to press statements from the GSD Training and Arms Department, this revised OMTE is the "new starting point" for the PLA to "adapt to the requirements of integrated joint operations."[79] Analysts from the DNI Open Source Center note the new OMTE focuses on five training areas—all intended to prepare the PLA for joint operations. The five focus areas are:

1. A press to implement joint operations exercises at all echelon levels.

2. An expanded range of combat and noncombat tasks—including international peacekeeping operations and a demand exercises occur at night, in adverse weather, and in complex electromagnetic environments.

3. An effort to develop a new corps of PLA personnel trained for conducting modern, high-tech warfighting operations.

4. A call for expanding technical and tactical training with high-tech weapons and systems.

5. A more objective and strict exercise evaluation system employing information technology.[80]

Not surprisingly, the press to realize these objectives continued in 2009. On January 6, 2009, *Jiefangjun Bao* reported the General Staff Department identified six major missions for military training in the coming year. These priorities were:

- Strengthen foundation training—this tasking included an emphasis on "training in key duty positions, specialized skills, and informatized content."
- Address mission subject training—including a requirement to "step up research and practice of strategy, campaign planning, and joint command."
- Conduct multi-arm, multi-service, joint training.
- Steadily advance training reform.
- Deepen reform of academy and school education—this specifically included a call to "step up the development of joint operations command talent," and to "enrich and improve the content involving complex electromagnetic environments and non-war actions."
- Boost the level of training support.[81]

This outline of PLA training objectives reveals the extent of military-wide efforts to realize Chinese Communist Party strategic guidance—specifically, an emphasis on "Integrated Joint Operations" in a highly technical battlefield environment where modern command and control meets advanced information and electronic warfare. "Integrated Joint Operations," however, is more than a buzz-phrase —it appears to drive significant programs for equipping, sustaining and training the PLA to conduct multi-service operations in an "informationized" environment.

A review of PLA press stories over the last three years strongly suggests that PLA units are training to meet this requirement—particularly the five key elements of integrated joint operations—unified command, unified planning, integrated operations, integrated C4ISR, and joint logistics. Furthermore, PLA press stories indicate the military is taking quite seriously the direction to prepare for operations in a "complex electromagnetic environment."[82]

The Chinese focus on training for operations in a "complex electromagnetic environment," reflects PLA understanding of the true nexus of successful joint operations—command, control, communications and a common picture of the battlefield. Pointing to U.S. military victories since 1991, Chinese military scholars argue, "the winner . . . maintained battlefield information supremacy, and from start to finish [so] kept the initiative of the war firmly in . . . grasp."[83] Given this situation, PLA strategic thinkers emphasize the need to field and train on modern communication systems, but also warn a dependence on such capabilities renders one susceptible to information and electronic warfare.

INTEGRATED JOINT OPERATIONS

An extensive review of military sources reveals a continuing debate as to how the PLA ultimately intends to define and develop doctrine for what the Chinese call integrated joint operations. Numerous authoritative Chinese authors agree, however, integrated joint operations are characterized by coordinated, simultaneous military operations employing real-time integration of C4ISR to efficiently and effectively conduct precision strikes intended to disrupt or destroy adversary capabilities in the most timely manner possible.

Chinese military thinkers also agree the five key elements of integrated joint operations are:

- Unified command
- Unified planning
- Integrated operations
- Integrated C4ISR
- Joint logistics

As such, Chinese military authors advocate training and preparing for information and electronic warfare on a widespread and continuing basis. More specifically, they call for the military to be prepared for information warfare in six areas—operational secrecy, military deception, electronic warfare, network warfare, psychological warfare, and physical destruction. Furthermore, they strongly recommend the PLA be prepared to conduct and operate within an environment characterized as integrated network-electronic warfare (INEW)—a battlespace where adversaries seek to deprive each other of information (network warfare) and the means of disseminating that information (electronic warfare).[84]

It is this combination of information and integrated-network electronic warfare—both offensive and defensive—PLA military units are being prepared to conduct when training guidance calls for operations in a "complex electromagnetic environment." The Chinese Communist Party is seeking to prepare the military for synergetic, precise joint operations, while simultaneously seeking the means of denying an adversary the opportunity to accomplish the same thing. While Chinese military writings suggest the PLA is just beginning to fully comprehend and train to these concepts, this will remain a focus for the foreseeable future and will dictate force modernization programs for the next 15–20 years.

I come to this conclusion for two reasons. First, the General Staff Department training directives since 2005—and revised OMTE—are probably directly correlated with recognized PLA shortfalls. The repeated emphasis on conducting realistic drills in complex electromagnetic environments strongly suggests the PLA leadership understands operational commanders and their subordinate units are not prepared for combat on today's battlefield. Furthermore, the repeated focus on joint training appears a clear assessment that the Chinese military is nowhere near ready to conduct the type of operations U.S. forces have repeatedly executed since 1991.

I am not the only one to reach this conclusion. Analysts at the U.S. Open Source Center (OSC) report that Chinese "military commentary routinely claims that virtually all elements of [the PLA] are deeply inadequate for performing it assigned missions."[85] As an example supporting this contention, the OSC analysts provide quotes from a January 1, 2006 *Jiefangjun Bao* editorial. According to *Jiefangjun Bao*, the PLA's capabilities will remain "incompatible" with the "demands of carrying out [Hu Jintao's] Historic Missions" and "winning informatized war" for "quite a long time to come."[86] The OSC analysts reach a similar conclusion in their comment on the overall agenda apparent in the revived OMTE—"this edition of the OMTE focuses on new areas . . . that the PLA deems it needs to improve in order to position itself to win future, high-tech wars."[87]

Nor, by the way, should one conclude these training challenges are limited to employing modern weapon systems. In their analysis of the 2008 GSD training directives, OSC writes, "the document mandates substantial and specific requirements for various aspects of joint operations training, suggesting that the PLA plans to take concrete steps to resolve chronic problems in this area."[88] In fact, if the GSD training directives issued from 2005 to 2009 are to be read at face value, it would appear the PLA has a long way to go in its effort to field a military capable of widespread joint operations. While Beijing certainly has aspirations for achieving this objective, the PLA is clearly a long way from realizing higher headquarters vision.

The second reason I assess the PLA will be engaged in a long-term effort to realize the efficiency and effectiveness of joint operations comes from observations made during the 2008 training year. In late December 2008, the *Kanwa Intelligence Review*—a respected unclassified source on Chinese military developments—published a study of People's Liberation Army exercises during the previous 12 months. The Toronto-based researchers particularly focused on three "major joint exercises: SWIRL WIND 082, the Fall Drill for the 38th Group Army, and LIBIN-98. These exercises took place in the Shenyang and Beijing Military Regions.

According to the *Kanwa* analysts, the exercises shared the following general characteristics:

- All of the drills reflected a PLA emphasis on "base-focused" training—that is, the employment of training facilities designed to support development of specific skill sets, i.e., mountain warfare.

- All of the exercises are becoming larger in scale and involve more personnel from other services.

- All of the drills are reportedly—at least the Chinese press would have us believe—conducted in complex electromagnetic environments.[89]

So much for the "strengths," let's turn to the "weaknesses" exhibited in these 2008 PLA exercises. First, as *Kanwa* notes, Chinese military training exhibits a tendency to employ older models. More specifically, *Kanwa* continues, "the modes of force integration in these exercises are very close to the combat drills of the Soviet Union in the 1970s and 1980s." The second weakness: a marked absence of cross-service data links. As *Kanwa* puts it,

> The construction of generic data link systems among the three major [PLA] services ... will need a huge amount of investment." As a result, the functions of the Chinese joint operation headquarters cannot be assessed against the standards of NATO or Japan, as such headquarters is pretty much for show only.[90]

In a similar vein, *Kanwa* reports during one of the major 2008 exercises "the command headquarters ... still used a large sand table, indicating the PLA's combat theater status display system is not yet electronic, nor are the maps digitized. As such, the widespread application of satellite positioning technologies is greatly restricted."[91]

Other weaknesses exhibited in 2008? Combat assault. According to *Kanwa*, "the combat and transport helicopters in service and the employment of mechanized airborne troops are still in the experimental stage." Furthermore, the Toronto-based researchers argue, "these platforms cannot yet be widely applied in large-scale campaign assault operations because the absolute number of these platforms is too small."[92] Night operations. *Kanwa* reports "there are multiple indications in the exercises that the capacity of the Chinese ground forces in engaging night combat operations is far behind the standard of NATO." This limitation on night operations ranges from a lack of thermal imaging systems on tanks to a lack of radar and front-view infrared search and track systems on PLA combat helicopters. Finally, *Kanwa* observes, it is impossible to accurately gauge Chinese joint capabilities, because Beijing has yet to conduct large-scale joint training with other countries. "As a consequence," *Kanwa* concludes, "China's real combat capability and equipment standard are not yet known to the outside world."[93] I agree with this observation, but if training guidance is any indication, the PLA is not ready for the type of joint operations a U.S. commander would be prepared to execute today.

U.S. DEFENSE DEPARTMENT ASSESSMENT OF PLA CAPABILITIES

In the 2009 "Annual Report to Congress: Military Power of the People's Republic of China," the U.S. Secretary of Defense offers this assessment of the People's Liberation Army's current operational capabilities:

> ... China will take until the end of this decade or longer to produce a modern force capable of defeating a moderate-size adversary. China will not be able to project and sustain small military units far beyond China before 2015, and will not be able to project and sustain large forces in combat operations far from China until well into the following decade. The PLA continues to face deficiencies in inter-service cooperation and actual experience in joint exercises and combat operations.

(2009, "Annual Report to Congress: Military Power of the People's Republic of China," Secretary of Defense, Department of Defense, Washington, DC, p. 20.)

PAYING FOR THE MODERN PEOPLE'S LIBERATION ARMY

China's defense expenditure mainly comprises expenses for personnel, training and maintenance, and equipment. Personnel expenses mainly cover salaries, insurance, food, clothing, and welfare benefits for officers, non-commissioned officers, and enlisted men, as well as for civilian employees. Training and maintenance expenses cover troop training, institutional education, construction and maintenance of installations and facilities, and other expenses on routine consumables. The equipment expenses mainly cover research on, experimentation with, and procurement, maintenance, transportation and storage of weaponry and equipment.

—China's National Defense in 2006[94]

China's military budget has historically been a "riddle wrapped in an enigma." While the biannual white papers on national defense issued since 2002 purportedly seek to address this mystery with a new air of transparency, the published figures do not include such large expenditures as strategic forces expenses, foreign acquisitions, state subsidies for the defense-industrial complex, and some military-related research and development. The result is wide-ranging estimates that vary from Beijing's self-proclaimed $52 billion in 2007 to U.S. Defense Department assessments of between $100 and $150 billion.[95]

In any case, since 1978, the published Chinese defense budget has grown more than 20-fold, from $2.5 billion (at conversion rates of 6.8 yuan to the dollar) to more than $52 billion in 2007. Beijing, however, is quick to place this increase in defense expenditures in a broader domestic political perspective. In the 2006 white paper on National Defense, Chinese officials argue:

> In the 1980s, China began to shift the focus of its work to economic development. At that time, it was decided that national defense should be both subordinate to and serve the country's overall economic development. As a result, national defense received a low input, and was in a state of self-preservation. From 1979 to 1989, the average annual increase of defense expenditure was 1.23 percent. However, the defense expenditure actually averaged registered an average annual decrease of 5.83 percent, given the 7.49 percent average annual increase in the consumer price index in the same period.[96]

The CCP is significantly less apologetic or conciliatory about what happened to defense spending between 1989 and 1997. In *China's National Defense 2008*, Beijing states that "to make up for the inadequacy of defense development and to maintain national security and unity, China gradually increased its defense expenditure on the basis of its sustained economic growth."[97] According to the Chinese military, during this time period annual defense spending rose by 14.5 percent. And from 1998–2007? Beijing unapologetically observes that "to maintain national security and development and meet requirement of the revolution in military affairs ... China continued to increase its defense expenditure"—at an average annual rate of 15.9 percent.[98]

Since 2002, Beijing has claimed the increase can be directly attributed to five factors:

- Increasing salaries and allowances for military personnel
- Increasing investment in equipment, infrastructure, and weapons
- Training costs
- Compensating for rising consumer costs
- Increasing expenses for international cooperation in nontraditional security fields (counterterrorism)[99]

The 2008 national defense white paper reiterates these costs, but then includes a rising technology expense to help explain "the increased part of China's defense expenditure." In a statement that reads remarkably like a Pentagon rising costs lament, Beijing confesses that pushing forward with RMA has resulted in "moderately increased funds for equipment and supporting facilities."[100]

CHINA'S DEFENSE BUDGET: WHAT WE KNOW AND DON'T KNOW

Beijing is increasingly sensitive about international criticism of its defense spending—or, more specifically, China's lack of transparency when it comes to defense spending. In *China's National Defense in 2008*, Beijing pointedly notes, "the relevant data of China's defense expenditure as been made public in the *China Economy Yearbook* since 1981." Nonetheless, questions remain.

What we know:

- The official "top line" of PLA expenditures.
- The official budget as a percentage of government spending and GDP.
- A rough breakdown of official defense expenditures by large category.

What we don't know:

- The complete "top-line" budget.
- Civilian government contributions to the PLA.

- Extra-budgetary expenditures.
- Expenditures by service branch.
- Expenditures by PLA budget functional category.
- Historical trends for all of the above.

In addition to these "traditional" explanations, Western scholars point to two other causes for increased Chinese defense appropriations. The first explanation is political—having been forced to almost completely divest from their commercial interests in the late 1990s, PLA officials are demanding an increasingly larger share of the national budget to meet taskings resident in the military strategic guidelines. The second, and related, explanation is that China's economic growth has compelled the military to compete for qualified manpower and pay higher prices for raw and finished material— Beijing is now confronting the cost of an economy expanding at record rates.[101]

CHINESE DEFENSE EXPENDITURES 1978–2007

In 2008 Beijing provided the first public disclosure of China's defense expenditures for the last 30 years. Included as an appendix in *China's National Defense in 2008*, this single page outlines a "rough" estimate of Beijing's defense costs. (Yuan to dollar exchange rate for conversion purposes below is 6.8 yuan to the dollar.)

Year	Defense Spending ($ Billion)	Percent of China's GDP That Year	Percent of Overall Government Spending
1978	$2.5	4.60%	14.96%
1979	$3.3	5.48%	17.37%
1980	$2.8	4.26%	15.77%

1981	$2.5	3.43%	14.75%
1982	$2.6	3.31%	14.34%
1983	$2.6	2.97%	12.57%
1984	$2.6	2.51%	10.63%
1985	$2.8	2.12%	9.56%
1986	$2.9	1.95%	9.10%
1987	$3.1	1.74%	9.27%
1988	$3.2	1.45%	8.75%
1989	$3.7	1.48%	8.91%
1990	$4.2	1.56%	9.41%
1991	$4.8	1.52%	9.75%
1992	$5.5	1.40%	10.10%
1993	$6.2	1.21%	9.17%
1994	$8.1	1.14%	9.51%
1995	$9.3	1.05%	9.33%
1996	$10.5	1.01%	9.07%
1997	$11.9	1.03%	8.80%
1998	$13.7	1.11%	8.66%
1999	$15.7	1.20%	8.16%
2000	$17.7	1.22%	7.60%
2001	$21.1	1.32%	7.63%
2002	$25.0	1.42%	7.74%
2003	$28.0	1.40%	7.74%
2004	$32.2	1.38%	7.72%
2005	$36.2	1.35%	7.29%
2006	$43.6	1.41%	7.37%
2007	$52.0	1.38%	7.14%

(Source: *China's National Defense in 2008*, p. 103.)

Given this situation, Chinese defense expenditures will continue to climb—at rates which outstrip inflation—particularly as the PLA seeks to meet deployment options resident in Hu's "Historic Missions." The PLA will not be allowed, however, to follow the Soviet model and spend the nation into bankruptcy. Instead, Chinese defense expenditures will be tailored to fund a military capable of meeting regional power projection requirements and will to ensure that a PLA commander has the equipment, personnel, and weapons required to counter and potentially defeat a modern adversary. Finally, I would contend China is not preparing to spend the funds necessary to meet U.S. defense expenditures in a "head on" manner. China likely sees no reason for a commitment of funds at such a level—large-scale global power projection is nowhere to be found in Beijing's military strategic guidelines.

A LONG WAY TO GO ...

China's military appears focused on assuring the capability to prevent Taiwan independence, and, if Beijing were to decide to adopt such an approach, to compel the island to negotiate a settlement on Beijing's terms. At the same time, China is laying the foundation for a force able to accomplish broader regional and global objectives.
—Military Power of the People's Republic of China 2009[102]

Beijing is intent on equipping, manning, and training a modern military capable of protecting the Chinese Communist Party, securing China's territorial claims, safeguarding her expanding national interests ... and ensuring world peace. Or so Hu's "Historic Mission" would have us believe. While these goals all appear reasonable expectations from a responsible international actor, China's military modernization has drawn no shortage of complaints—particularly from Washington. The American Enterprise Institute has called for "more aggressive steps" to "combat China's modernization efforts,"[103] and members of Congress have declared concern about "continuing trends and ambiguities regarding China's military modernization, including ... the steady increase of China's power projection capabilities."[104] But one really has to wonder if all this angst is really warranted.

THE EMPLOYMENT OF MILITARY FORCE —CHINA'S CATCH-22?

Beijing's military modernization efforts generate frequent debates about China's eventual plans for resolving the question of Taiwan's reunification with the mainland. Some Western analysts argue Beijing's decision to appeal to an employment of force is only a matter of time—that eventually Chinese leaders will grow weary of waiting for Taipei and, based upon a carefully calculated evaluation of military forces on either side of the Taiwan Strait, resort to a use of coercive force, which could include an amphibious invasion of Taiwan. Many advocates of this hypothesis suggest such a coercive campaign could occur within the next 10 years, and China will fill such a key role in international economic markets that any cost—lost trade and/or sanctions—would be relatively minimal and short-lived.

On the other side of the coin are scholars who argue the CCP's survival hinges on economic development and associated domestic political stability. Proponents of this view contend the economic and political costs—lost trade, foreign investment, and domestic employment—associated with an invasion of Taiwan would cause China's emerging middle and upper classes to publicly question the legitimacy of continued Communist rule. This "rebellion within the urban elite" could rapidly spread to the lower class blue collar and rural communities, thereby setting the stage for a nationwide regime change. Advocates of this hypothesis claim the CCP will never be ready for such a challenge, and therefore is simply willing to wait for economic forces to pull Taiwan irrevocably into China's arms—possibly under the guise of one nation.

I fully agree that Beijing is prepared to use force—if necessary—to prevent a declaration of independence on Taiwan. I also agree that China is prepared to forcibly evict perceived intrusions on her claimed territories. Neither I, nor her neighbors,[105] however, are convinced that the PLA is an imperialist force in the making. In fact, I am comfortable in concluding China understands the PLA to be an integral element of any regional hierarchy. Consider, for example, the following quote from a colonel assigned to Beijing's Academy of Military Sciences.

The armed forces need to cope with traditional security threats, and also need to cope with non-traditional security threats; need to safeguard the state's survival interests, and also need to safeguard the state's development interests; need to safeguard the homeland security, and also need to safeguard the overseas interests security; need to safeguard the overall state interests of reform, development, and stability, and also need to safeguard world peace and promote common development.[106]

This summary of Hu's tasking for the PLA is telling—and reminiscent of the broad mission statement provided to the U.S. Defense Department. That is to say, the PLA is being asked to keep up with the times, and that requires new capabilities and perspectives.

The CCP, unsurprisingly, does appear intent on providing the PLA with these new capabilities and perspectives. The CCP has chosen this path because Beijing believes a modern military is necessary for the Party's survival. The Party leadership has come to this conclusion via the school of bitter experience. Having abandoned communist ideology, the Party cannot afford to be perceived as failing to meet its other obligations. At the top of this list is protection and preservation of China's territorial integrity, and continued economic development. Beijing can ill-afford a repeat of the humiliation suffered during the 1996 Taiwan Strait crisis, and the Party cannot be perceived as allowing outsiders to threaten China's access to natural resources and export markets. To that end, the PLA is being modernized . . . and we need to accept that fact and understand the underlying causes.

Now, the real question is do we need to fear a modernizing People's Liberation Army? I would contend the answer to that question is—not anytime in the foreseeable future. Regardless of how much money Beijing is willing to spend, the PLA confronts unique cultural and historical challenges as it proceeds with through the modernization process. Allow me to offer an example to make the point—and perhaps help explain why the PLA is unlikely to be ready for a sustained conflict with any major military power in the coming 10 years. Let's begin with China's Confusionist culture. Confronted with a traditional deference for age and seniority—coupled with a bureaucracy that all but enshrines a many-tiered organizational structure—the PLA often finds its hands tied on efforts to flatten command-and-control processes. As a result, the rapid flow of information necessary for modern combat operations is frequently bogged-down in a process that appears intentionally designed to hinder operational efficiency.

These problems are not trivial. According to Chinese military analysts, the command and control shortfalls confronting the PLA repeatedly appear during joint military exercises and could be expected to hinder completion of a real-world mission.[107] These critical issues fall within six categories:

- Duplicative command responsibilities
- Low quality of commanders
- Bloated headquarters
- Uncoordinated regional organization and force structure
- Obsolete command and control technologies
- Questionable survivability[108]

I would note many of these shortfalls are currently the subject of intense study within the PLA, but suspect progress in fixing any one of the six is going to be slow and painful.

As the Chinese are willing to openly admit, this process requires time—potentially not reaching completion until 2050—and considerable expenditure of national treasure.

This struggle for a more efficient command and control system is critical for realizing the effects and efficiencies resident in the revolution in military affairs. The four elements abetting a revolution in military affairs—operational innovation, organization adaptation, evolving military systems, and emerging technologies—really only come to complete fruition when synthesized into a whole that is more powerful than the parts.

This was a lesson Marshal Ogarkov, the great Soviet military thinker, sought to emphasize in his evaluations of U.S. military power in the early 1980s.[109] For Ogarkov, the most impressive capability the United States demonstrated during DESERT STORM was the tightly synchronized, highly integrated joint operations across the depth of the theater—striking at strategic and operational centers of gravity. By their own admission, the Chinese have not achieved this status—and likely will not reach a comparable competence level until 2020.[110]

A strikingly similar argument was offered by Karl Lautenschlager in 1983. As a staff defense analyst at Los Alamos National Laboratory, Lautenschlager examined the relationship between technology and naval warfare. His study of naval developments led to conclusions which apply to RMA writ large.

According to Lautenschlager, it was not one technological breakthrough that made the difference on a battlefield. Rather, he argued, it was the "synthesis of different technologies and how that synthesis can produce fundamental change in mission capabilities."[111] Lauten-schlager concluded with three observations that still resonate on the indications and warning side of defense. First, he noted, "change is usually evolutionary but it can be dramatic." Second, new technology has not revolutionized warfare—in many ways we are still confronted with troops in a field exchanging volleys. Finally, "important changes are seldom reflected in obvious physical features."[112]

BEIJING'S AIRCRAFT CARRIER

Rumors of China's interest in deploying an operational aircraft carrier have been making the rounds for more than 30 years. In 1975, Admiral Liu Huaqing, vice chairman of the Central Military Commission, publicly declared China must establish its own aircraft carrier battle group(s) as a means of securing sea lines of communication and protecting her national sovereignty. Liu's foresight was remarkable, as he went on to note Beijing's aircraft carrier ambitions were not driven by an arms race with Moscow or Washington, but rather were intended to bolster China's ability to:

• Effectively engage in potential conflict with Taiwan.

• Settle potential conflicts in the South China Sea.

• Protect maritime resources.

• Maintain parity with other regional actors—including India and Japan.

• Provide the Chinese military a decisive edge in future warfare.

• Participate in worldwide peacekeeping operations.

In 1998, China appeared to take a significant step in this direction when Beijing purchased the 70 percent complete Russian-built Varyag. While stories of Varyag refurbishing efforts periodically surfaced, China did not seem to be moving forward with an aircraft carrier program until November 2008. On November 16, 2008, the *Financial Times* published a story in which the director of the foreign affairs office of the Chinese Ministry of Defense declared:

The navy of any great power ... has the dream to have one or more aircraft carriers ... The question is not whether you have an aircraft carrier, but what you do with your aircraft carrier ... Even if one day we have an aircraft carrier, unlike another country, we will not use it to pursue global deployment or global reach.

In December 2008, media outlets reported China would begin construction of two conventionally powered aircraft carriers in 2009—with plans for having the ships afloat in 2015, and fully operational by 2020. The news sources also claimed China is planning to build two nuclear-powered flattops. In March 2009, East Fleet Commander Admiral Xu Hongmeng appeared to substantiate these reports when he gave an interview including the following comment: "China will soon have its own aircraft carrier."

Why proceed down this path? James Holmes, a professor at the U.S. Naval War College offers three explanations: (1) Regional power projection; (2) Protection of sea lanes of communication used for oil deliveries and export of goods; (3) A status symbol—China is the only permanent member of the United Nations Security Council without a flattop.

This diversion into military thinkers from the 1980s is not accidental. Moscow, like Beijing, confronted at least one potential adversary who probably could not be defeated in a conventional military conflict. The issue then becomes, how might the Chinese seek to level the playing field in a regional conflict with a high-tech adversary. The answer is to be found in work done at the U.S. Army War College in the mid-1990s.

In 1994, Steven Metz and James Kievit published a paper on RMA and conflicts short of war in which they argued future opponents could attempt to counter high-tech U.S. forces through three means: (1) strike at domestic support for U.S. engagement; (2) target friends and allies; and (3) directly counter deployed American forces.[113] Furthermore, Metz and Kievit warned, not all conflict situations lend themselves to a full application of U.S. military prowess. In what might best be described as remarkable prescience, the two military thinkers argued, "The use of new technology may also run counter to basic American values. Information age—and in particular information warfare—technologies cause concerns about privacy."[114] These warnings remain valid and valuable more than 10 years after they were written—and certainly apply to the issues at stake in this project, China need not invest an excessive number of "new toys" when she can effectively hold the United States or any other adversary hostage by shutting down national power grids.[115]

Finally, I offer a comment on the potential long-term—or lack thereof—impact the current revolution in military affairs may have on the balance of power in Northeast Asia. In a 1999 study on the systemic effects of military innovation, Emily Goldman and Richard Andres note, there is a possibility "new and proven military methods, even if they are truly revolutionary, will have no lasting effect on the balance of international influence because diffusion [of the technology] occurs quickly among the states that are in range of each other's war-making ability."[116]

Goldman and Andres go on to state "the spread of innovations have been accelerating over time and there is little reason to believe the trend will be reversed. The result has been a steady decline in the amount of time that a state that first leverages the innovation can expect to maintain a monopoly on the methods." They go on observe the Mongols under Genghis Khan held a military lead for 50 years, while the French artillery advantage lasted only 4 years, and the Swedish advance in drill techniques held for a short 24 months.[117] The bottom line, China may be racing to achieve technological advances on the military front that have—at best—a fleeting life-span.

Where does this leave us? First, while the Chinese are indeed expending considerable energy and national treasure on modernizing the PLA this should not be cause for alarm. The PLA is being recrafted so as to more effectively meet Hu's "Historic Missions." As such, we can expect the PLA to gradually exhibit a greater regional presence, and perhaps become even more effective in overseas peacekeeping missions. These enhanced capabilities may indeed make Beijing's neighbors nervous, but they should not be cause for loss of sleep in Washington. China is at least 10 years from fielding an operational aircraft carrier, and is likely equally distant from learning to employ a truly joint military force. In other words, the PLA may begin to take on the appearance of a world-class military over the coming decade, but realization of the operational capabilities there within seem unlikely during the same time period.

RETURN OF THE RAPID DEPLOYMENT FORCE?

As the PLA wrestles with means of accomplishing Hu's "Historic Missions," there is a possibility someone in China will dust-off the Pentagon's concept of a rapid deployment force. In the late 1970s, the U.S. Defense Department engaged in a full-court campaign to establish capabilities for addressing contingencies outside existing alliance structures. Washington's answer, the Rapid Deployment Joint Task Force (RDJTF).

As envisioned by defense department planners, the RDJTF was not a fixed set of particular air, ground or naval units, but rather a reservoir of forces suitable and available for addressing non-NATO contingencies. The core of this reservoir was composed of highly mobile forces, including various Air Force fighter units, the 82nd Airborne Division, a Marine Amphibious Force, and the carrier battle groups. This mix was intended to facilitate rapid assembly of forces that could operate independently, with neither forward bases nor friendly nation support, in geographical areas that ranged from Korea to the Persian Gulf and Middle East.

In April 1981, Secretary of Defense Casper Weinberger announced the RDJTF would evolve into a separate command with specific geographic responsibilities. In 1983 the RDJTF became a separate unified command known as the U.S. Central Command.

China may be considering a similar RDJTF construct, particularly as Beijing has shown no inclination of establishing commands with geographical responsibilities outside the nation's claimed territorial boundaries. The PLA already has the requisite aircraft (fighters and transport), airborne units, and marines. What China has yet to establish is the naval support—specifically aircraft carriers or amphibious assault ships.

Given Hu's demand the PLA prepare to defend China's expanding national interests and engage in international peacekeeping operations, Beijing's version of the RDJTF may be put into effect before 2020. (See April 1978, "U.S. Projections Forces: Requirements, Scenarios and Options," Congressional Budget Office, Washington, DC; and, Paul Davis, June 1982, "Observations on the Rapid Deployment Joint Task Force: Origins, Direction and Mission," Rand Corporation, Santa Monica.)

Second, China's willingness to use this military force to participate in international peacekeeping and law-enforcement missions should be welcomed. Communication among military officers representing different states is a welcome development. China's officer corps has historically been an isolated lot whose nationalist sentiments could prove detrimental to efforts aimed at resolving differences without a resort to force. Exposing this cadre to U.S. and other military professionals could help alleviate this problem. Furthermore, international military ties have a potential educational effect that could serve to enhance professionalism. The PLA understands the importance of continuing education for its military—exposure to international officers could offer lessons no classroom can duplicate.

Finally, we should understand that Beijing's maintenance of a large, modern military is driven by history, an anarchic international system, and the CCP's desire to remain atop the nation's political hierarchy. None of these observations are novel or particularly difficult to understand. And yet many of China's harshest critics appear willing to ignore all three considerations when casting doubt on the intentions of Beijing's military expenditures. China's leaders have no intention of ever repeating the "century of humiliation," no desire of being left defenseless in our Westphalian world, and will not brook any obvious challenge to their single-party rule of the Middle Kingdom—a modern PLA is critical to realizing these objectives.

CHAPTER 5

Pondering Taiwan's Future

It is Taiwan's moves toward de jure statehood that pose the most
significant threat to China's long-term ambitions.
—John Lewis and Xue Litai, 2006[1]

China's political maturation on the global stage is perhaps most evident in Beijing's approach to dealing with Taiwan. While Taipei
remains the headquarters for a "renegade province," the saber rattling
and bluster that characterized China's dealings with the island during
the 1990s has been replaced with diplomacy and a tangible reconciliation campaign. I'm not going to contend Beijing has abandoned all
plans to forcibly reunify Taiwan with the mainland—particularly if
Taipei unilaterally declares independence. But I will argue China-
Taiwan relations in the coming 10 years may appear more analogous
to Beijing's current relations with Hong Kong than two pugilists preparing for battle.

Most American military and political decision makers are not prepared for this development. As we have previously noted, a potential
conflict between China and Taiwan has served U.S. Navy procurement interests for years, and many conservative Republicans still
believe Beijing is determined to replace Taipei's democracy with a
dictatorship of the proletariat. The Department of Defense 2009
report on Chinese military power provides a stellar example of this
mindset. According to the U.S. Secretary of Defense,

China's military appears focused on assuring the capability to
prevent Taiwan independence and, if Beijing were to decide to

adopt such an approach, to compel the island to negotiate a settlement on Beijing's terms.[2]

Oh, by the way, the Pentagon continues, "at the same time China is laying the foundation for a force able to accomplish broader regional and global objectives."[3] I would highlight the fact this second statement always appears in U.S. Department of Defense reports on China's military as a lingering afterthought. I would suggest it is time we reverse the order of those arguments.

Before turning to events that have caused me to reach this conclusion, we need to examine why so many U.S. military and political leaders appear stuck in an outdated mindset. Admittedly, China's role in the Korean War and her perceived unholy alliance with the former Soviet Union are in no small part to blame. But it has now been more than 30 years since Richard Nixon made his historic trip to Beijing— and exactly three decades since President Carter signed the Taiwan Relations Act.

In the Shanghai Communiqué China and the United States signed on February 27, 1972, Washington tacitly acknowledged both Taipei and Beijing agree there is only one China, and reaffirmed our interest in a peaceful settlement of the Taiwan question ... by the Chinese.[4] In the Taiwan Relations Act the United States made it clear we expected this settlement to be determined peacefully, and that Washington would provide Taipei with the military equipment necessary to defend the island.[5]

As further proof of our commitment to Taiwan's *de facto* independence ... and Washington's willingness to meet Beijing halfway on the entire issue ... on August 17, 1982 the United States issued a second Communiqué concerning the island's defense. In this Communiqué, the Reagan administration declared it did not seek to carry out a long-term policy of arms sales to Taiwan; that arms sales to Taiwan would not exceed, either in qualitative or quantitative terms, the level of those supplied since the establishment of diplomatic relations between the United States and mainland China. In addition, Washington announced an intention to reduce the sales of arms to Taiwan gradually.[6] However, as a fellow at Harvard University's Weatherhead Center for International Affairs noted in 2001, while the August 17, 1982 Communiqué pledged a general reduction in U.S. weapons supply to Taiwan so long as conditions in the Strait remained peaceful, neither the Reagan nor subsequent administrations ever adhered fully to the spirit of the agreement.[7]

One of the primary reasons for this repeated slip in protocol—and the cause for continuing problems between China and the United States when it comes to arms sales to Taiwan—a July 14, 1982 back channel communication between Washington and Taipei. In an attempt to appease U.S. congressional critics of the then-forthcoming August 17, 1982 Communiqué, the Reagan administration made six assurances to Taiwan:

1. Washington had not agreed to set a date certain for ending arms sales to Taiwan.
2. The United States had not agreed to engage in prior consultations with Beijing on arms sales to Taiwan.
3. Washington would not play any mediation role between Taipei and Beijing.
4. The United States had not agreed to revise the Taiwan Relations Act.
5. Washington had not altered its long-standing position on the issue of sovereignty over Taiwan.
6. The United States would not attempt to exert pressure on Taiwan to enter into negotiations with mainland China.[8]

The level of U.S. commitment to this back-channel set of assurances? In 1992 President George H. Bush decided to sell Taipei 150 F-16 fighters as a means of balancing the threat presented by China's acquisition of Su-27/FLANKER from the former Soviet Union.

This delicate balancing act likely would still largely be in effect were it not for the Tiananmen Square democracy demonstration in 1989. Beijing's decision to end the demonstration through an application of brute force caused American politicians to once again rethink our relations with Taiwan. The events in Tiananmen Square caused U.S. politicians to once again pigeonhole Beijing as a repressive communist regime—a second Soviet Union. Taiwan, on the other hand, was emerging as a promising democracy.

As a result of these developments, in 1992, President Bill Clinton initiated a comprehensive review of American policy toward Taiwan. In the late summer of 1994, the Clinton administration finally announced the results of this review. During testimony on the Taiwan Policy Review before the Senate Foreign Relations Committee on September 27, 1994, Assistant Secretary of State Winston Lord announced Washington would now approach Taipei in the following manner:

- The Taiwan Relations Act and the three communiqués will continue to be the heart of U.S. policy.
- The United States recognized cross-strait talks between Taiwan and mainland China as important for prompting stability in the region and the security of Taiwan. The United States will neither interfere in nor mediate this process, but we would welcome any evolution in relations between Taipei and Beijing that are mutually agreed upon and reached peacefully.
- Taiwan's top leadership would be permitted to transit U.S. territory for their travel convenience, for periods of time normal for transits, but without undertaking any public activities.
- Washington would initiate a sub-cabinet economic dialogue with Taiwan.
- The United States would more actively support Taiwan's membership in international organizations accepting non-states as members, and look for ways to have Taiwan's voice heard in organizations of states where Taiwan's membership is not possible.
- Washington would allow all American Institute in Taiwan (AIT, de facto embassy) employees, including the Director and Deputy Director, access to the Taiwan Ministry of Foreign Affairs.
- U.S. cabinet-level officials from economic and technical departments would be permitted to meet with Taiwan representatives and visitors in official settings.[9]

This apparent fundamental change in Washington's rules of engagement set the stage for the 1996 Taiwan Strait standoff—and the emergence of a new U.S. academic and policy hobby, touting the "China Threat."

On May 2, 1995, the U.S. House of Representatives voted 396 to 0 in favor of granting Taiwan President Lee Teng-hui an entry visa. The Senate followed 6 days later, voting 97 to 1 on a motion to permit Lee to make a visit to Cornell University. On May 22, 1995, Washington announced Lee had been granted a visa to enter the United States. Following this announcement the State Department and other officials repeatedly tried to assure Beijing that Washington's policy

concerning China and Taiwan had not fundamentally changed—
that the mainstay of President Clinton's mainland China policy
remained constructive engagement.[10] Needless to say, Beijing was
not impressed.

On May 23, 1995, Beijing's Ministry of Foreign Affairs issued a
statement accusing Washington of abetting the establishment of two
Chinas, violating the one-China principle of the three joint communiqués, and jeopardizing future U.S.-China relations. For Beijing,
Washington's decision to grant Lee a visa was tangible evidence of a
shift in U.S. policy—from engagement to containment, and that the
United States was seeking to heighten Taiwan's international profile.
As Andrew Nathan and Robert Ross observe in *The Great Wall and
the Empty Fortress: China's Search for Security*, President Lee's visa suggested the United States was willing to ignore mainland China's interests. Coming just as Taiwan's presidential election was entering its
final stage; the visa decision had the potential to encourage Taiwan's
candidates to openly declare support for the island's independence.[11]

The events which transpired next served to change U.S. military
perceptions of China in much the same way Tiananmen Square had
done for American politicians. In an effort to dissuade the Taiwan
population from reelecting President Lee, in March 1996 China
staged a dramatic show of force consisting of military exercises and
missile tests bracketing Taiwan. The U.S. response, an unmistakable
demonstration of armed might—the deployment of two aircraft carrier battle groups to the region. As James Chang notes, "deployment
of one aircraft carrier battle group could be seen as a symbol, a
demonstration, or political theater; two represented a more real
capability."[12] The bottom line: in 1996 Taiwan had brought the
United States and China to a state of crisis not witnessed since the
early 1950s.

ONE CHINA POLICY

In August 1993, Beijing issued a white paper officially describing the Chinese Communist Party's "One China" policy.
According to the document:

From 1979, the Chinese government has striven for the
peaceful reunification of China in the form of 'one country,

two systems' with the greatest sincerity and the utmost effort. Economic and cultural exchanges and people-to-people contacts between the two sides of the Taiwan Straits have made rapid progress since the end of 1987. Unfortunately, from the 1990s, Lee Teng-hui, the leader of the Taiwan authorities, has progressively betrayed the One-China Principle, striving to promote a separatist policy with 'two Chinas' at the core, going so far as to openly describe the cross-Straits relations as 'state to state relations, or at least special state to state relations.' This action has seriously damaged the basis for peaceful reunification of the two sides, harmed the fundamental interests of the entire Chinese nation including the Taiwan compatriots, and jeopardized peace and stability in the Asia-Pacific region.

As a means of resolving this dangerous standoff, Beijing proposed the principle of "peaceful reunification, and one country, two systems." The key points of this principle are as follows:

- China will do its best to achieve peaceful reunification, but will not commit itself to ruling out the use of force.
- China will actively promote people-to-people contacts and economic and cultural exchanges between the two sides of the Taiwan Straits, and start direct trade, postal, air and shipping services as soon as possible.
- China will seek to achieve reunification through peaceful negotiations and, on the premise of the One-China Principle, any matter can be negotiated.
- After reunification, the policy of "one country, two systems" will be practiced, with the main body of China (Chinese mainland) continuing with its socialist system, and Taiwan maintaining its capitalist system for a long period of time to come.

The bottom line for Beijing: "Taiwan is an inalienable part of China." (August 6, 1993, White Paper—The One-China Principle and the Taiwan Issue," Beijing.)

THE "CHINA THREAT"

In retrospect, we now know that China's decision to employ a demonstration of force in the run-up to Taiwan's election was a strategic mistake. Rather than detract from Lee's popularity, Beijing's belligerent behavior actually appeared to strengthen support for the feisty politician. Furthermore, the People's Liberation Army (PLA) was revealed to largely be a paper tiger.[13] The military exercises China tasked the PLA with accomplishing proved a daunting venture for uniformed personnel who had become almost single-mindedly focused on commercial enterprises.[14] The degree of these shortcomings would only become fully apparent to the West two years later, when Jiang Zemin gave a speech in which he declared: "To make concerted efforts to properly develop the army in an all-around manner, the central authorizes decided ... the army and the armed police ... shall not carry our any commercial activities in the future."[15]

In the United States, China's reaction to Taiwan's increasing independence—and Beijing's clear dismay with Washington—generated a new industry, authoring frightening tales of the Middle Kingdom's emerging threat to the American way of life. Perhaps the earliest—and most popular—of these works was Richard Bernstein and Ross Munro's *The Coming Conflict with China*. Originally published in 1997, *The Coming Conflict with China* warned, "The People's Republic of China, the world's most populous country, and the United States, its most powerful, have become global rivals, countries whose relations are tense, whose interests are in conflict, and who face tougher, more dangerous times ahead."[16] As best Bernstein and Munro could tell, "The 1996 face-off in the Taiwan Strait could presage future face-offs as an ever more powerful, assertive, nationalistic China maneuvers to retake what it deems to be a part of its national territory."[17] They darkly conclude, "China has given numerous signals that it views the West as its spiritual and practical adversary, and in this scheme of things, the United States and the West are one and the same."[18]

In 2000, Bill Gertz—a reporter with the conservative *Washington Times*—followed in Bernstein and Munro's footsteps with the publication of *The China Threat: How the People's Republic Targets America*. According to Gertz, the Clinton administration's policies had resulted in the creation of "a new superpower threat to world peace and stability in the decades to come."[19] According to Gertz, Taiwan's importance to Beijing cannot be overstated. He goes on to argue,

> It is not just fervent nationalism mixed with communism that is driving China's demands for reunification. The strategic motivation is China's desire to expand its influence far beyond Chinese shores ... China is seeking hegemony over strategic waters stretching several hundred miles, including Taiwan.[20]

In a classic bit of fear mongering, Gertz warns his readers, "China's patient communist leaders have a strategy that stretches over the next several decades. They rightly regard the United States as their main enemy and primary obstacle to China's goal of achieving world status and Pacific domination."[21]

A less sinister, but equally grim scenario is offered in Ted Galen Carpenter's book, *America's Coming War with China: A Collision Course over Taiwan.*[22] According to Carpenter, the most dangerous topic in any dialogue between Beijing and Washington is the fate of Taiwan. Carpenter—mistakenly, as we shall see in a moment—contends a growing number of Taiwan's residents seek independence and regard mainland China as an alien nation. He goes on to argue Mainland Chinese believe Taiwan was stolen from Beijing more than a century ago, and are increasingly impatient about reclaiming the lost territory. How impatient? Carpenter would have us believe the Taiwan question could provoke a war between China and the United States in the coming 5–10 years.

I would be remiss if the reader walks away believing all popular texts on China simply emphasize Beijing's potential threat to the West. A case-in-point, Will Hutton's 2007 manuscript, *The Writing on the Wall: China and the West in the 21st Century.* In a refreshing break from the ominous "China threat" crowd, Hutton argues, "it is wrong for so many Western politicians, business leaders and opinion formers to use China as an ominous threat before which the West must change or else wilt."[23] Hutton instead contends:

> China is not such a threat. Rather, it is a sophisticated civilization beset by profound and deepening problems that is making a difficult transition from a primitive and poor peasant society to modernity. It requires our understanding and engagement—not our enmity and suspicion.[24]

That said, Hutton too admits that Taiwan is "the most potentially dangerous" dispute in Asia. In an effort to defeat Taipei's seemingly endless dalliance with independence, he continues, Beijing has pulled out almost every trick in the book. This includes cross-strait trade and investment, support for Taiwan politicians who favor the current status quo, and the anti-secession law passed in 2005.[25]

TAIWAN'S INTERNATIONAL ISOLATION

As a means of further emphasizing Taiwan's status as little more than a "renegade province" the Chinese Communist Party has sought to strip Taipei of foreign diplomatic recognition. The origins of this campaign can be traced back to 1949, but the effort did not really gain traction until the 1970s. In October 1971, the United Nations General Assembly passed Resolution 2758 expelling "the representatives of Chiang Kai-shek" and replacing the China seat on the Security Council (and all other UN organs) with delegates from the People's Republic of China. In the following 10 years, the United States, Japan, and Canada announced plans to transfer diplomatic recognition from the Republic of China to the People's Republic of China.

In 2009, only 23 states still officially recognize the Republic of China. Beijing has encouraged this isolation by insisting states break ties with Taipei and then demanding recognition of the People's Republic of China as the sole legitimate government of the Middle Kingdom (including Taiwan) before establishing formal diplomatic relations. China's growing economic clout—many states want access to the Chinese market—and Beijing's willingness to engage in "checkbook diplomacy" have further speeded this process. A classic case of this "checkbook diplomacy," Dominica who ended its recognition of Taiwan in 2004 after Beijing offered to provide the Caribbean nation $117 million over a six year time period.

Nations that Recognize Taiwan in 2009

Central & South America (12 states)	*Africa (4 states)*
–Belize	–Burkina Faso
–Dominican Republic	–Gambia
–El Salvador	–Sao Tome and Principe

–Guatemala	–Swaziland
–Haiti	
–Honduras	*Europe (1 state)*
–Nicaragua	–Vatican City
–Panama	
–Paraguay	*Oceana (6 states)*
–Saint Kitts and Nevis	–Kiribati
–Saint Lucia	–Marshall Islands
–Saint Vincent and the Grenadines	–Nauru
	–Palau
	–Solomon Islands
	–Tuvalu

There are no signs China intends to back away from this policy. In May 2009, the Chinese Foreign Ministry told reporters, "The Chinese government adheres to the one-China policy and opposes Taiwan having official exchanges with any country. This position remains unchanged." (May 21, 2009, "China Opposes Taiwan Having Official Exchanges with Any Country," Xinhua, Beijing.)

Given the continuing problems Taiwan causes for China's relations with the West—to say nothing of the negative publicity highlighted above—one has to ask, why does Beijing persist? Certainly, there are scholars who contend it is only a matter of time before Taiwan is drawn back to the mainland . . . either by economics or politics. The problem, as Bates Gill noted in 2007, is that for China's current rulers Taiwan maybe the straw that broke the camel's back. That is, Beijing might be able to balance the economic, environmental, and social issues on her plate, but losing Taiwan could bring the whole act to a crashing halt. As Gill so ably concludes, "discussions with Chinese politicians and leaders make clear their view of what the 'loss' of Taiwan could mean to China: the chaotic breakup of China and downfall of the Chinese Communist Party."[26]

Chen Shui-bian's election as Taiwan's president in 2000 did little to reassure Beijing's worried leadership. Chen's pro-independence stance suggested the "one China, two governments," policy Beijing sought to promote as an amicable compromise was about to be cast into the wind. While Chen informed his Chinese counterparts that he would be willing to discuss "One China" with Beijing, he only did under the caveat that mainland leaders would have to treat Taipei as an equal.[27] Chen's selection of Annette Lu as his running mate did not help matters. Lu's tendency to issue inflammatory remarks only further aggravated the Chinese.

As far as Chinese commentators were concerned, Lu was worse than Lee Teng-hui. On April 20, 2000, Xinhua, Beijing's official news agency, went so far as to publish a commentary declaring: "Lu has outdone Lee [on the independence issue], consistently trying to make distinctions between Taiwan and China, and the Taiwanese and Chinese. She has foolishly claimed that 'Taiwan's sovereignty is independent and nobody can deny it.'" The commentary goes on to note, "Taiwan independence elements—like Lu—ignore logic and historical fact in their desire to split China."[28]

China's clear pique with Chen and Lu, however, did not culminate with a repeat of the military shows of force that had preceded the 1996 Taiwan presidential election. Instead, Beijing chose to beat the rhetorical drums of war. In white paper titled "China's National Defense in 2000," the CCP bluntly warned:

> ... if a grave turn of events occurs leading to the separation of Taiwan from China in any name, or if Taiwan is invaded and occupied by foreign countries, or if the Taiwan authorities refuse, sine die, the peaceful settlement of cross-Straits reunification through negotiations, then the Chinese government will have no choice but to adopt all drastic measures possible, including the use of force, to safeguard China's sovereignty and territorial integrity, and achieve the great cause of reunification. The "Taiwan independence" means provoking war again, and fomenting splits means relinquishing peace across the Straits. The Chinese People's Liberation Army unswervingly takes the will of the state as its supreme will and the national interests as its supreme interests. It has the absolute determination, confidence, ability and means to safeguard state sovereignty and territorial integrity, and will never tolerate, condone or remain indifferent to the realization of any scheme to divide the motherland.[29]

Stated in a simpler manner, China had drawn her "red-lines," those events that might cause the PLA to be charged with forcibly dragging

Taipei back into the fold. According to the U.S. Department of Defense, these red-lines were: a formal declaration of independence by Taipei; undefined moves "toward independence;" foreign intervention in Taiwan's internal affairs; indefinite delays in the resumption of cross-Strait dialogue; Taiwan's acquisition of nuclear weapons; and internal unrest in Taiwan.[30]

That Chen Shui-bian and Annette Lu managed to avoid crossing these boundaries during their rocky eight-year tenure atop Taiwan's political hierarchy is relatively amazing. Until one realizes that popular support for independence on Taiwan is not as unanimous as Beijing's rhetoric might have one think. In December 2002, a poll of Taiwan's residents found about 32 percent of the people questioned said that Taiwan independence is better for the nation's interest than unification with China. Nearly 20 percent said they preferred the status quo—de facto independence. Approximately 21 percent said that unification with China would be better for the nation's interest than independence, and 27 percent were undecided.[31]

In December 2008, a poll conducted by Taiwan's Mainland Affairs Council showed a dramatic shift from even this lukewarm support for independence. A poll of 1,068 adults found 91.8 percent per cent favored maintaining the status quo, up from 78.6 percent in the Council's October 15, 2008 survey. This was the highest level of support for maintaining the status quo since Taiwan began to conduct surveys on cross-strait ties in the 1980s. Only 6 percent of the respondents backed Taiwan immediately declaring independence and just 2 percent wanted immediate unification with the mainland—compared to 14.8 percent and 1.7 percent in the October 15, 2008 poll.[32]

How do we explain these numbers? Two phenomena are at work. The first is primarily economics, the second is sociological.[33] In 1991, the volume of cross-Strait trade—a distance of less than 150 miles between two populations who largely spoke the same language—accounted for just $8 billion. In 2006, that same figure was $115 billion . . . and in 2008 it reached approximately $130 billion. Furthermore, Taiwan businesses have spent a fortune developing facilities on the mainland. As the U.S. Council on Foreign Relations observed in 2006, investments on mainland China accounted for more than half of Taiwan's overseas spending. Taiwan officials claim businesses on the island have invested over $74 billion on the mainland as of January 2009.[34] All told, by 2006 China had become Taiwan's top export partner and its second-largest import partner.[35] In addition to these monetary links, Taipei now estimates up to one million

Taiwan citizens live on mainland China—the bulk of this population is said to be businessmen and their families.[36]

The sociological explanation for this diminished interest in a formal declaration of independence is less obvious. As you will recall, more than a few Western scholars believe a growing sense of nationalism among Taiwan's population will cause the island to permanently separate itself from the mainland. A comprehensive study published by the East-West Center in 2006 boldly refutes this claim. Using data from surveys, interviews, focus groups and previous research, the East-West Center found "holding a Taiwanese identity does not equate to supporting independence or opposing better cross-Strait relations."[37]

Even more significantly, the East-West Center research discovered nationalism on Taiwan varies by generation. To quote the study, nationalism "is a strong force mainly among [Taiwan residents] born between the early 1930s and the early 1950s, while younger [Taiwan citizens] generally hold pragmatic views about cross-Strait economic and political interactions."[38] For the moment, this generational difference is problematic because the older cohort largely dominates the island's political leadership. In the future, however, as the younger Taiwan residents shift into the leadership roles "we can expect them to adjust the island's mainland policy to promote engagement without surrendering [Taipei's] political autonomy."[39]

In fact, there are already signs of this shift in emphasis. The election of Ma Ying-jeou as President of Taiwan on March 22, 2008 is now perceived as a repudiation of the pro-independence politics that played so prominently during Chen Shui-bian's administration. We should also note Ma's victory was not in dispute. Ma defeated his opponent by more than 2 million votes, winning with a margin of 58 to 42 percent. As the Congressional Research Service observed, Ma's walked into office with a promise to address the island's economic woes and to improve Taiwan's damaged relationship with the mainland.[40]

MORE ACCURATELY DEFINING
TAIWAN NATIONALISM

Scholars on Taiwan now contend the sense of "nationalism" Western pundits find alarming is actually more an ethnic consciousness than a Westphalian political identity. As one researcher put it, "the rapid nativization is only partially reflected in positions on national identity and the independence-unification question, and its influence on concrete policy positions is even more limited ... Put simply, the trend toward Taiwanization in basic ethnic consciousness has not evolved into a political demand for Taiwan independence." (Wu Yu-shan, 2001, as translated and published in Shelly Rigger, 2006, "Taiwan's Rising Rationalism: Generations, Politics, and 'Taiwanese Nationalism,'" Policy Studies 26, East-West Center, Washington, DC, p. 7.)

Ma's first step toward realizing the latter ambition came during his inaugural address. Calling for China to work with Taiwan to "achieve peace and co-prosperity," Ma sought to bridge the political distance between Beijing and Taipei by appealing to "our common Chinese heritage."[41] Ma's employment of the term *zhonghua minzu*, was particularly telling. The phrase *zhonghua minzu* is a reference to the "Chinese nation," a vision of the Chinese people that transcends ethnic divisions and incorporates populations—like the indigenous Taiwanese—who have historically interacted and assimilated with Chinese society. As a student on Taiwan has since noted, Ma has been careful to continue cultivating this sense of being *zhonghua minzu* rather than highlighting a separate Taiwanese identify. Examples of Ma's efforts on this front include public participation in ancestor worship (Ma is the first Taiwan president to do so), presiding over ceremonies for Confucius's birthday, and officiating at a ceremony honoring the Yellow Emperor—the mythical ancestor of all Han Chinese.[42]

What does this appeal to *zhonghua minzu* do for Ma? First, it makes for good domestic politics. A 2005 survey found 46.9 percent of Taiwan's residents thought of themselves as both Chinese and Taiwanese. This sentiment was notably higher among younger voters—over 50 percent of who identified themselves as ethnically Taiwanese and Chinese.[43] Second, and more importantly, the emphasis on Chinese culture plays well with Beijing, where officials have been increasingly stressing Taiwan's cultural ties to China. As one observer noted, Ma's actions "are a strong reassurance to officials in Beijing."[44]

Ma's efforts to restore ties with Beijing have not been limited to cultural niceties. In his inaugural address, the Taiwan president also outlined his three principles for engaging with the mainland and reiterated a call for resumption of cross-Strait talks based on the "1992 Consensus." Ma's three principles—no unification, no independence, and no use of force—are largely intended to maintain the status quo in the Taiwan Strait. A wise political move given the overwhelming support for this position. His reference to the "1992 Consensus," however, was a bid to reopen talks with his CCP counterparts. As Ma summed his position, "we are ready to resume consultations."[45]

THE 1992 CONSENSUS

The "1992 Consensus" emerged from a sequence of meetings between the mainland's Association for Relations Across the Taiwan Straits (ARATS) and Taiwan's Straits Exchange Foundation (SEF). The consensus is that "both sides of the (Taiwan) Straits adhere to the 'one-China' principle," but explain that principle in separate manners. For Beijing, the "one-China principle" means there is one, undivided sovereign China—and that state is governed by the Chinese Communist Party. For Taipei, the "one-China principle" means there is one, undivided sovereign China—and that the government on Taiwan is the sole legitimate representative of that nation.

As Chinese officials have publicly stated, one of the intended consequences of the "1992 Consensus" is a tacit agreement mainland China and Taiwan belong to the same country. This position has been disputed on Taiwan. Former president Lee Teng-hui raised ire on the mainland with his "Two-states Theory," and former president Chen Shui-bian supported those who argued no consensus on the "one-China principle" had been reached during the 1992 talks.

Taiwan President Ma Ying-jeou has publicly declared the "1992 Consensus" undoubtedly exists. In his inaugural address Ma argued, "In 1992, the two sides reached a consensus on 'one China, respective interpretations.'"

In August 2008, President Ma sought to reiterate his support for the "1992 Consensus" by telling a Mexican newspaper, "We don't think the relationship between the two sides is one between two Chinas, but a special one."[46] During his August 26, 2008 interview with *Sol de Mexico*, Ma went on to contend, "The relationship is a special one, but that relationship is not between two countries." Ma's read on the situation:

> While it is unlikely that double recognition of both sides of the Taiwan Strait can be obtained from any foreign country, we must maintain a peaceful and prosperous relationship with Beijing and at the same time we would like to see both sides enjoy dignity in the international community. This is our goal.[47]

On September 3, 2008, Ma's spokesman was asked to clarify the President's remarks. Presidential Office Spokesman Wang Yu-chi sought to accomplish this task by suggesting the relationship between China and Taiwan is defined in the 11th Amendment to the Republic of China constitution. According to the 11th Amendment, "Rights and obligations between the people of the Chinese mainland area and those of the free area, and the disposition of other related affairs may be specified by law." As such, Wang's position was that the two regions are equal and have two ruling authorities whose relationship is not between the central and local governments—but one that is equal between the "free area" and the "mainland area."[48]

HISTORY IN THE MAKING

I could be rushing to judgment, but Ma Ying-jeou may ultimately be remembered as the man who paved the road to China-Taiwan reconciliation. Ma's insistence on reviving the "1992 Consensus" and dismissal of his predecessor's "two states" rhetoric has certainly opened a new chapter in relations between Beijing and Taipei. The result has been tangible progress on issues that suggest Washington's focus on the potential for a cross-Strait conflict is now overwrought. Stated more simply, we are watching history in the making. In less than a year Taipei and Beijing have made more progress on cross-Strait relations than had occurred in the previous five decades.

The first sign of this sea change occurred in Taipei on November 4, 2008. On that day, envoys from the mainland's Association for

Relations Across the Taiwan Straits and Taiwan's Straits Exchange Foundation signed 13 agreements—including a pact allowing for daily direct flights between China and Taiwan. The Chinese side was represented by Beijing's top Taiwan envoy, Chen Yunlin. Chen was the highest ranking CCP member to visit Taiwan since Chiang Kai-shek's Kuomintang government fled to the island almost 60 years ago. Under the new agreement, the number of direct China-Taiwan flights was tripled to 108 a week, and corporations are now allowed to use their private jets to ferry passengers across the Strait.[49] The agreement eliminated the previous requirement that flights between China and Taiwan pass though Hong Kong airspace. A total of 21 mainland Chinese airports will eventually be used to support the passenger flights to and from Taiwan, up from the five that had originally served in that role. Taiwan and China will also allow 60 cargo flights a month.[50] The savings for airlines and passengers—an estimated $90 million a year.[51]

While seemingly unremarkable, the flight agreement put a formal end to a ban on direct travel between China and Taiwan that had been in effect since 1949. It is only fair to note, the decision to proceed with daily direct flights had been in the making for some time. In June 2006, Beijing and Taipei had agreed allow six Taiwanese and six Chinese airlines to offer a total of 168 non-stop passenger flights during the four major Chinese holidays—the lunar new year, tomb sweeping day, and the Dragon Boat and the Mid-Autumn festivals. In July 2008, the two sides had agreed to allow for direct weekend flights between China and Taiwan.[52]

In addition to the direct flights, the November 4, 2008 agreements also provided for direct cargo shipments between China and Taiwan, and regular cross-Strait postal service. The direct cargo shipment agreement allows ships to pass between 11 Taiwan seaports and 63 harbors on the mainland. The direct shipping agreement won almost immediate acclaim from Taiwan businessmen, who contended the previous arrangement—forced stops in Hong Kong—was costing them time and an unnecessary $100 million a year.[53] Shippers had also circumnavigated the ban by making a brief stop at the Japanese island of Ishigaki. The mail agreement—once a key issue in cross-Strait talks—drew less attention, but is expected to shave about four days off the transit time for a package sent from China to Taiwan.

This progress in restoring the "three links"—direct trade, transport and postal ties—cannot be completely attributed to noble political ambitions. Ma's outreach efforts have also been promoted by his pledge to address Taiwan's economic woes. As more than one Western media service observed, by boosting ties with China, Taiwan's biggest trading partner, Ma Ying-jeou also hopes to revive the island's economy. Suffice it to say Ma's domestic political opponents have been quick to use this monetary link to criticize his efforts. On November 3, 2008—the day before the historic agreements were signed—the pro-independence Democratic Progressive Party staged a rally in Taipei protesting what they claimed was Ma's sellout of Taiwan's sovereignty in exchange for economic benefits.[54] In any case, on December 15, 2008 the agreements went into effect . . . with significant press coverage in Taipei and Beijing.

The next step in this reconciliation process occurred on December 31, 2008. In a speech commemorating the 30th anniversary of the "Message to Compatriots in Taiwan,"[55] Hu Jintao outlined a six-point proposal for normalizing cross-Strait relations. The "six-points" in Hu's speech are:

1. Firm adherence to the "one China" principle.
2. Strengthening commercial ties, including negotiating an economic cooperation agreement.
3. Promoting personnel exchanges.
4. Stressing common cultural links between the two sides.
5. Allowing Taiwan's "reasonable" participation in global organizations.
6. Negotiating a peace agreement.[56]

According to the director of the Institute of Taiwan Studies at the Chinese Academy of Social Sciences, Hu's "six-points" are intended to serve as the "guiding blueprint" for the future "peaceful development" of cross-Strait relations.[57] Perhaps the full extent of Hu's outreach is better understood by my noting the December 31, 2008 speech also included an unprecedented public effort to woo pro-independence forces on Taiwan. In his speech, Hu called on Chen Shui-bian's Democratic Progressive Party to accept the "One China" principle and "change" its pro-independence stance. Not surprisingly, Hu's efforts on this front were rebuffed. Democratic Progressive Party Chairwoman Tsai Ing-wen declared Hu's "demand that a political party must first abandon its main principles as a precondition for interaction is not in accord with democratic principles."

How significant was Hu's proposal? One Chinese scholar went so far as to argue Hu was laying the foundation for only the third strategic adjustment in Beijing's policy toward Taiwan over the last 30 years. These three strategic adjustments are said to be: (1) the shift in the mainland's policy from "armed liberation" to "peaceful liberation" before 1979; (2) the subsequent shift from "peaceful liberation" to "peaceful unification;" and (3) Hu's speech that move from "peaceful unification" to "peaceful development."[58]

I am not certain that Hu's "six-points" warrant such a grandiose interpretation, but do want to highlight a proposal in the address that holds the real possibility of preventing renewed cross-Strait armed violence. In a bid to reduce tensions, Hu declared:

> China will pursue a policy of peaceful development and the two sides can pick the right time to engage in exchanges on military issues and explore setting up a military and security mechanism to build mutual trust, which would help improve the situation in the Taiwan Strait and lesson military and security concerns.[59]

This, quite frankly, is an open invite to proceed with China-Taiwan military confidence building measures—a move Washington and all other interested parties should welcome with open arms.

Before the ink had even dried on Hu's speech, rumors began to circulate concerning Beijing's willingness to begin enacting such military confidence building measures. On January 4, 2009, *Yazhou Zhoukan*, a Hong Kong-based magazine, claimed Chinese officials were debating the issue of gradually decreasing the number of missiles Beijing has aimed at Taiwan once military exchanges had begun.[60] Taiwan's Ministry of National Defense also appears aware of such an offer. Speaking with reporters on January 4, 2009, Taiwan Defense Ministry Spokeswoman Chih Yu-lan stated "we have some grasp of this situation," when asked to comment on stories suggesting Beijing may be planning to remove some of the approximately 1,300 short- and medium-range missiles said to be targeting the island.[61] And how could Taiwan reciprocate this confidence-building measure? As one Hong Kong media pundit so ably observed, Taipei "should immediately announce that it will stop buying advanced weapons from the United States and other countries in line with Ma Ying-jeou's concept of a 'truce in military affairs.' "[62] For the moment Taiwan has limited its military confidence-building measures to setting up a think tank to coordinate contact with the People's Liberation Army.[63]

In mid January 2009, Taiwan officials began a public campaign seemingly designed to facilitate just such a move. Speaking at a monthly luncheon of the European Chamber of Commerce in Taipei, Mainland Affairs Council chairwoman Lai Shin-yuan declared Taiwan should no longer simply treat China as a threat, but instead should consider the present cross-Strait relationship as an opportunity. She then went on to state that, "faced with such closeness in cross-Strait relations, the Taiwanese government has the responsibility to adjust the unreasonable restrictions created by previous regulatory policies . . . and to resolve the wide range of problems in order that cross-Strait economic and trade relations can advance toward normalization."[64] While this statement was not widely circulated, Lai's words carry weight. The Mainland Affairs Council is responsible for supervising the Straits Exchange Foundation—the organization that negotiated and signed the historic November 4, 2008 cross-Strait contact agreements.

Perhaps the most remarkable development in this reconciliation process was Beijing's decision to allow Taipei's attendance at the May 2009 World Health Assembly. The World Health Assembly is the forum used to govern the World Health Organization. At first blush, this grand gesture seemed anything but a done deal. On March 20, 2009, Ma Ying-jeou told reporters Taiwan would not accept joint representation with China in international organizations. Instead, Ma announced Taipei the island would be willing to consider joining international organizations using one of three monikers: The Republic of China, Chinese Taipei, or Taiwan.[65] Beijing, on the other hand, appeared to ignore Ma.

On March 26, 2009, an official with China's Taiwan Affairs Office told reporters both sides should continue to "put forward efforts to create favorable conditions" for Taipei's attendance at the World Health Assembly—as an observer.[66] According to press sources on Taiwan, China had apparently agreed to support Taiwan's bid to become an "observer" under the name of Chinese Taipei.[67] On April 29, 2009, the World Health Organization informed Taiwan's Department of Health that Taipei was invited to attend the May World Health Assembly as an observer.[68] The invite signaled an apparently successful end to Taiwan's 12-year long campaign to participate in the World Health Organization and may portend an opportunity to attend other United Nations specialized agencies functions—something Taipei has been prohibited from doing since 1971. More importantly, the invite could only have come with Beijing's approval, and should be read as China's implicit understanding that Ma has no intention of using this opportunity to advocate for Taiwan's formal independence.

In his comments on the World Health Organization announcement President Ma was cautious—and mindful of Beijing's role in the decision. Ma was quick to praise his Chinese counterparts for working with his administration to improve cross-Strait relations and sought to depict the decision as a humanitarian gesture. But he was also willing to contend, "This shows that harmonious and amiable cross-Taiwan Strait relations complement rather than conflict with Taiwan's goal of international participation."[69]

Beijing's response was equally measured. An official with the mainland's Taiwan Affairs Office told reporters that China's decision to allow Taipei's participation in the World Health Assembly showed sincerity and goodwill from the mainland. Xinhua, China's official news agency, did however, tie the development to Hu Jintao's December 31, 2008 speech. Xinhua's perspective? Taiwan's observer status was granted as an element of Hu's willingness to allow Taipei "proper and reasonable arrangements" for participation in international organizations so long as this did not result in "two Chinas" or "one China and one Taiwan." Beijing's final thought on the World Health Organization announcement, "the two sides have properly settled Taiwan's participation ... through down-to-earth consultations in line with the spirit of building mutual trust ... seeking consensus ... and jointly creating a win-win situation."[70]

Beijing's hesitance is not surprising. As should be expected after 60 years of acrimony, all recent developments in China-Taiwan relations have not been pain-free. Consider, for example, Taipei's response to remarks Chinese Premier Wen Jiabao made on March 5, 2009. In a speech before China's legislature, Wen announced, "Cross-Strait relations have embarked on the track of peaceful development ... We are ... ready to hold talks on cross-Strait political and military issues and create conditions for ending the state of hostility and concluding a peace agreement between the two sides of the Taiwan Strait."[71] The response from Taipei, "a peace deal has advantages for both sides, but our thought is first to seek economic deals and political ones later."[72] Why this reticence? Analysts on Taiwan believe Ma does not have the political capital necessary to survive such a step. Struggling with a 30 percent approval rating, the Taiwan president is not prepared to resolve the domestic debate that would accompany such a move.[73]

In September, Taipei quietly rewarded Beijing's decision on the World Health Assembly by publicly announcing Taiwan would not be submitting a bid to reenter the United Nation's during the 64th General Assembly. Speaking with reporters, Taiwan's newly appointed foreign minister declared Taipei was still evaluating what approach the island should take in terms of seeking representation in the United Nations.[74] This move put an end to Taiwan's annual effort to rejoin the United Nations, a campaign that Taipei had pursued since 1993. This move apparently cleared the way for further forward progress in the China-Taiwan reconciliation process. In mid-October press sources reported Taiwan and China were preparing to open tourism offices in their respective capitals,[75] and in late October Taipei announced a relaxation of regulations concerning Chinese media representation on Taiwan.[76] I would caution, however, against reading too much into this latter development. As it turns out, Taipei only allowed the Chinese media to increase its presence on Taiwan from two to five people. And Beijing hedged on making any announcement concerning Chinese restrictions concerning Taiwan media operations on the mainland.

CHINA'S ANTI-SECESSION LAW

On March 14, 2005, the third session of the Tenth National People's Congress adopted the infamous "Anti-Secession Law." Specifically targeted at keeping Chen Shui-bian "in the box," the law includes the following provisions:

- There is only one China in the world. Both the mainland and Taiwan belong to one China.
- Solving the Taiwan question and achieving national reunification is China's internal affair, which subjects to no interference by any outside forces.
- The state shall do its utmost with maximum sincerity to achieve a peaceful reunification.
- The state stands for the achievement of peaceful reunification through consultations and negotiations on an equal footing between the two sides of the Taiwan Straits ... the two sides ... may consult and negotiate on the following matters:

- ○ Officially ending the state of hostility between the two sides.

- ○ Mapping out the development of cross-Straits relations.

- ○ Steps and arrangements for peaceful national reunification.

- ○ The political status of the Taiwan authorities;

- ○ The Taiwan region's room of international operation that is compatible with its status.

- • In the event that the "Taiwan independence" secessionist forces should act under any name or by any means to cause the fact of Taiwan's secession from China, or that major incidents entailing Taiwan's secession from China should occur, or that possibilities for a peaceful reunification should be completely exhausted, the state shall employ non-peaceful means and other necessary measures to protect China's sovereignty and territorial integrity.

A second potential glitch made news on March 14, 2009. In an apparent effort to appease his domestic critics, President Ma publicly requested Beijing remove China's anti-secession law. A presidential spokesman said Ma had called the law "unnecessary and unfeasible." According to the spokesman, Ma "believes the Chinese authorities are wise enough to know how to deal with [the anti-secession law] properly."[77] The Mainland Affairs Council issued a similar statement later the same day. According to the Mainland Affairs Council, annulling the "outdated" anti-secession law is key to maintaining peace and stability in the Taiwan Strait and would abet establishment of a "win-win" situation.[78] Ma's domestic critics, by the way, were not impressed with this gesture. And Beijing made no public comment on the entire affair.

THE PATH AHEAD

The next step in this China-Taiwan reconciliation process is the establishment of a trade agreement between Beijing and Taipei. There is some evidence that proposals for a formalization of closer economic ties with China had been an element of Ma's agenda since he came to power in May 2008. The issue, however, had been placed on a back burner awaiting completion of the agreements on cross-Strait aviation, shipping, and postal links. With the signing of these agreements in November 2008, the most obvious obstacles to such a move were cleared from table. That said, Taipei and Beijing have discovered politics on Taiwan can delay and/or derail even the best laid plans.

The public debate in Taiwan over the wisdom of establishing a broad economic partnership with China began to heat up in October 2008. On October 17, 2008, a panel of Taiwanese experts held a forum to evaluate the peril and potential of signing a Closer Economic Partnership Agreement (CEPA) with the mainland. The CEPA model was chosen as China had signed such an agreement with Hong Kong in June 2003 and with Macau on January 1, 2004.[79] While the assembled experts agreed the CEPA opened a huge market for Hong Kong goods and services, they were suspicious of Beijing's willingness to sign a similar document with Taipei. As the chairman of a pro-independence think tank put it, "what China is doing is trying to secure political power through the support of the business community and speed up reunification by economic means."[80]

Hu Jintao's "six-points" proposal on December 31, 2008 did little to allay these fears. The head of the opposition Democratic Progressive Party noted in an editorial for the *Taipei Times*, Hu had used his "six-points" proposal to reiterate there is only one China and that its sovereignty and territorial integrity cannot be changed. As such, Ma's chief domestic opponent continued, "the premise of signing a [comprehensive economic agreement] would be that Taiwan and China share the same understanding of what the "one China" principle means. Taiwan would have to adhere to the "one China" principle and become a part of China."[81] The bottom line: Ma's domestic opponents are convinced the proposed economic agreement is a de facto surrender of Taiwan's sovereignty.

Ma's response to this criticism, change the name of the agreement. By February 2009 the proposed trade pact was no longer being referred to as a Closer Economic Partnership Agreement, it was now the Comprehensive Economic Cooperation Agreement. The goal, however, remained the same . . . to facilitate the free flow of goods and services across the Taiwan Strait.[82] Interestingly, the name change came with a none-too-subtle variance in the motivations driving Ma's interest in this agreement. While the original press for such an agreement may have been primarily political—by February 2009 Taipei was hurriedly seeking a means of addressing the islands ailing economy. Like the rest of the developed world, Taiwan was suffering the fallout from the international financial crisis. Taipei's gross domestic product shrank a record 8.36 percent during the last quarter of 2008[83]—and economists on Taiwan were predicting an overall contraction of 3.6 percent in 2009.[84] Further darkening the picture, plans for China to sign a free-trade agreement with 10 members of the Association of Southeast Asian Nations in 2010.[85]

The semantic battles did not end with the move to Comprehensive Economic Cooperation Agreement. In late February 2009, Ma's cabinet announced that term would no longer be applied to the proposed agreement—instead the pact would now be referred to as the Economic Cooperation Framework Agreement (ECFA).[86] This rhetorical change was intended to further distance the proposal from Beijing's 2003 agreement with Hong Kong, but did little to ease concerns about the agreement's potential consequences for Taiwan. In addition to expressing concerns about Ma's apparent willingness to surrender the island's sovereignty, his critics now also began to claim ECFA was going to gut Taiwan's economy.

During a forum on cross-Strait business cooperation held on March 15, 2009, an economist from National Taiwan University warned the ECFA would abet further relocation of businesses to China, worsen the island's unemployment rate, and render Taiwan a minor spoke in a new China-focused "hub and spoke distribution network."[87] This grim prediction was repeated elsewhere. In mid-March, the Chung-Hua Institution for Economic Research released a study indicating the ECFA would put 120,000 Taiwan residents out of work.[88] Not to be outdone, the opposition Democratic Progressive Party declared the agreement would actually threaten up to four million jobs.[89]

Ma, and his Kuomintang counterparts, were not deterred. On March 29, 2009, Taiwan's Minister of Economic Affairs announced Taipei was considering the addition of an "opt out" clause in the proposed trade pact. According to Minister Yiin Chii-ming, "once ECFA talks get underway, the potential addition of an opt out clause will be considered [to protect us] if China fails to follow the guidelines or to demonstrate good faith in the execution."[90] Academics on Taiwan agreed this was a viable plan, arguing many international trade agreements have such clauses. For his part, Ma welcomed the public debate over ECFA—telling reporters, "The more opinions, the better the job the government will do."[91] A similar press came in addressing concerns the ECFA would be tantamount to surrendering Taiwan's sovereignty. On April 11, 2009, the chair of

Taiwan's Mainland Affairs Council stated the ECFA was purely an economic agreement. She went on to declare, "We are clear about China's intentions on unification, but the government will insist on the Republic of China's freedom, democracy, and sovereignty."[92]

By mid April 2009 it was quite clear that Ma had no intentions of backing away from the ECFA. On April 20, 2009, Taiwan Economics Vice Minister Lin Sheng-chung told lawmakers in the island's legislative yuan the government intended to sign the ECFA with China by the end of the year.[93] Reminding lawmakers of the forthcoming Southeast Asia free-trade agreement, Lin argued Taipei needed to act rapidly. In response to concerns the agreement was being forced upon an unwilling public, the Mainland Affairs Council revealed a poll during mid-April showed that over 70 percent of the island's residents supported proceeding with the Economic Cooperation Framework Agreement.[94]

And what about Beijing? As we have previously noted, Chinese leaders have learned to avoid commenting on Taiwan's domestic political disputes. Instead, Beijing has emphasized she is here to help the ailing Taiwan economy. On March 29, 2009, a Chinese spokeswoman for the Taiwan Affair's Office told reporters, "The mainland is willing to push forward such an agreement as long as it can benefit the peaceful development of cross-Strait ties, the wellbeing of people on both sides, and can help Taiwan's economy tide over the challenges it faces."[95] On April 18, 2009, Chinese Wen Jiabao told a delegation of Taiwan officials Beijing has a five-point proposal to help Taiwan's economy. According to Wen, the mainland will promote investment in Taiwan, encourage mainlanders to visit the island, buy more Taiwan goods and encourage Taiwan enterprises to tap the mainland market. He also said the two sides should try and set up an economic cooperation mechanism.[96] My observation—the Chinese have discovered progress on the Taiwan front starts with the pocketbook, and killing them with kindness.

These Chinese statements of goodwill concerning the development of closer economic ties with Taiwan continued in May 2009. During a mid-May meeting with the Straits Forum on China-Taiwan Relations, Wang Li—the director of Beijing's Taiwan Affairs Office—told his counterparts, "The mainland is willing to cooperate, ready to negotiate an agreement with Taiwan on their economic cooperation framework at the earliest possible date."[97]

While the Ma administration welcomed Beijing's gestures of largess, Taiwan's continuing economic contraction likely caused Taipei to race ahead with formalization of cross-Strait business ties. On June 30, Taiwan's Ministry of Economic Affairs announced Taipei will open 64 sectors in manufacturing, 25 in services, and 11 public infrastructure projects to investment from the mainland. Under the new regulations, Chinese companies and individuals will be allowed to invest in real estate on Taiwan,[98] to purchase up to 49 percent of an airport or harbor facility, and to place funds in the island's energy sector—including oil and gas exploration, wholesaling, and fuel retailing. Furthermore, Taiwan financial institutions are now permitted to offer services to mainland customers.[99]

This invitation for mainland investment on Taiwan was not as open-ended as might appear at first blush. Under the new guidelines, Chinese funds cannot enter Taiwan without government permission. The mainland investors are prohibited from entering monopoly industries such as water, electricity or fuel suppliers, nor can they participate in sectors considered key to the island's future economic development, financial stability or national security. Furthermore, the regulations ban investment by the Chinese military or from Chinese companies related to military purposes.[100] In other words, the Ma administration sought to lure mainland investment without drawing opposition charges of selling Taiwan's autonomy and security to Beijing.

Despite this effort to appease domestic critics, Ma's new investment regulations have generated political friction. The president's opponents claim the new regulations are likely not the speediest remedy for the island's ongoing recession, they question what Chinese businessmen are really interested in purchasing from Taiwan—the suspicion is the island's leading edge technology in display panels, integrated circuits, and silicon wafer manufacturing—and there are concerns about the source and amounts of cash Beijing could bring to bear on achieving any nefarious objective. As the director of one Taipei-based political organization put it, "Opening Taiwan to Chinese investment will create a tidal wave that will engulf Taiwan."[101] A second critic charged Ma's efforts played into Beijing's hands. "There's an intention or plan to try to enmesh Taiwan's economy, to consolidate links between the two sides, so in that way it will be more difficult for Taiwan's independence."[102]

The domestic outcry has done little to slow or alter Ma's agenda. On July 26, 2009, Ma was elected to serve as the Kuomintang chairman—a position that would allow for him to meet with Hu without violating China's self-imposed prohibition on dealing with Taiwan's leader as a head of state.[103] As the Kuomintang chairman, Ma could meet with Hu in his capacity as the head of the CCP, thereby avoiding charges Taipei or Beijing had granted the other recognition as co-equal national leaders. Hu certainly seems to understand the significance of Ma's new position. On July 27, Hu sent Ma a telegram congratulating him on his election as the Kuomintang chair—prompting the first exchange of letters between China and Taiwan's leaders in over 60 years. Hu's 73-word telegram applauded Ma's election and expressed hope the CCP will be able to work with the Kuomintang to promote peaceful relations between the two sides. Ma responded with his own short note, in which he called for continued efforts to establish cross-Strait peace and rebuild regional stability.[104]

This written exchange renewed rumors of a pending meeting between Hu and Ma. In June 2009, Beijing's official *China Daily* had published a story suggesting Ma's election as Kuomintang chair could pave the way for such a face-to-face session.[105] Taipei's mayor had also urged Ma to arrange such a meeting.[106] Ma, however, has been more reticent. In a televised interview conducted on 29 July, he called for signing a comprehensive trade pact with China—but downplayed fears such an agreement was a move toward reunification or that he was eager to meet with Hu Jintao. As Ma told his interviewer, "Once the [trade] pact is signed, it will not contain words such as 'one China' and 'peaceful unification.'" As for scheduling a sit down with the Chinese president, Ma explained, "The icy ties are just beginning to thaw and the construction of a bridge [for dialogue] is just starting. So it's better to wait until the ice has completely thawed and the remaining barriers entirely removed."[107] When is such a meeting likely? Taiwan media sources speculate the session is likely to occur in 2012—when Hu's term as the CCP is coming to an end and Ma would only have a year left in his position.[108]

Where is Ma headed? In June 2009, the Taiwan president told a magazine interviewer that his "no unification" policy did not exclude eventual reunification with the mainland. Ma then went on to note such an event certainly would not occur before 2016, when his potential second term as Taiwan's leader would come to an end. Ma's logic —he believes 80 percent of the island's resident's support his policy of maintaining the status quo, and that the issue of reunification would have to be decided by Taiwan's 23 million citizens.[109] In the meantime, Ma has continued to insist Beijing must stop targeting Taiwan with hundreds of missiles in order to extend the current thaw in cross-Strait relations. As Ma summed the situation in July 2009,

"People feel uneasy if we go to the negotiating table on security issues while still under the threat of missile attack."[110] Nonetheless, Taiwan is moving forward with tangible efforts to demonstrate a mounting trust in Beijing's long-term intentions. In July 2009, Taipei began removing anti-ship barricades that had lined the beaches of Kinmen Island[111] and there are continuing rumors of the potential for a meeting between military leaders from both sides of the Strait.[112] Ma may be moving forward on this reconciliation process cautiously, but he is moving forward—and is likely to do so regardless of opposition or public pressure to the contrary.

WRESTLING WITH THE FUTURE

It is impossible to adequately emphasize the central role Taiwan plays in Beijing's military and political calculus. This focus can be traced back to 1949—and has only become more evident over the last 15 years. For instance, in 1995 the Central Military Commission formulated the *wen nan bao bei* policy—a dictate that caused the PLA to shift planning priorities from the South China Sea to Taiwan and Taipei's "foreign supporters." The policy called for Chinese diplomats to resolve outstanding border disputes in the south, and instead focus on addressing the threat to China's territorial integrity presented by the "separatists" in Taipei.[113]

As we have seen, this press to curtail Taiwan's independence movement has apparently succeeded—but not without a cost to China. Beijing's heavyhanded tactics in 1996–96 and punitive rhetoric in 2000 caused many in Asia and the United States to question China's long term intentions. This is particularly true of China's military modernization efforts—many of which are perceived as nothing more than preparations for an amphibious assault of Taiwan. Hu's "harmonious world" campaign and "Historic Missions" expansion of the PLA's taskings may help alleviate these concerns ... but it will not make them go away.

A case in point, Western scholars continue to specifically link China's military developments to Beijing's focus on Taiwan. The 2005 Anti-Succession Law, of course, only further enforced this academic bias. An example of this tendency to inexorably link PLA modernization to Taiwan, John Lewis and Xue Litai's critically acclaimed books on the PLA. Lewis and Litai argue, "without the [Taiwan] crisis looming ever larger, Beijing's military preparations would undoubtedly atrophy, diminish as they did in the early and mid-1990s, and [China's] national programs and social energies would concentrate almost exclusively . . . on China becoming a global economic and political power."[114]

Other scholars have some to a similar conclusion. In a May 2008 article titled "China's Relations with the West: The Role of Taiwan and Hong Kong," the author declares "Hong Kong and Taiwan are fundamental to the very legitimacy of the Chinese Communist Party and China's government. They have constituted a continuing challenge to Chinese nationalism and China's potential as a great power." The scholar then states, "China's sense of itself as a burgeoning great power, increasingly wealthy and modernizing militarily, has been coupled with changes in Taiwan."[115] Following his May 27, 2009 meeting with Hu, then Kuomintang chairman Wu Poh-hsiung told reporters the Chinese president declared Beijing was prepared to negotiate and conclude the Economic Cooperation Framework Agreement before the end of the year.[116] In an apparent bid to reiterate Hu's offer, Chinese officials announced Beijing will be dispatching buying missions to Taiwan with orders for billions of dollars in an effort to bolster the island's struggling economy. According to China's Taiwan Affairs Office, between June and September at least seven Chinese business delegations would visit Taipei with the express purpose of inking deals designed to assist the island's agricultural and manufacturing sectors.[117]

Taiwan is not only critical to Beijing's focus on maintaining national integrity; the island also plays a pivotal role in China's emergence as a respected international actor. In a world where military power is largely defined by terrestrial capabilities, the "loss" of Taiwan would essentially confine China to an area west of the first island chain—Japan, Taiwan, the Philippines. This would eliminate the "strategic space" some Chinese military analysts see as critical to securing the nation's long term interests and its self-perceived role as one of the international community's primary leaders.

All of which begs the question, how will President Ma's outreach efforts affect Chinese military modernization efforts? In the short run, it does not appear the Kuomintang victory will slow the PLA's drive toward realizing the revolution in military affairs. I come to this conclusion because Beijing—regardless of events on Taiwan—likely remains convinced of the need to develop a truly regional military reach. Furthermore, the PLA is now tasked with a potentially global mission—either in defending China's economic interests, or in supporting international humanitarian/peacekeeping campaigns.

The shape of this continued military modernization, specifically weapons platforms and lift, however, may be directly impacted by events on Taiwan. If President Ma convincingly proceeds with his three nos (no independence, no unification, and no use of force), and strives to implement his five dos (adhere to the "1992 Consensus;" conclude a peace accord that is reinforced with confidence-building measures; enhance finance and economic exchanges, leading to a common market; fashion a *modus vivendi* based on pragmatism concerning Taiwan's role in the international community; and, accelerate interchange in the cultural and educational arenas) the PLA may indeed find itself owning fewer mobile missiles and a diminished number of transport ships.

For the moment, the jury on future China-Taiwan relations remains in sequestration. During the May 2008 Asian Security Summit, PLA Deputy Chief of Staff Ma Xiaotian was pleased to note cross-Strait relations have undergone positive changes since the March 22, 2008 Taiwan elections, but then also warned "Taiwan independence" forces remain problematic and serious thought about "Taiwan independence is still active within Taipei."[118]

Ma Xiaotian's optimistic comments now appear warranted given the November 2008 accords on cross-Strait links and ongoing efforts to sign a China-Taiwan Economic Cooperation Framework Agreement. However, his clear hedging on the future of cross-Strait relations likely reflects Beijing's understanding the issue of Taiwan's independence has not been permanently resolved. Mainland politicians have been burned by Taiwan's feisty electorate in the past—and are quite aware the debate over Taipei's status could once again become a rallying cry for a political party vying for support in future campaigns.

What does this mean for the PLA? First, we caution against reading too much into Ma Xiaotian's guarded assessment. Ma is not being alarmist or sending a "tough signal"—he is simply providing a pragmatic read on the current state of cross-Strait relations. Second, regardless of how rosy cross-Strait relations may currently appear; the PLA will remain tasked with preparing for a possible independence bid in Taipei. As one Hong Kong columnist so aptly noted:

> "Taiwan independence," "Tibet independence" and "Xinjiang independence" are actual threats to [Chinese] national security and territorial integrity, and "Taiwan independence" is the most serious threat of all the threats. [As such,] the PLA's strategic

requirements have not changed ... Its strategic tasks [remain] ...
safeguarding state sovereignty, national security, and territorial
integrity.[119]

Furthermore, it would be unreasonable for Beijing to relax the
PLA's modernization requirements simply because the United States,
European Union, or Japan have expressed positive attitudes about the
current state of cross-Strait relations. Beijing is well aware these "outside" sentiments could rapidly change—and that this change may not
be entirely linked to developments in China or Taiwan. Finally, "Taiwan independence" will remain a rallying cry for PLA modernization
as all good military thinkers understand "thriving in calamity and per-
ishing in soft living" is no way to prepare armed forces for countering
future threats. As more than one philosopher has declared, all militaries need an enemy—Taiwan serves that purpose for the PLA's leadership, and rank-and-file.

Indeed, Hu Jintao seems to be hedging his bets on cross-Strait
developments. In his December 31, 2008 "six-points" statement Hu
continued to frame cross-Strait negotiations under the "one-China"
principle ... and has yet to positively respond to President Ma's calls
for a "cross-Strait diplomatic truce." Nor, as a scholar at the Brookings Institution has pointed out, has Hu openly endorsed Ma's declaration of the "1992 Consensus" as "one China, with each side
having its own interpretation."[120] Instead, Hu has continued to rule
out any hints of "two Chinas" or "one China, one Taiwan" during
discussions of Taipei's international status.

The result is significant wariness among some elements of the Taiwan electorate. A former member of Chen Shui-bian's government
summed these concerns for the Brookings Institute this way:

> ... the fact that the current cross-Strait détente initiated by
> Taiwan's government has not received sufficient goodwill
> response from Beijing—especially when it comes to Taiwan's
> international space and China's reduction of military threats to
> the island—suggests a potential for instability in the near
> future.[121]

Some elements within the U.S. intelligence community also seem
worried. In his testimony before congress on March 11, 2009, the
U.S. Director of National Intelligence declared, "Taiwan ... has substantially relaxed. Leaders on both sides of the Straits are cautiously

optimistic about less confrontational relations. Nonetheless, preparations for a Taiwan conflict drive the modernization goals of the People's Liberation Army."[122] I am not—as evidence presented throughout this text has demonstrated—so sure that is really the case.

I agree that the Taiwan Strait will remain a potential source of regional instability—but less as a possible site of a conflict between Beijing and Taipei than as a constant irritant, like issues that continually crop up between South Korea and Japan. Seoul and Tokyo may issue belligerent statements and rattle their equally capable proverbial military sabers, but they are not preparing for a war in the near future. We need to learn to think of China and Taiwan in a similar manner— particularly if President Ma is able to continue to pursue his efforts at cross-Strait détente.

All of which begs the question, how should Washington approach China-Taiwan relations in the coming 10 years? Well, the U.S. intelligence community and Department of Defense appear determined to keep the United States on watch . . . to continually be preparing for a war with China over Taiwan. As we noted at the beginning of this discussion, many Western China-watchers seem to believe this watchfulness is warranted. Fortunately, they are not the only voices in the crowd. In early March 2009, Robert Sutter—a Visiting Professor of Asian Studies at the School of Foreign Service, Georgetown University—opened the debate by arguing U.S. policy makers need to reevaluate China's growing influence over Taiwan. For Sutter, a former member of the U.S. intelligence community and Congressional Research Service—Beijing's mounting sway over Taipei was evident economically, diplomatically and militarily. Sutter thus concludes, "The longstanding notion of U.S.-supported balance in the Taiwan Strait is no longer viable in the face of ever-increasing Chinese influence over Taiwan."[123] His bottom line: Washington may be well-served by adapting to this new reality and stepping away from a Taiwan policy largely based on armed defense of Taipei's democracy.

ONE COUNTRY, TWO SYSTEMS

Beijing has long argued the most obvious solution to the China-Taiwan standoff is to employ the policy that was used for Hong Kong in 1997 and Macau in 1999—one country, two systems. Deng Xiaoping reportedly advanced the concept of "one country, two systems" in January 1979 and stated that "so long as Taiwan returns to the embrace of the motherland, we will respect the realities and the existing system there." On September 30, 1981, Ye Jianying, chairman of the Standing Committee of China's National People's Congress, officially put forward a nine-point proposal for bringing about the peaceful reunification of the mainland and Taiwan. Ye reportedly declared that "after China is reunified, Taiwan may become a special administrative region. It may enjoy a high degree of autonomy and may keep its military forces. The national government will not intervene in the local affairs of Taiwan. Taiwan's current social and economic systems will remain unchanged, its way of life will not change, and its economic and cultural ties with foreign countries will not change." In 1982, a provision on setting up special administrative region was added to the Constitution of the People's Republic of China, thereby providing a legal basis for accomplishing "one country, two systems." (————, May 17, 2004, "A Policy of 'One country, two systems' on Taiwan," Embassy of the People's Republic of China.)

Members of the Brookings Institution, a nonprofit, nonpartisan public policy think tank based in Washington, took umbrage with Sutter's argument. First, the Brookings's scholars wrote, the U.S. role in the Taiwan Strait has not been to maintain a balance of power that favors Taipei—but rather to maintain peace and stability in the Strait.[124] Second, they continued, while China's ability to influence Taiwan is growing, "the mere creation of capabilities does not mean that they will or can be used—nor that efforts to do so would be unopposed." As such, the solution to Taipei's perceived problem is exercise of Taiwan's democratic system and by "strengthening the fundamental pillars of its security." In this case five pillars are identified: Taiwan's internationally competitive economy; her effective, two-party political system; a modest military deterrent; sensible diplomacy; and, a strong relationship with Washington. Proper application of these pillars—Brookings concludes—could serve to lay "a foundation for a cross-Strait relationship on terms acceptable to both sides, which is the goal not just of the United States but Taiwan and [China] as well."[125]

Finally, David Shambaugh—a longtime China watcher—weighed in on this topic with an evaluation of the Obama administration's strategic agenda with China. Shambaugh, the director of George Washington University's China policy program and the Elliott School of International Affairs, argued in April 2009 that the Obama administration has a unique opportunity to reshape Washington's role by not proceeding with arms sale to Taiwan and seeking to address Beijing's military threat to the island.[126] As best Shambaugh could tell, the United States could facilitate further advancement in the China-Taiwan reconciliation effort by urging Beijing to curtail elements of the PLA modernization that specifically threatened Taipei. In closing, he went on to note a probable requirement for Washington to "undertake a thorough Taiwan Policy Review given the dramatic and positive changes in cross-Strait relations."[127]

I tend to agree with Shambaugh—the United States needs to conduct a bottom-up review of Washington's ties to Taipei. I am not suggesting we abandon the island—or relinquish pressure on China to complete military confidence-building measures that could serve to further diminish the cross-Strait tensions. I suspect Robert Sutter is correct, Taiwan is increasingly under China's thumb . . . and the only way to prevent negotiations from becoming dictation is for the United States to continue demonstrations of our support for Taipei's democratic system. This support, however, does not have to include armed might. Washington needs to engage Beijing with the intent of causing Hu to formally commit to his "Harmonious World" policy—particularly in regard to dealing with Taiwan. Given President Ma's continued press for China-Taiwan détente such a move should come with little domestic political cost for Hu, and might serve to help remove the largest impediment to improved U.S. -China relations. The long-term solution? Somehow I suspect we are going to be revisiting the concept of "one country, two systems" in the not-so-distant future.

CHAPTER 6

The China Model

Chinese-style socialism has exhibited nonpareil superiority. The China model has demonstrated strong vigor and energy.
—Liu Yunshan, Director of the Department of Publicity, October 2008[1]

Chinese Communist Party leaders are understandably proud of what Deng Xiaoping's "reform and opening" policy has accomplished. But we need not depend on Beijing's propaganda machine to discover the underlying reasons for this pride. My favorite bit of data on this subject comes from the World Bank, whose analysts have argued that since the economic reform program began in 1978 approximately 400 million Chinese have been rescued from absolute poverty—and another 400 million were spared entering those miserable ranks as a result of China's one-child policy.[2] As Paul Wolfowitz—then the World Bank president and a renowned neoconservative—declared, "That's never happened before in history." Wolfowitz is not alone in coming to this conclusion. Some academics now argue China's modern poverty reduction has occurred on a scale unprecedented in mankind.[3]

Beijing's success has not passed unnoticed. There is a growing chorus of academics, policy makers, and popular pundits who believe China may be the paradigm for developing states in the twenty-first century. These advocates of the so-called China model point to six areas as a means of explaining why the Chinese Communist Party has succeeded where so many others have failed. These six pillars of success are:

1. A pragmatic approach to reform—resisting the advice of international financial institutions and experts to engage in shock therapy, choosing instead to implement reform gradually

2. Active state intervention in the economy—setting policy, establishing regulatory agencies, controlling foreign investment, and mitigating the adverse effects of globalization

3. Pursuit of economic reform before democratization

4. Acknowledgment of the importance and legitimacy of human rights while challenging the Western claim there is a universal consensus as to what those rights are—arguing instead human rights are contingent on local circumstances

5. Establishment of an alternative to liberal democracy—authoritarian capitalism—thereby potentially addressing perennial problems with social inequality and human well-being that democracy fails to resolve

6. A foreign policy focused on sovereignty, self-determination, and mutual respect—a professed intent to peacefully coexist and avoid power politics[4]

This admiration is not limited to academics, as Randy Peerenboom notes in his landmark text, *China Modernizes: Threat to the West or Model for the Rest?* "Vietnam has closely followed the economic, legal, and political reforms in China. Laos ... followed China's lead in implementing market reforms," and "Iran and other Middle Eastern countries have invited experts on Chinese law, economics and politics to give talks to government officials and academics."[5] Why all this adulation? Quite simply, the China model works. The Chinese Communist Party has facilitated unprecedented economic growth and a historic elimination of poverty and is working to establish a legal and governance system that surpasses similar institutions found in most African, Middle Eastern, and Latin American Nations.[6]

For all this success, the China model is not wanting for critics—particularly in the West. As a case-in-point, in November 2007 the American Enterprise Institute—a Washington-based conservative think tank—published a lengthy critique of the China model claiming the system is actually "economic freedom plus political repression."[7] According to the American Enterprise Institute, China's new system of governance's only advantage over "the standard authoritarian or totalitarian approach is obvious: it produces growth, which keeps people happy." Despite this adamant rejection of the China model's political philosophy, the American Enterprise Institute could not answer its own fundamental question about Beijing's Chinese-style socialism: Can it be sustained over the long run?

A similarly critical evaluation of the China model appeared in a November 2008 article published by the Jamestown Foundation.[8] Written by Willy Lam—a senior fellow at Jamestown who has long expressed concerns about Beijing's political system—the piece contends the China model under Hu Jintao has become a means of "striking a balance between growth and stability—and between market initiatives and state control." According to Lam, the current Chinese leadership would have us believe the China model "is an antidote to the kind of unbridled capitalism that underpins the financial woes in Western world."[9] But, Lam goes on to argue, the complacency bred by this perceived success could undermine implementation of "bold reforms" necessary for China's continued economic and political evolution. Where are these "bold reforms" to ultimately lead? I will allow Lam to explain in his own words. "And should the party elite succumb to a kind of triumphalism over the supposed superiority of authoritarian socialism with Chinese characteristics; the prospects for liberalization could be dealt a severe blow."[10] In other words, for Lam the China model will only be successful when it "evolves" into Western-style democracy and free-market capitalism.

Perhaps the most thoughtful recent critique of the China model was offered by the Glasshouse Forum—a nonpartisan consortium of academics and private enterprise charged with reflecting on the merits and problems of capitalism. In a 2008 report titled "The Limits of the China Model," the Stockholm-based Glasshouse Forum contends:

> There is little reason to conceive of a wholesale China model. First, there never was one model, as different economic experiments were tried in different places. Second, there have been both successes and failures. Third, the gravest and most important test still awaits the Chinese leadership. This is how to solve the growing problem of a democratic deficit and the demands from a changed social landscape in the future.[11]

More specifically, the Glasshouse Forum holds that the current China model fails to provide the "clear vision" required for the Chinese Communist Party's continued claim to legitimacy. According to the Swedish researchers, Beijing's long-term political dilemma cannot be repeatedly addressed through budgetary formulations. Instead of this economic focus, China's leaders will have to tackle an expected demand for greater political participation within their "middle-income country."[12] As the Glasshouse team puts it, "The challenges ahead for the Chinese leadership will be more political than economic—demands for legal rights, transparency, and democratic accountability."[13]

This is indeed an interesting debate. On the one hand we have those who appear to see the China model as a viable alternative to Western free-market, liberal democracy. On the other we are confronted by critics who contend the China model is little more than an evolutionary step on the way to arriving at free-market capitalism and liberal democracy. I am not so certain the future is that black and white. The Chinese Communist Party has clearly stumbled—I use the term purposely; this result was not planned—into what appears a sustainable form of governance. The current China model has done more to alleviate the suffering of the Middle Kingdom's vast peasant population than any previous form of governance. Furthermore, the current China model seems to have provided for a more responsible form of capitalism than that practiced in the United States or Europe. But, I will readily admit, the current China model seems destined to run headlong into a Chinese citizenry intent on winning greater say in their governance.

Is there a way out of this dilemma? My position is yes, and Beijing—contrary to Willy Lam's argument—is taking steps to address the problem. The challenge is to convince Western policy makers that this is indeed the case—that they do not need to be planning for the "Coming Collapse of China" or the "Coming Conflict with China" because Chinese leaders failed to adequately prepare for the future. This will be no easy task. As we shall see, Western academics have poorly prepared the policy community for understanding China's adaptability.

WHY THE WEST BELIEVES THE CHINA MODEL MUST FAIL

American foreign policy is not an intellectual orphan. That is to say, Washington's relations with other nations are rarely simply based on pragmatism. Instead we find policy makers are often pursuing an agenda that can be traced to academic arguments and philosophies that—at first blush—seemed little more than idle chatter among the denizens of various ivory towers.[14] Unfortunately, as the Neocons have now discovered, the philosophers and academic speculators don't always arrive at an appropriate conclusion. Sometimes these deep thinkers are significantly off the mark.

Allow me to demonstrate. In 1989, Francis Fukuyama, a former Rand analyst and then-Deputy Director of the State Department's policy planning staff, published an essay titled "The End of History?" Written as the former Soviet Union visibly collapsed and China's dalliance with capitalism transitioned into a permanent state of affairs, Fukuyama's piece heralded "the total exhaustion of viable systemic alternatives to Western liberalism."[15] More specifically, Fukuyama told the policy community:

> What we may be witnessing is not just the end of the Cold War, or the passing of a particular period of postwar history, but the end of history as such: that is, the end point of mankind's ideological evolution and the universalization of Western liberal democracy as the final form of human governance.[16]

In this brave new world, national governments would be "liberal insofar as [they] recognize and protect through a system of laws man's universal right to freedom, and democratic insofar as [they] exist only with the consent of the governed."[17] This is a noble vision—and one that won much acclaim, even among American political scientists.

In September 1989, Lucian Pye, a renowned sinologist and then-President of the American Political Science Association, stood before his assembled colleagues and declared they were witness to the "crisis of authoritarianism." Pye insisted political science needed to get busy studying and explaining the imminent demise of what he argued were "all manner of authoritarian systems."[18] According to Pye, authoritarian regimes were fundamentally challenged by the rise of global communications systems, expanding educational opportunities, international trade, and the effects of contemporary science and technology. Furthermore, Pye was willing to argue "the presumed advantages of totalitarian practices for economic development have apparently evaporated."[19] All of these points led him to conclude, "The long historical trend that favored the strengthening of centralized state power has seemingly come to an end, and the trend now favors the pluralism of decentralized authority."[20] For Pye, like Fukuyama, the future promised national governments who worshiped at the West's temple of free markets and liberal democracy.

As it turns out, everyone was not reading from the same script. The economic success realized by the so-called Asian tigers (China, Hong Kong, Indonesia, Japan, Malaysia, Singapore, South Korea, Thailand, and Taiwan) coupled with their clear deviation from the principles espoused by Western liberal democracy caused some academics to wonder if there wasn't another option. The living embodiment of this so-called authoritarian capitalism was Lee Kuan Yew, Singapore's prime minister from 1959 to 1990. According to Lee, while there was much to respect in West's concept of liberal democracy, there were also no end of shortcomings. In an interview published in *Foreign Affairs*, Lee declared:

> [There are] things that I have always admired about America . . . a certain openness in argument about what is good or bad for society; the accountability of public officials; none of the secrecy and terror that's part and parcel of communist government. But as a total system, I find parts of it . . . unacceptable: guns, drugs, violent crime, vagrancy, unbecoming behavior in public—in sum the breakdown of civil society. The expansion of the right of the individual to behave or misbehave as he pleases has come at the expense of orderly society. In the East the main object is to have a well-ordered society so that everybody can have maximum enjoyment of his freedoms. This freedom can only exist in an ordered state and not in a natural state of contention and anarchy.[21]

Needless to say, Lee's regime and his comments drew significant flack from the West—particularly from academics who took umbrage with his contention that individualism and materialism might undermine "Asian values" and thereby detract from the tigers' economic performance.[22]

The critics, however, faced a steep uphill battle. While they could criticize the authoritarian practices resident within many of the tiger governments, it was difficult to dispute their economic successes. This argument was rendered even more difficult by a 1993 World Bank report titled *The East Asian Miracle: Economic Growth and Public Policy*. According to the World Bank, "the East Asia miracle—achieving high growth with equity—is due to a combination of fundamentally sound development policies, tailored interventions, and an unusually rapid accumulation of physical and human capital." But, the authors continued, there was more to the story:

> In most of these economies the government intervened—systematically and through multiple channels—to foster development, and in some cases the development of specific industries. Policy interventions took many forms. Policies to bolster savings, build strong financial markets, and promote investment with equity included keeping deposit rates low and maintaining ceilings on borrowing rates to increase profits and retained earnings, establishing and financially supporting government banks, and sharing information widely between public and private sectors. Policies to bolster industry included targeting and subsidizing credit to selected industries, protecting domestic import substitutes, supporting declining industries, and establishing firm- and industry-specific export targets.[23]

Stated more succinctly, in addition to maintaining good social order—which frequently meant suppressing individual political activities—the Asian tiger leadership frequently, and in some cases successfully, intervened in Adam Smith's marketplace but chose to maintain the fundamentals of a capitalist system.

Academic and policy maker interest in this authoritarian capitalism might have continued to flourish had it not been for the 1997–1998 Asian financial crisis. The International Monetary Fund's $40 billion bailout package—coupled with the organization's call for afflicted governments to implement strict monetary and contractory fiscal policies—called into question the staying power of this emerging governance model. More than one academic claimed the entire fiasco could be attributed to "crony capitalism,"[24] and Paul Krugman, an economist who subsequently was awarded the Nobel Prize, declared the growth realized in Asia's tiger economies was probably caused by an "extraordinary mobilization of resources" rather than authoritarian policies.[25] In short, by the late 1990s many Western policy makers were convinced authoritarian capitalism was a temporary phenomena, a stage in the gradual evolution to liberal democracy. They were wrong.

Rather than fading away, the authoritarian capitalists appeared to develop a remarkable staying power. Vladimir Putin's perceived rescue of Moscow's moribund economy and China's continued high growth rates suggested that perhaps there was more to the story.

Instead of disappearing, the authoritarian capitalists actually seemed to be thriving. This disconcerting development was brought to the fore for Washington's policy elite in July 2007, when *Foreign Affairs* published Azar Gat's "The Return of Authoritarian Great Powers." Gat, the Ezer Weizman Professor of National Security at Tel Aviv University, used his essay to argue Russia and China's rise suggested "capitalism's ascendancy appears to be deeply entrenched, but the current predominance of democracy could be far less secure."[26] As Gat put it, "all that can be said at the moment is that there is nothing in the historical record to suggest a transition to democracy by today's authoritarian capitalist powers is inevitable."[27]

In George W. Bush's Washington these were fighting words. The first shot back across Gat's bow came from Michael Mandelbaum, the Christian A. Herter Professor and Director of the American Foreign Policy program at the Johns Hopkins University School of Advanced International Studies. In an essay titled "Democracy Without America," Mandelbaum hoisted the torch for those who believed authoritarian capitalist states were simply at a way point on the path to democracy. According to Mandelbaum, "the key to establishing a working democracy . . . has been the free-market economy. The institutions, skills, and values needed to operate a free-market economy are those that, in the political sphere, constitute democracy."[28] For Mandelbaum, free-market capitalism did more than build institutional and social skills requisite for a democracy. The Johns Hopkins professor went on to argue participating in a free-market economy cultivates two habits essential for democratic government: trust and compromise. His bottom line, "For a government to operate peacefully citizens must trust it not to act against their most important interests and, above all, to respect their political and economic rights."[29] So where is China in this process?

Mandelbaum dodges the question. While he admits China has undergone a "dizzying change" that has installed "many of the building blocks of political democracy," Mandelbaum notes the Chinese Communist Party is "determined to retain its monopoly on political power."[30] As such, he believes the Chinese Communist Party is willing to forcefully squelch any organized political opposition and bid for popular support by pointing to the country's economic successes. Furthermore, Mandelbaum holds many Chinese are loath to be plunged back into the chaos that so traumatized pre-1976 China. This does not mean Mandelbaum thinks Beijing will be able to ward off democracy forever. Revealing his determinist tendencies,

Mandelbaum ultimately concludes democracy may come to China because pressure for adopting this form of governance "grows wherever nondemocratic governments adopt the free-market system of economic organization."[31]

Unfortunately for Mandelbaum, this predilection for democracy in free-market economies does not appear permanent. As Larry Diamond—coeditor of the *Journal of Democracy*—noted in March 2008, "If democracies do not more effectively contain crime and corruption, generate economic growth, relieve economic inequality, and secure freedom and the rule of law, people will eventually lose faith and turn to authoritarian alternatives."[32] So how to avoid this problem? Diamond contends democratic institutions "must listen to their citizens' voices, engage their participation, tolerate their protests, protect their freedoms, and respond to their needs."[33] The assertion here, of course, is that the Chinese Communist Party does none of these things—a premise we now know to be erroneous. In fact, Beijing appears headed down the very path Diamond would have us believe essential for any democracy—"rigorous rules and impartial institutions."[34] This would lead me to believe we are coming full circle and Gat was right—we are preparing for a revival of authoritarian great powers.

But not before "The End of History" fans get in their two cents. In January 2009, Daniel Deudney—a professor of political science at Johns Hopkins—and G. John Ikenberry—the Albert G. Milbank Professor of Politics and International Affairs at Princeton—took their shot at rebutting Gat's hypothesis. In an essay bluntly titled "The Myth of Authoritarian Revival: Why Liberal Democracy Will Prevail," Deudney and Ikenberry argue "the proposition that autocracies have achieved a new lease on life and are emerging today as a viable alternative within the capitalist system is wrong."[35] According to the two professors, today's authoritarian regimes may be more competent and capitalist compatible, but they remain "fundamentally constrained by deep-seated incapacities that promise to limit their viability." What are these "incapacities"? Deudney and Ikenberry identify three: corruption, inequality, and limitations on governmental performance due to weak accountability and insufficient flows of information.[36]

Here's how this argument works. First, on the issue of corruption, Deudney and Ikenberry contend authoritarian regimes struggle with bribery and graft because officials are not restrained by institutional checks on state power. Liberal democracies, they claim, solve this problem with constitutions and the rule of law. Inequality, Deudney and Ikenberry continue, is resolved in a democracy through universal franchise and the rise of political parties who cater to various socio-economic classes within a society. Authoritarian capitalists, for the two professors, have no such option and thus are at a stage "where the other shoe has not dropped in their political evolution." And the limits on performance? According to Deudney and Ikenberry, "closed political systems are prone to policy mistakes arising from bad information." Liberal democracies, on the other hand, are said to "flourish" as a result of a capacity to "mutate in the face of new problems."

At this point the cynic is allowed a loud guffaw. A review of the last week's *Washington Post* or *New York Times* indicates the same three flaws abound within liberal democracies. Washington's continuing battles with campaign finance abuse, lobbying, and members of Congress under criminal investigation suggests there is no shortage of corruption in liberal democracies—even one as open and mature as the United States. Nor has the debate over socioeconomic inequality been successfully addressed—witness the labor unions continuing battles with corporate America or the sad plight of many African Americans. And poor government performance? The ongoing international financial crisis—largely a result of lax government regulation—clearly indicates poor policy can be crafted even with full access to all the information. (We shall pass on a conversation concerning the limits and filters on information making its way to elected representatives on Capitol Hill—suffice it to say all voices are not granted an equal hearing; normally those with money get the final say.)

Back to Deudney and Ikenberry. Given these fundamental "incapacities," the representatives from Johns Hopkins and Princeton become advocates of a determinist philosophy. Like Mandelbaum, the two professors believe that authoritarian capitalist regimes are little more than an evolutionary stage en route liberal democracy. To wit, they argue, "autocratic capitalism is not an alternative model; it is only a way station" on the path to liberal democracy.[37] As such, Deudney and Ikenberry recommend the policy community do little more than acknowledge authoritarian states' grievances and "inherited vulnerabilities" and then "mollify and ameliorate them." "A successful foreign policy," Deudney and Ikenberry continue, "should also seek to integrate, rather than exclude, autocratic ... powers." Why? "The foreign policy of the liberal states should ... be based on the broad assumption that there is ultimately one path to modernity—and that is essentially liberal in character."[38]

In short, we should not be surprised the U.S. policy community does not know how to deal with a rising China—they have been repeatedly told the Chinese Communist Party is actually facilitating its own obsolescence. But what if this advice is wrong? What happens if the Chinese Communist Party's abandonment of Marx, Lenin, and Mao has set the stage for establishment of a permanent fixture? That is to say, the China model may not be an evolutionary way point, but rather a viable means of long-term governance. Then it would seem imperative to offer policy makers a new perspective and provide a more comprehensive understanding of their Chinese counterparts. Yes, counterparts. Using the term "adversary" also would be deterministic—just because the Chinese are not practicing liberal democracy does not *ipso facto* make them an enemy. It is from this premise that we begin the next stage of our investigation.

BEIJING'S CONCEPT OF THE CHINA MODEL

The Chinese Communist Party is confronted with a very real dilemma. The economic miracle spurred by Deng's "reform and opening" has undermined the socialist ideology that once served as the Party's claim to legitimacy. Beijing's pragmatic response to this development—Jiang Zemin's "three represents" and Hu Jintao's "harmonious society"—has arrested the emergence of potential political challengers, but cannot completely staunch the bleeding. By introducing and expanding forms of private ownership, encouraging income disparities, and inadvertently abetting widespread corruption, the Chinese Communist Party appears destined for the fate Deudney and Ikenberry so vividly outlined—liberal democracy.

Or maybe not. Before we step aboard Deudney and Ikenberry's deterministic speeding bus a moment of contemplation is in order. Western critics of China's current dictatorship of the proletariat should always recall the Middle Kingdom has a long history of extraconstitutional rule. Perhaps it would be more appropriate to declare China has an almost 4,000-year-long history of single party governance. One can argue Sun Yat-sen set the stage for democratic revolution, but I would counter by noting the chaos that accompanied this experiment is not fondly remembered in China. The Chinese citizenry wants a stable, fair hand at the tiller. Hu Jintao and his fellow travelers are working diligently to meet that expectation. More specifically, the Chinese Communist Party is diligently seeking to correct the three "incapacities"—corruption, inequality, and limitations on governmental performance due to weak accountability and insufficient flows of information—that Deudney and Ikenberry use to predict a change in Beijing's chosen form of governance.

This brings us back to Beijing's concept of the China model. In September 2003, Hu Jintao and other Chinese leaders began promoting a new approach to managing China's growth called the "scientific development concept." This new approach aims to correct the perceived overemphasis on economic expansion and address China's mounting social and ecological concerns. As Hu put it:

> It is necessary to solidly adopt the scientific development concept of coordinated development, all-round development, and sustainable development, [and to] actively explore a new development path that conforms to reality, further improves the socialist market economic structure, combines intensified efforts to readjust structure with the promotion of rural development, combines efforts to bring into play the role of science and technology with efforts to bring into play the advantages of human resources, combines the development of the economy with the protection of resources and the environment, combines opening up to the outside world with opening up to other parts of the country, and strives to take a civilized development path characterized by the development of production, a well-off life, and a good ecological environment.[39]

This is no modest agenda. In one fell swoop Hu is seeking to address sustainable development, social welfare, a person-centered society, increased democracy, and, ultimately, the creation of a harmonious society. In the United States we would dismiss such a grandiose proposal as campaign rhetoric—in China this was a call to action.

Hu's "scientific development concept" received an official endorsement from the Chinese Communist Party in October 2003. During the Third Plenary Session of the 16th Central Committee, Chinese officials decreed "[We] take the people as the main thing, [and thus seek to] establish a concept of comprehensive, coordinated, sustainable development, and promote comprehensive economic, social, and human development."[40] This statement is a concise summary of Hu's thoughts—now let's turn to a discussion of what the Party is doing to meet these tasks. As we have previously addressed Hu's efforts on the economic and social welfare front, the following discussion examines the Chinese Communist Party's current and future efforts to combat corruption, contend with increasing demands for political participation, and assure constituents it fully intends to protect their fundamental human rights.

Chinese Communist Party leaders are clearly engaged in a campaign to realize the "scientific development concept." The initial efforts came in December 2003, when the Party convened Beijing's first-ever conference on "human resources." While the sessions were ostensibly focused on more effectively employing China's total workforce, i.e., matching skills with economic requirements, the conference now appears to have been intended to begin a thorough Chinese Communist Party house cleaning. In his address to the assembled cadre, Hu stressed the Party needed to establish "a selection and appointment mechanism that is open, competitive, and selective."[41] Chinese Premier Wen Jiabao was equally adamant. Taking direct aim at the Party's selection processes, Wen called for disregarding seniority and doing away with nepotism.[42] The goal was management of Party membership in a manner that rewarded performance and tackled a very visible problem with cadre corruption.

This bid to check official corruption continued in February 2004, when the party promulgated the "Regulations of the Communist Party of China on Inner-Party Supervision" and the "Communist Party of China Regulations on Disciplinary Measures." According to Chinese media sources, these regulations were primarily designed to address official corruption and to regularize procedures within the Party by "balancing the distribution of power."[43] These objectives were said to be facilitated by a requirement for annual reports from discipline inspection commissions, and through a stipulation that there be votes on all major Party decisions. In short, Hu Jintao was taking the visible steps toward curtailing China's corruption problem.

The next step in this "scientific development concept" was publication of a white paper on democracy in China. Speculation on Beijing's response to perceived popular demands for greater political participation on the mainland have been on the rise since the July 2003 mass demonstrations in Hong Kong. Dissatisfied with China's heavy hand on their city's governance, Hong Kong residents had taken to the streets in a bid to demand a transition to the more complete exercise of democratic principles within the Special Administrative Region. More specifically, the Hong Kong citizenry was seeking popular election of their chief executive. Although these demands were effectively placed on hold until 2020,[44] Chinese leaders evidently realized they needed to confront this phenomenon head on.

BEIJING'S RESPONSE TO "CHINESE DEMOCRACY"

The Chinese Communist Party has demonstrated a remarkable willingness to engage in self-criticism, but has little sense of humor when similar critiques are offered by outsiders—particularly musicians. While music fans may have waited more than 15 years for Guns and Roses to complete "Chinese Democracy," Beijing quickly dismissed the new album as "noisy and clamorous." Chinese bloggers were equally downbeat. Some bloggers condemned the album as an effort to stir up ill will against China. Other Chinese Internet users simply followed the government's lead—one going so far as to declare, "Forgive them; they haven't been on top of the world for hundreds of years. It's tough to avoid becoming outdated." (Ben Blanchard, November 25, 2008, "Beijing Brushes off 'Chinese Democracy,'" REUTERS, Beijing.)

"Building of Political Democracy in China," the white paper likely generated as a result of this realization, was published in mid-September 2005. Released through the State Council Information Office, "Building of Political Democracy in China" is a 33-page compendium of Hegel, Marx, Mao, Deng, and Jefferson. This paper is painful reading even for those of us used to wading through such ponderous tomes—the document does, nonetheless, provide a few glimpses into Beijing's vision of mass political participation now and into the future. Let us begin with the here and now. According to the white paper, China currently practices socialist political democracy with "distinctive Chinese characteristics." The characteristics are as follows:

- China's democracy is a people's democracy under the leadership of the Chinese Communist Party
- China's democracy is a democracy in which the overwhelming majority of the people act as masters of state affairs

- China's democracy is a democracy guaranteed by the people's democratic dictatorship
- China's democracy is a democracy with democratic centralism as the basic organizational principle and mode of operation. Democratic centralism requires that full play be given to democracy and that matters of concern are discussed collectively[45]

As I said, the document reeks of Hegel, Marx, and Mao, but there are moments of Deng and Jefferson, specifically a lengthy discussion on "grassroots democracy."

According to the authors of "Building of Political Democracy in China," the "inevitable trend and ... important base for the improvement and development of political democracy with Chinese characteristics" rests with expanding the scope of China's grassroots democracy.[46] Practiced in both rural and urban areas, grassroots democracy is said to allow "the Chinese people to directly exercise their legal rights of democratic election, democratic decision-making, democratic management and democratic supervision."[47] What does this really mean? Well, the white paper would have us believe that this grassroots democracy ensures local officials are fully accountable to their constituency. In practice, however, the theory is far from being in effect.

In the white paper's conclusion Beijing admits all is not well in China's version of socialist democracy. According to the document, China's political democracy suffers a number of "major" problems—including:

- The democratic system is not yet perfect
- The people's right to manage state and social affairs, and economic and cultural undertakings as masters of the country in a socialist market economy, are not yet fully realized
- Laws that have already been enacted are sometimes not fully observed or enforced, and violations of the law sometimes go unpunished
- Bureaucracy and corruption still exist
- The mechanism of restraint and supervision over the use of power needs further improvement
- Political participation of citizens in an orderly way should be expanded[48]

In short, China's whole system of socialist democracy is falling short of the mark. But this does not mean Beijing is preparing to throw the baby out with the bath water. Instead the Chinese Communist Party declares it will build political democracy by adhering to four principles:

1. Upholding the Chinese Communist Party's national leadership role
2. Giving play to the characteristics and advantages of the socialist system—the primary elements being Chinese Communist Party leadership and unity in striving to realize socialist modernization
3. Being conducive to social stability, economic development, and continuous improvement of the people's lives
4. Facilitating the safeguarding of national sovereignty, territorial integrity, and state dignity[49]

By now I think we all get the central message. Beijing is going to foster development of a very specific form of democracy—a form that retains the Chinese Communist Party as the nation's unchallenged leadership, abets economic development, prevents chaos, and preserves the Middle Kingdom's sovereign status. More importantly, however, this form of democracy is also intended to curtail corruption and prompt government accountability, at least at the local level. Grassroots democracy is really nothing more than a public evaluation of official performance. By meeting citizen expectations local cadre members are allowed to retain their position. Failure to meet constituent demands could cause some Chinese Communist Party members to go looking for work.

Hu Jintao has been adamant about adhering to this Party line. In his October 15, 2007, report to the 17th National Congress, the Chinese President outlined his vision of China's future governance by arguing, "We must keep to the path of political development under socialism with Chinese characteristics, and integrate the leadership of the Party, the position of the people as masters of the country, and the rule of law."[50] Hu then went on to identify six areas necessary for achieving this objective:

1. Expand the people's democracy and ensure they are masters of the country. We need to improve institutions for democracy, diversify its forms and expand its channels, and we need to carry

out democratic elections, decision-making, administration, and oversight in accordance with the law to guarantee the people's rights to be informed, to participate, to be heard, and to oversee.

2. Develop primary-level (grassroots) democracy and ensure that the people enjoy democratic rights in a more extensive and practical way. The most effective way for the people to be masters of the country is that they directly exercise their democratic rights in accordance with the law to manage public affairs and public service programs at the primary level, practice self-management, self-service, self-education, and self-oversight, and exercise democratic oversight over cadres.

3. Comprehensively implement the rule of law as a fundamental principle and speed up building of a socialist society under the rule of law to ensure that all citizens are equal before the law, and safeguard social equality and justice and consistency, sanctity and authority of the socialist legal system.

4. Expand the patriotic united front and unite with all forces that can be united.

5. Accelerate the reform of the administrative system and build a service-oriented government.

6. Improve the mechanism of restraint and oversight and ensure that power entrusted by the people is always exercised in their interests. We will focus on tightening oversight over leading cadres and especially principle ones, over the management and use of human, financial and material resources, and other key positions.[51]

In short, Hu is demanding the people be granted authority to exercise local authority as a means of holding Chinese Communist Party cadre accountable. He is not—repeat not—suggesting China become a liberal democracy as understood in a Western context.

Some observers inside and outside China appear to have a hard time accepting this fact. Perhaps the most celebrated example is the ongoing "Charter 08" movement. "Charter 08,"—an eight-page document inspired by Czechoslovakia's "Charter 77"[52]—went into public circulation on December 10, 2008. In the document, the signatories declare "authoritarianism is in general decline throughout the world; in China too, the era of emperors and overlords is on the way out."[53] Rather than continuing with Chinese Communist Party rule, "Charter 08" states "the path that leads out of our current predicament is to divest ourselves of the authoritarian notion of reliance on an 'enlightened overlord' or an 'honest official' and to turn instead toward a system of liberties, democracy, and the rule of law."[54] The document then goes on to highlight 19 areas in need of reform—ranging from a new constitution to protection of the environment. Originally signed by approximately 2,000 Chinese citizens, by late March 2009 over 8,500 persons had attached their name to the document.[55]

Needless to say, Chinese authorities have been less than enthusiastic about the "Charter 08" movement. Some of the more prominent signatories have been questioned and detained,[56] but the Party does not seem inclined to suppress this exercise in civil disobedience in as draconian a manner as that used on Falun Gong members.[57] That said, Chinese Communist Party leaders have forthrightly stated China will never adopt a Western-style democracy with a multiparty system. In a March 2009 speech before the National People's Congress, Wu Bangguo—then China's chief legislator—bluntly observed, "We will never simply copy the system of Western countries or introduce a system of multiple parties holding office in rotation. Although China's state organs have different responsibilities, they all adhere to the line, principles and policies of the Party."[58] The bottom line: Don't expect a significant deviation from single-party rule in the foreseeable future.[59]

This insistence on maintaining a single-party political system has not prevented Chinese authorities from seeking to address domestic and international concerns about Beijing's human rights record. In April 2009, Chinese authorities released the government's first-ever working plan on human rights protection. Titled the "National Human Rights Action Plan of China," the document pledges progress on a wide array of economic, political, and social issues. Economic promises include a right to work, right to basic living conditions, and a right to education. Political concerns covered in the document include rights of the person—a prohibition on extortion of confessions by torture—right to a fair trial, and right to oversee state implementation of laws and regulations. Social rights to be addressed include women's rights, senior citizen rights, and the rights of the disabled.[60] I realize it is tempting to dismiss this document as little more than propaganda, but the very fact Beijing felt it was necessary to publish such a statement speaks volumes about where the Chinese leadership believes they should head. This candor is even evident in the human rights plan. In the document's introduction Beijing admits

"China has a long road ahead in its efforts to improve its human rights situation."

Where does this leave us? I would argue China's leadership is intent on establishing a functional authoritarian regime that maintains its claim to legitimacy based on economic and political performance. The efforts to address corruption, battle various forms of inequality, and hold Party officials accountable suggest Hu Jintao and company are also working to resolve "incapacities" that may have contributed to the demise of other authoritarian regimes. In some senses, the Chinese Communist Party is thus being prepared to transition from a dictatorship of the proletariat to a dictatorship for the proletariat. But it will remain a dictatorship.

As Andrew Nathan and Bruce Gilley observe in *China's New Rulers: The Secret Files*, Hu and Wen "want to soften authoritarian rule, make it more responsive, and use the media and some political institutions, such as elections and courts, as tools to discipline the lower bureaucracy. But they think that their society is too complex and turbulent to be governable by a truly open, competitive form of democracy."[61] My thought is that Hu's China model is a beneficent form of authoritarian capitalism—a system where one's political and economic freedom ends where the perceived requirement to protect the state and Party begins. This precarious balancing act is successful, and probably sustainable, because the Party realizes it must periodically redraw the lines and remain sensitive to the population's demands. It is also sustainable because the Chinese citizenry believe this form of governance works.

WHAT THE CHINESE THINK OF HU'S CHINA MODEL

I come to this conclusion as a result of reviewing polling data collected over the last 10 years. In 2002, the East Asia Barometer, a comparative study of popular attitudes toward politics in Asia, found 94.4 percent of surveyed Chinese agreed "our form of government is best for us."[62] In June and August 2005, a Western public polling organization[63] discovered 76 percent of Chinese respondents agreed, "The free enterprise system and free market economy work best in society's interests when accompanied by strong government regulations."[64] And in 2008, the Pew Global Attitudes survey found 86 percent of Chinese were satisfied with the direction their country was headed.[65]

This is not to say the Chinese are completely satisfied with the way the government is handling all the nation's problems. The 2008 Pew Global Attitudes survey found 78 percent of the respondents complained about official corruption. The same survey shows 89 percent of Chinese identify the gap between rich and poor as a major problem. Nonetheless, 65 percent said they believe the government is doing a good job addressing issues that are most important to them—suggesting accountability had not become a major problem for the Chinese Communist Party.[66] These findings, of course, beg the question: are Chinese respondents truthful when responding to pollsters? If one felt there might be negative consequences for responding in a manner Beijing found unacceptable the tendency to be less than completely truthful would also explain these results. As it turns out, academic research on this subject has found Chinese survey respondents tend to be honest.[67] So it appears the Chinese are concerned about corruption and equality—as Deudney and Ikenberry would have predicted—but perhaps not so concerned as to suggest a growing demand for a transition to liberal democracy.

While the average Chinese citizen may be largely satisfied with how the Chinese Communist Party is attempting to govern the country, the same cannot be said of China's opinion leaders. Reporters working in China now claim the country is being pulled in two directions. On the left are proponents of a more traditional socialist system, on the right are advocates of increased democratization. As China struggles to recover from the current global recession these two camps have made a vocal bid to alter Beijing's policy priorities. The left—largely composed of young or middle-aged intellectuals—support maintaining a market economy, but are pushing for a stronger government hand in guiding that economy and in ensuring a more equitable distribution of the nation's wealth. The right—a much larger group consisting of liberal intellectuals, party veterans, and economists—support capitalist-style reforms and China's continuing "opening up."[68]

According to a professor at Shanghai's Fudan University, the leftists believe they represent grassroots interests, particularly in rural areas. The right, on the other hand, advocate political reforms that would foster "universal values"—such as democracy, human rights, and liberty. The leftists argue this shift would too closely align China with the West and damage China's sovereignty.[69] The common ground for both camps? Criticizing the government. The left faults Beijing for abetting social injustice via rapid development of a capitalist economy. The right condemns the government for the slow pace of political reforms leading to democratization.[70] The solution: a characteristically Chinese campaign to find a compromise and/or middle ground.

In fact, this search for a compromise is exactly where Hu Jintao appears to be heading. In October 2007 Hu surprised many China watchers by naming two, rather than a single, heir apparents. Xi Jinping—who is now destined to replace Hu in 2012—and Li Keqiang—who will be taking Wen Jiabao's position—represent opposite sides of two informal coalitions that currently jockey for control over China's policy apparatus. Xi is said to side with the elitist coalition, the "princelings" who aim to advance the interests of entrepreneurs and middle class. Conversely, Li is thought to be a member of the populist coalition, a group of policy makers set on realizing Hu's "harmonious society" by attending to the needs of farmers, migrant workers, and the urban poor. Xi is known to favor market liberalization and continued development of the private sector—he will likely push continued economic growth and further Chinese integration into the world economy. Li is more concerned about the unemployed and providing affordable housing, and he advocates further development of China's social safety net—he is thought to favor reduction of economic disparities over enhancing economic efficiency.[71]

As Cheng Li, the research director and senior fellow at the Brookings Institution's John L. Thorton China Center, observes, this policy divide at the top may be just what the doctor ordered. Instead of magnifying the political divisions—and thereby potentially setting the stage for emergence of competing parties—Xi and Li may prove a complementary pairing. Cheng Li puts it this way:

> The economic prowess of the princelings will be essential to responding to the macroeconomic challenges the country will face [in 2009] and beyond. And the sensibilities [Li Keqiang represents] ... will be invaluable as China responds to social problems born of—and exacerbated by—economic stagnation. The rise of the team of rivals arrangement may result in fewer policies aimed at maximizing GDP growth rates at all costs. Instead, it might give way to policies that provide due consideration to both economic efficiency and social justice.[72]

In other words, Hu may have come upon a means for ensuring the Chinese Communist Party satisfies the maximum number of constituent demands without surrendering to liberal democracy. Such a development would only add further popular support for Hu's China model and likely ensure Beijing's authoritarian capitalism remains a viable contender for other political systems.

THE CONFUCIAN OPTION

As might be expected in a nation with 1.3 billion residents, the debate over China's political evolution includes more than two options. Rather than simply focusing on democracy or authoritarianism, some Chinese scholars have suggested reviving Confucianism. Advocates of this argument contend enduring political reform in China must be founded on the country's traditions. One element of this transition to a more "Chinese" form of governance would be to revive instruction in Confucian values. The Confucianist contention is that if communism is dead as a unifying principle, it is time to revive Chinese classics. At least one Chinese university has already made the "four Confucian classics" compulsory reading, setting the stage for a phasing out of texts authored by Lenin or Marx. This movement is still in its nascent stages, and seems unlikely to replace Hu Jintao's "scientific development concept" anytime in the foreseeable future. That said, the Muslim world's rejections of globalization and Western cultural imperialism could find a Chinese equivalent in the Confucianist movement—a cause that could result in Beijing's adoption of a true China model. (Daniel Bell, May 12, 2009, "The Confucian Party," *New York Times*, New York.)

UNHAPPY CHINA

As we have seen, Chinese Communist Party efforts to hone the China model are in no small measure driven by domestic constituencies. Beijing is certainly guilty of seeking to impress foreign audiences—the capitol city overhaul that proceeded the 2008 summer Olympics is a case in point—but this public image campaign does not explain Hu Jintao's political reform efforts or Deng Xiaoping's decision to adopt free-market practices. These initiatives are driven by demands at home and have been tweaked along the way in order to meet an increasingly politically sophisticated citizenry.

The problem with this approach is that Deng's move to "socialism with Chinese characteristics" stripped the Party of the communist ideology that had been used to buttress Mao's, Deng's, and even Jiang Zemin's claim to legitimacy. As Christopher Hughes, a reader in International Relations at the London School of Economics, has observed, Deng's reform and opening policy transitioned the Party from leading a class struggle and press for socialist egalitarianism to directing a campaign calling for loyalty to the nation—and thereby the Chinese Communist Party.[73] Deng actually set the stage for this transition by defining the Party's "three major tasks" for the 1980s as "opposing international hegemonism, Taiwan's reunification with mainland China, and economic construction." For Deng, "modernization is at the core of all these three major tasks, because it is the essential condition for solving both our domestic and our external problems."[74] This sweeping call for modernization through economic development set the Party adrift from Marx, Lenin, and Mao. It also set the stage for the rise of modern Chinese nationalism.

Now we have wandered into an intellectual minefield. Chinese and Western scholars have struggled mightily to describe and define China's new nationalist fervor. Some academics argue Chinese nationalism is little more than a "natural outgrowth of China's recent accomplishments and very unhappy narratives."[75] Others contend Chinese nationalism stems from public anger over perceived foreign slights and a citizenry dismayed over perceived mishandling of domestic issues.[76] There is a third school, however, who hold China's nationalism is pragmatic—that it is "state-led and largely reactive ... is not fixed, objectified, and defined for all time; nor is it driven by any ideology, religious beliefs, or other abstract ideas."[77] Advocates of this theory assert nationalism is an instrument the Chinese Communist Party uses to rally public support and maintain a sense of unity during the transition from Mao's socialism to Hu Jintao's moderately prosperous society.[78] As such, Chinese nationalism is said to pair China with the Party, making one indistinguishable from the other.

This pragmatic nationalism seems to have emerged in a sequence of three stages. The first occurred following the Tiananmen Square demonstrations in 1989. Seeking to repair its political legitimacy in the aftermath of the Tiananmen crackdown, the Chinese Communist Party engaged in a campaign emphasizing patriotism and nationalism. The second stage occurred in the early 1990s, when Chinese intellectuals began to criticize what they believed was the West's cultural imperialism. During this period the Chinese began calling for a "Sinoization" of learning and culture, largely abandoning a previous propensity for Western ideas. The third stage, the spread of mass nationalism, emerged with the publication of *China Can Say "No."* Released in 1996, this polemic critique of Chinese fascination with Western culture and a broad condemnation of American foreign policy was a surprise best seller. As one scholar put it, "this book fanned the spread of nationalism among the general public."[79]

What is this Chinese nationalist identity? Peter Gries, the author of *China's New Nationalism*, describes the sentiment as a product of history and the century of humiliation. According to Gries, "Chinese nationalists today find pride in stories about the superiority of China's '5000 years' of 'glorious civilization.' "[80] I agree but suggest we need to add one more element—a distinct pride in China's recent accomplishments, specifically her economic miracle and demonstration of international prowess, as illustrated by the 2008 Olympics. The Chinese Communist Party uses this new national pride both to drive continued modernization and to enhance Beijing's negotiating position on the international front.[81] Furthermore, the Party uses this nationalism to enhance its legitimacy—who else should take credit for China's economic growth and be entrusted with continuing this push for prosperity?

Sometimes, however, this new Chinese nationalism can get out of hand. The first such incident appears to have taken place in 1996, when Chinese citizens participated in a violent anti-Japanese demonstration caused by a continuing dispute over ownership of the Senkaku islands. Large-scale anti-American rallies—including stoning of the U.S. embassy in Beijing—took place following the 1999 accidental bombing of a Chinese diplomatic facility in Kosovo. In 2001, the collision between a Chinese fighter and U.S. reconnaissance aircraft ignited further anti-American demonstrations. In 2003, the Senkaku dispute again spurred anti-Japanese rallies, and in 2005 Tokyo was widely condemned for seeking a permanent seat on the United Nations Security Council. Finally, in 2008 Chinese citizens returned to the streets to protest some Western nations' announced plans to boycott the Olympic Games opening ceremony as a means of demonstrating unhappiness with China's crackdown in Tibet.

While none of these incidents threatened the Chinese Communist Party's hold on power, the demonstrations caused renewed international concerns about China's "peaceful rise" and prompted some academics to begin debating the potential double-edged sword Chinese nationalism represented for Hu Jintao. As it turns out, Chinese nationalism could not only serve to legitimize Party rule, it could also provide a standard for evaluating the Chinese Communist Party's performance—at home and abroad. Nicholas Kristof, coauthor of *China Wakes: The Struggle for the Soul of a Rising Power*, summarized the Party's dilemma this way: "All this makes nationalism a particularly interesting force in China, given its potential not just for conferring legitimacy on the government but also for taking it away."[82] This problem, as we shall see, is not going to be resolved in the foreseeable future. If anything, it is going to get worse. The Chinese Communist Party increasingly finds itself criticized "as neither confident nor competent enough to safeguard China's vital national interests."[83]

The most recent example of just such a critique appeared in March 2008. *Unhappy China: The Great Time, Grand Vision and Our Challenges* chastises the Chinese Communist Party leadership for being too deferential to the West and contends Beijing should use the nation's economic clout to establish a position in the international community commensurate with China's stature.[84] The authors of *Unhappy China* sum their position as follows:

> With Chinese national strength growing at an unprecedented rate, China should stop debasing itself and come to recognize the fact that it has the power to lead the world, and the necessity to break away from Western influence . . . . From looking at the history of human civilization we are most qualified to lead this world; Westerners should be second.[85]

Taking direct aim at the international financial crisis spurred by the investment strategies practiced on Wall Street, the *Unhappy China* authors declare, "If China stood as the world's top country, it would not act like the United States, which has been irresponsible, lazy and greedy, and engaged in robbery and cheating. [Washington has] brought economic recession to the whole world."[86] The authors' proposed solution—China should exercise the ambition necessary to reestablish the world order. Beijing should assume a leadership role among nations and seek to upgrade the country's industries while other nations are busy struggling to resolve the global financial crisis.[87]

The message resident in *Unhappy China* likely was of little surprise to Beijing. Several of the text's authors were also contributors to *China*

Can Say "No." In fact, while newspapers in Hong Kong[88] and New York[89] were busily warning this latest publication was sure to stoke further nationalist fever in China, Beijing was apparently working to ensure that was not the case. On March 25, 2009, less than two weeks after *Unhappy China* appeared in bookstores, China's official news agency published a story titled "Book Rallying for Social Change Fails to Inspire Masses."[90] According to the Xinhua news release, "although the book is a hit among academicians and scholars, it seems to poorly resonate among ordinary readers." The story also provided scathing reviews from professors at two of China's most prestigious universities. Shen Dingli, the Deputy Dean of the International Relations Department at Shanghai's Fudan University, was quoted as condemning the book for being "too extreme and nationalistic." Shi Yinhong, a professor at the Renmin University of China, declared the book was full of leftist criticism but lacked "constructive suggestions."[91]

Chinese official news agencies were not the only source of domestic criticism for *Unhappy China.* Two days after the Xinhua story was distributed, a professor of history at Shanghai Normal University provided an interview to *Xinmin Weekly* summarized as "I Oppose the Nationalism of False Pride—A Criticism of *Unhappy China.*" The professor's observation: "There is no question that what the authors of this book are promoting is a high-pitched, vainly arrogant and radical form of nationalism . . . this form of nationalism is by its own logic a Pandora's Box that will release monsters that cannot be put back."[92] On March 31, 2009, *Southern Metropolis Daily*, a newspaper distributed in the Pearl River delta, published a commentary headlined " 'Unhappy China' is All for Show." Written by a professor at Nanjing University, the commentary argues *Unhappy China* "surged with naked Darwinism," and that the authors "disregard all facts and all logic and sink into their own fantasies, saying what they please without presenting an argument."[93] China's bloggers were divided over the book's value. Some rejected the text as a bitter rant from the left, while others felt there may be merit in the arguments but worried China was not ready for such a leadership role.[94]

The bottom line is that China's citizens are proud of their nation— and they expect the Chinese Communist Party to tirelessly work to restore the prestige once claimed by the Middle Kingdom. What is more telling, however, is Beijing's apparent willingness to allow debate over how the Party should proceed to occur in public. That *Unhappy China* was published and then widely sold (estimates of over

150,000 copies by May 2009[95]) is indicative of a regime that recognizes it must allow for a more open debate of ideas. I would also note that the message resident in *Unhappy China* suggests that even Hu Jintao's critics believe his China model is working. China's economic successes are the foundation for *Unhappy China's* boldest declarations concerning Beijing's future. And the fact they were allowed to publish such claims are evidence Hu's calls for "political participation of citizens in an orderly way" are now coming to fruition. Finally, I contend we have little to fear in Chinese nationalism. As Beijing has demonstrated in its response to *Unhappy China*, the Party is learning to control this emotional energy so that it does not serve to alarm the neighbors or endanger the existing domestic political hierarchy. Given Beijing's increasingly sophisticated employment of media and public messages, I believe this ability to keep a lid on the pot will only improve in the coming years.

CONCLUSION

So we return to the question of whether the current China model is sustainable—more specifically, is it a viable alternative to liberal democracy or simply a way point en route that final destination? As we have seen, Chinese leaders are quite sensitive to the three "incapacities" Deudney and Ikenberry identified in January 2009. This sensitivity comes across in a number of manners, from Hu Jintao identifying fixes for the Party to an official abetting of nationalism, and is likely to remain in place for the foreseeable future. But I am not at all convinced Beijing's answer to this sensitivity is a wholesale adoption of Western liberal democracy. China's history, culture, and current political system all suggest single party rule is a fixture Washington needs to learn to accept.

What do the Chinese mean by democracy? The best response I have seen to this query was provided by Wen Jiabao during a 2006 session with a delegation from the Brookings Institution. Wen told the group, "When we talk about democracy, we usually refer to three components: elections, judicial independence, and supervision based on checks and balances."[96] If we recall that Deudney and Ikenberry's three "incapacities" are corruption, inequality, and accountability, it seems Wen is quite aware of the China model's greatest challenges. So what does Wen envision? According to the Brookings delegation, the Chinese Premier predicted elections in China would expand gradually from villages, to towns, then counties, and possible provinces. The goal is to select and promote competent local leaders. (Wen made no comment about elections reaching the national level.) In discussing the judiciary, Wen stressed the need for reform to assure "dignity, justice and independence." As for 'supervision," Wen told his audience this was necessary to restrain abuses of official power and called for the implementation of checks and balances within the Chinese Communist Party to promote greater accountability.[97]

Much of Wen's vision is beginning to happen in China, but at a pace Westerners might find maddening. Competitive popular elections occur in over 700,000 villages representing nearly 700 million residents—but the democracy movement has yet to gain significant traction above this level. China is working to realize impartial rule of law. Over the last 30 years the Chinese have passed over 250 new laws, and are in the midst of establishing a national code from nothing. While the Chinese constitution was amended in 1999 to declare the nation is officially "governed according to law," this is an event in the making. The primary hurdle will be implementation at the local level and in politically sensitive cases. As we have also seen, the checks and balances Wen calls for are starting to appear in the Chinese Communist Party. That said, a movement to more complete accountability is an uphill battle. Hu Jintao and Wen Jiabao know that rooting out corruption is critical to maintaining the Party's legitimacy, but they also need to retain the loyalty of local officials, so do not expect a nationwide ethics and standards crackdown any time soon.

All of this suggests some form of democracy is taking root in China. The timeline for a more compete adoption of what one suspects will become "democracy with Chinese characteristics," however, remains relatively open-ended. Chinese officials have told U.S. scholars: "No one predicts 5 years. Some think 10–15. Some say 30–35. And no one says 60."[98] That observation reminds me of the People's Liberation Army modernization guidelines—progress by 2020, but no major breakthrough until 2050. Nonetheless, Beijing clearly is doing more than simply thinking about how to transition from the more traditional authoritarian model to a more sustainable version of beneficent single-party rule, one with answers to the three "incapacities."

Policy makers in Washington and the West should be aware of these specific efforts and timelines. The Chinese Communist Party is not planning to serve as a way point on the path to liberal democracy —and will not appreciate being treated as though they can simply be waited out. The same is now true of the Chinese citizenry.

Emboldened by China's economic performance and her growing international stature, the Chinese people will likely not accept a leadership that appears to kowtow to outside demands. Thus the success of the China model becomes a blessing and a curse: A blessing in that China's success at home has earned respect and admiration abroad. A curse in that a little success breeds demands for more. China's leaders are going to find it increasingly difficult to meet the demands for continued economic development generated by previous performance. I suspect that meeting—or at least perceptibly striving to meet—these demands is, and will continue to be, the predominate effort for China's leaders.

Epilogue

The future pattern of China-East Asia relations will be one featuring China in East Asia, instead of China's East Asia .... As
China increasingly grows into a stabilizing force ion the region
and as China's rise is unstoppable, the United States needs to further readjust its thinking toward China, change its erroneous
practice of viewing China as its major rival in its security strategy
in this region, and regard China not only as an important partner
in the economic field bit also an important partner in political
and security fields.
—Wu Xinbo, Associate Dean of the School of International
Relations and Public Affairs, Fudan University, 30 June 2009[1]

In June 2009, I had the opportunity to teach a seminar on China's
future for students enrolled in a master's degree program at the
National Defense Intelligence College. The 15 individuals in the
seminar came from a wide swath of U.S. government agencies and
were typically well on their way to a successful career in Washington.
What they all surprisingly lacked was something more than a cursory
understanding of China. Over the course of two weeks, I heard arguments ranging from "China doesn't matter," to "Beijing is Washington's coercive competitor in waiting." In short, it appears as though
even well-educated Americans have ignored developments in China
for the last 10 years ... perhaps awaiting the day "they" would become
more like "us."

If we accept the thesis of Martin Jacques' *When China Rules the
World: The Rise of the Middle Kingdom and the End of the Western World,*

it's going to be a long, fruitless wait. Jacques, an advocate of economic determinism, uses a 2007 Goldman Sachs study as the launching point for his argument. According to Goldman Sachs, China's economy will surpass the United States in 2027 and be approximately twice as large in 2050.[2] As economic might is the foundation of at least political and military prowess, Jacques contends China's rise will result in a world where Shanghai will overshadow New York, the renimbi will replace the dollar, Mandarin will join English as the global *lingua franca*, and Chinese learning and values will supplant Western culture. For Jacques, "The debate over values will be rooted in culture rather than ideology, since the underlying values of society are primarily the outcome of distinctive histories and cultures."[3] And, he continues, because China in 2050 will be the dominant international economy, the West will have to adapt to operating in an environment where the community trumps the individual, social relationships are more important than law, and stability is more desirable than freedom.

Disquietingly, Jacques apparently does not believe the West will have much say in this matter. He contends, "As the dominant global power, China is likely to have a strongly hierarchical view of the world, based on a combination of racial and cultural attitudes."[4] On this we can agree, China as the Middle Kingdom perceives international relations as a hierarchy based on "rightful rule." If we have learned anything from Beijing's behavior over the last 10 years it is that the Chinese are more interested in becoming a responsible international actor than assuming Washington's role as the global policeman. However, Chinese history strongly suggests the Middle Kingdom is more likely to focus on cultural developments at home than seek to impose them on barbarians abroad. It is always useful to recall the Chinese chose to burn their fleet in the fifteenth century after purportedly discovering the world had little new to offer. Jacques has clearly forgotten this lesson, as he discovers a new menace from China—cultural imperialism. In fact, Jacques would have us believe Beijing's perception of China as the center of civilization will lead to a "profound cultural and racial reordering of the world in the Chinese image."[5]

So, I tell the students, rather than looking more like us, at least one author believes we will begin to look more like them. This is an uncomfortable notion for Americans, particularly those employed within the U.S. federal bureaucracy. More than one of the master's candidates immediately chimed in with the contention "it's time we did something" about China's rising economic might. This, of course, resulted in a long conversation about Beijing's monetary policy and the true value of the yuan. It also, not unexpectedly, refreshed a class-wide debate over the real nature of the China "threat."

Yes, despite Beijing's best efforts, many Americans still believe the Chinese harbor ill-intentions for our future. Consider, for example, the following e-mail I received from Bill Gertz—a *Washington Times* reporter and author of *The China Threat: How the People's Republic Targets America*—in the midst of my preparations to teach the master's seminar:

Sent: Thu 5/28/2009 11:18 PM
Subject: Re: The China Threat

Well, since you asked: The problem is the legacy of what I call the "benign China" school of China affairs specialists who have come to dominate both the policy and intelligence communities and who brook no dissent from those who regard China as a threat, or even a potential threat. The reading lists and academic agenda at all the service schools and academies reflect this misguided view. The political advisers at Pacific Command and elsewhere in Asia also are adherents of this view.

This benign China view is an outgrowth of the Joe Nye "self-fulfilling prophecy" straw man argument that if China is treated as a threat (by the United States) it will become a threat. This outlook also jives nicely with Chinese strategic deception and influence operations that are calculated to play down China's military buildup as non-threatening, even though by almost any measure, China's forces appear to be developing on a war-footing. Our senior leaders continue to scratch their heads about "China's intentions" being opaque, when it is more than clear what their intentions are: they are preparing for a war with the United States, over Taiwan, over sea lanes of communication, over island chains, etc.

In recent years this false outlook is becoming more and more difficult to sell. Take the issue of China's nuclear forces buildup, something that the benign China specialists feel they can mitigate by seeking to engage China's Second Artillery in "talks." In April 2006 at the DC summit President George Bush specifically asked Hu Jintao if Second Artillery commander Gen. Jing Zhiyuan to visit Stratcom as part of this engagement effort. Hu indicated he would make the visit happen. More than three years later, no

Gen. Jing (who by the way visited South American military leaders in 2007 but could not find the time to stop off in the U.S.

Similarly, the "responsible stakeholder" strategy also has
failed. China's communist and military leaders believe they cannot hold stakes with their ultimate main enemy. And the idea that
China can be drawn into responsible international behavior is a
self-delusion.

The ultimate solution to the problem of the China threat is
recognize that the strategy of just trading with China as a way
to mitigate the threat is not and will not work. That ultimately
China's leaders need to be convinced that the current path
of economic reform without political reform will not work
and ultimately will lead to the break up of China as a unitary
state. The solution is some form of democracy with Chinese
characteristics.

Bill Gertz[6]

The essence of Gertz's position—a not uncommon response, by the
way—we should avoid becoming more like them, by making them
more like us. This is an argument that is unlikely to advance the
conversation or do policy makers much good. With the exception of
chastising perceived threats to China's security or national unity, Beijing has used the last 10 years to learn how to successfully operate
inside of an international political and financial system the United
States has dominated since World War II.

Gertz, I would note, is not alone in this perspective. In May 2009,
Foreign Affairs published an article titled "The G-2 Mirage: Why the
United States and China Are Not Ready to Upgrade Ties." The essay,
written by two senior members of the Council on Foreign Relations,
argued "the current lack of U.S. Chinese cooperation does not stem
from a failure on Washington's part to recognize how much China
matters . . . . It derives from mismatched interests, values, and capabilities."[7] The authors then proceed to tick off a short list of these fundamental mismatches. At the top, different views on sovereignty,
sanctions and the use of force. They condemn Beijing for being
focused on resources and export markets, while the West is praised
for seeking to "prevent human rights abuses and improve governance
in the developing world."[8] In other words, Chinese pragmatism is
misguided, while the West's cultural imperialism is to be praised and
emulated on a global scale.

The next mismatch the Council on Foreign Affairs chooses to highlight: "China's authoritarian but decentralized political and economic system." The apparent problem with this system—Beijing cannot be depended upon to cooperate on product safety or environmental issues. Furthermore, the Chinese are condemned for lacking the legal infrastructure necessary to enforce intellectual property rights. We already know the Chinese are aware of these problems and are seeking to address same.[9] But what the authors seem to have forgotten is that Washington has long been the most prominent opponent to the Kyoto Protocols, the international environmental treaty intended to provide for the "stabilization of greenhouse gas concentrations in the atmosphere at a level that would prevent dangerous anthropogenic interference with the climate system."

And then there is the issue of transparency—specifically on military front. While the Council on Foreign Relations acknowledges Beijing's rational decision to not highlight her military shortfalls, they take Washington's side in arguing transparency on this front might help avoid miscalculation and mishaps. On this point they lose me. Beijing, as we have seen, is certainly aware of the People's Liberation Army's (PLA) strengths and weaknesses. With the exception of seeking to defend her claimed territorial waters and meet Hu Jintao's taskings under the new "historic missions," the PLA has been kept on a very short leash. Nonetheless, the Council on Foreign Relations would have us believe the perceived lack of Chinese transparency makes it difficult to gauge China's intentions.[10] Apparently there is no sleep to be had until the Chinese show us the keys to the castle—a demand no rational actor will completely accept in today's Westphalian international system.

Finally, the Council on Foreign Relations is concerned because China pursues an economic agenda that is not entirely in synch with Washington's expectations. Apparently Beijing's insistence on boosting employment through strict currency management, protection of shaky domestic markets, and lack luster protection of intellectual rights is not in meeting with international standards.[11] But I have a hard time reconciling these demands with the buy American clauses written into Washington's 2009 economic stimulus act, our continued efforts to strictly limit Mexican trucking in the United States , and the rampant industrial espionage that continues to occur within Western corporations. It does appear the Council is suggesting we have one set of standards for China—and another for ourselves. No wonder the Chinese appear set to pursue their own agenda.

In fact, the Chinese are now clearly champing at the bit. Beijing's continuing efforts to level the playing field include: lobbying for a greater say in the International Monetary Fund;[12] participation in the Group of Eight (G-8) summits;[13] and, chastising the West for failing to properly regulate the financial institutions that caused the 2007–09 global economic crisis.[14] (A saying circulating on the internet is indicative of Chinese thinking when it comes to the 2007–08 financial meltdown: "In 1949, only Socialism could save China. In 1989, only China could save Socialism. In 2009, only China can save Capitalism."[15]) Beijing is not likely to back away from this increasingly activist role.

Data released in mid-summer 2009 suggest China is poised to demand a greater say in a number of international forums. In July 2009, the National Bureau of Statistics of China announced that the country had realized an annual increase in her gross domestic product of 7.1 percent and appeared to be reaping the benefits of Beijing's $586 billion stimulus package.[16] This announcement came only a day after we learned China's foreign exchange reserves now total $2.13 trillion[17]—the largest on the planet by twice—and a mere 24 hours before Western press sources announced China had overtaken Japan as the world's second-largest stock market.[18] Western impressions of China's rise? George Soros, the famous American billionaire, offered this telling quote: "China is going to be a positive force in the world and the market, and as a consequence, its power and influence are likely to grow. Personally, I think it's going to grow faster than most people now expect."[19]

These demonstrated successes have not, however, put a halt to the debate over the utility of the China model. While British Prime Minister Gordon Brown declared the "the old Washington consensus is over" during his press conference at the conclusion of the April G-20 summit,[20] and Great Britain's foreign secretary told reporters "[China] has become an indispensable power economically, and . . . will become an indispensable power across a wider range of issues,"[21] Western pundits continue to dismiss Beijing's approach to governance as overrated. A set of articles published at the end of May 2009 is illustrative of this mindset.

On 25 May 2009, *Newsweek*, published an article titled "Why Bow to China?" After acknowledging the accolades Beijing has received from academics and politicians, the *Newsweek* authors declare, "China is much bigger than its neighbors in terms of the size of its economy, but by other measures—technology, per capita GDP or the strength of its institutions—its far from supreme." Furthermore, they argue, "The China model is hardly superior to its rivals for Asian leadership." Japan, they contend, is less corrupt and better managed, South Korea is more innovative, and Singapore has proven sophisticated employment of information technology can more than compensate for sheer size. Rather than recognize China as a predominate entity in the region, the authors conclude "There are ways to promote an Asia of many powers."[22] (As we have seen, this is exactly what the Chinese have been attempting to accomplish—apparently my students are not the only Americans who have not been watching and listening to Beijing.)

An op-ed published in the *Wall Street Journal* on the same day comes to a similar conclusion. In "China's Modern Authoritarianism" Perry Link and Joshua Kurlantzick posit:

China's material successes . . . suggest the government's top priority is economic growth. The increasing socioeconomic diversity in Chinese society suggests the regime seeks liberalization and might one day throw open its political system. These are dangerous misconceptions. The Party's top priority remains what it has always been: the maintenance of absolute political control.[23]

Link and Kurlantzick then go on to observe, "The Party's adaptive methods of disruption and distraction have helped maintain control during a period of rapid change, suggesting a durable domestic model of authoritarian governance." That said, the two authors are not convinced Beijing's system has staying power. As they put it, "The China model, although a definite threat to democratic values, is no juggernaut. Its appeal abroad will depend in large part on how the Chinese economy weathers the global downturn, and how any stumbles it might encounter are perceived in the developing countries."[24]

In a sign of just how broadly this condemnation of the China model has spread on 26 May 2009 the *Economist* published an article advising readers to be cautious of Beijing's siren song. In "Beware the Beijing Model," the *Economist* frames the conversation by contending, "The economic downturn has . . . opened the door to a seemingly alternative ideology to the West's liberal-market approach . . . . Instead of placing one's trust in the market, the future of economic growth is seen to be coming from a more muscular state hand on the levers of capitalism."[25] However, the *Economist* continues, "What the Beijing model means in practice is unclear." The magazine's editors agree the

Chinese Communist Party's adherence to centralized control of the nation's economy has spurred extraordinary growth. But, the author's then note, this success would not have been possible without the associated American appetite for foreign goods. All of which causes the *Economist* to rhetorically ask, "Would this China model exist at all, but for its American counterpart?" Their conclusion, no. As the far as the *Economist* can tell, "A new dustbin awaits this new model."[26]

It is only fair to note this skepticism is not limited to Western observers. Chinese academics are also debating the geostrategic significance of the China model. In the mid-1990s, some Chinese scholars began to forecast the emergence of a new world order—one that featured greater balance among the major powers, a resistance to Western values, and a focus on diplomatic and economic prowess rather than military might.[27] The global financial crisis of 2007–08 renewed Chinese interest in this topic. On 18 May 2009, the assistant president of the China Institute of Contemporary International Relations published an op-ed in which he proclaimed, "The global financial crisis offers global leaders a chance to change the decades-old world political and economic orders. But a new order cannot be established until an effective multilateral mechanism to monitor globalization and countries actions comes into place."[28] The implied message—Washington and the West need to look east . . . specifically to China. That said, Chinese academics are not convinced the West is willing to listen. As a scholar from Shanghai's Fudan University told a panel discussing the China model in May 2009, "China had the capacity to learn from the West, but the West does not have the same capacity to learn. We need new thinking and China can humbly offer some wisdom."[29]

This perceptible arrogance concerning the success of Beijing's model is not universally shared in China's academic ivory towers. The dean of Beijing University's School of International Studies has publicly contended, "To date, no country has been able to constitute a comprehensive challenge to the United States, and the current international power structure of 'one superpower and many great powers' will continue for the foreseeable future."[30] Instead of becoming embroiled in world politics, the dean recommends Beijing "concentrate on managing its own affairs first."[31] Liu Jianfei, associate director of the International Strategy Institute at the Communist Party Central School, is equally cautious about Beijing overplaying China's hand. In an essay published in May 2009, Liu declared, "Many are calling for China to be the new leader in the new world order, but we need to continue down the road of reform and development and not adopt hegemonic tendencies. China also needs the cooperation and trade of the United States and other Western countries in order to succeed."[32]

These comments and press stories are telling. We are witnessing a very real debate over how the West—and China—should evaluate Beijing's rise to global prominence. Is China the next great threat to the West? Or is Beijing a responsible international actor who should be invited to join the Group of 8? Is the China model a viable alternative to liberal democracy? Or is the China model simply an ongoing experiment that facilitates the survival of an authoritarian regime? I would argue that Beijing certainly wants to be perceived as a responsible international actor—albeit one with national interests she is willing to defend, diplomatically, economically, and militarily. This does not mean China intends to go toe-to-toe with the United States. Rather, Washington can expect cooperation when it is in Beijing's interest to work with us. And, Washington can expect belligerence when Beijing believes China's national security, however defined, is endangered.

As for the arguments concerning the China model; my suspicion is that we are witnessing the evolution of a political system—and the emergence of a new political ideology. The Chinese Communist Party understands its long-term survival is contingent upon meeting constituent needs, but that does not mean those constituents are going to be invited to participate in nation-wide elections. Furthermore, in the wake of the 2007–08 financial crisis and the riots in Tibet and Xinjiang, I am not so certain the Chinese citizenry wants Beijing to loosen her grip on the nation's economy or society. This may change over time, but probably not in the next 10 years. China's 1.3 billion residents largely recognize they have been the beneficiaries of the Chinese Communist Party's experiment and see no preferable alternative standing in the wings. What really remains to be seen is how many other nations choose to follow in Beijing's footsteps, and what that means for Washington's bid to peddle liberal democracy across the planet.

BEIJING'S WAY AHEAD

As my comments above indicate, there is no shortage of speculation concerning the path China will follow in the coming 10 years. As we have seen, there seems little reason to subscribe to collapse theories, but that does not mean all will be smooth sailing for Beijing. While the Chinese Communist Party's adoption of pragmatism should help calm the seas, unforeseen developments have a way of derailing even the best laid plans. As a result, the best one can offer is a broad set of potential futures ranging from best to worst case.

In 2007, the National Bureau of Asian Research attempted to outline these potential scenarios in sequence of short papers focused on China in 2020. Prepared by prominent academics, the scenarios examine Beijing's possible ways ahead on the political, economic, and national security fronts. Cheng Li, a Senior Fellow at the John L. Thornton China Center of the Brookings Institution, offered the predictions concerning Beijing's political future. According to Li, "China's political future is unlikely to develop along a direct, linear trajectory." Rather, he continues, the interplay of current trends, key players, and demographic factors will serve to shape China's governance in the years to come.[33]

Li then sketches out three possible scenarios: emergence of a democratic China; prolonged chaos, and a resilient, authoritarian China. A democratic China, Li argues, could emerge as a result of the nation's increased urbanization, rising middle class, and the information revolution.[34] Li's mid-ground political scenario for China's leaders comes under the rubric of "prolonged chaos." Prolonged chaos, Li holds, could result from the significant demographic and economic challenges confronting China's leaders. The potential for a state of prolonged political hubris could also be brought about by corruption scandals, tensions between the national and local governments, and/or a global economic crisis that largely decimates China's middle class.[35] Li's third scenario—a resilient, authoritarian China—is predicated upon the assumption "China's authoritarian system is not stagnant; instead, its resiliency—its constant ability to adjust to new environments and its introduction of some legal, administrative, social, and political reforms—may actually make the system sustainable." Furthermore, Li continues, the various economic, political and social problems that plague liberal democracies elsewhere may serve to curtail Chinese domestic interest in adopting such a system. His bottom line, "by 2020 China will neither have made the transition to democracy nor have become chaotic. Instead, China will remain under the authoritarian rule of a 99-year old Chinese Communist Party."[36]

Pieter Bottelier, the Senior Adjunct Professor of China Studies at Johns Hopkins University's School of Advanced International Studies, provides a similar set of three scenarios for China's economic future. Like Li, Bottelier opens with the contention that China's economic future is dependent upon the interplay of multiple variables and challenges. Among the most important variables and challenges, access to energy, environmental protection, reducing dependency on exports, and stimulating domestic consumption.[37]

Bottelier then outlines three potential scenarios for China's economy in 2020. A word of clarification is required before we examine his findings. Bottelier refers to scenarios using the term "second transition." China's second economic transition according to Bottelier, "involves reducing the relative importance of low value-added manufacturing, increasing reliance on domestic innovation, making China's economy more energy efficient, reducing social inequality; and providing better environmental protection."[38] Given these objectives, Bottelier sets about describing his economic scenarios. The first, a successful second transition, meets the goals described above and is accompanied by timely reforms that deliver sustained growth. Should Beijing be able to pull this off, Bottelier believes China's leaders "will be well positioned for continued growth with stability, a substantial increase in outward investment, and a global leadership role well beyond 2020."[39]

His second scenario, a failed second transition, finds Beijing entering 2020 confronted with declining productivity, falling real wages, and growing urban unemployment. This scenario, Bottelier argues, could lead to popular revolt or even revolution and serious economic contraction. The final scenario, crisis management, envisions a stalled or delayed second transition. However, the Chinese Communist Party manages to adroitly manage events in such a way that Beijing avoids or fends off a "perfect storm."[40] Unfortunately, Bottelier does not reveal which of the three scenarios is most likely. My suspicion, given Beijing's demonstrated success in contending with the 2007–08 global recession, scenario one—a successful second economic transition.

This leads us to the scenarios associated with China's national security and foreign policy in 2020. As envisioned by David Lampton, the Dean of Faculty and Director of the China Studies Program at John Hopkins University's School of Advanced International Studies, these scenarios are contingent upon three variables: China's internal development, major power alignments, and the degree of Asian and international economic and security integration.[41] When Lampton looks forward to 2020, he sees three scenarios for Beijing on the security/foreign policy front: broadly cooperative, at odds, and mixed.

A "broadly cooperative" Chinese foreign policy would find a Beijing that "sees its own interests as generally consistent with the requirements of maintaining the international system of the last 60 years." In this situation, Lampton contends China would continue to modernize her military, and continue to emphasize employment of economic and soft power.[42] She could also be expected to act in a reasonably cooperative manner on questions concerning global security. Lampton's second scenario, "at odds," envisions a China whose national interests and well-being are incompatible with the prevailing international system. In this environment Beijing would place substantial emphasis on improving her coercive power and suffer problematic relations with Washington and Tokyo.[43] The final scenario, "mixed," depicts China as neither pleased, nor completely displeased with the current international system. Beijing's propensities are different enough from Washington and Tokyo's so as to cause friction—but not so severe as to result in international armed conflict. According to Lampton, such a situation would cause China to place greater emphasis on military modernization and economic power. The international security environment would be characterized as competitive, while the international economic climate would be cooperative.[44]

As it turns out, Lampton favors scenario three—"mixed." After evaluating the key variables he identified at the outset, Lampton contends China's push for economic development will result in spillovers—environmental and regulatory—that the international community will find unacceptable. The John Hopkins professor concludes Beijing will push back, thereby causing periodic tensions and misunderstandings. The bottom line for Lampton, "even a China that wants to be broadly cooperative with a receptive world . . . will often be torn between the demands of its citizens for improved life opportunities and a world Beijing sees as demanding things that the Chinese leadership will resist for fear of slowing down China's progress."[45]

What are we to take away from these predictions? First, there seems little reason to believe the Chinese government is going to significantly alter in form or function in the coming 10 years. A pragmatic, resilient, authoritarian regime will still be sitting in Beijing in 2020. Second, China's efforts to foster sustainable economic growth over the coming 10 years are unlikely to subside. The Chinese Communist Party understands its legitimacy is inexorably tied to further improving a large constituency's life styles. Progress in this campaign may not be linear, but Beijing's demonstrated ability to rapidly respond to challenging international economic developments

suggests a regime focused on the art of the possible—delays and pla-
teaus in the continued economic transition are inevitable, but not
insurmountable. Finally, China's foreign policy is likely to be neither
altruistic nor belligerent. Beijing, like all rational actors in the current Westphalian international system, will look out for China's best
interests. As such, China can be expected to be cooperative when it is
to Beijing's benefit and contrarian when the situation appears less
favorable.

MIDDLE KINGDOM REDUX

In November 1997, Jiang Zemin—then president of the People's
Republic of China—stood before a packed theater at Harvard and
sought to lay the foundation for a closer relationship between the Chinese and Americans. Likely aware a majority of his audience had little
more than a passing knowledge of his country, Jiang prefaced his
remarks with a short lesson on China's history—and then offered four
observations intended to help Americans better understand the
Middle Kingdom. Jiang referred to these observations as traditions
that have "exerted a profound impact on the values and way of life of
the Chinese people, and on China's road of development today."[46]
These four traditions are:

- The tradition of solidarity and unity – "China became a vast unified country more than 2,000 years ago. The deep-rooted Chinese culture has become a strong bond for ethnic harmony and
  national unity. Solidarity and unity have been inscribed in the
  hearts of the Chinese people as part of their national identity."
- The tradition of maintaining independence – "Today, in finding
  a road to development suited to us, we will proceed from our
  own national conditions to address the issue of how to conduct
  economic construction and political and cultural advancement
  without blindly copying other countries' models. In handling
  international affairs, we decide our positions and policies from
  an independent approach."
- The peace-loving tradition – "China's foreign policy is peace-
  oriented. We will establish and develop friendly relations and cooperation with all countries in the world on the basis of the Five
  Principles of Peaceful Coexistence .... We will never impose
  upon others the kind of suffering we once experienced."

- The tradition of constantly striving for self-perfection – "The reform and opening-up endeavor is an embodiment and a creative
development of the Chinese spirit of constantly striving for self-
perfection and renovation in modern times."[47]

Jiang's conclusion, China's choice of social systems, her economic policies, and approach to domestic and foreign affairs were all products of
these traditions and reality. According to the Chinese president, these
choices not only served the fundamental interests of his constituents,
"but also world peace, stability, prosperity, and progress. This is the
key to understanding of the present-day China and its future."[48]

Ten years after Jiang offered these remarks I would contend he did not
lead his audience astray. Beijing has indeed emphasized the importance of
solidarity and unity—Hong Kong and Macau have rejoined the fold, and
Taiwan appears on the verge of reconciling its long-standing differences
with the mainland. China, to be certain, is confronted with ethnic strife
at home, but any nation with a plethora of unique populations living
inside a single border is going to struggle with "troubles." I think there
is little doubt China has adhered to the tradition of independence. Beijing
continues to insist it will pursue democracy, economic development, foreign relations, and military modernization in its own way. Furthermore—
much to Washington's chagrin—Beijing continues to insist other nations
are also entitled to this sense of independence. China's neighbors know
this . . . as we have seen, they find it reassuring . . . it now seems the United
States must come to grips with this reality.

Is China a peace-loving state? In the decade that has passed since
Jiang made his remarks the Chinese have not gone to war with their
neighbors, nor have they engaged in proxy battles elsewhere on the
planet. Instead, Beijing has stepped up her participation in United
Nations Peace Keeping operations and has advocated the use of diplomacy as a means of handling the North Koreans. More to the point,
China has largely resolved her territorial squabbles with Russia, and
has refrained from employing force when dealing with disputed claims
in the East and South China Sea. And what of the tradition of striving
for self-perfection? The Chinese model of economic development is
now widely touted as the future for many emerging markets. The Chinese Communist Party's campaign to reduce corruption, increase
government accountability and implement rule of law—while far from
perfect—also appear a product of this tradition. I hesitate to suggest
this struggle for self-perfection will resolve China's environmental
and social concerns, but one cannot rule out the possibility.

All of which leads me to conclude Beijing is indeed intent on reviving the Middle Kingdom—a China that sits atop a regional hierarchy by dint of political authority, not coercion or co-option. I am also convinced China's leaders have a time line for achieving this objective. Hu Jintao has called for realization of a "moderately prosperous society" by 2020 and a "moderately developed country by 2050. In a similar vein, the People's Liberation Army is charged with making progress toward full informatization by 2020 and is to be a modernized force by 2050. Barring some unforeseen development, the Chinese are well on their way to meeting these objectives.

This, of course, begs the question of what China will do once the Middle Kingdom is no longer an aspiration—but has, instead, become a realization. In July 2009, the Brookings Institution and Taiwan's National Chengchi University held a conference focused on that very topic. While the presenters covered a broad range of materials, the paper that came closest to answering our question was prepared by David Finkelstein, the Director of China Studies at the CNA Corporation. Speaking on China's external grand strategy, Finkelstein offered the following observation: there is little evidence to suggest Beijing actually has a "grand external strategy"—and even if she did these "aspirations . . . are dashed, as often as not, by the realities of the immediate overtaking the long-term and the urgent sweeping aside the important."[49] Finkelstein also noted China's leaders are now operating in uncharted waters. As he put it, "There is no precedent in the history of the People's Republic of China for a China so enmeshed in the international system. Neither is there any precedent for China's emerging status as a global actor of consequence."[50] In one fell swoop Finkelstein has laid bare the problem confronting China watchers charged with predicting Beijing's behavior —there is no track record to use as a guide.

Nonetheless, Finkelstein suggests we can potentially discern China's grand external strategy by understanding Beijing's objectives. This, he continues, is a relatively straight-forward task, as Chinese official documents and leadership statements have made clear the Chinese Communist Party's ultimate goal—the attainment of a strong modern, and prosperous China.[51] On this point I think we can all agree. Finkelstein then goes on to highlight the fact China's leaders understand this objective cannot be accomplished in isolation, Beijing must reach out to the international community. (The Chinese phrase this realization as follows: "China cannot develop in isolation from the rest of the world, nor can the world enjoy prosperity or stability without China."[52]) The result, China is employing all elements of her national power—diplomatic, informational, military, and economic—to pursue this agenda on a global stage.

Is it working? Finkelstein, and I, would argue yes. Will it continue to work? That depends on Beijing's ability to overcome domestic challenges and reassure a nervous international community. The China model may not be a juggernaut, but there is widespread fear a reconstituted Middle Kingdom could be an inexorable force that crushes all in its path. I am loath to assume this worst case scenario, but do agree a Middle Kingdom redux is likely to operate in a manner very different from that China has exhibited in the past. The China of 2020 will no longer seek to belligerently confront the international community, nor, however, will she be satisfied with simply participating in global developments. Instead, I believe the China of 2020 will strive to assume a prominent voice in helping shape the international system.[53] This is no minor aspiration, but it does not have to be worrisome.

The Middle Kingdom of 2020 will neither be imperial nor exclusionist. The Chinese harbor no colonial aspirations and see little benefit in refusing to establish relations with states that adhere to a different ideological perspective. This open mind—even if driven by little more than business concerns—suggests the Middle Kingdom is not intent on driving the United States out of Asia or in changing our form of governance. Stated more bluntly, the Middle Kingdom of 2020 will not be a revival of the former Soviet Union. Beijing is not seeking a renewal of the Cold War.

So what do the Chinese want? First, to be left to peacefully govern their own affairs. Second, to realize the material and social benefits of a rapidly expanding economy. And, third, to be respected as a great power within the international community. These objectives are neither unreasonable —nor unexpected. In many ways the same goals could be identified within the United States in the 1820s, 1950s, and perhaps in 2020. The problem is that Washington, and many Americans, have yet to assimilate this possibility. It is time to clear that mental hurdle. In 2020, China will remain focused on economic development, she will be the dominant policy leader in Asia, and Beijing will be a senior, respected member of the international community—truly, the Middle Kingdom redux.

—Eric C. Anderson
September 1, 2009

Notes

INTRODUCTION

1. Gordon Chang, 2001, *The Coming Collapse of China*, Random House, New York.

2. James Kynge, 2007, *China Shakes the World: A Titan's Rise and Troubled Future—and the Challenge for America*, First Mariner Books, New York.

3. John Mearsheimer, 2005, "Better to be Godzilla than Bambi," *Foreign Policy*, a special report prepared in conjunction with the Carnegie Endowment for International Peace.

4. Roughly the period between the first Opium War (1839–1842) and Mao's victory over Chiang Kai Shek in 1949.

5. Vladimir Lenin, 1916, *Imperialism: The Highest Stage of Capitalism*, Resistance Books, New York.

6. John K. Fairbank, 1969, "China's Foreign Policy in Historical Perspective," *Foreign Affairs*, Volume 47, Number 3.

7. The overthrow of the Song Dynasty by the Mongols and the subsequent forming of the Yuan Dynasty in 1271 is the preeminent example of dynastic succession of non-Han Chinese rulers.

8. John K. Fairbank, 1969.

9. Tribute states that were pulled into Chinese cultural orbit include Japan, Vietnam, and Korea.

10. There has been considerable academic debate over the utility of understanding ancient Chinese foreign relations through the lens of the "tribute system." Many contemporary historians—the most prominent arguably being John E. Wills, Jr.—have argued that the "tribute system" as explained and championed by John Fairbank grossly oversimplified the Chinese court's efforts to win and maintain influence outside the Great Wall.

11. Pan Yihong, 1987, "Traditional Chinese Theories of Foreign Relations and Tang Foreign Policy," *British Columbia Asian Review*, Number 1, Vancouver, Canada.

12. ———, 1987. See also: Harriet Zurndorfer, January 2004, "Tribute, Trade and the Demise of the 'Chinese World Order' in Ming (1368–1644) and Qing (1644–1911) China," *Leidschrift*, Volume 18, Number 3; and, Harriet Zurndofer, August 2004, "Imperialism, Globalization, and Public Finance: The Case of Late Qing China," Working Paper 06/04, University of Leiden, Leiden, Netherlands.

13. ———, 1987.

14. Takeshi Hamashita, 1994, "The Tribute System and Modern Asia," *Japanese Industrialization and the Asian Economy*, edited by A. J. H. Latham and Heita Kawashita, Routledge, New York; and, Takeshi Hamashita, 1997, "The Intra-Regional System in East Asia in Modern Times," *Network Power: Japan and Asia*, edited by Peter Katzhstein and Takashi Shiraishi, Cornell University Press, Ithaca, New York.

15. John K. Fairbank, 1969.

16. This would include the Boxer Rebellion, Second Anglo-Chinese War, Sino-Japanese War, etc.

17. Kenneth Lieberman, 1983, "China in 1982: A Middling Course for the Middle Kingdom," *Asian Survey*, Volume 23, Number 1, pp. 26–37.

18. Bo Yang, 1992, *The Ugly Chinaman and the Crisis of Chinese Culture*, Sydney Allen & Unwin.

19. Song Xianlin and Gary Sigley, 2000, "Middle Kingdom Mentalities: Chinese Visions of National Characteristics in the 1990s," *Communal/Plural*, Volume 8, Number 1, pp. 47–64.

20. June Teufel Dreyer, 2003, "Encroaching on the Middle Kingdom? China's View of Its Place in the World," *U.S.-China Relations in the Twenty-First Century: Policies, Prospects and Possibilities*, Lexington Books, pp. 85–104.

21. ———, 2008, "Annual Report to Congress: Military Power of the People's Republic of China 2008," Office of the Secretary of Defense, Washington, DC, p. 8.

22. Song Qiang, Zhang Zangzang, Qiao Ben, Gu Qingsheng, and Tang Zhengyu, 1996, *China Can Say No*, Zhonghua Gongshang Lianhe Chubanshe, Beijing.

23. Peter Gries, 1997, "Reviews," *The China Journal*, Number 37, pp. 180–185.

24. Nicholas Kristof, 1993, "The Rise of China," *Foreign Affairs*, Volume 72, Number 5, pp. 59–74.

25. Gerald Segal, 1999, "Does China Matter?" *Foreign Affairs*, Volume 78, Number 5, pp. 24–36.

26. Minxin Pei, 2006, "Assertive Pragmatism: China's Economic Rise and Its Impact on Chinese Foreign Policy," Proliferation Papers, Ifri Security Studies Department, Paris.

27. Gerald Segal, 1999, "Does China Matter?" *Foreign Affairs*, Volume 78, Number 5, p. 33.

28. Alastair Iain Johnston, 2003, "Is China a Status Quo Power?" *International Security*, Volume 27, Number 4, pp. 5–56.

29. David Shambaugh, 2005, "China Engages Asia: Reshaping the Regional Order," *International Security*, Volume 29, Number 3, pp. 64–99.

30. ———, 2005, p. 64.

31. ———, 2005, p. 72.

32. ———, 2005, p. 85.

33. ———, 2005, p. 89.

34. Alastair Iain Johnston, 2003, pp. 35–36.

35. Byung-Joon Ahn, 2004, "The Rise of China and the Future of East Asian Integration," *Asia-Pacific Review*, Volume 11, Number 2, pp. 18–35. By "interdependence," Ahn means: "the degree to which economic conditions in one country influence or harm those of other countries; the degree of influencing is generally referred to as *sensitivity* and the degree of harming as *vulnerability*" (p. 19).

36. Zhou Bian, April 9, 2004, "A Gentle Giant," *Beijing Review*, Beijing. Wen Jiabao provided this response during a press conference at the Second Session of the 10th National People's Congress in Spring 2004.

37. ———, April 9, 2004.

38. ———, June 16, 2005, "China's New Road of Peaceful Rise and China-US Relations," Speech at the Brookings Institution, Washington, DC.

39. Tiejun Zhang, 2005, "China's Role in East Asian Community Building: Implications for Regional and Global Governance," Shanghai Institute for International Studies, Shanghai.

40. André Laliberté, December 2004, "China's 'Peaceful Emergence': Hegemonic Transition or 'Neo-Bismarckian Moment'?" Paper presented to the CANCAPS annual meeting, Quebec City, Canada.

41. Shogo Suzuki, 2004, "China's Perceptions of International Society in the Nineteenth Century: Learning More About Power Politics?" *Asian Perspective*, Volume 28, Number 3.

42. Eric Teo Chu Cheow, September 16, 2004, "Asian Security and the Re-emergence of China's Tributary System," *China Brief*, Volume 4, Issue 18, The Jamestown Foundation.

43. Arthur Waldron, 2005, "The Rise of China: Military and Political Implications," *Review of International Studies*, Number 31, pp. 715–733.

CHAPTER 1

1. Gerald Segal, September 1999, "Does China Matter? *Foreign Affairs*, Volume 78, Number 5, Council on Foreign Relations, Washington, DC.

2. For more on "peer competitors," see: Thomas Szayna, Daniel Byman, Steven Bankes, Derek Eaton, Seth Jones, Robert Mullins, Ian Lesser, and William Rosenau, 2001, *The Emergence of Peer Competitors: A Framework for Analysis*, Rand Corporation, Santa Monica, CA; and, Michael Klare, November 1997, "Rogue States and 'Peer Competitors,'" *Le Monde Diplomatique*, Paris.

3. Kevin Hamlin and Li Yanping, July 15, 2009, "China's Foreign-Exchange Reserves Surge, Exceeding $2 Trillion," www.bloomberg.com.

4. Gerald Segal, September 1999. Unfortunately, Gerald Segal died of cancer on November 2, 1999. His untimely demise at age 46 deprived him of an opportunity to readdress his question ten years after the fact. (See: Michael Richardson, 9 November 1999, "Gerald Segal: An Appreciation," *International Herald Tribune*, London.)

5. ———, September 1999.

6. Ariana Cha, January 15, 2009, "China Passes Germany with 3rd-Highest GDP," *The Washington Post*, Washington, DC, p. A16; and ———, October 28, 2008, "China's GDP Accounts for 6% of the World," Xinhua, Beijing. (For comparison purposes, in 2007 the United States had the highest GDP—an estimated $13.8 trillion—while Japan was in second place with $4.38 trillion.)

7. ———, January 21, 2008, "China says Foreign Direct Investment Rose to $83 Billion in 2007 amid Export Boom," *International Herald Tribune*, London.

8. Andrew Batson, January 11, 2008, "China's 2007 Trade Surplus Surges," *The Wall Street Journal*, New York.

9. Norihiko Shirouzu, February 5, 2008, "China's Auto Industry to Consolidate," *The Wall Street Journal*, New York, p. B1.

10. Ariana Cha and Maureen Fan, November 10, 2008, "China Unveils $586 Billion Stimulus Plan," *The Washington Post*, Washington, DC.

11. ———, August 2007, *Temasek Review 2007: Creating Value*, Singapore, p. 10.

12. ———, August 2007, *Temasek Review 2007: Creating Value*, Singapore, p. 38.

13. Jason Leow, December 5, 2007, "The $2 Billion China Bet," *The Wall Street Journal*, New York.

14. Henny Sender, August 24, 2007, "How a Gulf Petro-State Invests its Oil Riches," *The Wall Street Journal*, New York.

15. Michael Flaherty, March 17, 2008, "Sovereign Funds Steer Clear of Wall Street," Reuters, New York.

16. Gerald Segal, September 1999.

17. Gordon Chang, 2001, *The Coming Collapse of China*, Random House, New York.

18. Gerald Segal, September 1999.

19. The pairings worked as follows (asset management company and associated bank): Cinda and the Construction Bank of China; Great Wall and the

Agricultural Bank of China; Huarong and the Industrial and Commercial Bank of China; and Orient and the Bank of China.

20. Weijian Shan, October 17, 2005, "Will China's Banking Reform Succeed?" *The Wall Street Journal*, New York.

21. Keith Bradsher, January 14, 2004, "China to Give Up $41 Billion Stake in 2 Big Banks," *The New York Times*, New York.

22. Victor Shih, August 16, 2005, "Beijing's Bailout of Joint-stock and State-owned Banks," *China Brief*, Volume 5, Issue 18, The Jamestown Foundation, Virginia.

23. Min Xu, April 1, 2005, "Resolution of Non-Performing Loans in China," The Leonard Stern School of Business, Glucksman Institute for Research in Securities Markets. The author reports that the China Banking Regulatory Commission claims that the asset management companies disposed of almost half of the loans acquired between 2000 and 2004 by December 31, 2004.

24. Kent Matthews, Jianguang Guo, and Nina Zhang, November 2007, "Non-Performing Loans and Productivity in Chinese Banks: 1997–2006," Cardiff Economics Working Papers, Cardiff Business School, Cardiff University, United Kingdom.

25. ———, May 15, 2006, "Ernst and Young Withdraws China Bank NPL Report After Acknowledging Errors," AFX News Limited, www.forbes.com.

26. ———, August 23, 2006, "China's Banks in Sound Shape: Bad Loans Drop," www.chinadaily.com.cn.

27. Sudip Roy, April 2, 2009, "China's Looming NPL Crisis," *Euromoney*, London.

28. Hidetaro Muroi, July 26, 2007. Of note, more than one analyst has argued that these statistics are skewed by the huge increase in loans made in China over the last five years. (———, February 24, 2008, "Chinese Banks: Non-Performing Loans Rising," www.seekingalpha.com and Keith Bradsher, November 29, 2007, "$200 Billion to Invest, But in China," *The New York Times*, New York.) I have no reason to dispute this claim, but would note that the figures above are still markedly illustrative of a separate issue—the degree to which China prepared at least three of the "big four" for commercial competition and thus the good common sense it made for the China Investment Corporation to sink a large chunk of its initial funding in these institutions.

29. Zhou Xin, February 15, 2008, "China AgBank's NPL Ratio Rises to 23.6% in 2007," Reuters, Beijing.

30. ———, January 28, 2008, "Lender Outlines Listing," *The Wall Street Journal*, New York.

31. ———, February 15, 2008.

32. Peter Walker, January 26, 2009, "Banking Crisis Brings down Iceland Government," *Guardian*, London.

33. Philip Pan, January 26, 2009, "Economic Crisis Fuels Unrest in Eastern Europe," *The Washington Post*, Washington, DC, p. A01.

34. Simon Kennedy, January 30, 2009, "Roubini Predicts More Global Gloom After Vindication at Davos," www.bloomberg.com.

35. William Branigin, February 2, 2009, "Obama Urges Lawmakers to Overcome Differences' on Stimulus Package," *The Washington Post*, Washington, DC.

36. Keith Bradsher, January 7, 2009, "China Losing Taste for Debt From U.S." *The New York Times*, New York.

37. ———, January 7, 2009.

38. Nouriel Roubini and Brad Setser, February 2005, "Will the Bretton Woods 2 Regime Unravel Soon? The Risk of a Hard Landing in 2005–2006," Paper for the Symposium on the "Revived Bretton Woods System: A New Paradigm for Asian Development?" Organized by the Federal Reserve Bank of San Francisco and University of California-Berkeley, San Francisco. As Roubini and Setser note, this group includes researchers at the Federal Reserve who predict rate increases of between 50 and 100 basis points; PIMCO, a global investment management firm, who put the increase closer to 100 basis points; and Morgan Stanley, who estimate borrowing costs could rise 100–150 basis points.

39. Zalmay Khalilzad, Abram Shulsky, Daniel Byman, Roger Cliff, David Orletsky, David Shlapak, and Ashley Tellis, 1999, *The United States and a Rising China: Strategic and Military Implications*, Project Air Force, Rand, pp. 45–47.

40. ———, p. 47.

41. ———, pp. 47–48.

42. Zalmay Khalilzad, January 2009, *China's National Defense in 2008*, Information Office of the State Council of the People's Republic of China, Beijing, p. 8. This document is the sixth biannual defense white paper Beijing has released since 1998.

43. Zalmay Khalilzad, January 2009, *China's National Defense in 2008*, p. 14.

44. Bill Gertz, March 2, 2007, "China Expands Sub Fleet," *The Washington Times*, Washington, DC, p. A-1.

45. Gerald Segal, September 1999.

46. ———, September 1999.

47. ———, September 1999.

48. The Great Leap Forward was Mao's economic and cultural "bootstrap" plan. Enforced between 1958 and 1961 (Second Five Year Plan), the Great Leap Forward was intended to rapidly transform China from a primarily agrarian economy dominated by peasant farmers into a modern, industrialized, communist society. The central idea behind the Great Leap was that rapid development of China's agricultural and industrial sectors should take place in parallel. The Great Leap Forward is now widely

perceived as an economic disaster, effectively being a "Great Leap Backward." Officially, Chinese authorities admit the Great Leap Forward caused up to 14 million deaths, but scholars have estimated the number of famine victims to be between 20 and 43 million (Peng Xizhe, 1987, "Demographic Consequences of the Great Leap Forward in China's Provinces," *Population and Development Review*, Volume 13, Number 4, pp. 639–670.)

49. The Cultural Revolution (1966–1976) was a prolonged struggle for power within the Chinese Communist Party. The struggle ultimately took on the form of wide-scale social, political, and economic chaos and violence. Mao launched the Cultural Revolution as a means of eliminating China's "liberal bourgeoisie." This class struggle was accomplished by mobilizing China's youth—the feared Red Guard. The Cultural Revolution is now widely understood as Mao's effort to regain control of the party after the disastrous Great Leap Forward.

50. Yasheng Huang, 2008, *Capitalism with Chinese Characteristics: Entrepreneurship and the State*, Cambridge University Press, Cambridge, p. 105. See also: Quangsheng Zhao, 1996, *Interpreting Chinese Foreign Policy*, Oxford University Press, New York, p. 42.

51. Wikipedia offers an equally pedestrian explanation for the Chinese Communist Party's approach to opening and reform: "Although Chinese economic reform has been characterized by many in the West as a return to capitalism, Chinese officials have insisted that it is a form of socialism, because to do otherwise would call into question the validity of Marxism and the legitimacy of the regime. However, they have not argued against the premise that many of the reforms involve adopting economic policies that are in use in capitalist nations, and one of the premises of Chinese economic reform is that China should not avoid adopting 'whatever works' for ideological reasons."

52. Minxin Pei, March 2006, "The Dark Side of China's Rise," *Foreign Policy*, Washington, DC, pp. 32–40.

53. GlobeScan, a Canadian firm, whose mission is: "to be the world's center of excellence for objective global survey research and strategic counsel."

54. ———, January 11, 2006, "20 Nation Poll Finds Strong Global Consensus: Support for Free Market System, But also More Regulation of Large Companies," Program on International Policy Attitudes, Washington, DC.

55. Polling performed by GlobeScan.

56. ———, October 12, 2006, "Chicago Council Releases Major Study of Opinion on the Rise of China and India," Program on International Policy Attitudes, Washington, DC. This study was conducted by the Chicago Council on Global Affairs (formerly known as the Chicago Council on Foreign Relations) and was touted as: "the most extensive study ever published of Chinese and Indian public opinion on their countries' role in the world and a wide range of international issues."

57. Paul Kennedy, January 14, 2009, "American Power Is on the Wane," *The Wall Street Journal*, New York.

58. Joshua Cooper Ramo, May 2004, *The Beijing Consensus*, The Foreign Policy Centre, London, p. 2.

59. ———, May 2004, p. 3.

60. ———, May 2004, pp. 11–12.

61. ——— May 2004, p. 39.

62. According to Nye, soft power is the "ability to shape the preferences of others . . . It is the ability to get what you want through attraction rather than coercion or payments. It arises from the attractiveness of a country's culture, political ideals, and policies." (Joseph Nye, 2004, "Soft Power: The Means to Success in World Politics," *Public Affairs*, p. xi.)

63. Kerry Dumbaugh, April 2008, "China's Foreign Policy and 'Soft Power' in South America, Asia, and Africa," Congressional Research Service, Library of Congress, Washington, DC, p. 3.

64. Michael Schiffer and Gary Schmitt, May 2007, "Keeping Tabs on China's Rise," The Stanley Foundation, Muscatine, IA, p. 1.

65. Roger Altman, January 2009, "The Great Crash, 2008: A Geopolitical Setback for the West," *Foreign Affairs*, Council on Foreign Relations, Washington, DC.

66. ———, January 2009.

67. ———, January 2009.

68. Azar Gat, July 2007, "The Return of Authoritarian Great Powers," *Foreign Affairs*, Volume 86, Number 4, pp. 59–69.

69. ———, July 2007, p. 59.

70. ———, July 2007, p. 63.

71. ———, July 2007, p. 65.

72. ———, July 2007, p. 68.

73. Jay Solomon and Siobhan Gorman, October 17, 2008, "Financial Crisis May Diminish American Sway," *The Wall Street Journal*, New York.

74. ———, November 2008, *Global Trends 2025: A Transformed World*, National Intelligence Council, Director for National Intelligence, Washington, DC, p. vi.

75. ———, November 2008, p. vii.

76. ———, November 2008, p. vii.

77. Robert Reich, January 10, 2006, "China: Capitalism Doesn't Require Democracy," Common Dreams New Center, commondreams.org.

78. Kerry Dumbaugh, April 2008, p. 12.

79. G. John Ikenberry, January 2008, "The Rise of China and the Future of the West: Can the Liberal System Survive?" *Foreign Affairs*, Council on Foreign Relations, Washington, DC.

80. Martin Jacques, 2009, *When China Rules the World: The Rise of the Middle Kingdom and the End of the Western World*, Allen Lane, New York.

81. Robert Triffin, 1978, "The International Role and the Fate of the Dollar," *Foreign Affairs*, Volume 57, Number 2, New York, pp. 269–286.

82. Michael Dooley, David Folkerts-Landau, and Peter Garber, September 2003, "An Essay on the Revived Bretton Woods System," National Bureau of Economic Research (NBER) Working Paper 9971, Cambridge. See also: Dooley, et al., March 2004, "The Revived Bretton Woods System: The Effects of Periphery Intervention and Reserve Management on Interest Rates and Exchange Rates in Center Countries," NBER Working Paper 10332, Cambridge; Dooley, et al., July 2004, "Direct Investment, Rising Real Wages and the Absorption of Excess Labor in the Periphery," NBER Working Paper 10626, Cambridge; Dooley, et al., September 2004, "The US Current Account Deficit and Economic Development: Collateral for a Total Return Swap," NBER Working Paper 10727, Cambridge; and, Dooley, et al., December 2004, "The Revived Bretton Woods System: Alive and Well," Deutsche Bank, London.

83. ———, September 2003.

84. ———, September 2003.

85. ———, September 2003.

86. Aaron Friedberg, November 2000, "The Struggle for Mastery in Asia," *Commentary*, New York, p. 19.

87. ———, November 2000, p. 20.

88. Robert Samuelson, August 20, 2008, "The Real China Threat," *The Washington Post*, Washington, DC, p. A15.

89. ———, August 20, 2008, p. A15.

90. Quansheng Zhao, 1996, *Interpreting Chinese Foreign Policy*, Oxford University Press, Oxford, p. 51.

91. Alastair Iain Johnston, Spring 2003, "Is China a Status Quo Power?" *International Security*, Volume 27, Number 4, p. 49.

92. ———, Spring 2003, p. 49.

93. Brian Simpson, March 1997, "China's Future Intent: Responsible World Power or International Rogue State," Research Paper, Air Command and Staff College, Montgomery, Alabama, p. 14.

94. Joseph Cheney, April 1999, "China: Regional Hegemon or Toothless Tiger?" Research Report, Air War College, Montgomery, Alabama, p. 42.

95. David Shambaugh, Summer 2005, "The Author Replies," *International Security*, Volume 30, Number 1, p. 210.

96. ———, Summer 2005, p. 210.

97. Robert Sutter, 2005, *China's Rise in Asia: Promises and Perils*, Rowman and Littlefield Publishers, New York, p. 5.

98. ———, 2005, p. 10.

99. David Kang, 2007, *China Rising: Peace, Power, and Order in East Asia*, Columbia University Press, New York, p. 4.

100. ———, 2007, pp. 67–71.

101. ———, 2007, p. 126.

102. Evan Medeiros, Keith Crane, Eric Heginbotham, Norman Levin, Julia Lowell, Angel Rabasa, and Somi Seong, 2008, *Pacific Currents: The Responses of U.S. Allies and Security Partners in East Asia to China's Rise*, Project Air Force, Rand, Santa Monica, CA, pp. 231–244.

103. Henry Kissinger, 1994, *Diplomacy*, Simon and Schuster, New York, pp. 826–828.

104. This balance-of-power approach is also referred to as the "realist" model. I hesitate to use this verbiage, as it is value weighted and incredibly biased. Apparently a model is "realistic" if it purportedly explains European politics, and something else—"idealist" perhaps?—if it does not.

105. David Lake, Summer 2007, "Escaping from the State of Nature: Authority and Hierarchy in World Politics." *International Security*, Volume 32, Number 1, Boston, p. 47.

106. ———, Summer 2007, p. 48.

107. ———, Summer 2007, pp. 50–51.

108. ———, Summer 2007, p. 51.

109. ———, Summer 2007, p. 52.

110. David Kang, 2007, p. 43.

111. David Kang, 2007, pp. 43–44.

112. John K. Fairbank, 1969, "China's Foreign Policy in Historical Perspective," *Foreign Affairs*, Volume 47, Number 3, p. 24.

113. The overthrow of the Song Dynasty by the Mongols and the subsequent forming of the Yuan Dynasty in 1271 is the preeminent example of dynastic succession of non-Han Chinese rulers.

114. John K. Fairbank, 1969.

115. David Shambaugh, 2005, "China Engages Asia: Reshaping the Regional Order," *International Security*, Volume 29, Number 3, p. 72.

116. ———, 2005, p. 85.

CHAPTER 2

1. David Shambaugh December 22, 2005, "China's Peaceful Development Road," White Paper, State Council Information Office, Beijing.

2. Glenn Kessler, February 21, 2009, "Clinton Criticized for Not Trying to Force China's Hand," *The Washington Post*, Washington, DC, p. A08.

3. Jay Solomon, February 21, 2009, "Clinton Meets with China's Leadership," *The Wall Street Journal*, New York.

4. Glenn Kessler, February 21, 2009.

5. ———, 24 February 2008, "Not So Obvious," *The Washington Post*, Washington, DC, p. A12.

6. Anne Applebaum, February 24, 2009, "How to Speak Human Rights," *The Washington Post*, Washington, DC, p. A13.

7. ———, February 22, 2009, "Hillary on Human Rights," *The Wall Street Journal*, Asian Edition, New York.

8. ———, February 24, 2009.

9. ———, February 22, 2009.

10. ———, 2008, "China's Strategic Modernization: Report from the ISAB Task Force," International Security Advisory Board, Department of State, Washington, DC, p. 1. (Report was passed to Bill Gertz of the *The Washington Times* in October 2008 and then posted on the Internet.)

11. ———, 2008, "China's Strategic Modernization: Report from the ISAB Task Force," p. 2.

12. Dan Blumenthal and Aaron Friedberg, January 2009, "An American Strategy for Asia," A Report of the Asia Strategy Working Group, American Enterprise Institute, Washington, DC, p. 8.

13. ———, p. 7.

14. ———, p. 7.

15. ———, p. 7.

16. Jay Solomon, February 21, 2009.

17. Robert Zoellick, September 21, 2005, "Whither China: From Membership to Responsibility," Remarks to the National Committee on U.S. -China Relations, New York.

18. Dan Blumenthal, June 11, 2007, "Is China at Present (or will China Become) a Responsible Stakeholder in the International Community?" Paper presented at Carnegie Endowment for International Peace "Reframing China Policy" debates, Washington, DC, p. 1.

19. Andrew Cooper and Gregory Chin, July 2008, "China's Knocking on the G8 Door," *Far Eastern Economic Review*, Hong Kong.

20. Gary Bertsch, July 12, 2007, "China's Strategic Trade Controls and U.S.-China Cooperation on Nonproliferation," Testimony before the U.S. -China Economic and Security Review Commission on China's Proliferation and the Impact of Trade Policy on Defense Industries in the United States and China, Washington, DC.

21. ———, March 4, 2009, "U.S. Notes Positive Transformation in Chinese Army," *International Herald Tribune*, London. The news story specifically quotes David Sedney, deputy assistant defense secretary for East Asia in the Obama administration, contending, "We believe that China, as a responsible international actor, should not be exporting conventional arms to Iran when Iran continues to supply arms to extremist groups in countries on its borders."

22. C. Fred Bergsten, Bates Gill, Nicholas Lardy, and Derek Mitchell, 2008, "International System," *China : The Balance Sheet*, Center for Strategic and International Studies, Washington, DC.

23. Wen Jiabao, 2004, cited in Esther Pan, April 2006, "The Promise and Pitfalls of China's 'Peaceful Rise,' " Backgrounder, Council on Foreign Relations, Washington, DC.

24. Michael Glosny, 2006, "Heading Toward a Win-Win Future? Recent Developments in China's Policy Towards Southeast Asia," *Asian Security*, Volume 2, Number 1, pp. 24–57.

25. ———, January 2009, *China's National Defense in 2008*, Information Office of the State Council of the People's Republic of China, Beijing, p. 7.

26. ——— 2006, *The National Security Strategy of the United States*, The White House, Washington, DC.

27. Alan Tonelson, October 7, 2005, "Washington Dreams on About China," *The Washington Times*, Washington, DC.

28. Joshua Ramo, September 2006, "Brand China," Foreign Policy Centre, London.

29. Esther Pan, April 2006, "The Promise and Pitfalls of China's 'Peaceful Rise,' " Backgrounder, Council on Foreign Relations, Washington, DC.

30. Yongnian Zheng and Sow Keat Tok, October 2007, " 'Harmonious Society' and 'Harmonious World': China's Policy Discourse under Hu Jintao," Briefing Series—Issue 26, China Policy Institute, The University of Nottingham, Nottingham, United Kingdom.

31. Zheng Bijian, 2005, *China's Peaceful Rise: Speeches of Zheng Bijian*, Brookings Institution Press, Washington, DC, pp. 27–28.

32. Evan Medeiros and M. Taylor Fravel, November 2003, "China's New Diplomacy," *Foreign Affairs*, Council on Foreign Relations, Washington, DC.

33. Quansheng Zhao, 1996, *Interpreting Chinese Foreign Policy*, Oxford University Press, Oxford, p. 57.

34. ———, 1996, pp. 56–57.

35. ———, 2008, "Annual Report to Congress: Military Power of the People's Republic of China 2008," Office of the Secretary of Defense, Washington, DC, p. 8.

36. Evan Medeiros and M. Taylor Fravel, November 2003. See also: Thomas Christensen, September 1996, "Chinese Realpolitik," *Foreign Affairs*, p. 38–40.

37. John Lewis and Xue Litai, 2006, *Imagined Enemies: China Prepares for Uncertain War*, Stanford University Press, California, p. 250.

38. Deng Xiaoping, June 18, 1995, "The Last Mutual Trust is Lost Between China and the United States," *Yazhou Zhoukan*, Beijing.

39. Yongnian Zheng and Sow Keat Tok, October 2007.

40. The Association of Southeast Asian Nations was established on August 8, 1967, in Bangkok. The five original members were Indonesia, Malaysia, Philippines, Singapore, and Thailand. Brunei joined on January 8, 1984, Vietnam on July 28, 1995, Laos and Burma on July 23, 1997, and Cambodia on April 30, 1999.

41. The Shanghai Cooperation Organization (SCO) is an intergovernmental international organization founded in Shanghai on June 15, 2001.

The six member countries are: China, Kazakhstan, Kyrgyzstan, Russia, Tajikistan, and Uzbekistan.

42. Yongnian Zheng and Sow Keat Tok, October 2007.

43. Joshua Ramo, September 2006.

44. Yongnian Zheng and Sow Keat Tok, October 2007.

45. ———, September 16, 2005, "Hu Makes 4-point Proposal for Building Harmonious World," Xinhua News Agency, Beijing.

46. Yongnian Zheng and Sow Keat Tok, October 2007.

47. Michael Yahuda, September 2007, "China's Foreign Policy Comes of Age," *The International Spectator*, Volume 42, Number 3, p. 349.

48. Esther Pan, April 2006. Of note, the Congressional Research Service (CRS) offers a slightly different list for China's "presumed" foreign policy goals. According to the CRS analysts, these are: enhancing sustainable economic growth, squeezing Taiwan's international space, maintaining regional and international stability, and increasing international stature and competing with U.S. supremacy. When the definitions for the CRS categories are reviewed, it is clear these four categories would all fit within the three identified by the Council on Foreign Relations; nonetheless, readers should be aware that other means of interpreting Hu's "harmonious world" objectives are present. (Kerry Dumbaugh, July 18, 2008, "China's Foreign Policy: What does it Mean for U.S. Global Interests," CRS Report for Congress, Congressional Research Service, Washington, DC.)

49. I would like to acknowledge Alex Liebman's initial employment of this title in his 2007 article, "China's Asia Policy: Strategy and Tactics," in *Assessing the Threat: The Chinese Military and Taiwan's Security*, edited by Michael Swaine, Andrew Yang, and Even Medeiros, Carnegie Endowment for International Peace, Washington, DC, p. 27.

50. Zheng Bijian, December 22, 2005, "China's Peaceful Development Road," p. 9.

51. ———, December 22, 2005.

52. Daniel Goma, 2006, "The Chinese-Korean Border Issue: An Analysis of a Contested Frontier," *Asian Survey*, Volume 46, Issue 6, University of California Press, pp. 867–880.

53. M. Taylor Fravel, Fall 2005, "Regime Insecurity and International Cooperation: Explaining China's Compromises in Territorial Disputes," *International Security*, Volume 30, Number 2, Harvard and Massachusetts Institute of Technology, Boston, p. 46. (For a broader examination of this topic see also: M. Taylor Fravel, 2008, *Strong Borders, Secure Nation: Cooperation and Conflict in China's Territorial Disputes*, Princeton University Press, Princeton.)

54. ———, Fall 2005, pp. 60–61.

55. ———, Fall 2005, p. 59.

56. ———, Fall 2005, pp. 61–62.

57. The 1982 United Nations Convention on the Law of the Sea formally established territorial claim limits, rules for innocent passage in territorial waters, and means for determining exclusive economic zones.

58. In the Treaty of Amity and Cooperation in Southeast Asia, the signatories (Indonesia, Malaysia, the Philippines, Singapore, and Thailand) agreed to "have the determination and good faith to prevent disputes from arising." When a dispute did emerge, the parties agreed to "refrain from the threat of the use of force" . . . and to "settle such disputes among themselves through friendly negotiations."

59. China and ASEAN, November 4, 2002, 2002 Declaration on the Conduct of Parties in the South China Sea, declaration 1.

60. ———, November 4, 2002, declarations 3–5.

61. ———, November 4, 2002, declaration 10.

62. China actually legally guarantees this right even within hits exclusive economic zones. Article 4 of China's 1998 *Exclusive Economic Zone and Continental Shelf Act* declares: "Any State, provided that it observes international law and the laws and regulations of the People's Republic of China, shall enjoy in the exclusive economic zone and the continental shelf of the People's Republic of China freedom of navigation and over flight and of laying submarine cables and pipelines, and shall enjoy other legal and practical marine benefits associates with these freedoms. The laying of submarine cables and pipelines must be authorized by the competent authorities of the People's Republic of China."

63. Cheng-yi Lin, February 29, 2008, Taiwan's Spratly Initiative in the South China Sea," *China Brief,* Jamestown Foundation, Washington, DC.

64. ———, March 11, 2009, "China Protests Philippine Law to Extend Territorial Claim in South China Sea," Xinhua, Beijing.

65. Li Yanlin, March 6, 2009, "Vice Admiral Zhao Guojun: China is Entirely Capable to Defend South China Sea," China Military Online, www.hinamil.com.

66. M. Taylor Fravel, Fall 2005, p. 63.

67. ———, June 26, 1998, *Exclusive Economic Zone and Continental Shelf Act*, Adopted at the third session of the Standing Committee of the Ninth National People's Congress, Beijing.

68. ———, June 26, 1998 .

69. For more on China's legal perceptive concerning U.S. operations in her waters, see: Yann-Huei Song, 2005, "Declarations and Statements with Respect to the 1982 UNCLOS: Potential Legal Disputes between the United States and China after U.S. Accession to the Convention," *Ocean Development & International Law*, Volume 36, pp. 261–289.

70. ———, June 26, 1998, *Exclusive Economic Zone and Continental Shelf Act*.

71. Robyn Meredith, 2008, *The Elephant and the Dragon: The Rise of India and China and What It Means for All of Us*, W. W. Norton and Company, New York, pp. 97–116.

72. ———, 2008, p. 107.

73. ———, December 13, 2006, "Global Economic Prospects 2007: Managing the Next Wave of Globalization," Global Economic Prospects, World Bank, Washington, DC.

74. ———, June 2005, "U.S.-China Trade in Perspective: Asia's Emerging Union and Implications for the United States," The China Business Forum, The U.S.-China Business Council, Washington, DC.

75. Malcom Moore, August 23, 2008, "China Replaces U.S. as Japan's Biggest Trading Partner," *Telegraph*, London.

76. ———, May 6, 2008, "Australian Minister Says China Is Largest Trade Partner," Xinhua, Beijing.

77. Bhartendu Kumar Singh, March 24, 2008, "China Emerges India's Largest Trade Partner," www.indiapost.com.

78. ———, February 29, 2008, "China, ASEAN Become 4th-Largest Trade Partners in 2007," Xinhua, Beijing.

79. Pasha Hsieh, 2008, "China-Taiwan Trade Relations: Implications of the WTO and Asian Regionalism," in *Trading Arrangements in the Pacific Rim: ASEAN and APEC*, edited by Paul Davidson, Oxford University Press, p. 10.

80. ———, 2008, p. 10.

81. Robert Sutter, 2006, "China's Regional Strategy and Why It May Not Be Good for America," in *Power Shift: China and Asia's New Dynamics*, edited by David Shambaugh, University of California Press, Berkeley, p. 297; and Alex Liebman, 2007, p. 42.

82. ASEAN member states: Brunei Darussalam, Cambodia, Indonesia, Laos, Malaysia. Myanmar, Philippines, Singapore, Thailand, and Vietnam.

83. ———, August 15, 2009, "China-ASEAN Investment Agreement Signed," Xinhua, Beijing.

84. Fang Lexian, October 2003, "Is China's Foreign Policy Becoming Less Ideological?" Paper for the International Workshop on "Regional Governance: Greater China in the 21st Century," University of Durham, United Kingdom.

85. Ann Kent, 2007, *Beyond Compliance: China, International Organizations, and Global Security*, Stanford University Press, Palo Alto, California.

86. Alex Liebman, 2007, pp. 32–39.

87. Zheng Bijian, 2005, p. 33.

88. Michael Glosny, December 2006, "China's Foreign Aid Policy: Lifting States Out of Poverty or Leaving Them to the Dictators?" CSIS Freeman Report, Center for Strategic and International Studies, Washington, DC.

89. Christopher Blanchard, Nicholas Cook, Kerry Dumbaugh, Susan Epstein, Shirley Kan, Michael Martin, Wayne Morrison, Dick Nanto, Jim Nichol, Jeremy Sharp, Mark Sullivan, and Bruce Vaughn, August 15, 2008,

"Comparing Global Influence: China's and U.S. Diplomacy, Foreign Aid, Trade, and Investment in the Developing World," CRS Report for Congress, Congressional Research Service, Library of Congress, Washington, DC, p. 33.

90. ——, April 25, 2008, "Understanding Chinese Foreign Aid: A Look at China's Development Assistance to Africa, Southeast Asia, and Latin America," Report prepared for the Congressional Research Service, New York University Wagner School, New York.

91. Christopher Blanchard, et al, 2008, p. 33.

92. Michael Glosny, December 2006.

93. Zheng Bijian, 2005, pp. 65–66.

94. Helmut Reisen, 2007, "Is China Actually Helping Improve Debt Sustainability in Africa?" G-24 Policy Brief Number 9, Organization for Economic Cooperation and Development, Paris.

95. ——, 2007.

96. For more on Chinese foreign direct investment see: ——, 2005, "China Spreads its Wings—Chinese Companies go global," Accenture, New York; and Bates Gill and James Reilly, Summer 2007, "The Tenuous Hold of China Inc. in Africa," *The Washington Quarterly*, Washington, DC, pp. 37–52.

97. Helmut Reisen, 2007.

98. Andrea Goldstein, Nicholas Pinaud, Helmut Reisen, and Xiaobao Chen, May 2006, "China and India: What's In It for Africa?" Development Center Studies, Organization for Economic Cooperation and Development, Paris; and Helmut Reisen, 2007.

99. Helmut Reisen, 2007.

100. Qi Quoqian, June 2007, "China's Foreign Aid: Policies, Structure, Practice and Trend," Paper prepared for Oxford and Cornell Universities' conference on "New Directions in Development Assistance," Oxford, United Kingdom.

101. Joshua Eisenman and Joshua Kurlantzick, May 2006, "China's Africa Strategy," American Foreign Policy Council, Washington, DC.

102. Christopher Blanchard, et al, 2008, pp. 33–34.

103. Ngaire Woods, 2008, "Whose Aid? Whose Influence? China, Emerging Donors and the Silent Revolution in Development Assistance," *International Affairs*, Volume 84, Number 6, p. 1220.

104. Kishore Mahbubani, March 2008, "Smart Power, Chinese-Style," *The American Interest*, p. 76.

105. Avery Goldstein, 2001, "The Diplomatic Face of China's Grand Strategy: A Rising Power's Emerging Choice," *The China Quarterly*, Volume 168, Cambridge University Press, p. 836.

106. ——, 2001, p. 846.

107. ——, 2001, p. 847.

108. Kishore Mahbubani, March 2008, p. 71.

109. Joshua Kurlantzick, 2007, *Charm Offensive: How China's Soft Power Is Transforming the World*, Yale University Press, p. 65. See also: Xiaohong Liu, 2001, *Chinese Ambassadors: The Rise of Diplomatic Professionalism Since 1949*, University of Washington Press.

110. Kishore Mahbubani, March 2008, p. 71.

111. ———, June 20, 1997, Planning Group for Integration of USIA into the Department of State.

112. Rumi Aoyama, 2007, "Chinese Diplomacy in the Multimedia Age," edited by Kazuko Mori and Kenichiro Hirano in *A New East Asia: Toward a Regional Community*, National University of Singapore.

113. Rumi Aoyama, December 2004, "Chinese Diplomacy in the Multimedia Age: Public Diplomacy and Civil Diplomacy," Research Institute of Current Chinese Affairs, Waseda University, Tokyo, p. 13.

114. John Mearsheimer, 2001, *The Tragedy of Great Power Politics*, W. W. Norton, New York, p. 402.

115. David Shambaugh, 1996, "Containment or Engagement of China?" *International Security*, Volume 21, Number 2, Harvard and Massachusetts Institute of Technology, Boston, pp. 180–209.

116. Mark Beeson, 2009, "Hegemonic Transition in East Asia? The Dynamics of Chinese and American Power," *Review of International Studies*, Volume 35, British International Studies Association, London, p. 96.

117. Robert Gilpin, 1981, *War and Change in World Politics*, Cambridge University Press, Cambridge, p. 48.

118. Dominic Ziegler, March 31, 2007, "Reaching for a Renaissance: A Special Report on China and Its Region," *The Economist*, London.

119. Mark Beeson, p. 107.

120. ———, p. 104.

121. ———, p. 111.

122. ———, p. 112.

123. Robert Sutter, 2005, *China's Rise in Asia: Promises and Perils*, Rowman and Littlefield Publishers, New York, p. 10.

124. ———, p. 10.

125. Jason Dean, James Areddy, and Serena Ng, January 29, 2009, "Chinese Premier Blames Recession on U.S. Actions," *The Wall Street Journal*, New York, p. A1.

126. ———, February 2, 2009, "Wen: China, U.S. Should Work Together to Fight Financial Crisis," Xinhua, Beijing.

127. ———, February 2, 2009.

128. David Barboza, March 24, 2009, "China Urges New Money Reserve to Replace Dollar," *The New York Times*, New York.

129. Andrew Batson, March 24, 2009, "China Takes Aim at Dollar," *The Wall Street Journal*, New York, p. A1.

130. Andrew Batson, March 31, 2009, "China Seeks More Involvement—and More Clout," *The Wall Street Journal*, New York, p. A10.

131. A———, March 31, 2009.

CHAPTER 3

1. Zheng Bijian, 2005, *China's Peaceful Rise: Speeches of Zheng Bijian*, Brookings Institution Press, Washington, DC, p. 17.

2. Hu Jintao, October 15, 2007, "Report to the Seventeenth National Congress of the Communist Party of China," Xinhua, Beijing. Hu first introduced this concept in a speech to a study session of the Chinese Communist Party Political Bureau in August 2003.

3. Gross National Product (GNP) is the total value added from domestic and foreign sources claimed by residents of a country. GNP is determined by adding Gross Domestic Product (GDP), the value of goods and services produced within a country, to the net income received by residents from non-resident sources. Using GNP rather than GDP as a measure of national wealth is a controversial decision, as the South Koreans proved in 2000, when Seoul chose to demonstrate a revival of the North Korean economy by switching from a study of Pyongyang's GDP to the North's GNP. By using GNP, which includes foreign aid, Seoul was able to claim a minor climb in Pyongyang's per capita earnings. Economists and policy-makers who tended to be more focused on specific developments in North Korea were not impressed. The common complaint: including aid in a measure of wealth distorts the numbers and really only serves to highlight donor income—not that of the average North Korean.

4. Hu Jintao, October 15, 2007.

5. ———, October 15, 2007.

6. ———, October 15, 2007.

7. This finding is not without controversy. In 2001, Thomas Rawski, an economist at the University of Pittsburgh, published a paper contending all Chinese GDP figures released after 1997 were suspect and probably more reflective of official exaggeration than actual growth. While widely circulated in China-critical media outlets, Rawski's work was never accepted as gospel within the international banking community. (Thomas Rawski, September 12, 2001, "What's Happening to China's GDP Statistics?" Prepared for the China Economic Review symposium on Chinese Statistics, Pittsburgh.)

8. Haruhiko Kuroda, March 23, 2008, "Toward Inclusive Economic Development in China," Speech by the President of the Asian Development Bank at the China Development Forum, Beijing.

9. Wayne Morrison, January 12, 2006, "China's Economic Conditions," CRS Issue Brief for Congress, Congressional Research Service, Library of Congress, Washington, DC.

10. Brian Klein, October 1, 2008, "The Great Crash of China," *Far Eastern Economic Review*, Hong Kong.

11. Andrew Batson, November 11, 2008, "China Bets Highways Will Drive Its Growth," *The Wall Street Journal*, New York.

12. While certainly beyond the scope of this text, it is interesting to note Beijing's trade surplus is almost exclusively an artifact of business conducted between China and the United States. Chinese specialization in finishing goods—completing products from imported raw materials—has limited China's take to approximately 20 percent of the value of the items exported. The consequence, China runs a trade deficit with many of its neighbors—most specifically, South Korea and Taiwan. At a broader scale, China's trade deficit with East Asia has actually increased over the last seven years. It grew from $39 billion in 2000 to $130 billion in 2007.

13. Andrew Batson, January 11, 2008, "China's 2007 Trade Surplus Surges," *The Wall Street Journal*, New York.

14. For a concise summary of China's historic exchange rate policy see: Nicholas Lardy, Winter 2005, "Exchange Rate and Monetary Policy in China," *Cato Journal*, Volume 25, Number 1, pp. 41–47.

15. Some economists argue Chinese management of the exchange rate has resulted in the yuan being undervalued by 15–25 percent. Beijing is sensitive to these claims and has sought to address the issue by allowing the yuan to increase in value against the dollar. In 2007, this policy resulted in the yuan increasing in value against the dollar by 6.9 percent. This was more than twice the "float" allowed in 2006, when the yuan only rose against the dollar by 3.4 percent. To help keep this change in perspective, China's official exchange rate for the yuan remained locked in place at 8.28 to $1 from 1996 to July 2005. As of April 2008, the yuan-dollar exchange rate was approximately 7.00 to $1. (For more on China's monetary exchange policy see Morris Goldstein, May 2004, "Adjusting China's Exchange Rate Policies," Paper presented at the IMF seminar on China's Foreign Exchange System, Peterson Institute for International Economics, Washington, DC.)

16. Stephen Green, July 2005, "Making Monetary Policy Work in China: A Report from the Money Market Front Line," Stanford Center of International Development, Working Paper 245, Stanford University, California.

17. For a layman's description of this process and other means the Chinese government uses to prevent inflation and rapid Yuan appreciation against the dollar see: James Fallows, January 2008, "The $1.4 Trillion Question," *The Atlantic*, Washington, DC, pp. 35–48.

18. Not all of the voices have been raised in complaint; there are some American scholars who argue revaluation of the yuan will do little to reduce the U.S. trade imbalance with China. As David Hale and Lyric Hale note in an essay *Foreign Affairs* published in January 2008, "the

growing Chinese trade surplus has actually produced numerous benefits for the world economy and U.S. corporations and consumers." (David Hale and Lyric Hale, January 2008, "Reconsidering Revaluation: The Wrong Approach to the U.S.-China Trade Imbalance," *Foreign Affairs*, Volume 87, Number 1, pp. 57–66.) A Morgan Stanley study makes the point more succinctly by noting cheaper exports from China have saved U.S. consumers an estimated $600 billion over the last 10 years—$521 a year in increased disposable income for every American household over that time period.

19. Zheng Bijian, 2005, p. 40.

20. ———, April 8, 2008, "China's Oil Consumption to Rise by 63 Percent in 2020," Xinhua, Beijing; and, Gal Luft, 2008, "Fueling the Dragon: China's Race into the Oil Market," Institute for the Analysis of Global Security, Washington, DC.

21. ———, November 8, 2008, "World Energy Outlook 2008," International Energy Agency, Paris.

22. Gal Luft, 2008.

23. ———, 2008. See also: Erica Strecker Downs, 2000, *China's Quest for Energy Security*, Project Air Force, Rand, Washington, DC.

24. Jim Yardley, September 28, 2007, "Beneath Booming Cities, China's Future Is Drying Up," *The New York Times*, New York.

25. ———, September 28, 2007.

26. Joseph Kahn and Jim Yardley, August 25, 2007, "As China Roars, Pollution Reaches Deadly Extremes," *The New York Times*, New York.

27. Jim Yardley, September 28, 2007.

28. ———, September 28, 2007.

29. Joseph Kahn and Jim Yardley, August 25, 2007.

30. ———, January 16, 2009, "Over 80% of China's Sea Areas Suffer from Pollution," Xinhua, Beijing.

31. ———, June 6, 2006, "Pollution Costs Equal 10% of China's GDP," www.chinadaily.com.cn.

32. ———, August 25, 2007. See also: Govindasamy Agoramoorthy and Minna Hsu, October 10, 2005, "China's Battle Against Escalating Environmental Pollution," *Current Science*, Volume 89, Number 7, pp. 1073–1074.

33. Govindasamy Agoramoorthy and Minna Hsu, October 10, 2005.

34. Joseph Kahn and Jim Yardley, August 25, 2007.

35. Ariana Cha, November 19, 2008, "China's Environmental Retreat," *The Washington Post*, Washington, DC.

36. The Sword of Damocles is frequently used as an allusion epitomizing the imminent and ever-present peril faced by those in positions of power. It is used to denote the sense of foreboding engendered by the leader's precarious situation, particularly in cases where the onset of tragedy is restrained only by a delicate trigger or chance.

37. Jiang Zemin, November 2002, "Report to the 16th National Congress," Xinhua, Beijing.

38. Jia Hepeng, 2004, "The Three Represents Campaign: Reform the Party or Indoctrinate the Capitalists?" *Cato Journal*, Volume 24, Number 3, Cato Institute, Washington, DC, p. 261.

39. Yongnian Zheng and Sow Keat Tok, October 2007, " 'Harmonious Society' and 'Harmonious World': China's Policy Discourse under Hu Jintao," Briefing Series—Issue 26, China Policy Institute, The University of Nottingham, Nottingham, United Kingdom.

40. ———, April 2008, "China: The Olympics Crackdown," AI Index: ASA 17/050/2008, Amnesty International, p. 1.

41. Murray Tanner, 2004, "China Rethinks Unrest," *The Washington Quarterly*, Volume 27, Number 3, p. 145.

42. ———, 2004, p. 146.

43. Zhu Rongji, March 19, 2003, "Report on the Work of the Government," Speech on 5 March 2003, Xinhua, Beijing.

44. Murray Tanner, April 14, 2005, "Chinese Government Responses to Social Unrest," Testimony before the U.S.-China Economic and Security Review Commission, Rand, Arlington, Virginia.

45. Albert Keidel, May 26, 2005, "The Economic Basis for Social Unrest in China," The Third European-American Dialogue on China, George Washington University, Washington, DC.

46. ———, May 26, 2005.

47. ———, May 26, 2005.

48. The "iron rice bowl" is a Chinese term used to refer to an occupation with guaranteed job security, income, and benefits. Historically "iron rice bowl" occupations included the military, civil service, and China's state-owned enterprises.

49. Thomas Lum, May 8, 2006, "Social Unrest in China," CRS Report for Congress, Congressional Research Service, Library of Congress, p. 5.

50. ———, May 8, 2006, p. 5.

51. Heungkyu Kim, October 4, 2007, "On China's Internal Stability," Paper presented at the Second Berlin Conference on Asian Security, Berlin, p. 5.

52. Keng Shu, Chang Chih-chung, and Hsu Chih-Chia, 2006, *Know Thyself, Know Others: The Neglected Risks of China*, Mainland Affairs Council, Taipei. (The Mainland Affairs Council is a cabinet-level administrative agency in the Taiwan government. The Mainland Affairs Council is responsible for the development and implementation of policies between Taiwan and the People's Republic of China.) Estimates on the size China's rural population range—Chinese sources claim the nation has 950 million registered famers, with 750 million still living in the countryside. (———, October 20, 2008, "China Extends Rural Reform and Development in New Party Document," China Economic Net, www.en.ce.cn.)

53. Heungkyu Kim, October 4, 2007, p. 5.

54. Keng Shu, Chang Chih-chung, and Hsu Chih-Chia, 2006.

55. As with the size of China's rural population, there are a number of estimates concerning the true scale of China's migrant labor population. Chinese sources claim 126 million (———, October 20, 2008, "China Extends Rural Reform and Development in New Party Document," China Economic Net, www.en.ce.cn), *The Wall Street Journal* says 130 million (Shai Oster, December 2, 2008, "China Fears Restive Migrants As Jobs Disappear in Cities," *The Wall Street Journal*, New York) and the U.S. Council on Foreign Relations refuses to assign a number (Carin Zissis, March 26, 2007, "China's Internal Migrants," Council on Foreign Relations, Washington, DC.).

56. ———, April 2, 2007, "China: Rural Migration and Plugging the Rural-Urban Gap," STRATFOR, Washington, DC.

57. ———, October 23, 2008, "Still Not to the Tiller: A Timid Approach to an Issue of Burning Concern to One-eighth of the World's People, *The Economist*, London.

58. ———, October 13, 2008, "Beijing Announces Landmark Agricultural Reform," AsiaNews, www.asianews.it.

59. ———, October 20, 2008, "China Shares up 2.3% on Expectation of more Economic Stimulus," Xinhua, Beijing.

60. Maureen Fan, October 20, 2008, "China to Allow Land Leasing, Transfer," *The Washington Post*, Washington, DC.

61. ———, October 12, 2006, "China's Party Leadership Declares New Priority: 'Harmonious Society,' " *The Washington Post*, Washington, DC, p. A18.

62. ———, July 22, 1999, "China Bans Falun Gong," Xinhua, Beijing.

63. Heungkyu Kim, October 4, 2007, p. 2.

64. Ibid.

65. ———, January 4, 2008, "China's per Capita GDP to Hit US$3,000 by 2010," Xinhua, Beijing.

66. Charles Wolf, K. C. Yeh, Benjamin Zycher, Nicholas Eberstadt, and Sung-Ho Lee, 2003, *Fault Lines in China's Economic Terrain*, Rand, Arlington, Virginia, pp. xvi–xx.

67. ———, 2003, p. xx.

68. Charles Wolf, et al., 2003, p. xx.

69. ———, 2003, p. 179.

70. ———, December 28, 2007, "Background Information: The Frequent Occurrence of Mass Incidents in China Pushes it into Becoming a 'Risky Society,' " Mainland Affairs Council, Taipei.

71. Keng Shu, Chang Chih-chung, and Hsu Chih-Chia, 2006.

72. ———, June 27, 2005, "Building Harmonious Society Crucial for China's Progress: Hu," Xinhua, Beijing. Of note, for unexplained reasons Xinhua—China's official news agency—did not release a full text of Hu's February 19, 2005 speech until June 26, 2005.

73. ———, June 27, 2005.

74. ———, June 27, 2005.

75. ———, October 8, 2006, "China Faces 8 Challenges in Building Harmonious Society: Experts," Xinhua, Beijing.

76. Hu Jintao, October 15, 2007, "Hold High the Great Banner of Socialism with Chinese Characteristics and Strive for New Victories in Building a Moderately Prosperous Society in All Respects," Report to the Seventeenth National Congress of the Communist Party of China, Beijing.

77. The Development Research Center (DRC) of the State Council Web site claims the organization "is a comprehensive policy research and consulting institution directly under the State Council, the central government of the People's Republic of China .... DRC has a team of prominent economists and qualified experts and researchers in the fields of macroeconomic policy, development strategy and regional economic policy, industrial economy and industrial policy, rural economy, technical economy, foreign economic relations, social development, market circulation, enterprise reform and development, finance as well as international economy."

78. Heungkyu Kim, October 4, 2007, p. 5.

79. Zukiu Hu and Mohsin Khan, April 1997, "Why Is China Growing So Fast?" Economic Issues Number 8, International Monetary Fund, Washington, DC, pp. 1–2. (Hu and Khan's first cut at this project appeared as IMF Working Paper 96/75, "Why Is China Growing So Fast?")

80. ———, April 1997, pp. 5–8.

81. ———, April 1997, p. 4.

82. Hong Liang and Eva Yi, November 11, 2005, "China's Ascent: Can the Middle Kingdom Meet Its Dreams?" Global Economics Paper Number 133, Goldman Sachs Economic Research Group, New York, p. 6.

83. ———, November 11, 2005, pp. 10–13.

84. ———, November 11, 2005, p. 13.

85. Bert Hofman and Louis Kuijs, October 19, 2007, "Rebalancing China's Growth," Paper presented at the Conference on China's Exchange Rate Policy, Peterson Institute for International Economics, Washington, DC, pp. 7–8.

86. ———, October 19, 2007, p. 13.

87. Heungkyu Kim, October 4, 2007, p. 5.

88. Bert Hofman and Louis Kuijs, October 19, 2007, p. 15.

89. ———, January 26, 2007, "Government Vows Social Security Net," China Daily, p. 3.

90. ———, March 5, 2008, "China Pledges to Expand Rural Medicare System," Xinhua, Beijing.

91. ———, March 5, 2008.

92. ———, March 5, 2008, "Premier Wen Announces Hefty Educational Investment," Xinhua, Beijing.

93. ———, March 5, 2008, "Premier Wen Announces Hefty Educational Investment."

94. ———, March 5, 2008.

95. John Chan, March 12, 2008, "China's National People's Congress Haunted by the Specter of Social Unrest," Center for Research on Globalization, Montreal, Canada.

96. Jason Leow, November 30, 2008, "Chinese President Warns Hurdles Ahead," *The Wall Street Journal*, New York.

97. ———, October 24, 2008, "Southern China to Shed Millions of Jobs as Economic Crisis Bites," Channel News Asia, www.channelnewsasia.com.

98. ———, November 6, 2008, "Chinese Job Losses Prompt Exodus," BBC News, news.bbc.co.uk.

99. Shai Oster, December 2, 2008, "China Fears Restive Migrants As Jobs Disappear in Cities," *The Wall Street Journal*, New York.

100. Ariana Cha, January 13, 2009, "As China's Jobless Numbers Mount, Protests Grow Bolder," *The Washington Post*, Washington, DC, p. A7.

101. ———, January 13, 2009.

102. ———, January 13, 2009.

103. ———, May 4, 2008, "GDP Growth 1952–2008," www.chinability.com.

104. Ian Johnson and Andrew Batson, February 3, 2009, "China's Migrants See Jobless Ranks Soar," *The Wall Street Journal*, New York.

105. ———, May 4, 2008, "GDP Growth 1952–2008," Chinability.com.

106. Tania Branigan, January 25, 2009, "China Fears Riots will Spread as Boom Goes Sour," *The Observer*, London.

107. Albert Keidel, May 26, 2005.

108. ———, November 19, 2008, "China Says Employment Situation 'Critical,'" Agence France-Presse, Beijing. This statistics is attributed to Ministry of Social Security.

109. Tania Branigan, January 25, 2009.

110. ———, December 5, 2008, "China 'Faces Mass Social Unrest,'" BBC News, London.

111. Chris Hogg, February 2, 2009, "Chinese Migrant Job Losses Mount," BBC News, Shanghai.

112. Ian Johnson and Andrew Batson, February 3, 2009.

113. Michael Bristow, November 20, 2008, "China Fears Grow Over Job Losses," BBC News, Beijing. Quote attributed to Yin Weimin, Minister of Human Resources and Social Security.

114. ———, November 20, 2008, "China Moves to Ease Social Tensions Amid Economic Crisis," Agence France-Presse, Beijing.

115. Kathrin Hille, December 8, 2008, "Chinese Media Put a Positive Spin on Crisis," *Financial Times*, London.

116. ———, October 20, 2008, "Chinese Economy Growth Rate Slows," BBC News, news.bbc.co.uk.

117. David Barboza, November 7, 2008, "Once Sizzling, China's Economy Shows Rapid Signs of Fizzling," *The New York Times*, New York.

118. ———, November 25, 2008, "World Bank: China's GDP to slow to 7.5% in 2009," www.chinadaily.com.cn.

119. Alan Wheatley, March 18, 2009, "World Bank Cuts China 2009 GDP Forecast to 6.5 Percent," Reuters, Beijing.

120. Ariana Cha and Maureen Fan, November 10, 2008, "China Unveils $586 Billion Stimulus Plan," *The Washington Post*, Washington, DC.

121. Andrew Batson, November 10, 2008, "China Sets Big Stimulus Plan in Bid to Jump-Start Growth," *The Wall Street Journal*, New York.

122. Tina Wang, November 10, 2008, "China's Stimulus: More Show than Substance," www.forbes.com.

123. ———, January 12, 2009, "China can be First to 'Recover' from Crisis," www.chinadaily.com.cn.

124. ———, March 5, 2009, "China 'Faces most Difficult Year,'" BBC News, London.

125. Andrew Batson, November 10, 2008.

126. Tina Wang, November 10, 2009.

127. Gordon Chang, December 22, 2008, "Thirty Years of Reform in China," *The Weekly Standard*, Volume 14, Issue 14, Washington, DC. For an equally grim assessment see: Ray Yep, April 10, 2009, "Economic Downturn and Instability in China: Time for Political Reform?" Brookings Northeast Asia Commentary, Number 28, The Brookings Institution, Washington, DC.

128. Gordon Chang, December 22, 2008.

129. Calla Wiemer, November 12, 2008, "China's Stimulus Will Work," *The Wall Street Journal Asia*, New York.

130. ———, November 12, 2008.

131. ———, April 2009, *East Asia and Pacific Update: Battling the Forces of Global Recession*, World Bank, Washington, DC, p. 45.

132. ———, April 2009.

133. ———, March 2009, *The China Quarterly Update*, World Bank, Washington, DC, p. 11.

134. ———, April 2009, *East Asia and Pacific Update*, p. 7.

135. Andrew Batson, April 11, 2009, "China Turns A Corner As Spending Takes Hold," *The Wall Street Journal*, New York, p. A1.

136. ———, April 11, 2009.

137. Tina Wang, March 6, 2009.

138. Wang Changyong, March 6, 2009, "Facelift for China's Economic Stimulus Plan," www.caijing.com.

139. Cheng Li, March 2009, "China's Team of Rivals," *Foreign Policy*, Washington, DC. See Also: Li Cheng and Lynn White, 2003, "The Sixteenth Central Committee of the Chinese Communist Party: Hu Gets What?" *Asian Survey*, Volume 43, Number 4, pp. 553–597. High-level debates over China's economic and political future are not new. As Philip Pan writes in *Out of Mao's*

Shadow, arguments over how far to proceed with Deng's "reform and opening" pitted those who advocated capitalist-style economic reforms and a political transition against CCP conservatives who considered such policies ideological heresy. (Philip Pan, 2008, *Out of Mao's Shadow: The Struggle for the Soul of a New China*, Simon and Schuster, New York, p. 11.)

140. ———, March 2009.

141. ———, March 2009.

142. ———, March 2009.

143. Andrew Batson, November 11, 2008.

144. Andrew Batson, August 5, 2009, "Fears of Migrant Unrest in China Have Faded," *The Wall Street Journal*, New York.

145. ———, August 5, 2009.

146. Peter Nolan, 2004, *China at the Crossroads*, Polity Press, Cambridge, pp. 58–59; Gordon Chang, 2002, *The Coming Collapse of China*, Random House, New York; and, Gordon Chang, December 22, 2008, "Thirty Years of Reform in China," *The Weekly Standard*, Volume 14, Issue 14, Washington, DC.

147. Johan Lagerkvist, 2008, "The Limits of the China Model," Glasshouse Forum, Stockholm; and, Daniel Deudney and G. John Ikenberry, January 2009, "The Myth of the Autocratic Revival," *Foreign Affairs*, Volume 88, Number 1, pp. 77–93.

148. Hu Jintao, October 15, 2007.

149. ———, October 15, 2007.

150. Steven Jackson, 2000, "A Typology for Stability and Instability in China," in *Is China Unstable*, editor David Shambaugh, M. E. Sharpe, New York, pp. 3–14.

151. ———, 2000, p. 14.

152. Susan Shirk, 2007, *China: Fragile Superpower*, Oxford University Press, Oxford, p. 6.

153. Jack Goldstone, Summer 1995, "The Coming Collapse," *Foreign Policy*, Number 99, Washington, DC, pp. 51–52.

154. Barry Naughton and Dali Yang, 2004, "Holding China Together," *Holding China Together: Diversity and National Integration in the Post-Deng Era*, edited by Barry Naughton and Dali Yang, Cambridge University Press, Cambridge, pp. 1–25.

CHAPTER 4

1. Wang Changyong, January 2009, *China's National Defense in 2008*, Information Office of the State Council of the People's Republic of China, Beijing, p. 3. This document is the sixth biannual defense white paper Beijing has released since 1998.

2. Francis Fukuyama, 1992, *The End of History and the Last Man*. Free Press. New York. In this oft cited essay, Fukuyama argues, "What we may be witnessing is not just the end of the Cold War, or the passing of a

particular period of postwar history, but the end of history as such: that is, the end point of mankind's ideological evolution and the universalization of Western liberal democracy as the final form of human government."

3. French for "a reason for being"—justification or purpose of existence.

4. For an insightful discussion of this topic, see: David Shambaugh, 2002, *Modernizing China's Military: Progress, Problems, and Prospects*, University of California Press, Los Angeles.

5. Solomon Karmel, 2000, *China and the People's Liberation Army: Great Power or Struggling Developing State?* St. Martin's Press, New York, p. 181.

6. ———, 2009, "Annual Report to Congress: Military Power of the People's Republic of China," Office of the Secretary of Defense, Department of Defense, Washington, DC.

7. Solomon Karmel, 2000, p. 2.

8. Henry Kissinger, June 13, 2005, "China: Containment Won't Work, *The Washington Post*, Washington, DC, p. A19.

9. ———, June 13, 2005, p. A19.

10. Zalmay Khalilzad, Abram Shulsky, Daniel Byman, Roger Cliff, David Orletsky, David Shlapak, and Ashley Tellis, 1999, *The United States and a Rising China: Strategic and Military Implications*, Project Air Force, Rand, p. 45–47.

11. ———, p. 47.

12. ———, pp. 47–48.

13. ———, January 2009, *China's National Defense in 2008*, p. 8.

14. ———, April 2004, "Study Guide for Jiang Zemin Thought on National Defense and Army Building," PLA National Defense University Army Building Research Department, Beijing. New guidelines are usually issued under the name of the Chairman of the Central Military Commission, who historically has also served as the Communist Party Chairman and the state President—i.e., Deng Xiaoping, Jiang Zemin, or Hu Jintao. A second Chinese source states, "Military Strategic Guidelines are the core of military strategy; they are the overall plan and the overall guiding principle of the Party and the nation for guiding the preparations and implementation of warfare within a particular period of time, and they are the driving force and assume the overall responsibility for the construction of national defense and the military. (Yao Youzhi, 2004, "On Academic Questions Related to the Military Strategic Guidelines.")

15. David Finkelstein, October 2006, "China's National Strategy Revisited," Strategic Studies Institute.

16. ———, October 2006.

17. Jiang Zemin, January 13, 1993, "The International Situation and Military Strategic Guidelines." (Republished in August 2006, Three Volumes: *Selected Works of Jiang Zemin*.)

18. David Finkelstein, October 2006.

19. Shen Yongjun and Su Ruozhou, January 11, 2006, "PLA Sets to Push Forward Informationalization Drive from Three Aspects," PLA Daily Online, PLAdaily.com.

20. For a comprehensive discussion of "informatization" objectives, see Zheng Zhidong, April 2005, "Thoughts on Improving Preparations for People's War Under Informatized Conditions," *Beijing Guofang*, pp. 19–20.

21. Zheng Zhidong, April 2005, "Thoughts on Improving Preparations for People's War Under Informatized Conditions," *Beijing Guofang*. See also: *China's National Defense in 2006*, p. 24 for a discussion of specialized technical units as the new "backbone" of the militia, replacing infantry units.

22. Wu Daxiang, January 13, 2003, "Clearly Recognize the New Mission of the Urban Militia," *Zhongguo Guofang Bao*, p. 3.

23. ———, 2005, *The Science of Military Strategy*, Military Science Publishing House, Academy of Military Science of the Chinese People's Liberation Army, Beijing.

24. ———, 2005.

25. ———, 2005.

26. ———, December 29, 2006, "China Issues White Paper on National Defense 2006," FEA200612300635508, Open Source Center, Washington, DC.

27. This is no minor concern—as evidenced by an essay published in the April 2009 CCP journal *Seeking Truth*. In his essay, Li Jinai, head of the PLA General Political Department and member of the Central Military Commission, declared: "The Chinese Communist Party is the leadership core of the cause of socialism with Chinese characteristics, and maintaining the Party's absolute leadership is our military's political priority." Li went on to argue China should "resolutely resist 'de-Partyising or de-politicizing the military' or 'nationalizing the military' and other mistaken thoughts and influences." (Ben Blanchard, 1 April 2009, "China General Tells Troops Party Trumps State," Reuters, Beijing.

28. Daniel Hartnett, June 2008, "Towards a Globally Focused Chinese Military: The Historic Missions of the Chinese Armed Forces," Project Asia, The CNA Corporation, Alexandria, VA.

29. ———, June 2008.

30. ———, February 6, 2008, "China—Strategic Guidance Establishes Basis for Expanding PLA Activity, Open Source Center, Washington, DC; and, ———, 1 October 2008, "China—Media Highlight Updates to Party's Military Guiding Theory," Open Source Center, Washington, DC.

31. ———, January 2007, "The New Mission of the People's Army," *Liaowang*, Beijing, pp. 26–28.

32. Chen Zhou, June 2007, "An Analysis of Defensive National Defense Policy of China for Safeguarding Peace and Development," *China Military Science*, Academy of Military Sciences, Beijing.

33. ———, January 2009, *China's National Defense in 2008*, p. 11

34. ———, January 2009, p. 12.

35. ———, January 2009, p. 12.

36. ———, January 2009, p. 15.

37. ———, January 2009, pp. 8–9.

38. Gary Feuerberg, April 13, 2009, "China's Military Plans Go Forward Despite the Economy," Epoch Times, www.theepochtimes.com.

39. ———, 2009, "Annual Report to Congress: Military Power of the People's Republic of China," p. 20.

40. Roger Cliff, Mark Burles, Michael Chase, Derek Eaton, and Kevin Pollpeter, 2007, *Entering the Dragon's Lair: Chinese Antiaccess Strategies and Their Implications for the United States*, Rand Corporation, Santa Monica, pp. 1–16.

41. Larry Wortzel, May 2007, "China's Nuclear Forces: Operations, Training, Doctrine, Command, Control and Campaign Planning," Strategic Studies Institute, Washington, DC, p. 9.

42. ———, 2007, "Over the Horizon Backscatter Radar," www .globalsecurity.org.

43. ———, 2007, "Type 052B Luyang Class Destroyer/Luyang Class Multirole Destroyer," www.globalsecurity.org.

44. Larry Wortzel, May 2007. pp. 30–33.

45. Carlo Kopp, 2007, "Almaz S-30-China's 'Offensive' Air Defense," International Assessment and Strategy Center, www.strategycenter.net.

46. Roger Cliff, et al., pp. 44–46.

47. Phillip Saunders and Charles Lutes, June 2007, "China's ASAT Test: Motivations and Implications," Institute for National Strategic Studies, Washington, DC.

48. Geoffrey Forden, 2007, "Measure of Success—Analyzing the Results of China's ASAT Test," *Janes Intelligence Review*, Janes, London.

49. ———, December 5, 2007, "Chinese ASAT Test," www.center forspace.com.

50. There is considerable academic debate over the revolution in military affair's intellectual "founding fathers." Scholars now contend RMA first emerged in the Soviet Union as the "Military-Technical Revolution." In any case, the overarching concepts are the same—intellectually capture the fundamental impact technological innovations were having on the conduct of military operations. (See: Dima Adamsky, April 2008, "Through the Looking Glass: The Soviet Military-Technical Revolution and the American Revolution in Military Affairs," *Journal of Strategic Studies*, Volume 31, Number 2, p. 258.)

51. Steven Metz and James Kievet, June 27, 1995, "Strategy and the Revolution in Military Affairs: From Theory to Policy," Strategic Studies Institute, U.S. Army War College, Carlisle Barracks, Pennsylvania, pp. 4–6. The Soviet military thinkers offered similar observations, calling for specific attention on automated decision-support systems; telecommunications; and

enhanced weapon accuracy, range, and precision. (Dima Adamsky, April 2008, "Through the Looking Glass: The Soviet Military-Technical Revolution and the American Revolution in Military Affairs," *Journal of Strategic Studies*, Volume 31, Number 2, p. 263.)

52. This PLA focus on defeating perceived U.S. military advantages has resulted in a growing body of Chinese thinking on asymmetric capabilities. This focus should come as little surprise; the Chinese are simply studying a principle of warfare already clearly recognized within the U.S. armed forces. Nor, by the way, should Chinese employment of asymmetric capabilities come as a surprise. As U.S. Army Field Manual 3–0 notes, "Asymmetry becomes very significant, perhaps decisive, when the degree of dissimilarities creates exploitable advantages . . . .[However,] asymmetry tends to decay over time as adversaries adapt to dissimilarities exposed in action."

53. Shen Yongjun and Su Ruozhou, January 11, 2006.

54. For a comprehensive discussion of informatization objectives, see Zheng Zhidong, April 2005, "Thoughts on Improving Preparations for People's War Under Informatized Conditions," *Guofang*, pp. 19–20.

55. ———, January 2009, *China's National Defense in 2008*. p. 11.

56. Qiao Liang and Wang Xiangsui, 1999, *Unrestricted Warfare: Assumptions on War and Tactics in the Age of Globalization*, PLA Literature and Arts Publishing House, Beijing. In late 1999, the Central Intelligence Agency's Foreign Broadcast Information Service (FBIS) (now the Director of National Intelligence's Open Source Center) provided a full translation of the text. According to the FBIS analysts, "the book was written by two PLA senior colonels from the younger generation of Chinese military officers and was published . . . in Beijing, suggesting that its release was endorsed by at least some elements of the PLA leadership." ———, August 24, 1999, "Excerpts from 'Unrestricted Warfare,'" FBIS, Washington, DC—FTS19990 823001254.)

57. ———, 1999, Part I, pp. 1–9.

58. ———, 1999, Chapter 8, pp. 223–240.

59. ———, 1999, Chapter 2, pp. 34–59.

60. ———, 1999, Part II, pp. 121–131.

61. ———, 1999, Part II, pp. 121–131.

62. ———, 1999, Chapter 2, pp. 34–59. The authors define "international law warfare" as: "seizing the earliest opportunity to set up the regulations." Media warfare is defined as: "manipulating what people see and hear in order to lead public opinion. Psychological warfare is defined as: "spreading rumors to intimidate the enemy and break down his will."

63. ———, October 23, 2004, "Chinese PLA Focusing on Media, Psychological, and Legal Warfare Training, *Wen Wei Po*, Hong Kong. At least one Chinese press report claims the "three warfare" concept can be traced back to a July 28, 2004, PLA General Political Department seminar.

Other sources claim the "three warfare" was formalized in the PLA Political Work Decree as revised in December 2003.

64. ———, March 20, 2007, " 'Three War' and the Role of the PLA Political Commissars," *Kanwa Intelligence Review*, Toronto.

65. ———, March 20, 2007.

66. Li Dapeng, July 2, 2007, "Introduction to Legal Warfare in Complex Electromagnetic Environment," *Zhanqi Bao*, Chengdu Military Region, China.

67. Liu Wan-lin, April 22, 2008, "Investigation into the Impact of PRC Military's Media Warfare on ROC Military," *Hai-chun Hsueh-shu Yueh-k'an*, Taipei.

68. Timothy Thomas, April 2003, "New Developments in Chinese Strategic Psychological Warfare," *Special Warfare*.

69. ———, June 13, 2005, "Armed Forces Psychological Warfare Drill Kicks Off," Central News Agency, Taipei.

70. ———, January 2009, *China's National Defense in 2008*, p. 15.

71. The General Staff Department carries out staff and operational functions for the PLA and has major responsibility for implementing military modernization plans. Headed by the chief of general staff, the department serves as the headquarters for the ground forces and contained directorates for the three other armed services: Air Force, Navy, and Strategic Missile Force. The General Staff Department includes functionally organized sub departments for artillery, armored units, engineering, operations, training, intelligence, mobilization, surveying, communications, quartermaster services, and politics.

72. ———, April 24, 2007, "Analysis: PRC Military Seeks Integrated Joint Operations," FEA20070424126867, Open Source Center, Washington, DC.

73. ———, January 17, 2005, "JFJB: General Staff Headquarters Training Plans Aim to Increase Combat Power," CPP20050117000085, Open Source Center, Washington, DC. (Liu, Chunjiang, and Su, Ruozhou, January 15, 2005, "The General Staff Headquarters makes Plans for this Year's Military Work in a Bid to Comprehensively Enhance Units' Combat Power," *Jiefangjun Bao*.)

74. ———, June 8, 2006, "China: PLA Military Training, Tasks for 2006," CPP2006060608318001, Open Source Center, Washington, DC.

75. ———, January 25, 2007, "OSC Analysis: PLA Training Directives for 2007 Emphasize 'Informationalized Conditions,'" CPF2007 0125443003, Open Source Center, Washington, DC.

76. ———, February 11, 2008, "OSC Analysis: China's 2008 Military Training Implements New Strategy," CPF20080211538001, Open Source Center, Washington, DC.

77. ———, February 11, 2008.

78. ———, February 11, 2008.

79. ——, July 25, 2008, "PLA General Staff Department Approves Release of Newly Amended 'Military Training, Examination Outline,'" *Jiefangjun Bao*, Beijing.

80. ——, September 8, 2008, "Analysis: Revised PRC Military Training Guidance Codifies Joint Operations," FEA20080909767592, Open Source Center, Washington, DC. (According to the Open Source Center, China's OMTE has been revised seven times since 1957. These revisions are reportedly performed in response to changes in the PLA structure or to leadership directives on military training. The major OMTE revisions are said to have occurred in 1957, 1978, 1980, 1989, 1995, 2001, and 2008.)

81. Wu Dilun and Liu Feng'an, 6 January 2009, "General Staff Department Lays Out Plan for Military Training Throughout the Armed Forces in the New Year," *Jiefangjun Bao*, Beijing.

82. For example, see: ——, June 26, 2006, "China: PLA Ground Force, Air Force Units Stage Joint Training Exercises," CPP2006060626702002, Open Source Center, Washington, DC; ——, August 17, 2006, "Nanjing Military Region Infantry Division Improves Communication Confrontation Skills," CPP20061010318007, Open Source Center, Washington, DC; ——, August 18, 2006, "PRC Second Artillery Unit Leaders on New Directions, Bottlenecks of Training," CPP200609143118009, Open Source Center, Washington, DC; ——, September 13, 2006, "Strengthening Realistic Opposing Force Exercises," CPP20060914476001, Open Source Center, Washington, DC; ——, October 9, 2006, "PRC Guangzhou Military Region Army Vessels Unit Plays a Supporting Role in Joint Operations," CPP20061010702002, Open Source Center, Washington, DC; ——, February 14, 2007, "Jinan Military Region Unit 71960 Writer Discusses Ways to Carry Out Integrated Joint Training," CPP20070406436011, Open Source Center, Washington, DC; and ——, March 13, 2007, "OSC Analysis: Group Army with Possible Taiwan Mission Perfecting Command Skills," FEA20070314102386, Open Source Center, Washington, DC.

83. Dai Qingmin, April 20, 2003, "On Seizing Information Supremacy," *Zhongguo Junshi Kexue*. (——, July 28, 2003, "Chinese Military's Senior Infowar Official Stresses Integrated Network/EW Operations," CPP200307280000209, Open Source Center, Washington, DC.)

84. Dai Qingmin, April 20, 2003.

85. ——, February 6, 2008, "China—Strategic Guidance Establishes Basis for Expanding PLA Activity," Open Source Center, Washington, DC.

86. ——, February 6, 2008.

87. ——, September 8, 2008, "Analysis: Revised PRC Military Training Guidance Codifies Joint Operations," Open Source Center, Washington, DC.

88. ——, February 11, 2008, "OSC Analysis: China's 2008 Military Training Implements New Strategy, " Open Source Center, Washington, DC.

89. ———, January 7, 2009, "Kanwa: Capability of Chinese Military in Recent Integrated Joint Operations," CPP20090107715016, Open Source Center, Washington, DC.

90. ———, January 7, 2009.

91. ———, January 7, 2009.

92. ———, January 7, 2009.

93. ———, January 7, 2009.

94. ———, December 29, 2006, "China Issues White Paper on National Defense 2006," FEA200612300635508, Open Source Center, Washington, DC.

95. ———, 2009, "Annual Report to Congress: Military Power of the People's Republic of China," p. 31.

96. ———, December 29, 2006.

97. ———, January 2009, *China's National Defense in 2008*, p. 65.

98. ———, January 2009, *China's National Defense in 2008*, pp. 65–66.

99. ———, December 29, 2006.

100. ———, January 2009, *China's National Defense in 2008*, p. 67.

101. Keith Crane, Roger Cliff, Evan Medeiros, James Mulvenon, and William Overholt, 2005, *Modernizing China's Military: Opportunities and Constraints*, Rand Corporation, Santa Monica, CA.

102. ———, 2009, "Annual Report to Congress: Military Power of the People's Republic of China," p. 20.

103. Thomas Donnelly and Tim Sullivan, April 2008, "Defense Issues for the Next Administration," American Enterprise Institute for Public Policy Research, Washington, DC.

104. Ike Skelton, March 25, 2009, "Skelton Statement on Annual Report to Congress on China's Military Power," House Armed Services Committee, Washington, DC. Ike Skelton (D-MO) is the House Armed Services Committee Chairman.

105. Evan Medeiros, Keith Crane, Eric Heginbotham, Norman Levin, Julia Lowell, Angel Rabasa, and Somi Seong, 2008, *Pacific Currents: The Responses of U.S. Allies and Security Partners in East Asia to China's Rise*, Project Air Force, Rand, Santa Monica, CA, pp. 231–244.

106. Zhou Chen, June 2007, "An Analysis of Defensive National Defense Policy of China for Safeguarding Peace and Development," *China Military Science*, Beijing, p. 7.

107. Sun Zhenjiang, 2000, "Exploration of the Factors Restricting Command in Joint Operations" *National Defense University Gazette*.

108. John Lewis and Xue Litai, 2006, *Imagined Enemies: China Prepares for Uncertain War*, Stanford University Press, California, pp. 140–143.

109. Marshal Ogarkov, March 25, 1982, "Always in Readiness to Defend the Homeland," Voenizdat, Moscow.

110. ———, December 29, 2006, "China Issues White Paper on National Defense 2006," Open Source Center, Washington, DC.

111. Karl Lautenschlager, Fall 1983, "Technology and the Evolution of Naval Warfare," *International Security*, Volume 8, Number 2, p. 4.

112. ———, Fall 1983, pp. 49–50.

113. Steven Metz and James Kievit, July 25, 1994, "The Revolution in Military Affairs and Conflict Short of War," Strategic Studies Institute, U.S. Army War College, Carlisle Barracks, Pennsylvania, pp. 13–14.

114. ———, July 25, 1994, p. 15.

115. Siobhan Gorman, 8 April 2009, "Electricity Grid in U.S. Penetrated by Spies," *The Wall Street Journal*, New York, p. A1.

116. Emily Goldman and Richard Andres, Summer 1999, "System Effects of Military Innovation and Diffusion," *Security Studies*, Volume 8, Number 4, p. 83.

117. ———, Summer 1999, p. 123.

CHAPTER 5

1. John Lewis and Xue Litai, 2006, *Imagined Enemies: China Prepares for Uncertain War*, Stanford University Press, California, p. 2.

2. ———, 2009, "Annual Report to Congress: Military Power of the People's Republic of China," Office of the Secretary of Defense, Department of Defense, Washington, DC, p. 20.

3. ———, 2009.

4. Text of the Joint Communiqué issued by the United States of America and the People's Republic of China (February 27 of 1972 in Shanghai), paragraph 12.

5. Under the Taiwan Relations Act (signed April 10, 1979), Washington is legally bound:

- To preserve and promote extensive, close, and friendly commercial, cultural, and other relations between the people of the U.S. and the people of Taiwan

- To declare that peace and stability in the area are in the political, security, and economic interests of the United States, and are matters of international concern

- To make clear that the United States rests upon the expectation that the future of Taiwan will be determined by peaceful means

- To consider that any effort to determine the future of Taiwan by other than peaceful means, including by boycotts, or embargoes, to be a threat to the peace and security of the Western Pacific area and of grave concern to the U.S.

- To provide Taiwan with defensive arms

- To assert the right to resist any resort to force or other forms of coercion that would jeopardize the security or social and economic systems of the people of Taiwan (Taiwan Relations Act, April 1979, section 2(b))

6. Text of Shanghai II Communiqué, August 17, 1982, paragraph 6.

7. James Chang, June 2001, "U.S. Policy Toward Taiwan," Weatherhead Center for International Affairs, Harvard University, p. 7. For a broader discussion of this history, see James Mann, 2000, *About Face: A History of America's Curious Relationship with China, from Nixon to Clinton*, Vintage Books, New York.

8. ———, August 17, 1982, "Press Release from the Ministry of Foreign Affairs," Taipei, pp. 4–5.

9. Winston Lord, September 27, 1994, "Testimony on Taiwan Policy Review," Presented before the Senate Foreign Relations Committee, Washington, DC, pp. 1–4.

10. James Chang, June 2001, p. 11.

11. Andrew Nathan and Robert Ross, 1997, *The Great Wall and the Empty Fortress: China's Search for Security*, W. W. Norton Company, New York, p. 74.

12. James Chang, June 2001, p. 13.

13. Michael O'Hanlon, Fall 2000, "Can China Conquer Taiwan?" *International Security*, Volume 25, Number 2, Harvard University, Cambridge.

14. James Mulvenon, 2001, *Soldiers of Fortune: The Rise and Fall of the Chinese Military-Business Complex, 1978–1998*, M. E. Sharpe, New York.

15. ———, July 22, 1998, "Jiang Orders PLA Firms to Close," Xinhua, Beijing.

16. Richard Bernstein and Ross Munro, 1997, *The Coming Conflict with China*, Vintage, New York, p. 3.

17. ———, 1997, p. 6.

18. ———, 1997, p. 21.

19. Bill Gertz, 2000, *The China Threat: How the People's Republic Targets America*, Regnery Publishing, Washington, DC, p. xix.

20. ———, 2000, p. 186.

21. ———, 2000, p. xxii.

22. Ted Carpenter, 2006, *America's Coming War with China: A Collision Course over Taiwan*, Palgrave Macmillan, New York.

23. Will Hutton, 2007, *The Writing on the Wall: China and the West in the 21st Century*, Little, Brown, London, pp. x–xi.

24. ———, 2007, p. xi.

25. ———, 2007, pp. 240–245.

26. Bates Gill, 2007, *Rising Star: China's New Security Diplomacy*, Brookings Institution Press, Washington, DC, p. 140.

27. Kitty McKinsey, March 3, 2000, "China: All Eyes on Beijing After the Taiwan Election," Radio Free Europe.

28. ———, April 20, 2000, "Lu's Description of Cross-Strait Relations as being that of Distant Relatives and Close Neighbors is Clearly a Denial of the One-China Principle," Xinhua, Beijing.

29. ———, October 16, 2000, "China's National Defense in 2000," Information Office of the State Council, Beijing.

30. ———, 2006, "Military Power of the People's Republic of China 2006," Annual report to Congress, Office of the Secretary of Defense, Washington, DC.

31. ———, December 2002, "Support for Independence Increasing," Poll for the Cabinet's Research, Development and Evaluation Commission, Taipei.

32. ———, December 25, 2008, "Poll: 91.8% of Taiwanese Support Keeping Status Quo," Asia World News, www.earthtimes.org.

33. See also: Robert Ross, March 2006, "Taiwan's Fading Independence Movement," *Foreign Affairs*, Volume 85, Number 2, Washington, DC, pp. 141–148.

34. Luis Yu, January 21, 2009, "Taiwan Must Not Simply Consider China as a Threat: MAC Head," www.cna.com.

35. Ester Pan and Youkyong Lee, March 24, 2008, "China-Taiwan Relations," Backgrounder, U.S. Council on Foreign Relations, Washington, DC.

36. Cindy Sui, November 8, 2008, "China's Envoy takes Taiwan in His Stride," *Asia Times*, Hong Kong.

37. Shelly Rigger, 2006, "Taiwan's Rising Rationalism: Generations, Politics, and 'Taiwanese Nationalism,'" Policy Studies 26, East-West Center, Washington, DC, pp. vii–viii.

38. ———, 2006, p. viii.

39. ———, 2006, pp. 3–4.

40. Kerry Dumbaugh, April 2, 2008, "Taiwan's 2008 Presidential Election," CRS Report for Congress, Congressional Research Service, Washington, DC.

41. Ma Ying-jeou, May 20, 2008, "Taiwan's Renaissance," President Ma's Inaugural Address, Taipei.

42. Michael Turton, April 9, 2009, "The Culture of Taiwan," *The Wall Street Journal*, New York.

43. Shelly Rigger, 2006, p. 24.

44. Michael Turton, April 9, 2009.

45. Ma Ying-jeou, May 20, 2008.

46. Ko Shu-ling, September 4, 2008, "'State to State' Theory Is Dead, Ma Says," *Taipei Times*, Taipei.

47. Ko Shu-ling, September 4, 2008. This not the first time Ma has used the word "dignity" when describing how he would like Taiwan to be treated. In his inaugural address, Ma issued the following statement: "We will also

enter into consultations with mainland China over Taiwan's international space and a possible cross-Strait peace accord. Taiwan doesn't just want security and prosperity. It wants dignity. Only when Taiwan is no longer being isolated in the international arena can cross-Strait relations move forward with confidence."

48. Ko Shu-ling, September 4, 2008.

49. ———, November 4, 2008, "Beijing, Taipei Sign Flight, Cargo Agreements," www.chinadaily.com.cn.

50. James Peng and Yu-huay Sun, November 4, 2008, "China, Taiwan Agree on Direct Flights, Shipping, Mail," www.bloomberg.com.

51. ———, December 15, 2008, "China, Taiwan celebrate launch of direct flights," Agence France-Presse, Shanghai.

52. Anthony Kuhn, July 5, 2008, "Direct Flights Take Off Between China, Taiwan," National Public Radio, Washington, DC.

53. James Peng and Yu-huay Sun, November 4, 2008.

54. ———, November 4, 2008.

55. The message was first issued by the Standing Committee of the National People's Congress on January 1, 1979. In the original message, the Chinese Communist Party announced the "abandonment" of its pledge for the "armed liberation" of Taiwan, calling instead for the island's "peaceful liberation."

56. Russell Hsiao, January 12, 2009, "Hu Jintao's 'Six-Points' Proposition to Taiwan," *China Brief*, Volume 9, Issue 1, Jamestown Foundation, Washington, DC. Hu is said to have reiterated these points in a meeting with former Kuomintang Party Chairman Wu Poh-hsiung on May 26, 2009. (Li Hanfang, May 26, 2009, "Experts: Hu Jintao's Important Opinion About Taiwan Will Expedite the Advance of Cross-Strait Relations from a New Starting Point," Xinhua, Beijing.)

57. Russell Hsiao, January 12, 2009.

58. ———, January 12, 2009.

59. Yu Tsung-chi, February 11, 2009, "The Shift in China's Taiwan Policy," *Taipei Times*, Taipei.

60. Rich Chang, January 4, 2009, "MND Unmoved by PRC Missile Report," *Taipei Times*, Taipei.

61. ———, January 4, 2009, "Taiwan Believes China may Cut Missiles Aimed at It," REUTERS, Taipei.

62. Lin Chuan, January 5, 2009, "Both Sides of the Taiwan Strait Wish to Establish a 'Mechanism of Mutual Trust in Military and Security Affairs,' " *Zhongguo Tongxun She*, Hong Kong.

63. Peter Enav, March 9, 2009, "Official: Taiwan Wants Chinese Military Contacts," Associated Press, Taipei.

64. Luis Yu, January 21, 2009.

65. ———, March 20, 2009, "Taiwan Leader: No Joint Representation with China," Associated Press, Taipei.

66. Xie Yu, March 26, 2009, "Beijing May Help Taipei in WHO Role," www.chinadaily.com.cn.

67. President Ma has publicly declared that the use of "Chinese Taipei" as a means of referring to Taiwan is not ideal, but he contends Taiwan should not forego opportunities to participate in international bodies simply because of dislike for that title. Ma also likes to argue his predecessor chose to ignore the nomenclature issue when Taiwan was bidding to become a member of the World Trade Organization in 2002. (———, May 20, 2009, "Ma puts up Spirited Defense of China Policies," *Taiwan News*, Taipei.)

68. ———, April 30, 2009, "Taiwan Gains WHA Observer Status," *The China Post*, Hong Kong.

69. Y. F. Low, April 30, 2009, "WHA Participation will not Harm Taiwan's Sovereign Status: President," Central News Agency, Taipei.

70. ———, April 30, 2009, "Resolving Issue of Taiwan's WHA Role Shows Mainland Sincerity: Official," Xinhua, Beijing.

71. Rachel Chan, September 15, 2009, "Taiwan likely won't bid to Enter the U.N. this Year: Foreign Minister," Taiwan News Online, Taipei.

72. Ralph Jennings, October 21, 2009, "China, Taiwan Break New Ground with Official Postings," REUTERS, Taipei.

73. Ralph Jennings and Ben Blanchard, October 28, 2009, "Once Seen as Spies, Taiwan Eases China Media Curbs," REUTERS, Taipei. See also: October 29, 2009, "Xinhua President Eyes Broader Exchanges with Taiwan Media," Xinhua, Beijing.

74. Ben Blanchard, March 5, 2009, "China Says Ready to Talk Peace with Taiwan," Reuters, Beijing.

75. ———, March 5, 2009.

76. Jane Rickards and Arianna Cha, March 6, 2009, "Taiwan Says It Is Not Ready for Peace Talks With China," *The Washington Post*, Washington, DC, p. A09. See also: Ko Shu-ling, March 6, 2009, "Talks Require '1992 Consensus,' Goodwill: Taiwan," *Taipei Times*, Taipei.

77. ———, March 15, 2009, "Anti-secession Law 'Unnecessary:' Ma," *The China Post*, Hong Kong.

78. ———, March 15, 2009.

79. Rich Chang, October 18, 2008, "CEPA Endangers Taiwan: Forum," *Taipei Times*, Taipei, p. 3.

80. ———, October 18, 2008.

81. Tsai Ing-wen, March 1, 2009, "CECA Comes with Big Hidden Costs," *Taipei Times*, Taipei, p. 8.

82. Ariana Cha, February 21, 2009, "Taiwan, China Negotiating a Landmark Free-Trade Agreement," *The Washington Post*, p. A09.

83. ———, February 21, 2009.

84. ———, April 20, 2009, "Taiwan's Economy to Contract 3.6% in 2009," Agence France-Presse, Taipei.

85. ———, February 21, 2009.

86. ———, March 4, 2009, "Editorial: CECA or ECFA: Who Cares?" *Taipei Times*, Taipei, p. 8.

87. Ko Shu-ling, March 16, 2009, "Experts Warn of ECFA Dangers," *Taipei Times*, Taipei, p. 3.

88. Elizabeth Tchii and Ko Shu-ling, March 30, 2009, " 'Opt Out' Clause Mulled for ECFA: MOEA Chief," *Taipei Times*, Taipei, p. 1.

89. Rich Chang and Ko Shu-ling, March 31, 2009, "DPP Calls for Open ECFA Talks," *Taipei Times*, Taipei, p. 3.

90. Elizabeth Tchii and Ko Shu-ling, March 30, 2009.

91. ———, March 30, 2009.

92. Rich Chang, April 12, 2009, "ECFA Unrelated to Sovereignty, Lai Says," *Taipei Times*, Taipei, p. 1.

93. ———, April 21, 2009, "MOEA Wants ECFA by End of 2009," *Taiwan News*, www.etaiwannews.com.

94. ———, April 21, 2009.

95. ———, March 26, 2009, "Chinese Mainland Would Consider Trade Pact to Help Taiwan," Xinhua, Beijing.

96. ———, April 21, 2009, "China-Taiwan—Taiwan Envoy Welcomes Mainland Proposal," www.chinadaily.com.cn.

97. ———, May 18, 2009, "Beijing Says It Is Prepared to Conclude ECFA with Taipei," *The China Post*, Hong Kong.

98. Under the new guidelines, Chinese businessmen and individuals who own real estate in Taiwan will be allowed to visit the island independently and stay as long as four months each year. Previously, mainland residents were compelled to travel in groups and could only obtain a visa for 14-day visits.

99. Chinmei Sung and Janet Ong, June 30, 2009, "Taiwan Opens 100 Industries to Chinese Investment," www.bloomberg.com. Taiwan financial institutions can provide foreign-currency loans to Chinese companies that have received permission to operate on the island. The banks can also extend local-currency loans and mortgages to Chinese companies and individuals who have been granted Taiwan residency permits. (Alex Pevzner, July 1, 2009, "Taiwan Banks Permitted to Lend to Chinese Companies," *The Wall Street Journal*, New York.)

100. ———, June 30, 2009, "Taiwan Officially Opens Doors to Chinese Investment," Central News Agency, Taipei.

101. Hsu Shu-fen, July 8, 2009, "The Chinese Agenda in Investing in Taiwan," *Taipei Times*, Taipei, p. 8.

102. Stuart Biggs and Dune Lawrence, August 1, 2009, "Ma Says Taiwan-China Economic Embrace Is Just 'the Beginning,'" www.bloomberg.com.

103. ———, July 27, 2009, "KMT Chairman Post for Ma Sign of Closer Ties," www.chinadaily.com.cn. Ma ran an uncontested campaign. He won 92.5 percent of the approximately 300,000 votes cast in the election.

104. William Ide, July 27, 2009, "China and Taiwan Leaders Exchange Letters for First Time," Voice of America, Hong Kong.

105. ———, June 11, 2009, "Taiwan President may Meet with China's Hu—Paper," Reuters, Beijing.

106. Mo Yan-chih, June 12, 2009, "Pressure Builds for Ma-Hu Meet," *Taipei Times*, Taipei, p. 1.

107. ———, July 29, 2009, "Taiwan Leader Calls for China Trade Pact, But no Rush to Meet Hu," Agence France-Presse, Taipei.

108. Mo Yan-chih, June 12, 2009, p. 1.

109. ———, June 18, 2009, "No Discussion of Unification before 2016: President," *Taiwan News*, Taipei, p. 1.

110. Stuart Biggs and Stephen Engle, July 31, 2009, "China must Remove Missiles for Taiwan Thaw, Ma Says," www.bloomberg.com.

111. ———, July 12, 2009, "Taiwan Removes Military Barrier as China Ties Warm," Reuters, Taipei.

112. ———, July 21, 2009, "No Plans for Taiwan-China Military Meeting," Reuters, Taipei.

113. John Lewis and Xue Litai, 2006, p. 32.

114. ———, 2006, p. 276.

115. Nancy Bernkopf Tucker, May 2008, "China's Relations with the West: The Role of Taiwan and Hong Kong," Foreign Policy Research Institute.

116. David Young, May 27, 2009, "Beijing Ready to Negotiate ECFA before Year's End," *The China Post*, Hong Kong.

117. ———, May 29, 2009, "China Says up to Nine Buying Teams to Head for Taiwan," *Taiwan News*, Taipei.

118. Ni Eryan, July 2, 2008, "Where Does the U.S. Military's 'Shock' Come From?" *Wen Wei Po*, Hong Kong.

119. ———, July 2, 2008.

120. Liu Shih-chung, February 3, 2009, "U.S. Inauguration Inspires, Worries Taiwan," *Taipei Times*, Taipei.

121. Liu Shih-chung, February 17, 2009, "Secretary Clinton: Seeking Balance Between Taipei and Beijing," The Brookings Institution, Washington, DC.

122. William Lowther, March 12, 2009, "Taiwan 'Driving Chinese Military Goals,'" *Taipei Times*, Taipei, p. 1.

123. Robert Sutter, March 5, 2009, "Cross-Strait Moderation and the United States—Policy Adjustments Needed," PacNet, Number 17, Pacific Forum CSIS, Honolulu.

124. Richard Bush III and Alan Romberg, March 12, 2009, "'Cross-Strait Moderation and the United States'—A Response to Robert Sutter," The Brookings Institution, Washington, DC.

125. ———, March 12, 2009.

126. David Shambaugh, April 2009, "Early Prospects of the Obama Administration's Strategic Agenda with China," The Brookings Institution, Washington, DC.

127. ———, April 2009.

CHAPTER 6

1. Liu Yunshan, October 24, 2008, "The Chinese System is Incomparably Superior," *Apple Daily*, Hong Kong.

2. Paul Wolfowitz, October 14, 2005, "China—A Model Country," Remarks by World Bank President at Lanzhou University, Lanzhou, China.

3. Barry Naughton, 2007, *The Chinese Economy: Transitions and Growth*, Massachusetts Institute of Technology Press, Cambridge.

4. Randy Peernboom, 2007, *China Modernizes: Threat to the West or Model for the Rest?* Oxford University Press, Oxford, pp. 4–9.

5. ———, 2007, p. 9.

6. ———, 2007, p. 20.

7. Rowan Callick, November 2007, "The China Model," *The American*, American Enterprise Institute, Washington, DC.

8. The Jamestown Foundation is a Washington-based think tank, whose stated mission is to "inform and educate" policy makers about events and trends which it regards as being of current "strategic" importance to the United States.

9. Willy Lam, November 18, 2008, "Beijing's Glorification of the 'China Model' Could Blunt Its Enthusiasm for Reforms," *China Brief*, Volume 8, Issue 21, Jamestown Foundation, Washington, DC.

10. ———, November 18, 2008.

11. Johan Lagerkvist, 2008, "The Limits of the China Model," Glasshouse Forum, Stockholm, p. 17.

12. ———, 2008, p. 7.

13. ———, 2008, p. 18.

14. For a contemporary discussion of this phenomena, see: Jacob Heilbrunn, 2008, *They Knew They Were Right: The Rise of the Neocons*, Doubleday, New York.

15. Francis Fukuyama, Summer 1989, "The End of History?" *The National Interest*, Number 16, National Affairs Incorporated, Baltimore, p. 3.

16. ———, Summer 1989, p. 4.

17. ———, Summer 1989, p. 5.

18. Lucian Pye, March 1980, "Political Science and the Crisis of Authoritarianism," *American Political Science Review*, Volume 84, Number 1, p. 5.

19. ———, March 1980, p. 7.

20. ———, March 1980, p. 8.

21. Fareed Zakaria, March 1994, "Culture Is Destiny; A Conversation with Lee Kuan Yew," *Foreign Affairs*, Volume 73, Number 2.

22. For instance, see: Christopher Lingle, 1996, *Singapore's Authoritarian Capitalism: Asian Values, Free Market Illusions, and Political Dependency*, Locke Institute, Fairfax, Virginia.

23. Nancy Birdsall, Ed Campos, W. Max Corden, Chang-Shik Kim, Howard Pack, Richard Sabot, Joseph Stiglitz, and Marilou Uy, 1993, *The East Asian Miracle: Economic Growth and Public Policy, World Bank*, Oxford University Press, Oxford.

24. Helen Hughes, Spring 1999, "Crony Capitalism and the East Asian Currency Financial 'Crises,' " *Policy*, Center for Independent Studies, Wellington, New Zealand, pp. 3–9.

25. Paul Krugman, November 1994, "The Myth of Asia's Miracle," *Foreign Affairs*, Volume 73, Number 6, Council on Foreign Relations, Washington, DC.

26. Azar Gat, July 2007, "The Return of Authoritarian Great Powers," *Foreign Affairs*, Volume 86, Number 4, Council on Foreign Relations, Washington, DC, p. 59.

27. ———, July 2007, p. 66.

28. Michael Mandelbaum, September 2007, "Democracy Without America," *Foreign Affairs*, Volume 86, Number 5, Council on Foreign Relations, Washington, DC, p. 34.

29. ———, September 2007, p. 35.

30. ———, September 2007, p. 38.

31. ———, September 2007, p. 39.

32. Larry Diamond, March 2008, "The Democratic Rollback: The Resurgence of the Predatory State," *Foreign Affairs*, Volume 87, Number 2, Council on Foreign Relations, Washington, DC, p. 40.

33. ———, March 2008, pp. 41–42.

34. ———, March 2008, p. 45.

35. Daniel Deudney and G. John Ikenberry, January 2009, "The Myth of Authoritarian Revival: Why Liberal Democracy Will Prevail," *Foreign Affairs*, Volume 88, Number 1, Council on Foreign Relations, Washington, DC, p. 78.

36. ———, January 2009, pp. 84–85.

37. ———, January 2009, p. 93.

38. ———, January 2009, p. 93.

39. ———, September 2, 2003, "Hu Jintao in Jiangxi," Xinhua, Beijing.

40. ———, October 14, 2003, "Comunique of the Third Plenary Session of the 16th Central Committee of the Chinese Communist Party," Xinhua, Beijing.

41. ———, December 20, 2003, "Hu Jintao: Implement the Strategy of Human Resources," Xinhua, Beijing.

42. ———, December 20, 2003, "Hu Jintao: Implement the Strategy of Human Resources."

43. ———, February 24, 2004, "New Regulations," www.chinadaily .com.cn.

44. ———, January 6, 2008, "Democracy Delayed, Again," *The Washington Post*, Washington, DC, p. B06.

45. ———, September 12, 2005, "Building of Political Democracy in China," White Paper, State Council Information Office, Beijing, p. 4.

46. ———, September 12, 2005, "Building of Political Democracy in China," p. 15.

47. ———, September 12, 2005, "Building of Political Democracy in China," p. 15.

48. ———, September 12, 2005, "Building of Political Democracy in China," p. 32.

49. ———, September 12, 2005, "Building of Political Democracy in China," pp. 32–33.

50. Hu Jintao, October 15, 2007, "Hold High the Great Banner of Socialism with Chinese Characteristics and Strive for New Victories in Building a Moderately Prosperous Society in All Respects," Report to the Seventeenth National Congress of the Communist Party of China, Xinhua, Beijing.

51. ———, October 15, 2007.

52. Charter 77 was initially circulated within Czechoslovakia in January 1977. The document criticized the government for failing to implement human rights provisions found in a number of documents it had signed, including the Czechoslovak Constitution, the Final Act of the 1975 Conference on Security and Cooperation in Europe, and the United Nations covenants on political, civil, economic, and cultural rights. Originally appearing as a manifesto in a West German newspaper and signed by 243 Czechoslovak citizens representing various occupations, political viewpoints, and religions, by the mid-1980s, the document had been signed by 1,200 people. According to Charter 77, the signatories were a "loose, informal and open association of people . . . united by the will to strive individually and collectively for respect for human and civil rights in our country and throughout the world."

53. ———, December 10, 2008, "Charter 08," p. 4. Reprinted in full: Perry Link, January 15, 2009, "China's Charter 08," *The New York Review of Books*, Volume 56, Number 1, New York.

54. ———, December 10, 2008, "Charter 08," p. 4.

55. ———, March 31, 2009, " 'Charter' Democrats in China," *The Wall Street Journal*, New York. See also: ———, January 30, 2009, "Virtual Groundswell," *The Washington Post*, Washington, DC, p. A18.

56. Austin Ramzy, December 17, 2008, "Beijing Clamps Down After Call for Democracy," *Time*, New York.

57. Beijing may be trying to avoid appearing as heavy handed as Prague in 1977. The official Czechoslovakian response to "Charter 77" has been characterized as harsh. State media described "Charter 77" as "an anti-state, anti-socialist, and demagogic, abusive piece of writing," and individual signers were variously described as "traitors and renegades." Punitive responses included dismissal from work; denial of educational opportunities for the signers' children; suspension of drivers' licenses; forced exile; loss of citizenship; and detention, trial, and imprisonment.

58. ———, March 9, 2009, "China 'Will Not have Democracy,'" BBC News, London.

59. We should note that Zhou Tianyong, an advisor to the Chinese Communist Party Central Committee and a known liberal voice, told reporters at the *Telegraph* something quite similar in October 2008. According to Zhou, "by 2020, China will basically finish its political and institutional reforms . . . there will be public democratic involvement at all government levels." But Zhou did not predict an end to single-party rule. (Malcolm Moore, October 15, 2008, "China will be a Democracy by 2020, says Senior Party Figure," *Telegraph*, London.)

60. ———, April 13, 2009, "National Human Rights Action Plan of China (2009–2010)," Information Office of the State Council, Beijing.

61. Andrew Nathan and Bruce Gilley, 2002, *China's New Rulers: The Secret Files*, The New York Review Books, New York, p. 235.

62. Andrew Nathan, April 20, 2007, "Political Culture and Regime Support in Asia," Paper presented at Conference on "The Future of U.S.-China Relations, USC U.S.-China Institute, Los Angeles, p. 5. (The China survey used in this study was conducted from March to June 2002. The pollsters spoke with 3183 Chinese citizens over the age of 18.)

63. GlobeScan, a Canadian firm, whose mission is: "to be the world's center of excellence for objective global survey research and strategic counsel."

64. ———, January 111, 2006, "20 Nation Poll Finds Strong Global Consensus: Support for Free Market System, But also More Regulation of Large Companies," Program on International Policy Attitudes, Washington, DC.

65. ———, July 22, 2008, "The Chinese Celebrate Their Roaring Economy, As They Struggle with its Costs," *Pew Global Attitudes Project*. (Results of face-to-face interviews with 3,215 Chinese adults conducted between March 28 and April 19, 2008.)

66. ———, July 22, 2008, "The Chinese Celebrate Their Roaring Economy, As They Struggle with its Costs."

67. Tianjian Shi, 1996, "Survey Research in China," in Michael Carpini, Huddy Leonie, and Robert Shapiro's *Research in Micropolitics*, JAL Press, Greenwich, Connecticut, pp. 213–250; and Tianjian Shi, 1997, *Political Participation in Beijing*, Harvard University Press, Cambridge.

68. ———, April 24, 2009, "China at a Crossroad: Right or Left?" *Asia Times*, www.atime.com.

69. ———, April 24, 2009.

70. ———, April 24, 2009.

71. Cheng Li, March 2009, "China's Team of Rivals," *Foreign Policy*, Washington, DC.

72. ———, March 2009.

73. Christopher Hughes, April 17, 2006, "Chinese Nationalism in the Global Era," Open Democracy News Analysis, www.opendemocracy.net.

74. Deng Xiaoping, January 16, 1980, "The Present Situation and the Tasks Before Us," Speech at a meeting of cadre called by the Central Committee of the Chinese Communist Party.

75. Jayshree Bajoria, April 23, 2008, "Nationalism in China," Backgrounder, Council on Foreign Relations, Washington, DC. Quote from Kenneth Lieberthal, a professor at the University of Michigan.

76. Richard Bernstein and Ross Munro, March 1997, "The Coming Conflict with America," *Foreign Affairs*, Volume 76, Number 2, Washington, DC, p. 29; and James Lilly, October 24, 1996, "Nationalism Bites Back," *The New York Times*, New York.

77. Suisheng Zhao, 2005, "China's Pragmatic Nationalism: Is it Manageable?" *Washington Quarterly*, Volume 29, Number 1, Washington, DC, p. 132.

78. ———, 2005, p. 132.

79. Lee Jung Nam, 2006, "The Revival of Chinese Nationalism: Perspectives of Chinese Intellectuals," *Asian Perspective*, Volume 30, Number 4, p. 146.

80. Peter Gries, 2004, *China's New Nationalism: Pride, Politics, and Diplomacy*, The University of California Press, Los Angeles.

81. Suisheng Zhao, 2005, "Nationalism's Double Edge," *Wilson Quarterly*, Washington, DC.

82. Nicholas Kristopf, April 22, 2001, "Guess Who's a Chinese Nationalist Now?" *The New York Times*, New York, Section 4, p. 1.

83. Suisheng Zhao, 2005, p. 133.

84. ———, April 12, 2009, "Unhappy China," *The China Post*, Hong Kong.

85. Fu Qi and Li Huizi, March 27, 2009, "Book 'Unhappy China' Stirs a Controversy," www.shanghaidaily.com.

86. Malcolm Moore, March 29, 2009, " 'Unhappy China' Bestseller Claims Beijing Should 'Lead the World,' " *Telegraph*, London.

87. Fu Qi and Li Huizi, March 25, 2009, "Book Rallying for Social Change Fails to Inspire the Masses," Xinhua, Beijing.

88. Kristine Kwok and Raymond Li, March 28, 2009, "Brash Bestseller Seen Adding Fuel to the Flames of Nationalism," *South China Morning Post*, Hong Kong.

89. Jason Dean, March 30, 2009, "Books Stokes Nationalism in China," *The Wall Street Journal*, New York, p. A18.

90. Fu Qi and Li Huizi, March 25, 2009.

91. ———, March 25, 2009.

92. ———, March 27, 2009, "Xiao Gongqin: I Oppose the Nationalism of False Pride—A Criticism of *Unhappy China*." *Xinmin Weekly*, Shanghai.

93. Jing Kaixuan, March 31, 2009, " 'Unhappy China' is All for Show," *Southern Metropolis Daily*, Guangzhou, China, p. A31.

94. Kathrin Hille, March 27, 2009, "China's 'Angry Youths' are Novel Heros," *Financial Times*, London.

95. ———, March 27, 2009.

96. John Thornton, January 2008, "Long Time Coming: The Prospects for Democracy in China," *Foreign Affairs*, Volume 87, Issue 1, Council on Foreign Relations, Washington, DC, p. 4.

97. ———, January 2008, p. 4.

98. ———, January 2008, p. 21.

EPILOGUE

1. Wu Xinbo, June 30, 2009, "New Trends in U.S.-East Asia Relations," *Jiefang Ribao*, Shanghai.

2. Dominic Wilson and Anna Stupnytska, 28 March 2007, "The N-11: More Than an Acronym," Global Economics Paper Number 153, Goldman Sachs, New York, p. 8.

3. Martin Jacques, 2009, *When China Rules the World: The Rise of the Middle Kingdom and the End of the Western World*, Allen Lane, New York.

4. ———, 2009, p. 365.

5. ———, 2009, p. 366.

6. For those who are interested, I did respond to the email. My comments follow:

Subject: Re: Re: The China Threat

Bill

The problem with "belligerent China" analysis begins with history and ends with the facts. While some in the intelligence community may still subscribe to "worst case" analysis, I would contend this is a poor excuse for doing one's homework—and tends to be very non-productive ... to say nothing of wasteful. You may recall the Russian missile gap, the North Korean plan to invade South Korea in 1995, or the slew of rumored follow-on terrorist attacks that were to come after 9–11 ... [all of which] caused us to needlessly spend taxes that could have been better used elsewhere.

The Chinese military build-up jibes quite well with Hu Jintao's new "historic missions" strategic guidelines, and is the type of activity any responsible government undertakes in our Westphalian international system. I have to chuckle at the nuclear comment ... the 20 (or so) intercontinental ballistic missiles the Chinese maintain are a poor match for Moscow or Washington's existing stockpile. Finally, I would suggest a long examination of PLA training guidelines and exercise performance—this is a force that may be ready for a modern adversary in 20–30 years.

Rather than subscribe to "belligerent China" we would be well suited to engaging with Asia's most important government as a true contemporary—who may just have stumbled into a form of governance that works better than our own ... at least when it comes to maintaining and monitoring economic development. My suspicion is that the China Model is not a way point on the path to liberal democracy ... it is a viable alternative that many other nations are going to find quite appealing.

V/R

Eric C. Anderson

7. Elizabeth Economy and Adam Segal, May 2009, "The G-2 Mirage: Why the United States and China Are Not Ready to Upgrade Ties," *Foreign Affairs*, Volume 88, Number 3, Council on Foreign Relations, Washington, DC, p. 15.

8. ———, May 2009, p. 16.

9. ———, May 2009, pp. 17–18.

10. ———, May 2009, p. 18.

11. ———, May 2009, p. 19.

12. Andrew Batson, March 24, 2009, "China Takes Aim at Dollar," *The Wall Street Journal*, New York, p. A1.

13. Canada, France, Germany, Italy, Japan, Russia, the United Kingdom, and the United States.

14. Jason Dean, James Areddy, and Serena Ng, 29 January 2009, "Chinese Premier Blames Recession on U.S. Actions," *The Wall Street Journal*, New York, p. A1.

15. See: Simon Elegant, April 10, 2009, "Is China's Economy Strong Enough to Save the World?" *Time*, New York; and ———, April 17, 2009, "China Not Capable of 'Saving' World Alone," Xinhua, Beijing.

16. ———, July 16, 2009, "China's Economy Stabilized with a Better Performance Trend While Its Upturn Yet to Consolidate," National Bureau of Statistics in China, Beijing.

17. ———, July 15, 2009, "China's Foreign Reserves Top $2 Trillion," BBC News, London.

18. ———, July 17, 2009, "China Market Value Overtakes Japan's," Bloomberg, New York.

19. ———, June 8, 2009, "George Soros: China a 'Positive Force,'" *People's Daily*, Beijing.

20. Gordon Brown, April 2, 2009, "London Summit Press Conference," Transcript of press conference given by Prime Minster Gordon Brown in London on 2 April 2009 at the end of the London Summit. The G-20—the Group of Twenty Finance Ministers and Central Bank Governors—is composed of Argentina, Australia, Brazil, Canada, China, France, Germany, India, Indonesia, Italy, Japan, Mexico, Russia, Saudi Arabia, South Africa, South Korea, Turkey, United Kingdom, United States, and the European Union.

21. Julian Borger, May 17, 2009, "David Miliband: China Ready to Join U.S. as World Power," *Guardian*, London.

22. Christian Caryl and May Hennock, May 25, 2009, "Why Bow to China?" *Newsweek*, New York.

23. Perry Link and Joshua Kurlantzick, May 25, 2009, "China's Modern Authoritarianism," *The Wall Street Journal*, New York.

24. ———, May 25, 2009.

25. ———, May 26, 2009, "Beware the Beijing Model," *Economist*, London.

26. ———, May 26, 2009, "Beware the Beijing Model."

27. Michael Pillsbury, October 19, 2001, "China's Perceptions of the USA: The View from Open Sources," Testimony prepared for the U.S.-China Economic and Security Review Commission, Washington, DC.

28. Fu Mengzi, May 18, 2009, "Old Order Should Yield Place to New," *People's Daily*, Beijing.

29. ———, May 26, 2009, "Beware the Beijing Model." Quote attributed to Wei-Wei Zhang, a faculty member at Fudan University.

30. Wang Jisi, October 20, 2008, "Roundtable on U.S.-China Relations," *Nanfeng Chuang*, Chengdu, China.

31. ———, October 20, 2008.

32. Liu Jianfei, May 2009, "Chinese Foreign Strategy in Wake of the Financial Crisis," *Sousuo yu Zhengming*, Volume 3, Shanghai Social Science Association, Shanghai.

33. Cheng Li, July 2007, "China in the Year 2020: Three Political Scenarios," *Asia Policy*, Number 4, National Bureau of Asian Research, Seattle, p. 18.

34. ———, July 2007, pp. 20–25.

35. ———, July 2007, pp. 25–27.

36. ———, July 2007, pp. 28.

37. Pieter Bottelier, July 2007, "China's Economy in 2020: The Challenge of a Second Transition," *Asia Policy*, Number 4, National Bureau of Asian Research, Seattle, p. 32.

38. ———, July 2007, p. 32. The "first transition," said to occur between 1978 and 2003 was primarily aimed at adopting market principles, creating market institutions, and maximizing economic growth. (Bottelier, July 2007, p. 36.)

39. ———, July 2007, p. 39.

40. ———, July 2007, p. 39.

41. David Lampton, July 2007, "Alternative Security and Foreign Policy Futures for China: 2020," *Asia Policy*, Number 4, National Bureau of Asian Research, Seattle, p. 8.

42. ———, July 2007, p. 9. In his book *Soft Power: The Means to Success in World Politics*, Joseph Nye outlines two concepts of national power: hard and soft. In Nye's construct, hard power is essentially the coercive capabilities (inducements or threats) a state can bring to bear in efforts to persuade other international actors to act in a chosen manner. Soft power, for Nye, is an ability to attract the support of others through getting them "to want the outcomes you want." (Joseph Nye, 2004, *Soft Power: The Means to Success in World Politics*, PublicAffairs, New York.)

43. ———, July 2007, p. 9.

44. ———, July 2007, p. 9.

45. ———, July 2007, p. 15.

46. Jiang Zemin, November 1, 1997, "Enhance Mutual Understanding and Build Stronger Ties of Friendship and Cooperation," Speech at Sanders Theater, Harvard University.

47. ———, November 1, 1997.

48. ———, November 1, 1997.

49. David Finkelstein, July 2009, "Commentary on China's External Grand Strategy," Paper presented at the 38th Taiwan-U.S. Conference on Contemporary China—"China Faces the Future"—sponsored by the Brookings Institution and National Chengchi University, Washington, DC, p. 12.

50. ———, July 2009, p. 4.

51. ———, July 2009, p. 3.

52. ———, 2007, "Report to the Seventeenth National Congress of the Chinese Communist Party of China on October 15, 2007," Foreign Language Press, Beijing, p. 62.

53. ———, July 2009, p. 11. Finkelstein contends China's approach to external work has gone through four phases since 1949:

- First, from the 1950s though the 1970s, China's approach was to confront the international system.

- Second, in the 1980s, China began to engage the international system to accrue modernization benefits.

- Third, from the 1990s through the end of the twentieth century, part of China's external strategy was to begin to participate in the international system.

- And, finally … since at least 2001, China's approach is to be a player that will shape the international system.

Selected Bibliography

Author's note: The bibliography that follows is listed alphabetically, by family name. In the case of Western authors—or Chinese writers who chose to use a Western format—the given name appears before the family name. For Chinese or other Asian authors who stick to the Eastern tradition, the family name appears before the given name.

"Annual Report to Congress: Military Power of the People's Republic of China 2008," Office of the Secretary of Defense, Washington, DC.

Dima Adamsky, April 2008, "Through the Looking Glass: The Soviet Military-Technical Revolution and the American Revolution in Military Affairs," *Journal of Strategic Studies*, Volume 31, Number 2, Routledge, New York.

Byung-Joon Ahn, 2004, "The Rise of China and the Future of East Asian Integration," *Asia-Pacific Review*, Volume 11, Number 2, Routledge, New York.

Roger Altman, 2008, January 2009, "The Great Crash, 2008: A Geopolitical Setback for the West," *Foreign Affairs*, Council on Foreign Relations, Washington, DC.

Rumi Aoyama, December 2004, "Chinese Diplomacy in the Multimedia Age: Public Diplomacy and Civil Diplomacy," Research Institute of Current Chinese Affairs, Waseda University, Tokyo.

———, 2007, "Chinese Diplomacy in the Multimedia Age," edited by Kazuko Mori and Kenichiro Hirano in *A New East Asia: Toward a Regional Community*, National University of Singapore.

Mark Beeson, 2009, "Hegemonic Transition in East Asia? The Dynamics of Chinese and American Power," *Review of International Studies*, Volume 35, British International Studies Association, London.

C. Fred Bergsten, Bates Gill, Nicholas Lardy, and Derek Mitchell, 2008, "International System," *China: The Balance Sheet*, Center for Strategic and International Studies, Washington, DC.

Richard Bernstein and Ross Munro, 1997, *The Coming Conflict with China*, Vintage, New York.

Nancy Birdsall, Ed Campos, W. Max Corden, Chang-Shik Kim, Howard Pack, Richard Sabot, Joseph Stiglitz, and Marilou Uy, 1993, *The East Asian Miracle: Economic Growth and Public Policy*, World Bank, Oxford University Press, Oxford.

Christopher Blanchard, Nicholas Cook, Kerry Dumbaugh, Susan Epstein, Shirley Kan, Michael Martin, Wayne Morrison, DC Nanto, Jim Nichol, Jeremy Sharp, Mark Sullivan, and Bruce Vaughn, August 15, 2008, "Comparing Global Influence: China's and U.S. Diplomacy, Foreign Aid, Trade, and Investment in the Developing World," CRS Report for Congress, Congressional Research Service, Library of Congress, Washington DC.

Dan Blumenthal, June 11, 2007, "Is China at Present (or Will China Become) a Responsible Stakeholder in the International Community," paper presented at Carnegie Endowment for International Peace "Reframing China Policy" debates, Washington, DC.

Dan Blumenthal and Aaron Friedberg, January 2009, "An American Strategy for Asia," Report of the Asia Strategy Working Group, American Enterprise Institute, Washington, DC.

Bo Yang, 1992, *The Ugly Chinaman and the Crisis of Chinese Culture*, Sydney Allen & Unwin, New York.

Pieter Bottelier, July 2007, "China's Economy in 2020: The Challenge of a Second Transition," *Asia Policy*, Number 4, National Bureau of Asian Research, Seattle.

Rowan Callick, November 2007, "The China Model," *The American*, American Enterprise Institute, Washington, DC.

Ted Carpenter, 2006, *America's Coming War with China: A Collision Course over Taiwan*, Palgrave Macmillan, New York.

Gordon Chang, 2001, *The Coming Collapse of China*, Random House, New York.

Joseph Cheney, April 1999, "China: Regional Hegemon or Toothless Tiger?" Research Report, Air War College, Montgomery, Alabama.

———, December 22, 2005, "China's Peaceful Development Road," White Paper, State Council Information Office, Beijing.

———, January 2009, *China's National Defense in 2008*, Information Office of the State Council of the People's Republic of China, Beijing.

Eric Teo Chu Cheow, September 16, 2004, "Asian Security and the Re-emergence of China's Tributary System," *China Brief*, Volume 4, Issue 18, The Jamestown Foundation, Washington, DC.

Roger Cliff, Mark Burles, Michael Chase, Derek Eaton, and Kevin Pollpeter, 2007, *Entering the Dragon's Lair: Chinese Antiaccess Strategies and Their Implications for the United States*, Rand Corporation, Santa Monica.

Keith Crane, Roger Cliff, Evan Medeiros, James Mulvenon, and William Overholt, 2005, *Modernizing China's Military: Opportunities and Constraints*, Rand Corporation, Santa Monica.

Deng Xiaoping, June 18, 1995, "The Last Mutual Trust Is Lost Between China and the United States," *Yazhou Zhoukan*, Beijing.

Daniel Deudney and G. John Ikenberry, January 2009, "The Myth of the Autocratic Revival," *Foreign Affairs*, Volume 88, Number 1, Council on Foreign Affairs, Washington, DC.

Larry Diamond, March 2008, "The Democratic Rollback: The Resurgence of the Predatory State," *Foreign Affairs*, Volume 87, Number 2, Council on Foreign Relations, Washington, DC.

Erica Strecker Downs, 2000, *China's Quest for Energy Security*, Project Air Force, RanDCrporation, Washington, DC.

June Teufel Dreyer, 2003, "Encroaching on the Middle Kingdom? China's View of Its Place in the World," *U.S.-China Relations in the Twenty-First Century: Policies, Prospects and Possibilities*, Lexington Books, New York.

Kerry Dumbaugh, April 2008, "China's Foreign Policy and 'Soft Power' in South America, Asia, and Africa," Congressional Research Service, Library of Congress, Washington, DC.

———, July 18, 2008, "China's Foreign Policy: What Does It Mean for U.S. Global Interests," CRS Report for Congress, Congressional Research Service, Washington, DC.

Elizabeth Economy and Adam Segal, May 2009, "The G-2 Mirage: Why the United States and China Are Not Ready to Upgrade Ties," *Foreign Affairs*, Volume 88, Number 3, Council on Foreign Relations, Washington, DC.

John Fairbank, 1969, "China's Foreign Policy in Historical Perspective," *Foreign Affairs*, Volume 47, Number 3, Council on Foreign Affairs, Washington, DC.

David Finkelstein, July 2009, "Commentary on China's External Grand Strategy," paper presented at the 38th Taiwan-U.S. Conference on Contemporary China—"China Faces the Future"—sponsored by the Brookings Institution and National Chengchi University, Washington, DC.

M. Taylor Fravel, Fall 2005, "Regime Insecurity and International Cooperation: Explaining China's Compromises in Territorial Disputes," *International Security*, Volume 30, Number 2, MIT Press, Cambridge.

M. Taylor Fravel, 2008, *Strong Borders, Secure Nation: Cooperation and Conflict in China's Territorial Disputes*, Princeton University Press, Princeton.

Aaron Friedberg, November 2000, "The Struggle for Mastery in Asia," *Commentary* (magazine), New York.

Francis Fukuyama, 1992, *The End of History and the Last Man*, Free Press, New York.

Azar Gat, July 2007, "The Return of Authoritarian Great Powers," *Foreign Affairs*, Volume 86, Number 4, Council on Foreign Affairs, Washington, DC.

Bill Gertz, 2000, *The China Threat: How the People's Republic Targets America*, Regnery Publishing, Washington, DC.

Bates Gill, 2007, *Rising Star: China's New Security Diplomacy*, Brookings Institution Press, Washington, DC.

Bates Gill and James Reilly, Summer 2007, "The Tenuous Hold of China Inc. in Africa," *The Washington Quarterly*, Washington, DC.

Robert Gilpin, 1981, *War and Change in World Politics*, Cambridge University Press, Cambridge.

———, November 2008, *Global Trends 2025: A Transformed World*, National Intelligence Council, Director for National Intelligence, Washington, DC.

Michael Glosny, 2006, "Heading Toward a Win-Win Future? Recent Developments in China's Policy Towards Southeast Asia," *Asian Security*, Volume 2, Number 1, Routledge, New York.

Michael Glosny, December 2006, "China's Foreign Aid Policy: Lifting States Out of Poverty or Leaving Them to the Dictators?" CSIS Freeman Report, Center for Strategic and International Studies, Washington, DC.

Andrea Goldstein, Nicholas Pinaud, Helmut Reisen, and Xiaobao Chen, May 2006, "China and India: What's In It for Africa?" Development Center Studies, Organization for Economic Cooperation and Development, Paris.

Avery Goldstein, 2001, "The Diplomatic Face of China's Grand Strategy: A Rising Power's Emerging Choice," *The China Quarterly*, Volume 168, Cambridge University Press, Cambridge.

Jack Goldstone, Summer 1995, "The Coming Collapse," *Foreign Policy*, Number 99, Washington, DC.

Daniel Goma, 2006, "The Chinese-Korean Border Issue: An Analysis of a Contested Frontier," *Asian Survey*, Volume 46, Issue 6, University of California Press, Los Angeles.

Peter Gries, 2004, *China's New Nationalism: Pride, Politics, and Diplomacy*, University of California Press, Los Angeles.

David Hale and Lyric Hale, January 2008, "Reconsidering Revaluation: The Wrong Approach to the U.S.-China Trade Imbalance," *Foreign Affairs*, Volume 87, Number 1, Council on Foreign Affairs, Washington, DC.

Takeshi Hamashita, 1994, "The Tribute System and Modern Asia," *Japanese Industrialization and the Asian Economy*, edited by A. J. H. Latham and Heita Kawashita, Routledge, New York.

Takeshi Hamashita, 1997, "The Intra-Regional System in East Asia in Modern Times," *Network Power: Japan and Asia*, edited by Peter Katzhstein and Takashi Shiraishi, Cornell University Press, Ithaca, New York.

Bert Hofman and Louis Kuijs, October 19, 2007, "Rebalancing China's Growth," paper presented at the Conference on China's Exchange Rate Policy, Peterson Institute for International Economics, Washington, DC.

Russell Hsiao, January 12, 2009, "Hu Jintao's 'Six-Points' Proposition to Taiwan," China Brief, Volume 9, Issue 1, Jamestown Foundation, Washington, DC.

Pasha Hsieh, 2008, "China-Taiwan Trade Relations: Implications of the WTO and Asian Regionalism," in *Trading Arrangements in the Pacific Rim: ASEAN and APEC*, edited by Paul Davidson, Oxford University Press, Oxford.

Hu Jintao, October 15, 2007, "Report to the Seventeenth National Congress of the Communist Party of China," Xinhua, Beijing.

Zukiu Hu and Mohsin Khan, April 1997, "Why Is China Growing So Fast?" Economic Issues Number 8, International Monetary Fund, Washington, DC.

Yasheng Huang, 2008, *Capitalism with Chinese Characteristics: Entrepreneurship and the State*, Cambridge University Press, Cambridge.

Helen Hughes, Spring 1999, "Crony Capitalism and the East Asian Currency Financial 'Crises,'" *Policy*, Center for Independent Studies, Wellington, New Zealand.

Will Hutton, 2007, *The Writing on the Wall: China and the West in the 21st Century*, Little, Brown, London.

G. John Ikenberry, January 2008, "The Rise of China and the Future of the West: Can the Liberal System Survive?" *Foreign Affairs*, Council on Foreign Relations, Washington, DC.

Steven Jackson, 2000, "A Typology for Stability and Instability in China," in *Is China Unstable*, edited by David Shambaugh, M. E. Sharpe, New York.

Martin Jacques, 2009, *When China Rules the World: The Rise of the Middle Kingdom and the End of the Western World*, Allen Lane, New York.

Jia Hepeng, 2004, "The Three Represents Campaign: Reform the Party or Indoctrinate the Capitalists?" *Cato Journal*, Volume 24, Number 3, Cato Institute, Washington, DC.

Jiang Zemin, November 2002, "Report to the 16th National Congress," Xinhua, Beijing.

Alastair Iain Johnston, Spring 2003, "Is China a Status Quo Power?" *International Security*, Volume 27, Number 4, MIT Press, Cambridge.

David Kang, 2007, *China Rising: Peace, Power, and Order in East Asia*, Columbia University Press, New York.

Solomon Karmel, 2000, *China and the People's Liberation Army: Great Power or Struggling Developing State?* St. Martin's Press, New York.

Albert Keidel, May 26, 2005, "The Economic Basis for Social Unrest in China," The Third European-American Dialogue on China, George Washington University, Washington, DC.

Ann Kent, 2007, *Beyond Compliance: China, International Organizations, and Global Security*, Stanford University Press, Palo Alto, California.

Zalmay Khalilzad, Abram Shulsky, Daniel Byman, Roger Cliff, David Orletsky, David Shlapak, and Ashley Tellis, 1999, *The United States and a Rising China: Strategic and Military Implications*, Project Air Force, Rand, Santa Monica.

Henry Kissinger, 1994, *Diplomacy*, Simon & Schuster, New York.

Nicholas Kristof, 1993, "The Rise of China," *Foreign Affairs*, Volume 72, Number 5, Council on Foreign Affairs, Washington, DC.

Paul Krugman, November 1994, "The Myth of Asia's Miracle," *Foreign Affairs*, Volume 73, Number 6, Council on Foreign Relations, Washington, DC.

Joshua Kurlantzick, 2007, *Charm Offensive: How China's Soft Power Is Transforming the World*, Yale University Press, New Haven.

Haruhiko Kuroda, March 23, 2008, "Toward Inclusive Economic Development in China," speech by the president of the Asian Development Bank at the China Development Forum, Beijing.

James Kynge, 2007, *China Shakes the World: A Titan's Rise and Troubled Future —and the Challenge for America*, First Mariner Books, New York.

Johan Lagerkvist, 2008, "The Limits of the China Model," Glasshouse Forum, Stockholm.

David Lake, Summer 2007, "Escaping from the State of Nature: Authority and Hierarchy in World Politics," *International Security*, Volume 32, Number 1, MIT Press, Cambridge.

David Lampton, July 2007, "Alternative Security and Foreign Policy Futures for China: 2020," *Asia Policy*, Number 4, National Bureau of Asian Research, Seattle.

Karl Lautenschlager, Fall 1983, "Technology and the Evolution of Naval Warfare," *International Security*, Volume 8, Number 2, MIT Press, Cambridge.

Lee Jung Nam, 2006, "The Revival of Chinese Nationalism: Perspectives of Chinese Intellectuals," *Asian Perspective*, Volume 30, Number 4, Institute for Far Eastern Studies, Kyungnam University, Seoul.

Vladimir Lenin, 1916, *Imperialism: The Highest Stage of Capitalism*," Resistance Books, New York.

John Lewis and Xue Litai, 2006, *Imagined Enemies: China Prepares for Uncertain War*, Stanford University Press, California.

Fang Lexian, October 2003, "Is China's Foreign Policy Becoming Less Ideological?" paper for the International Workshop on "Regional

Governance: Greater China in the 21st Century," University of Durham, United Kingdom.

Cheng Li, July 2007, "China in the Year 2020: Three Political Scenarios," *Asia Policy*, Number 4, National Bureau of Asian Research, Seattle.

Cheng Li, March 2009, "China's Team of Rivals," *Foreign Policy*, Washington, DC.

Hong Liang and Eva Yi, November 11, 2005, "China's Ascent: Can the Middle Kingdom Meet Its Dreams?" Global Economics Paper Number 133, Goldman Sachs Economic Research Group, New York.

Kenneth Lieberman, 1983, "China in 1982: A Middling Course for the Middle Kingdom," *Asian Survey*, Volume 23, Number 1, University of California Press, Los Angeles.

Cheng-yi Lin, February 29, 2008, Taiwan's Spratly Initiative in the South China Sea," *China Brief*, Jamestown Foundation, Washington, DC.

Christopher Lingle, 1996, *Singapore's Authoritarian Capitalism: Asian Values, Free Market Illusions, and Political Dependency*, Locke Institute, Fairfax, Virginia.

Xiaohong Liu, 2001, *Chinese Ambassadors: The Rise of Diplomatic Professionalism Since 1949*, University of Washington Press, Seattle.

Gal Luft, 2008, "Fueling the Dragon: China's Race into the Oil Market," Institute for the Analysis of Global Security, Washington, DC.

Ma Ying-jeou, May 20, 2008, "Taiwan's Renaissance," President Ma's Inaugural Address, Taipei.

Kishore Mahbubani, March 2008, "Smart Power, Chinese-Style," *The American Interest*, Washington, DC.

Michael Mandelbaum, September 2007, "Democracy Without America," *Foreign Affairs*, Volume 86, Number 5, Council on Foreign Relations, Washington, DC.

John Mearsheimer, 2001, *The Tragedy of Great Power Politics*, W. W. Norton, New York.

John Mearsheimer, 2005, "Better to Be Godzilla than Bambi," *Foreign Policy*, special report prepared in conjunction with the Carnegie Endowment for International Peace, Council on Foreign Affairs, Washington, DC.

Evan Medeiros, Keith Crane, Eric Heginbotham, Norman Levin, Julia Lowell, Angel Rabasa, and Somi Seong, 2008, *Pacific Currents: The Responses of U.S. Allies and Security Partners in East Asia to China's Rise*, Project Air Force, Rand, Santa Monica.

Evan Medeiros and M. Taylor Fravel, November 2003, "China's New Diplomacy," *Foreign Affairs*, Council on Foreign Relations, Washington, DC.

Robyn Meredith, 2008, *The Elephant and the Dragon: The Rise of India and China and What It Means for All of Us*, W. W. Norton and Company, New York.

Steven Metz and James Kievit, July 25, 1994, "The Revolution in Military Affairs and Conflict Short of War," Strategic Studies Institute, U.S. Army War College, Carlisle Barracks, Pennsylvania.

James Mulvenon, 2001, *Soldiers of Fortune: The Rise and Fall of the Chinese Military-Business Complex, 1978–1998*, M. E. Sharpe, New York.

Andrew Nathan and Bruce Gilley, 2002, *China's New Rulers: The Secret Files*, New York Review Books, New York.

Andrew Nathan and Robert Ross, 1997, *The Great Wall and the Empty Fortress: China's Search for Security*, W. W. Norton, New York.

Barry Naughton, 2007, *The Chinese Economy: Transitions and Growth*, MIT Press, Cambridge.

Barry Naughton and Dali Yang, 2004, "Holding China Together," *Holding China Together: Diversity and National Integration in the Post-Deng Era*, edited by Barry Naughton and Dali Yang, Cambridge University Press, Cambridge.

Peter Nolan, 2004, *China at the Crossroads*, Polity Press, Cambridge.

Michael O'Hanlon, Fall 2000, "Can China Conquer Taiwan?" *International Security*, Volume 25, Number 2, MIT Press, Cambridge.

Philip Pan, 2008, *Out of Mao's Shadow: The Struggle for the Soul of a New China*, Simon & Schuster, New York.

Pan Yihong, 1987, "Traditional Chinese Theories of Foreign Relations and Tang Foreign Policy," *British Columbia Asian Review*, Number 1, Vancouver, Canada.

Randy Peernboom, 2007, *China Modernizes: Threat to the West or Model for the Rest?* Oxford University Press, Oxford.

Minxin Pei, 2006, "Assertive Pragmatism: China's Economic Rise and Its Impact on Chinese Foreign Policy," Proliferation Papers, Ifri Security Studies Department, Paris.

———, March 2006, "The Dark Side of China's Rise," *Foreign Policy*, Slate Group, Washington, DC.

Lucian Pye, March 1980, "Political Science and the Crisis of Authoritarianism," *American Political Science Review*, Volume 84, Number 1, Cambridge University Press, Cambridge.

Qi Quoqian, June 2007, "China's Foreign Aid: Policies, Structure, Practice and Trend," paper prepared for Oxford and Cornell universities' conference on "New Directions in Development Assistance," Oxford, United Kingdom.

Qiao Liang and Wang Xiangsui, 1999, *Unrestricted Warfare: Assumptions on War and Tactics in the Age of Globalization*, PLA Literature and Arts Publishing House, Beijing.

Joshua Cooper Ramo, May 2004, *The Beijing Consensus*, The Foreign Policy Centre, London.

Joshua Ramo, September 2006, "Brand China," Foreign Policy Centre, London.

Thomas Rawski, September 12, 2001, "What's Happening to China's GDP Statistics?" prepared for the China Economic Review symposium on Chinese Statistics, Pittsburgh.

Helmut Reisen, 2007, "Is China Actually Helping Improve Debt Sustainability in Africa?" G-24 Policy Brief Number 9, Organization for Economic Cooperation and Development, Paris.

Shelly Rigger, 2006, "Taiwan's Rising Rationalism: Generations, Politics, and 'Taiwanese Nationalism,'" Policy Studies 26, East-West Center, Washington, DC.

Robert Ross, March 2006, "Taiwan's Fading Independence Movement," *Foreign Affairs*, Volume 85, Number 2, Council on Foreign Affairs, Washington, DC.

Nouriel Roubini and Brad Setset, 2005, *The Science of Military Strategy*, Military Science Publishing House, Academy of Military Science of the Chinese People's Liberation Army, Beijing.

———, February 2005, "Will the Bretton Woods 2 Regime Unravel Soon? The Risk of a Hard Landing in 2005–2006," paper for the symposium on the "Revived Bretton Woods System: A New Paradigm for Asian Development?" organized by the Federal Reserve Bank of San Francisco and University of California at Berkeley, San Francisco.

Michael Schiffer and Gary Schmitt, May 2007, "Keeping Tabs on China's Rise," The Stanley Foundation, Muscatine, Iowa.

Gerald Segal, 1999, "Does China Matter?" *Foreign Affairs*, Volume 78, Number 5, Council on Foreign Affairs, Washington, DC.

David Shambaugh, 1996, "Containment or Engagement of China?" *International Security*, Volume 21, Number 2, MIT Press, Cambridge.

David Shambaugh, 2002, *Modernizing China's Military: Progress, Problems, and Prospects*, University of California Press, Los Angeles.

David Shambaugh, 2005, "China Engages Asia: Reshaping the Regional Order," *International Security*, Volume 29, Number 3, MIT Press, Cambridge.

David Shambaugh, 2005, "The Author Replies," *International Security*, Volume 30, Number 1, MIT Press, Cambridge.

Susan Shirk, 2007, *China : Fragile Superpower*, Oxford University Press, Oxford.

Keng Shu, Chang Chih-chung, and Hsu Chih-Chia, 2006, *Know Thyself, Know Others: The Neglected Risks of China*, Mainland Affairs Council, Taipei.

Brian Simpson, March 1997, "China's Future Intent: Responsible World Power or International Rogue State," research paper, Air Command and Staff College, Montgomery, Alabama.

Song Qiang, Zhang Zangzang, Qiao Ben, Gu Qingsheng, and Tang Zhengyu, 1996, *China Can Say No*, Zhonghua Gongshang Lianhe Chubanshe, Beijing.

Song Xianlin and Gary Sigley, 2000, "Middle Kingdom Mentalities: Chinese Visions of National Characteristics in the 1990s," *Communal/Plural*, Volume 8, Number 1, Carfax Publishing, Abingdon, England.

Robert Sutter, 2005, *China's Rise in Asia: Promises and Perils*, Rowman and Littlefield Publishers, New York.

Robert Sutter, 2006, "China's Regional Strategy and Why It May Not Be Good for America," in *Power Shift: China and Asia's New Dynamics*, edited by David Shambaugh, University of California Press, Berkeley.

Shogo Suzuki, 2004, "China's Perceptions of International Society in the Nineteenth Century: Learning More about Power Politics?" *Asian Perspective*, Volume 28, Number 3, The Institute for Far Eastern Studies, Kyungnam University, Seoul.

Thomas Szayna, Daniel Byman, Steven Bankes, Derek Eaton, Seth Jones, Robert Mullins, Ian Lesser, and William Rosenau, 2001, *The Emergence of Peer Competitors: A Framework for Analysis*, Rand Corporation, Santa Monica.

Murray Tanner, 2004, "China Rethinks Unrest," *The Washington Quarterly*, Volume 27, Number 3, Washington, DC.

John Thornton, January 2008, "Long Time Coming: The Prospects for Democracy in China," *Foreign Affairs*, Volume 87, Issue 1, Council on Foreign Relations, Washington, DC.

Robert Triffin, 1978, "The International Role and the Fate of the Dollar," *Foreign Affairs*, Volume 57, Number 2, Council on Foreign Affairs, Washington, DC.

————, April 25, 2008, "Understanding Chinese Foreign Aid: A Look at China's Development Assistance to Africa, Southeast Asia, and Latin America," report prepared for the Congressional Research Service, New York University Wagner School, New York.

Arthur Waldron, 2005, "The Rise of China: Military and Political Implications," *Review of International Studies*, Number 31, Cambridge University Press, Cambridge.

Wen Jiabao, 2004, cited in Esther Pan, April 2006, "The Promise and Pitfalls of China's 'Peaceful Rise,'" Backgrounder, Council on Foreign Relations, Washington, DC.

Dominic Wilson and Anna Stupnytska, March 28, 2007, "The N–11: More than an Acronym," Global Economics Paper Number 153, Goldman Sachs, New York.

Charles Wolf, K. C. Yeh, Benjamin Zycher, Nicholas Eberstadt, and Sung-Ho Lee, 2003, *Fault Lines in China's Economic Terrain*, Rand, Arlington, Virginia.

Ngaire Woods, 2008, "Whose Aid? Whose Influence? China, Emerging Donors and the Silent Revolution in Development Assistance," *International Affairs*, Volume 84, Number 6, Wiley, New York.

Larry Wortzel, May 2007, "China's Nuclear Forces: Operations, Training, Doctrine, Command, Control and Campaign Planning," Strategic Studies Institute, Washington, DC.

Michael Yahuda, September 2007, "China's Foreign Policy Comes of Age," *The International Spectator*, Volume 42, Number 3, Routledge, New York.

Fareed Zakaria, March 1994, "Culture Is Destiny; A Conversation with Lee Kuan Yew," *Foreign Affairs*, Volume 73, Number 2, Council on Foreign Relations, Washington, DC.

Zhang Tiejun, 2005, "China's Role in East Asian Community Building: Implications for Regional and Global Governance," Shanghai Institute for International Studies, Shanghai.

Quangsheng Zhao, 1996, *Interpreting Chinese Foreign Policy*, Oxford University Press, Oxford.

Suisheng Zhao, 2005, "Nationalism's Double Edge," *Wilson Quarterly*, Washington, DC.

Zheng Bijian, June 16, 2005, "China's New Road of Peaceful Rise and China-US Relations," Speech at the Brookings Institution, Washington, DC.

Zheng Bijian, 2005, *China's Peaceful Rise: Speeches of Zheng Bijian*, Brookings Institution Press, Washington, DC.

Yongnian Zheng and Sow Keat Tok, October 2007, " 'Harmonious Society' and 'Harmonious World': China's Policy Discourse under Hu Jintao," Briefing Series—Issue 26, China Policy Institute, University of Nottingham, United Kingdom.

Zhou Bian, April 9, 2004, "A Gentle Giant," *Beijing Review*, Beijing.

Zhu Rongji, March 19, 2003, "Report on the Work of the Government," speech on March 5, 2003, Xinhua, Beijing.

Robert Zoellick, September 21, 2005, "Whither China: From Membership to Responsibility," Remarks to the National Committee on U.S.-China Relations, New York.

Index

National Bureau of Statistics (China), 2, 109, 110, 240
National Chengchi University, 249
National Defense Authorization Act for Fiscal Year 2000 (U.S.), 121
National Defense Intelligence College (China), 235
National defense policy (China), 8. *See also* People's Liberation Army
National Defense University (China), 124
"National Human Rights Action Plan of China," 222–23
National Intelligence Council, 16–17
Nationalism, xviii, xxi, xxiii, 23, 227–30; Taiwan and, xvii, 181–82
National People's Congress (China), xvii
National Security Strategy (2006), 36–37
Natural resources, 79–81
Navy, Chinese, 8, 145, 164–65; anti-piracy patrol, 135–36
Navy, U.S., 46–47, 169
Nehru, Jawaharlal, 39
New America Foundation, 141
New Republic (magazine), 85
Newsweek (magazine), 240–41
New World Order, 123
New York Times, 7, 81, 109
New York University study, 56
Nigeria, Chinese aid to, 59
"1992 Consensus," 183–84, 199, 200
Nixon, Richard, 170
Non-performing loans, 4–6, 7, 117
North Atlantic Treaty Organization (NATO), 136, 154, 167
North Korea, 120, 139
Nuclear weapons, 7, 122, 138–39, 237
Nye, Joseph, 12, 237

Obama, Barack, 32, 202–3
Ogarkov, Marshal, 163
Oil-consumption rates, 79
Oil-exploitation rights, xvii, 79–80
Olympics (Beijing, 2008), xi, 84, 226, 228
One-child policy, 205
"One China" principle, 62, 173–74, 178, 186, 192; Lee Teng-hui and,

174, 179; "1992 Consensus" and, 183, 200. *See also* Taiwan
"On the Middle Kingdom" (Shi), xi
Opening and reforms, of Deng, 67, 82, 102, 117, 205; foreign policy and, 39; ideology and, 9–10
Open Source Center (OSC), 130, 148, 149, 152–53
Operation DESERT STORM, 8, 123, 124, 127, 143, 163
Operation IRAQI FREEDOM, 127
Organization for Economic Cooperation and Development, 59
Outline for Military Training and Evaluation (OMTE), 149, 152–53
Over-the-horizon targeting (OTHT), 137–38

Pakistan, 139
"Peaceful development" policy (China), 37. *See also* Economic development
"Peaceful rising" strategy, xxi–xxii, 36; Hu Jintao and, xx, 28, 42
Peace of Westphalia. *See* Westphalian system
Peerenboom, Randy, 206
Pentagon, 4, 119, 157, 167; Taiwan and, 170. *See also* Defense Department, U.S.; Military, U.S.
People's Bank of China, 5, 6, 22, 71–72, 78
People's Daily (newspaper), xxi–xxii
People's Liberation Army (PLA), xvii, 7–9, 119–68; active defense, 133; ASAT testing and, 139, 140–41; budgeting for, 155–60; C4ISR infrastructure and, 127–28, 137, 138, 139–40, 142; Hu's historic missions and, 132–33, 135, 148, 159, 160, 162, 166–67, 197, 239; informatized warfare, 126, 127–31, 134, 142–43, 148, 150, 152, 166; modernization of, 119, 200, 201, 203, 232; national security and modernization, 124–35; naval strength, 8, 47, 135–36, 145, 164–65; non-kinetic capabilities, 143–46; nuclear weapons, 7, 122, 138–

About the Author

Eric C. Anderson is faculty member at the National Intelligence University. As a long-standing member of the U.S. intelligence community, he has written over 600 articles for the National Intelligence Council, International Security Advisory Board and the Department of Defense. In addition, he is a leading scholar on the rise of sovereign wealth funds. His book, *Take the Money and Run: Sovereign Wealth Funds and the Demise of American Prosperity*, was published in March 2009.

Prior to assuming his current position, Mr. Anderson served as a national security consultant. In addition he has been a senior intelligence officer for the Defense Intelligence Agency, a senior intelligence analyst for the Multi National Forces-Iraq in Baghdad and at the U.S. Pacific Command in Hawaii. From 1990-2000, Mr. Anderson was an active duty intelligence officer in the United States Air Force—with assignments in Japan, Korea and Saudi Arabia. He remains on duty as an Air Force reserve officer, teaching at the National Defense Intelligence College. He has also taught for the University of Missouri, University of Maryland, and the Air Force Academy.

Mr. Anderson has a PhD in political science from the University of Missouri, an MA from Bowling Green State University in Ohio, and a BA from Illinois Wesleyan University. He is also a graduate of the Air Force Squadron Officer's School, Air Command and Staff College, and the Air War College. A long-time Harley rider, Mr. Anderson claims to have put over 200,000 miles on motorcycles during the last 20 years.